KING SPAWN

VOLUME 1

SEAN LEWIS

JAVI FERNANDEZ

TODD McFARLANE

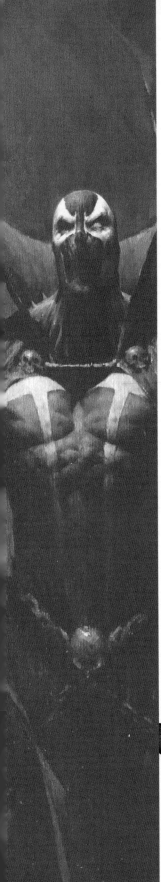

Sean Lewis
Todd McFarlane
SCRIPT / PLOT

Javi Fernandez
Stephen Segovia (HAUNT)
Marcio Takara (NIGHTMARE)
Philip Tan (THE HERO)
Brett Booth (GUNSLINGER)
ARTISTS

Daniel Henriques (THE HERO)
Adelso Corona (GUNSLINGER)
INKERS

Editor-in-Chief
THOMAS HEALY

Production Artist
RYAN KEIZER

President of Comic Operations
SHANNON BAILEY

Creative Director
TODD McFARLANE

Publisher for Image Comics
ERIC STEPHENSON

SPAWN CREATED BY
TODD McFARLANE

FCO Plascencia
Andrew Dalhouse (Haunt, The Hero, Gunslinger)
Marcelo Maiolo (Nightmare)
Ulises Arreola (Cover)
COLOR

Andworld Design
Tom Orzechowski (Shorts)
LETTERING

Javi Fernandez
COLLECTED EDITION COVER

Puppeteer Lee
Don Aguillo
Jonathan Glapion
Jason Shawn Alexander
Björn Barends
COVER ARTISTS

King Spawn Volume 1. May 2022. First Printing. Published by Image Comics, Inc. Office of publication: PO BOX 14457, Portland, OR 97293 USA. Originally published in single issue format as King Spawn issues #1-6. Spawn, its logo and its symbol are registered trademarks © 2022 Todd McFarlane Productions, Inc. All other related characters are TM and © 2022 Todd McFarlane Productions, Inc. All rights reserved. The characters, events and stories in this publication are entirely fictional. "Image" and the Image Comics logos are registered trademarks of Image Comics, Inc. No part of this publication may be reproduced or transmitted, in any form or by any means (except for short excerpts for journalistic or review purposes), without the express written permission of Todd McFarlane Productions, Inc., or Image Comics, Inc. Printed in the USA. ISBN: 978-1-5343-2311-7.

image i
TODD McFARLANE
P R O D U C T I O N S
McFARLANE.COM

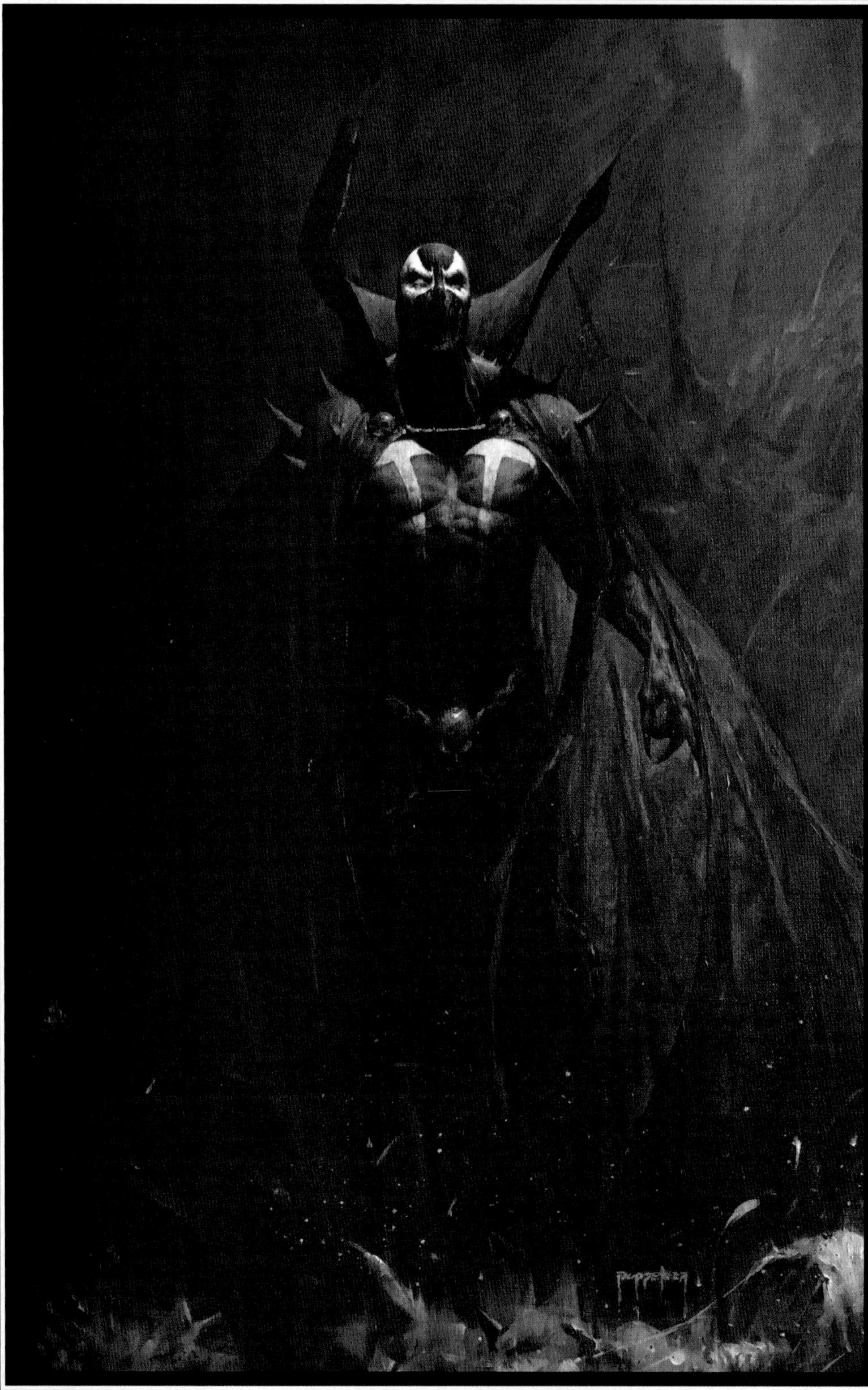
PUPPETEER

King Spawn #1 Cover by Puppeteer Lee

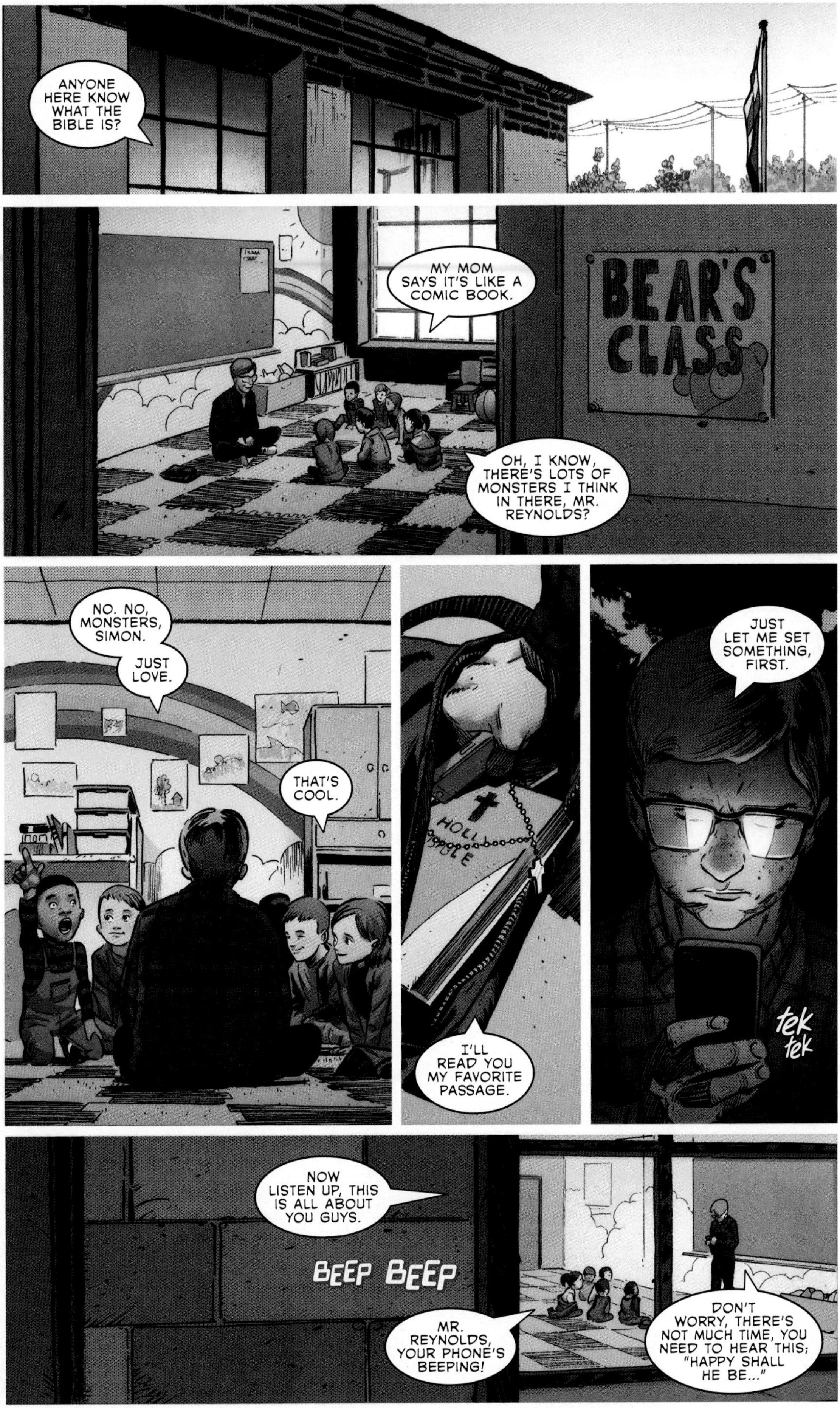
ANYONE HERE KNOW WHAT THE BIBLE IS?
BEAR'S CLASS
MY MOM SAYS IT'S LIKE A COMIC BOOK.
OH, I KNOW, THERE'S LOTS OF MONSTERS I THINK IN THERE, MR. REYNOLDS?
NO. NO, MONSTERS, SIMON.
JUST LOVE.
THAT'S COOL.
I'LL READ YOU MY FAVORITE PASSAGE.
JUST LET ME SET SOMETHING, FIRST.
tek tek
NOW LISTEN UP, THIS IS ALL ABOUT YOU GUYS.
BEEP BEEP
MR. REYNOLDS, YOUR PHONE'S BEEPING!
DON'T WORRY, THERE'S NOT MUCH TIME, YOU NEED TO HEAR THIS; "HAPPY SHALL HE BE..."

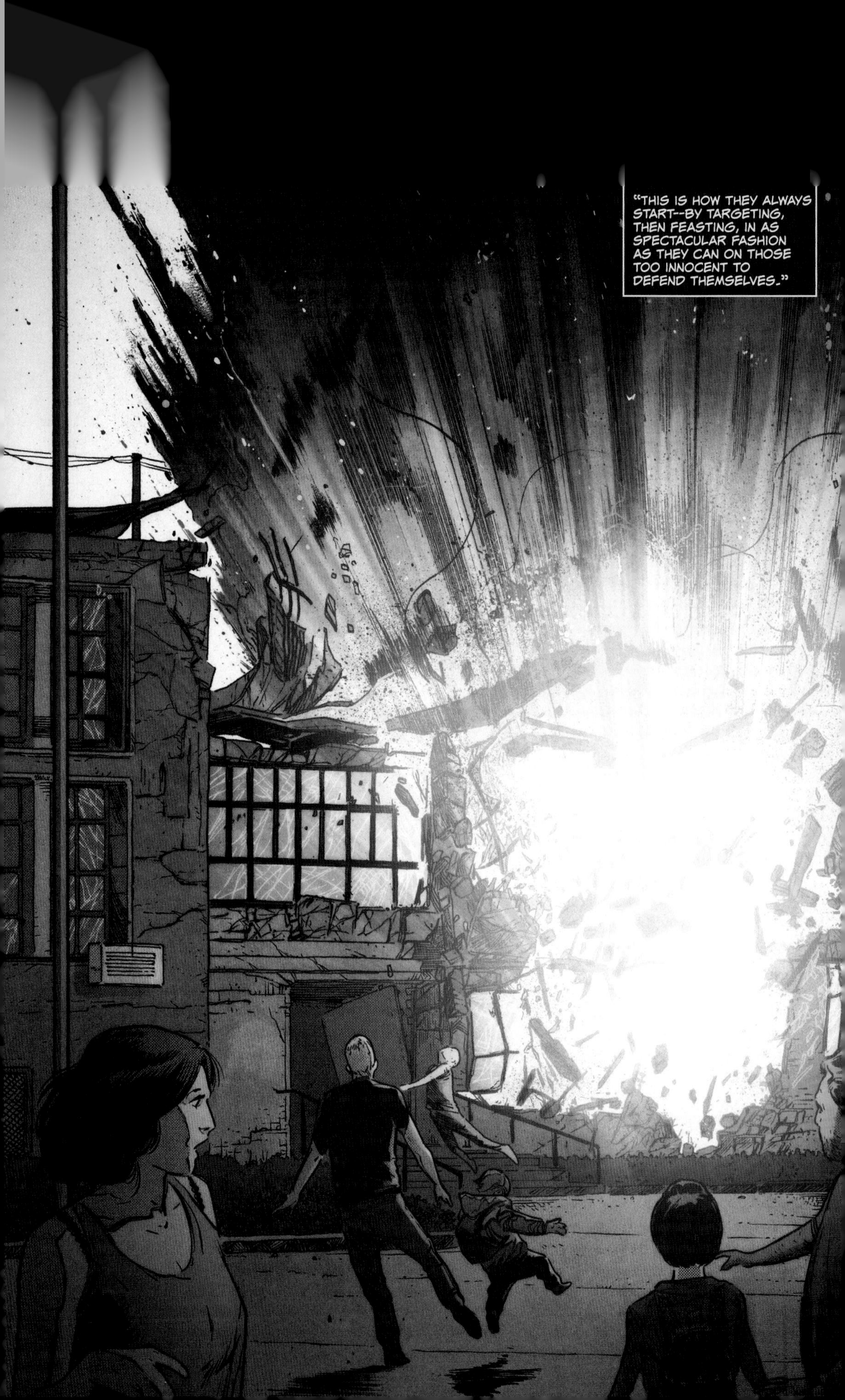
"THIS IS HOW THEY ALWAYS START--BY TARGETING, THEN FEASTING, IN AS SPECTACULAR FASHION AS THEY CAN ON THOSE TOO INNOCENT TO DEFEND THEMSELVES."

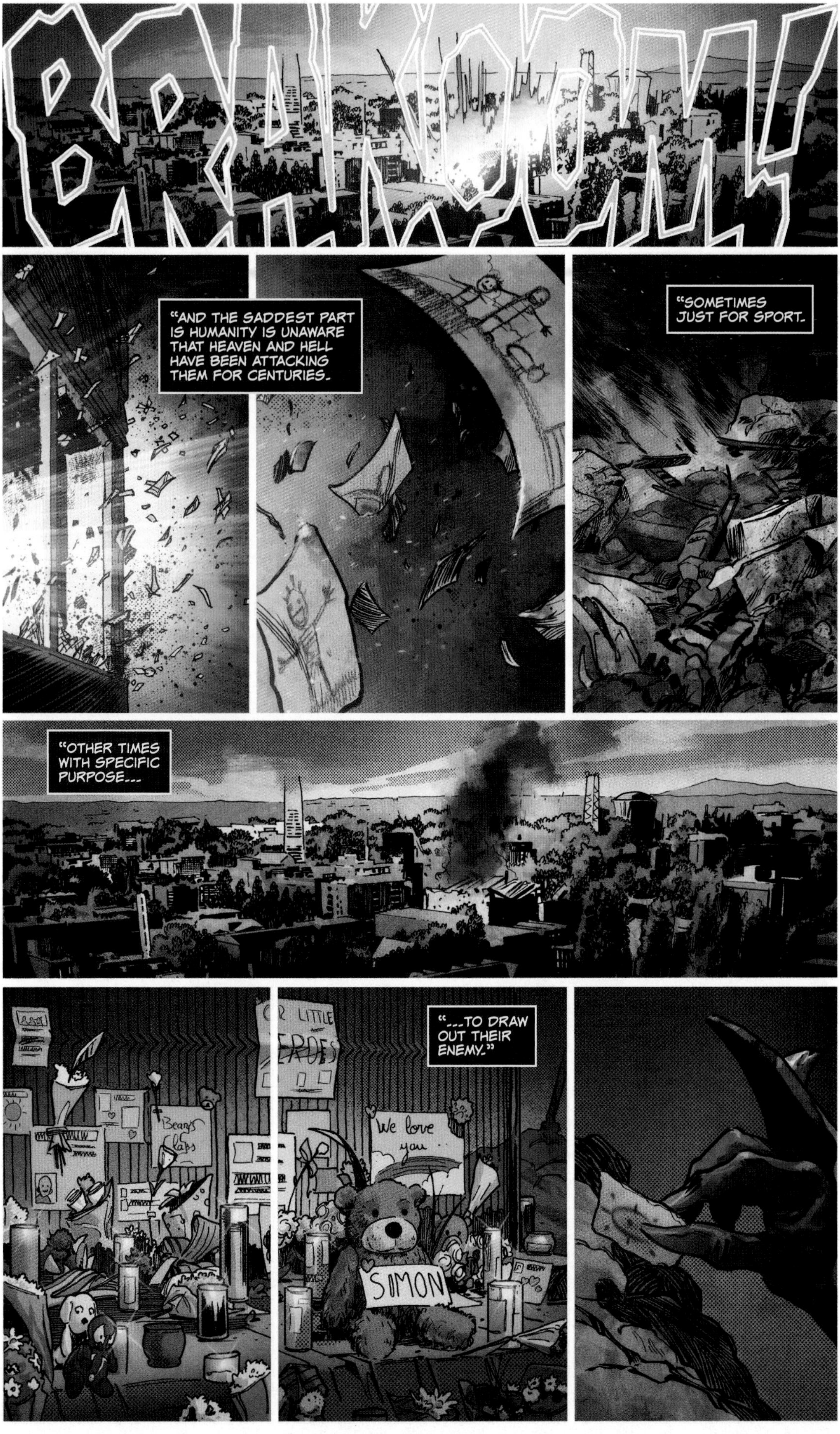

BRAKOOOM!
"AND THE SADDEST PART IS HUMANITY IS UNAWARE THAT HEAVEN AND HELL HAVE BEEN ATTACKING THEM FOR CENTURIES.
"SOMETIMES JUST FOR SPORT.
"OTHER TIMES WITH SPECIFIC PURPOSE...
"...TO DRAW OUT THEIR ENEMY."
We love you
SIMON

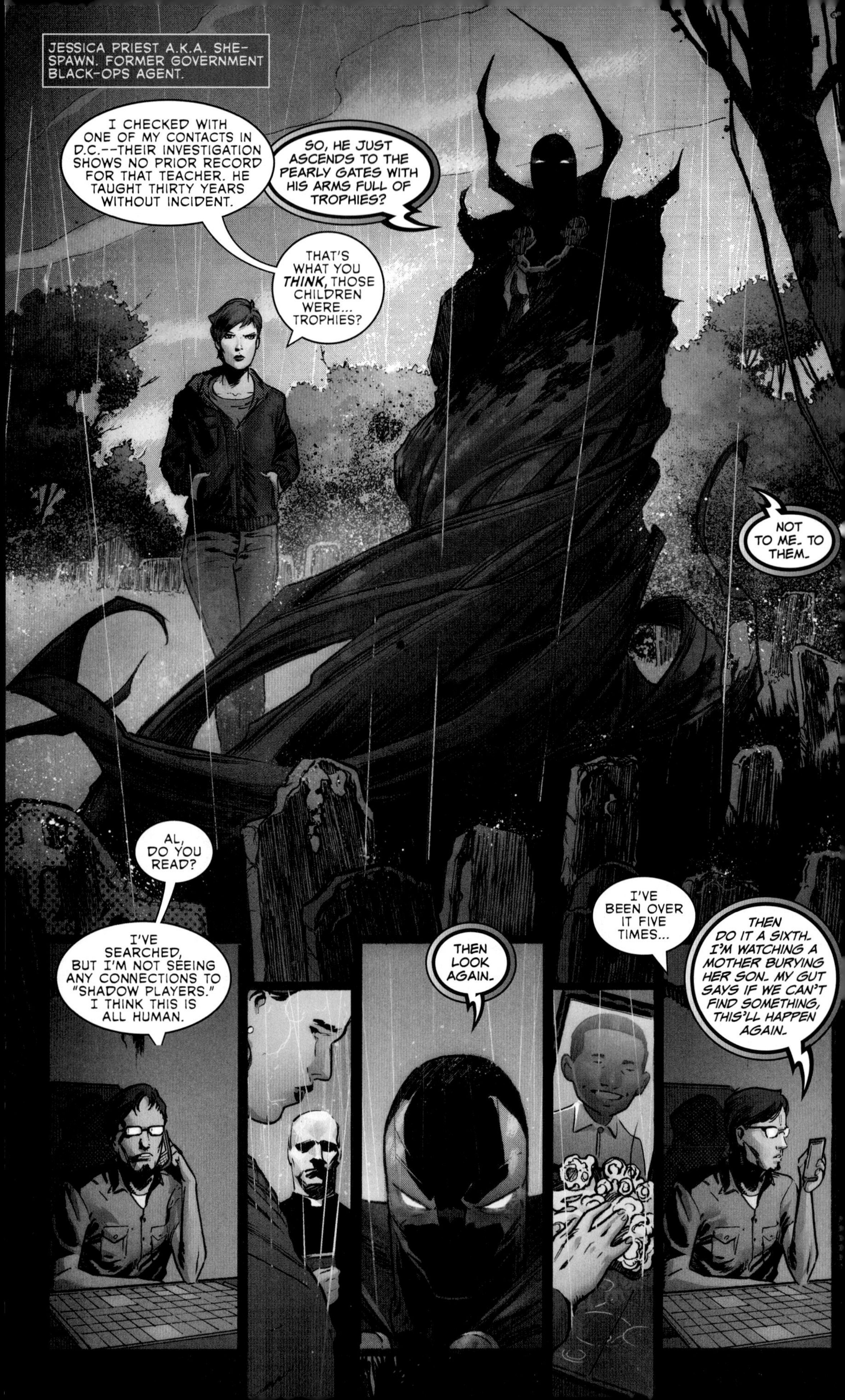
JESSICA PRIEST A.K.A. SHE-SPAWN. FORMER GOVERNMENT BLACK-OPS AGENT.
I CHECKED WITH ONE OF MY CONTACTS IN D.C.--THEIR INVESTIGATION SHOWS NO PRIOR RECORD FOR THAT TEACHER. HE TAUGHT THIRTY YEARS WITHOUT INCIDENT.
SO, HE JUST ASCENDS TO THE PEARLY GATES WITH HIS ARMS FULL OF TROPHIES?
THAT'S WHAT YOU *THINK*, THOSE CHILDREN WERE... TROPHIES?
NOT TO ME. TO THEM.
AL, DO YOU READ?
I'VE SEARCHED, BUT I'M NOT SEEING ANY CONNECTIONS TO "SHADOW PLAYERS." I THINK THIS IS ALL HUMAN.
THEN LOOK AGAIN.
I'VE BEEN OVER IT FIVE TIMES...
THEN DO IT A SIXTH. I'M WATCHING A MOTHER BURYING HER SON. MY GUT SAYS IF WE CAN'T FIND SOMETHING, THIS'LL HAPPEN AGAIN.

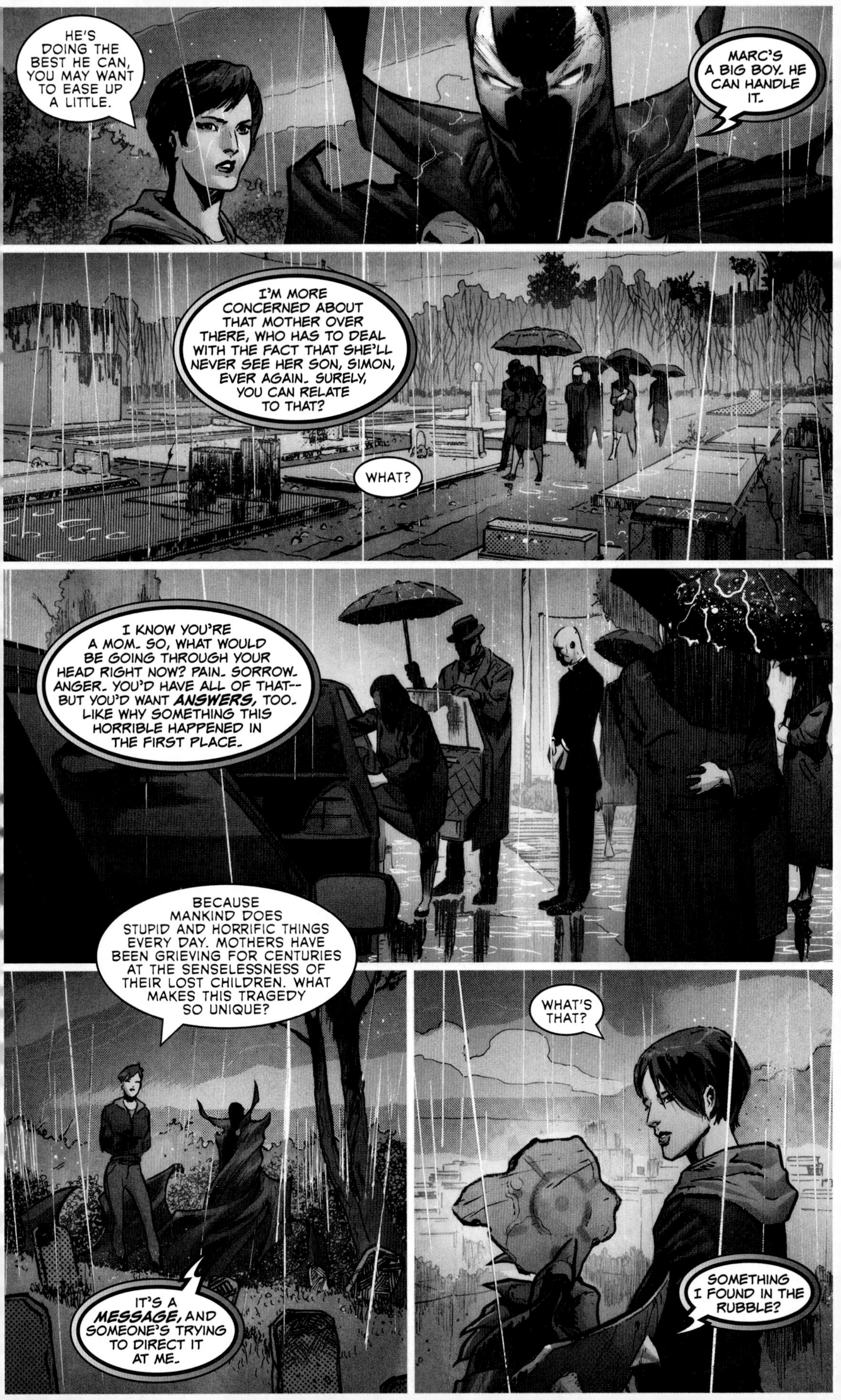
HE'S DOING THE BEST HE CAN, YOU MAY WANT TO EASE UP A LITTLE.
MARC'S A BIG BOY. HE CAN HANDLE IT.
I'M MORE CONCERNED ABOUT THAT MOTHER OVER THERE, WHO HAS TO DEAL WITH THE FACT THAT SHE'LL NEVER SEE HER SON, SIMON, EVER AGAIN. SURELY, YOU CAN RELATE TO THAT?
WHAT?
I KNOW YOU'RE A MOM. SO, WHAT WOULD BE GOING THROUGH YOUR HEAD RIGHT NOW? PAIN. SORROW. ANGER. YOU'D HAVE ALL OF THAT-- BUT YOU'D WANT ANSWERS, TOO. LIKE WHY SOMETHING THIS HORRIBLE HAPPENED IN THE FIRST PLACE.
BECAUSE MANKIND DOES STUPID AND HORRIFIC THINGS EVERY DAY. MOTHERS HAVE BEEN GRIEVING FOR CENTURIES AT THE SENSELESSNESS OF THEIR LOST CHILDREN. WHAT MAKES THIS TRAGEDY SO UNIQUE?
IT'S A MESSAGE, AND SOMEONE'S TRYING TO DIRECT IT AT ME.
WHAT'S THAT?
SOMETHING I FOUND IN THE RUBBLE?

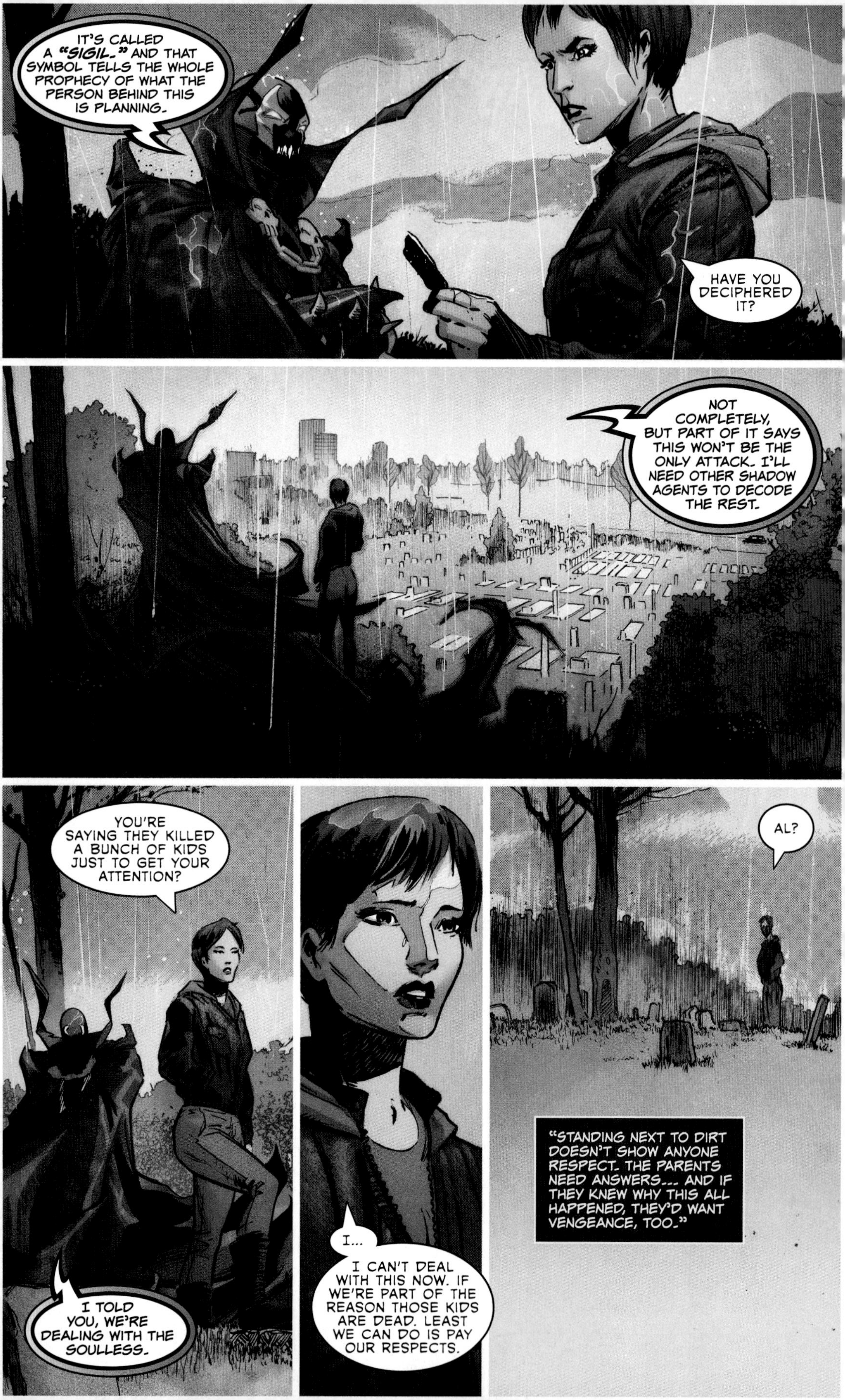
IT'S CALLED A "SIGIL." AND THAT SYMBOL TELLS THE WHOLE PROPHECY OF WHAT THE PERSON BEHIND THIS IS PLANNING.
HAVE YOU DECIPHERED IT?
NOT COMPLETELY, BUT PART OF IT SAYS THIS WON'T BE THE ONLY ATTACK. I'LL NEED OTHER SHADOW AGENTS TO DECODE THE REST.
YOU'RE SAYING THEY KILLED A BUNCH OF KIDS JUST TO GET YOUR ATTENTION?
I TOLD YOU, WE'RE DEALING WITH THE SOULLESS.
I...
I CAN'T DEAL WITH THIS NOW. IF WE'RE PART OF THE REASON THOSE KIDS ARE DEAD. LEAST WE CAN DO IS PAY OUR RESPECTS.
AL?
"STANDING NEXT TO DIRT DOESN'T SHOW ANYONE RESPECT. THE PARENTS NEED ANSWERS... AND IF THEY KNEW WHY THIS ALL HAPPENED, THEY'D WANT VENGEANCE, TOO."

ZEALOT19 15 mins ago
Yes god Metatron has struck!!!!

SONICisnotaHEDGEHOG 15 mins ago
Fucking troll. Kids are DEAD!

thetruthisoutthere 14 mins ago
Well he has a point kids die every day and ppl don't care

BIGMEECH 13 mins ago
Where was that big hombre Spawn thought his gig was stopping that shit or does he just do photo shoots

ZEALOT19 13 mins ago
This will not be the last attack!

BIGMEECH 12 mins ago
Not me Bot. I tap that and you dump porn in my hard drive

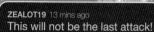

SONICisnotaHEDGEHOG 13 mins ago
Out of the comments asshole!

CHLOE (Admin) 10 mins ago
User what's your name?

UNKNOWN USER 11 mins ago
What if Spawn is watching you?

ZEALOT19 12 mins ago
Follow the link… psalms.link

BIGMEECH 10 mins ago
Yo, the user total hasn't gone up. It still says there are four of us and the admin. But there's 5.

SONICisnotaHEDGEHOG 9 mins ago
Wtf creepy

thetruthisoutthere 9 mins ago
I'm live recording

UNKNOWN USER 8 mins ago
Zealot tell me about psalms.

ZEALOT19 8 mins ago
Fuck you! We are legion!

UNKNOWN USER 7 mins ago
Tell your LEGION I'm coming for all of you.

CHLOE (Admin) 6 mins ago
He's gone? What the hell was that. I'm closing the room for the night.

ZEALOT19 6 mins ago
There will be more dead kiddies!!!!!!

BIGMEECH 3 mins ago
Fuck I wished it'd just been porn.

SONICisnotaHEDGEHOG 5 mins ago
Asshole leave!

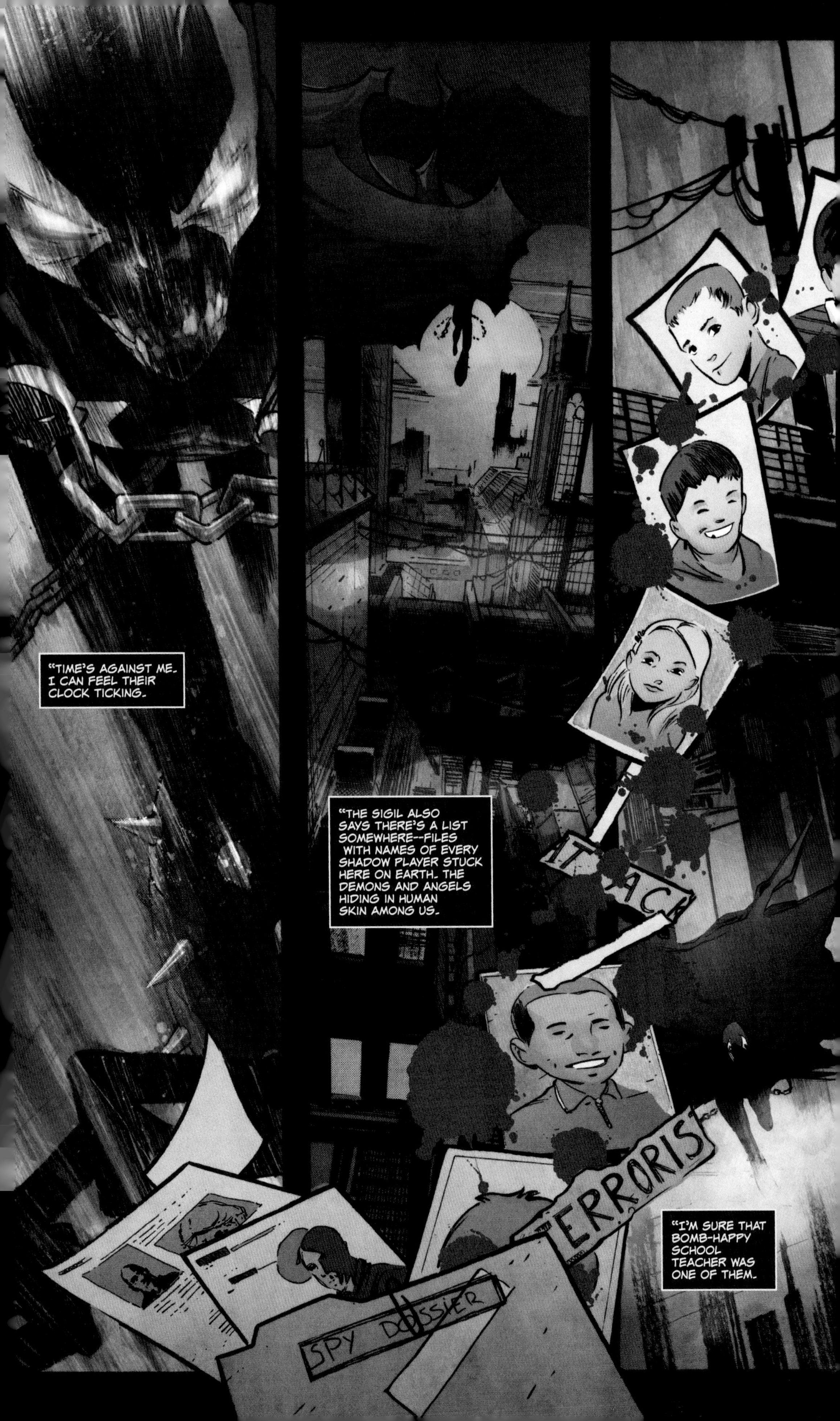
"TIME'S AGAINST ME. I CAN FEEL THEIR CLOCK TICKING.
"THE SIGIL ALSO SAYS THERE'S A LIST SOMEWHERE--FILES WITH NAMES OF EVERY SHADOW PLAYER STUCK HERE ON EARTH. THE DEMONS AND ANGELS HIDING IN HUMAN SKIN AMONG US.
ERRORIS
SPY DOSSIER
"I'M SURE THAT BOMB-HAPPY SCHOOL TEACHER WAS ONE OF THEM.

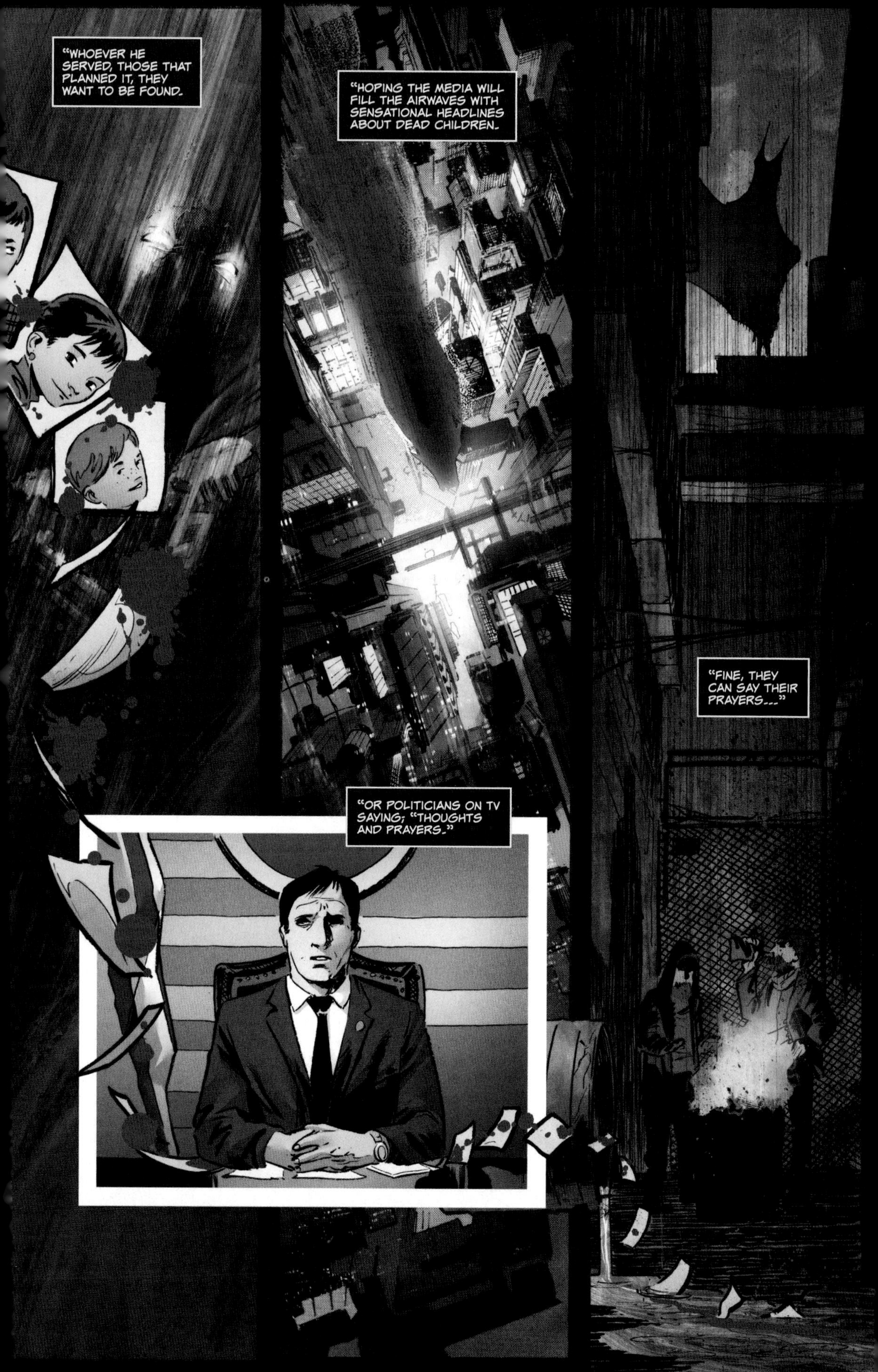
"WHOEVER HE SERVED, THOSE THAT PLANNED IT, THEY WANT TO BE FOUND.
"HOPING THE MEDIA WILL FILL THE AIRWAVES WITH SENSATIONAL HEADLINES ABOUT DEAD CHILDREN.
"FINE, THEY CAN SAY THEIR PRAYERS..."
"OR POLITICIANS ON TV SAYING; "THOUGHTS AND PRAYERS."

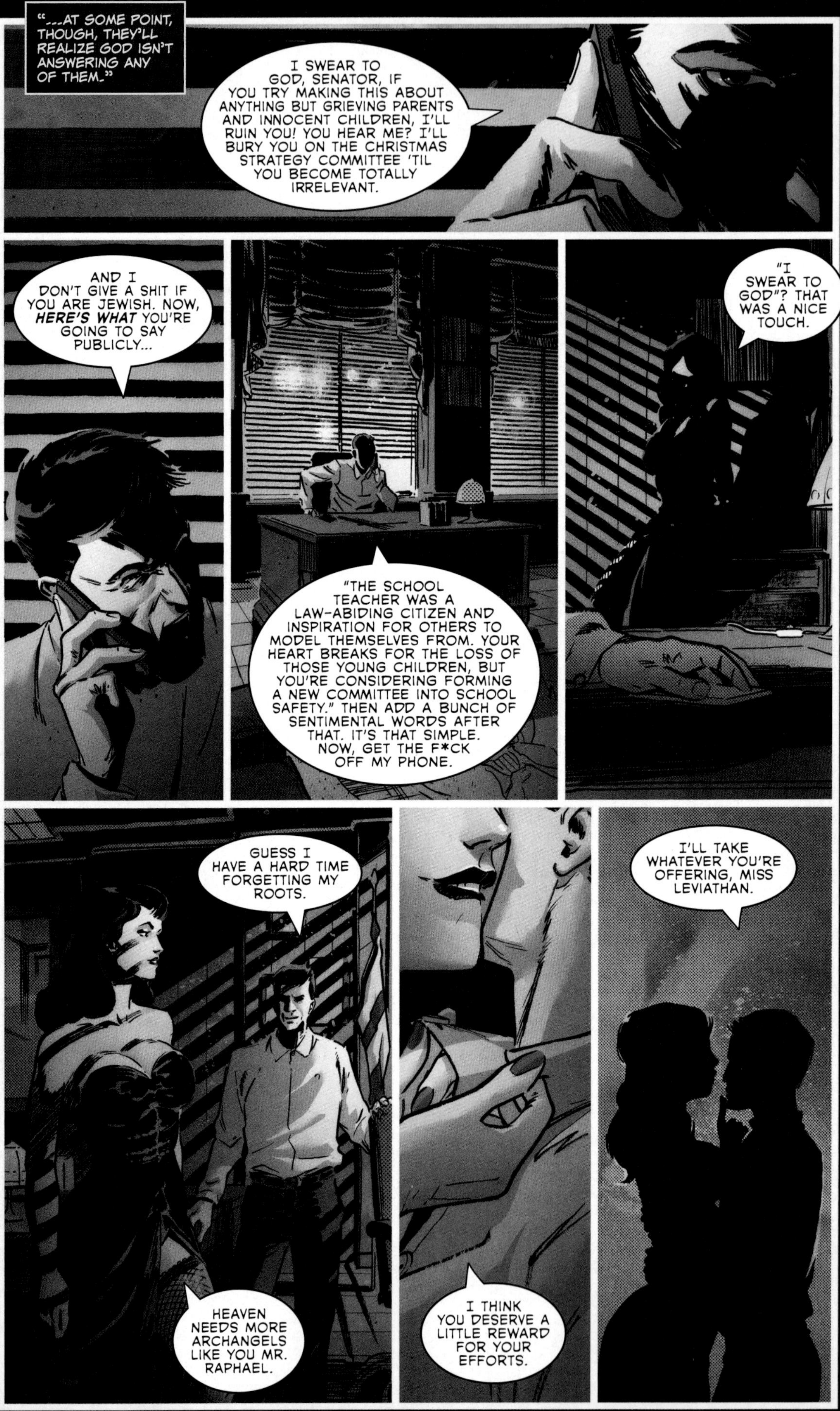
"...AT SOME POINT, THOUGH, THEY'LL REALIZE GOD ISN'T ANSWERING ANY OF THEM."
I SWEAR TO GOD, SENATOR, IF YOU TRY MAKING THIS ABOUT ANYTHING BUT GRIEVING PARENTS AND INNOCENT CHILDREN, I'LL RUIN YOU! YOU HEAR ME? I'LL BURY YOU ON THE CHRISTMAS STRATEGY COMMITTEE 'TIL YOU BECOME TOTALLY IRRELEVANT.
AND I DON'T GIVE A SHIT IF YOU ARE JEWISH. NOW, ***HERE'S WHAT*** YOU'RE GOING TO SAY PUBLICLY...
"THE SCHOOL TEACHER WAS A LAW-ABIDING CITIZEN AND INSPIRATION FOR OTHERS TO MODEL THEMSELVES FROM. YOUR HEART BREAKS FOR THE LOSS OF THOSE YOUNG CHILDREN, BUT YOU'RE CONSIDERING FORMING A NEW COMMITTEE INTO SCHOOL SAFETY." THEN ADD A BUNCH OF SENTIMENTAL WORDS AFTER THAT. IT'S THAT SIMPLE. NOW, GET THE F*CK OFF MY PHONE.
"I SWEAR TO GOD"? THAT WAS A NICE TOUCH.
GUESS I HAVE A HARD TIME FORGETTING MY ROOTS.
HEAVEN NEEDS MORE ARCHANGELS LIKE YOU MR. RAPHAEL.
I THINK YOU DESERVE A LITTLE REWARD FOR YOUR EFFORTS.
I'LL TAKE WHATEVER YOU'RE OFFERING, MISS LEVIATHAN.

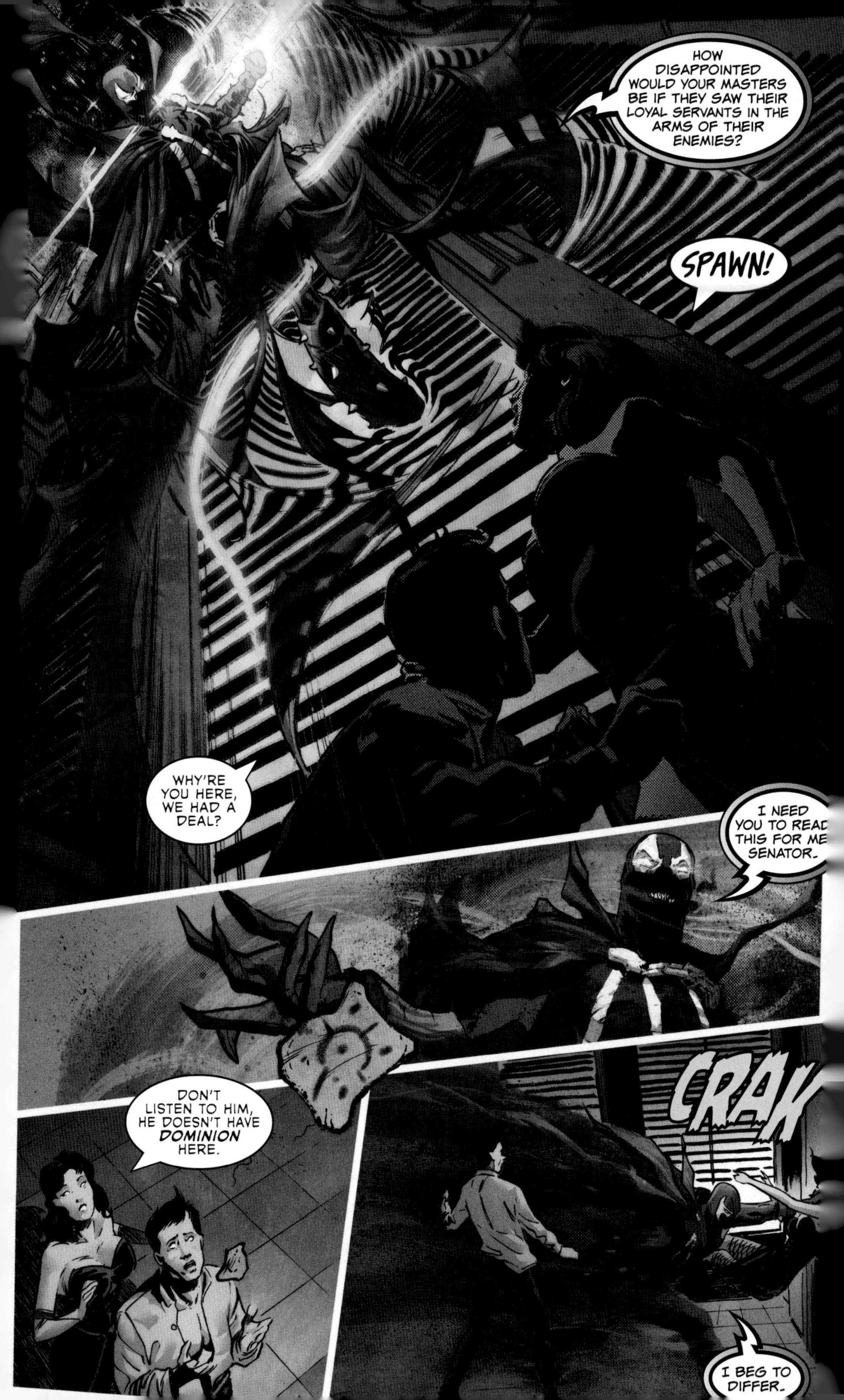
HOW DISAPPOINTED WOULD YOUR MASTERS BE IF THEY SAW THEIR LOYAL SERVANTS IN THE ARMS OF THEIR ENEMIES?
SPAWN!
WHY'RE YOU HERE, WE HAD A DEAL?
I NEED YOU TO READ THIS FOR ME SENATOR.
DON'T LISTEN TO HIM, HE DOESN'T HAVE *DOMINION* HERE.
CRAK
I BEG TO DIFFER.

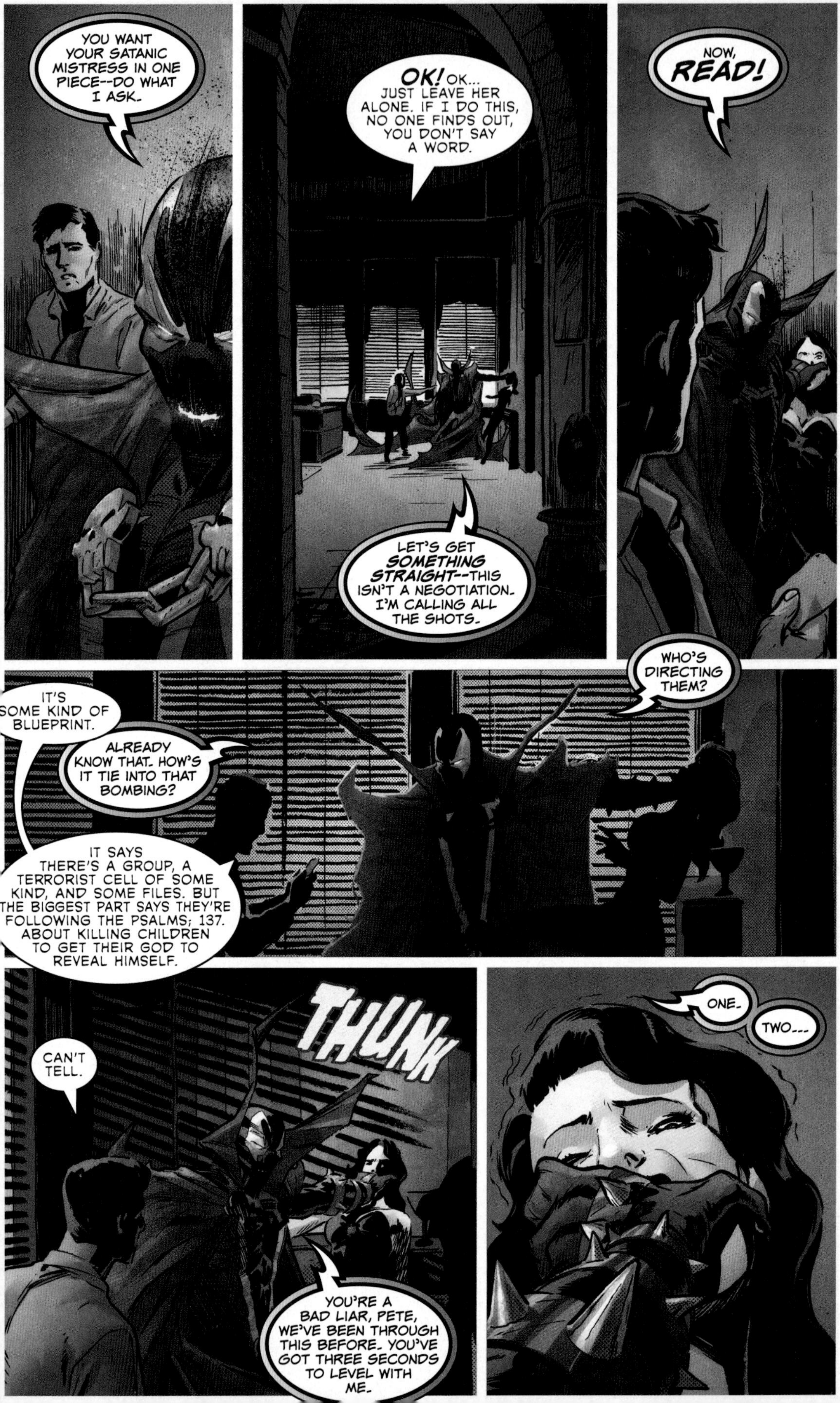
YOU WANT YOUR SATANIC MISTRESS IN ONE PIECE--DO WHAT I ASK.
OK! OK... JUST LEAVE HER ALONE. IF I DO THIS, NO ONE FINDS OUT, YOU DON'T SAY A WORD.
LET'S GET SOMETHING STRAIGHT--THIS ISN'T A NEGOTIATION. I'M CALLING ALL THE SHOTS.
NOW, READ!
IT'S SOME KIND OF BLUEPRINT.
ALREADY KNOW THAT. HOW'S IT TIE INTO THAT BOMBING?
IT SAYS THERE'S A GROUP, A TERRORIST CELL OF SOME KIND, AND SOME FILES. BUT THE BIGGEST PART SAYS THEY'RE FOLLOWING THE PSALMS; 137. ABOUT KILLING CHILDREN TO GET THEIR GOD TO REVEAL HIMSELF.
WHO'S DIRECTING THEM?
CAN'T TELL.
THUNK
YOU'RE A BAD LIAR, PETE, WE'VE BEEN THROUGH THIS BEFORE. YOU'VE GOT THREE SECONDS TO LEVEL WITH ME.
ONE.
TWO...

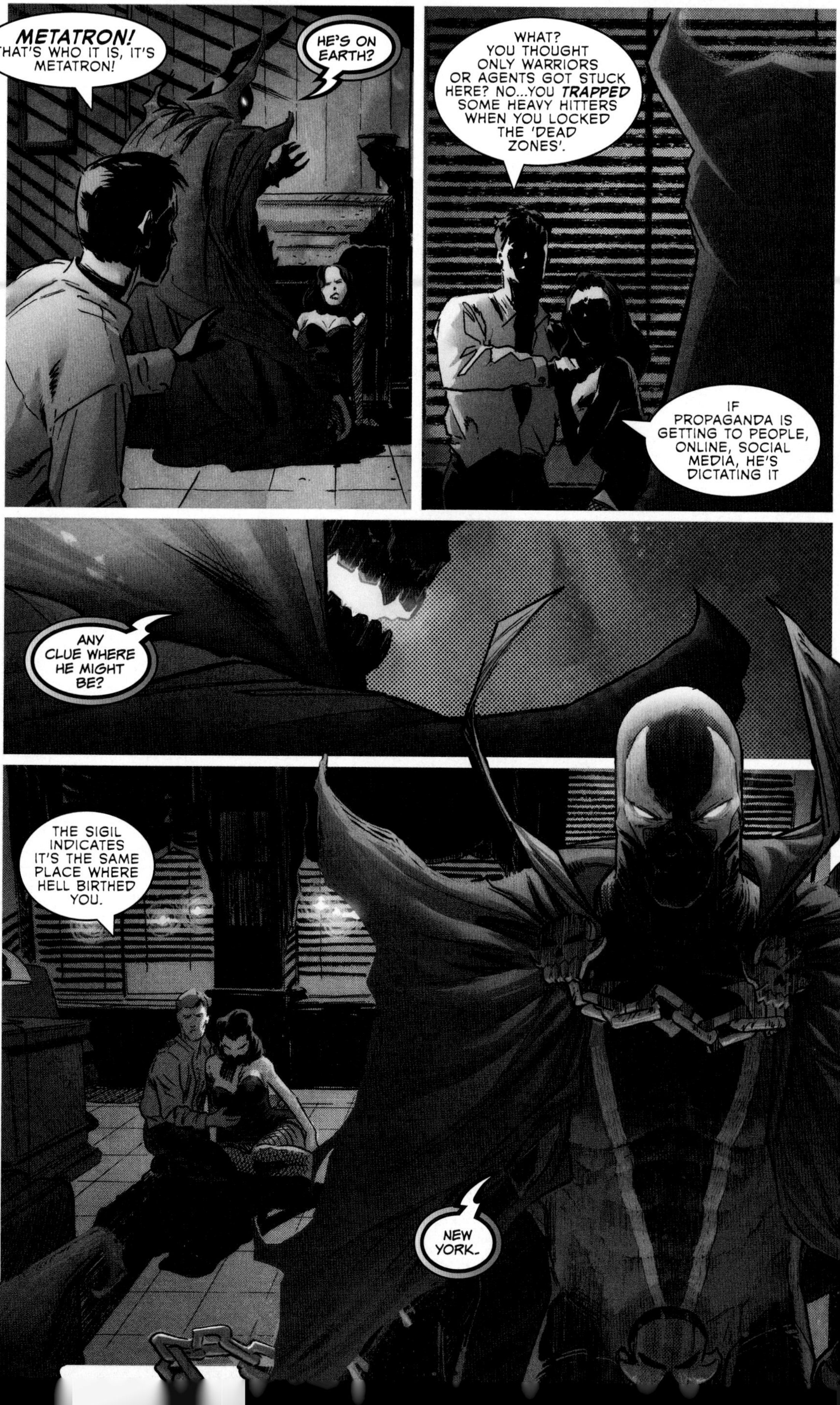
METATRON! THAT'S WHO IT IS, IT'S METATRON!
HE'S ON EARTH?
WHAT? YOU THOUGHT ONLY WARRIORS OR AGENTS GOT STUCK HERE? NO...YOU TRAPPED SOME HEAVY HITTERS WHEN YOU LOCKED THE 'DEAD ZONES'.
IF PROPAGANDA IS GETTING TO PEOPLE, ONLINE, SOCIAL MEDIA, HE'S DICTATING IT
ANY CLUE WHERE HE MIGHT BE?
THE SIGIL INDICATES IT'S THE SAME PLACE WHERE HELL BIRTHED YOU.
NEW YORK.

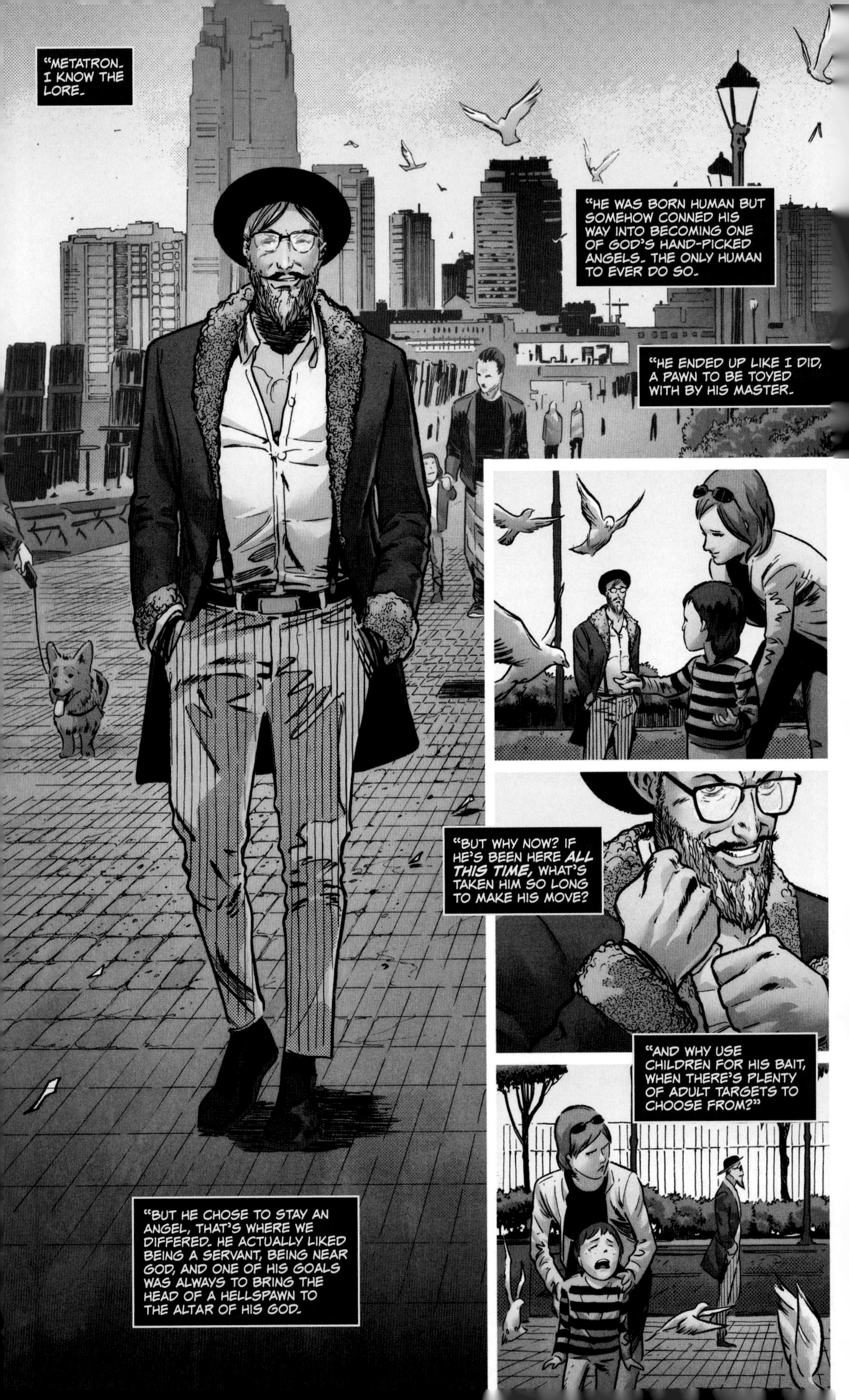
"METATRON. I KNOW THE LORE.
"HE WAS BORN HUMAN BUT SOMEHOW CONNED HIS WAY INTO BECOMING ONE OF GOD'S HAND-PICKED ANGELS. THE ONLY HUMAN TO EVER DO SO.
"HE ENDED UP LIKE I DID, A PAWN TO BE TOYED WITH BY HIS MASTER.
"BUT HE CHOSE TO STAY AN ANGEL, THAT'S WHERE WE DIFFERED. HE ACTUALLY LIKED BEING A SERVANT, BEING NEAR GOD, AND ONE OF HIS GOALS WAS ALWAYS TO BRING THE HEAD OF A HELLSPAWN TO THE ALTAR OF HIS GOD.
"BUT WHY NOW? IF HE'S BEEN HERE *ALL THIS TIME,* WHAT'S TAKEN HIM SO LONG TO MAKE HIS MOVE?
"AND WHY USE CHILDREN FOR HIS BAIT, WHEN THERE'S PLENTY OF ADULT TARGETS TO CHOOSE FROM?"

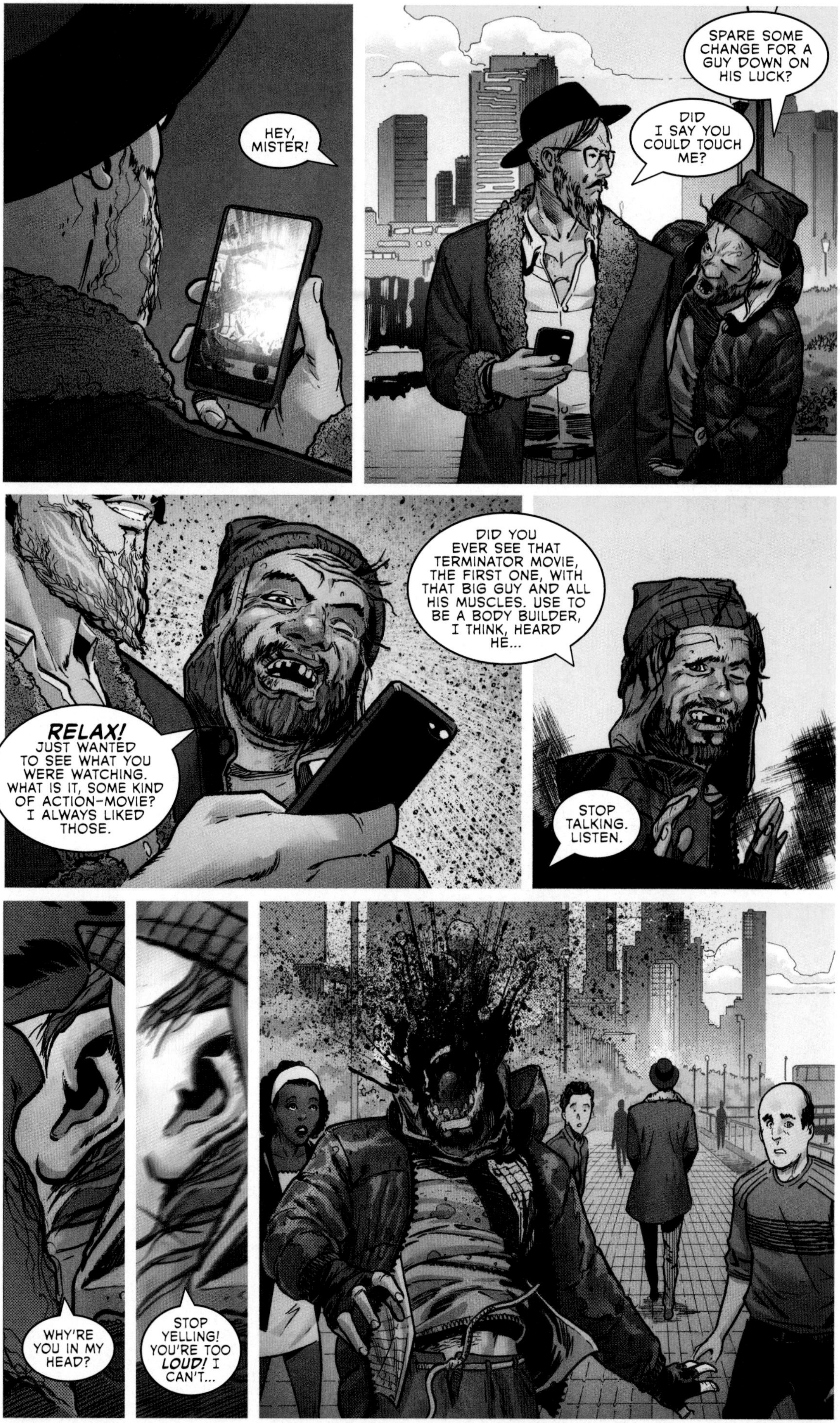
HEY, MISTER!
SPARE SOME CHANGE FOR A GUY DOWN ON HIS LUCK?
DID I SAY YOU COULD TOUCH ME?
RELAX! JUST WANTED TO SEE WHAT YOU WERE WATCHING. WHAT IS IT, SOME KIND OF ACTION-MOVIE? I ALWAYS LIKED THOSE.
DID YOU EVER SEE THAT TERMINATOR MOVIE, THE FIRST ONE, WITH THAT BIG GUY AND ALL HIS MUSCLES. USE TO BE A BODY BUILDER, I THINK, HEARD HE...
STOP TALKING. LISTEN.
WHY'RE YOU IN MY HEAD?
STOP YELLING! YOU'RE TOO LOUD! I CAN'T...

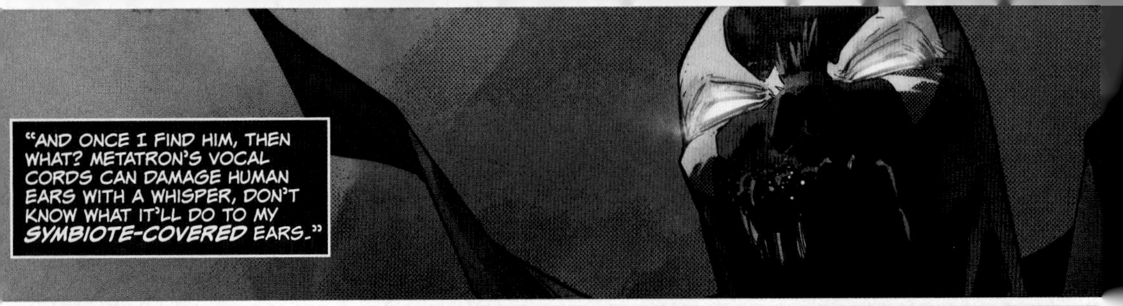
"AND ONCE I FIND HIM, THEN WHAT? METATRON'S VOCAL CORDS CAN DAMAGE HUMAN EARS WITH A WHISPER, DON'T KNOW WHAT IT'LL DO TO MY SYMBIOTE-COVERED EARS."

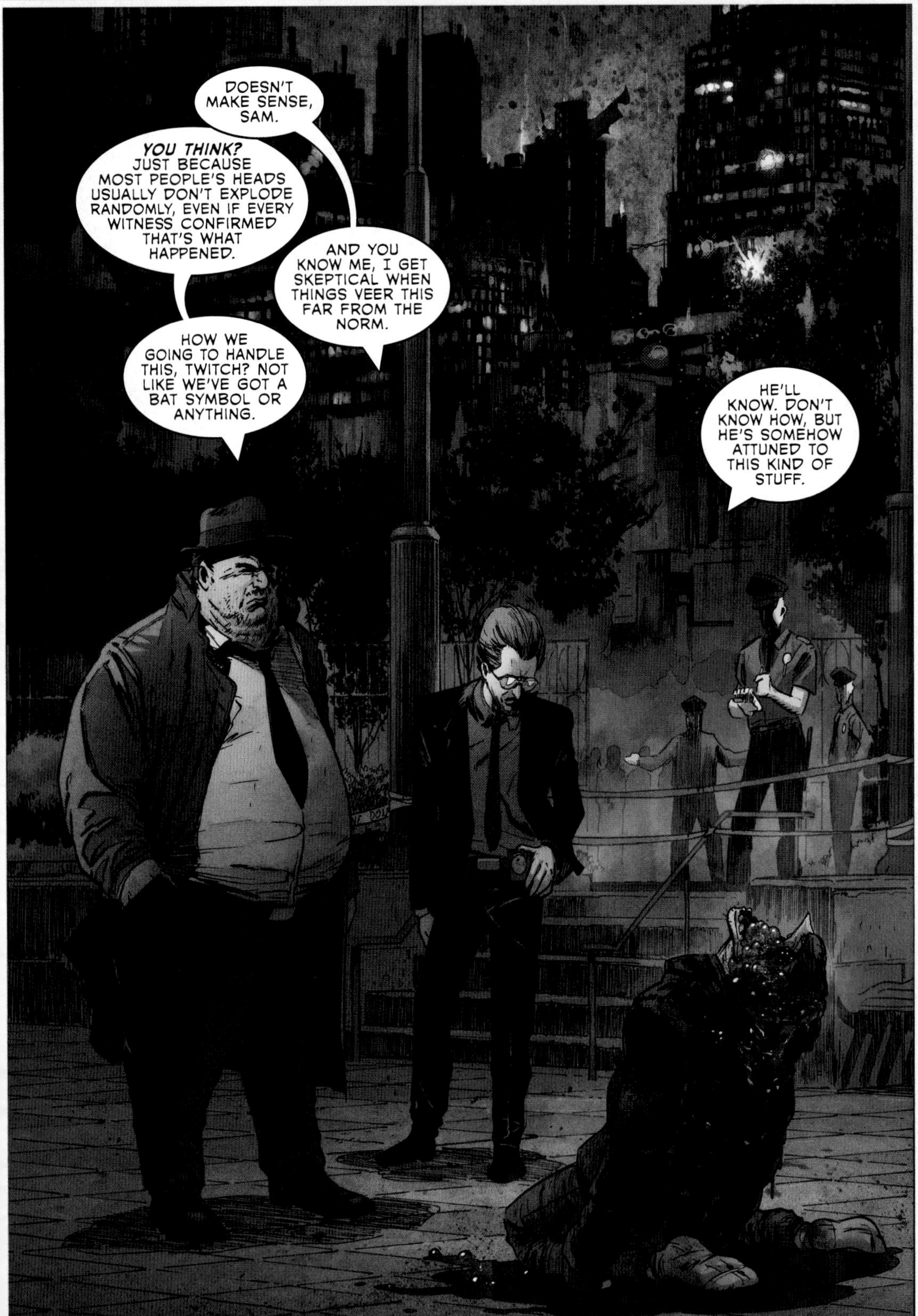
DOESN'T MAKE SENSE, SAM.
YOU THINK? JUST BECAUSE MOST PEOPLE'S HEADS USUALLY DON'T EXPLODE RANDOMLY, EVEN IF EVERY WITNESS CONFIRMED THAT'S WHAT HAPPENED.
AND YOU KNOW ME, I GET SKEPTICAL WHEN THINGS VEER THIS FAR FROM THE NORM.
HOW WE GOING TO HANDLE THIS, TWITCH? NOT LIKE WE'VE GOT A BAT SYMBOL OR ANYTHING.
HE'LL KNOW. DON'T KNOW HOW, BUT HE'S SOMEHOW ATTUNED TO THIS KIND OF STUFF.

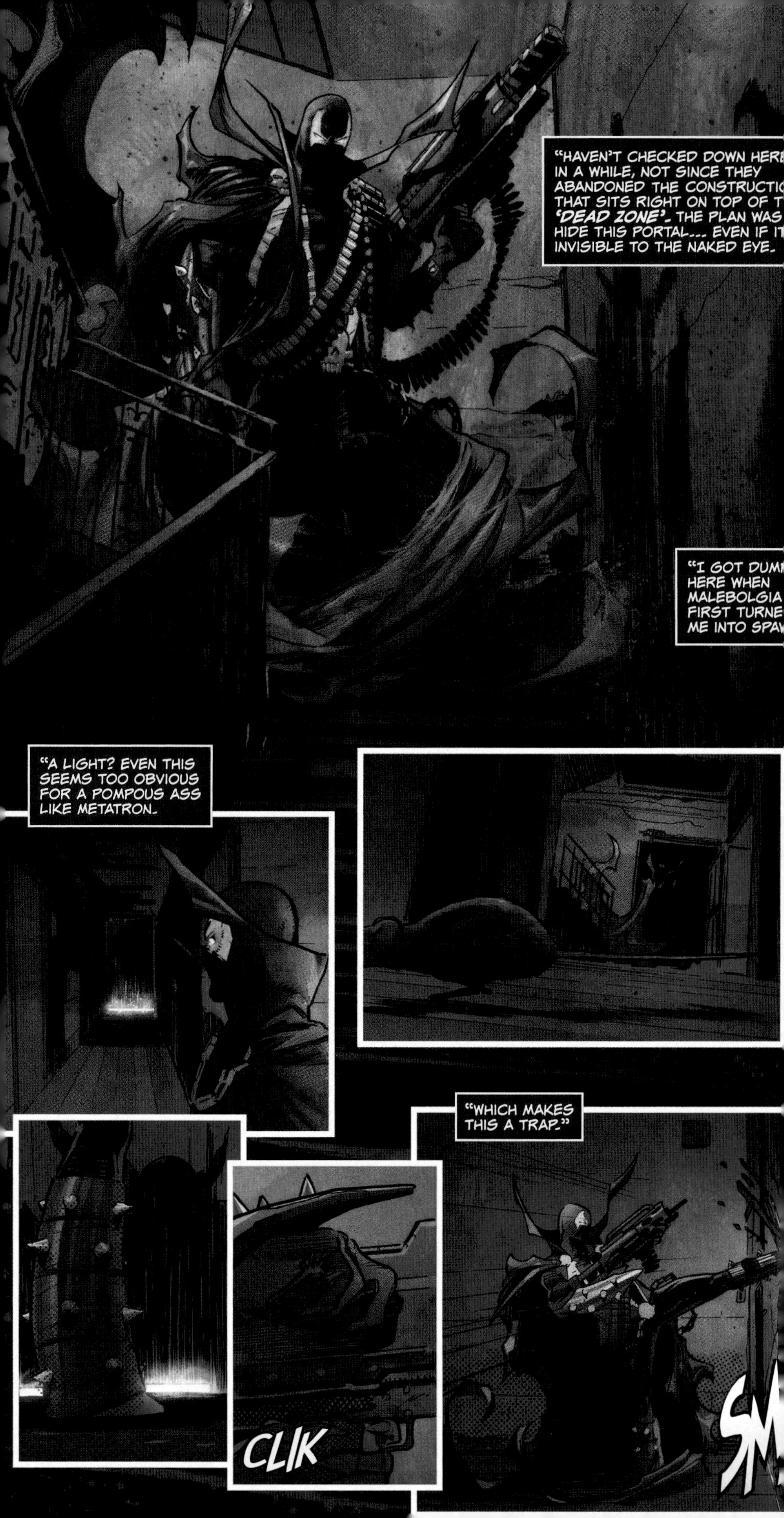
"HAVEN'T CHECKED DOWN HERE IN A WHILE, NOT SINCE THEY ABANDONED THE CONSTRUCTIC THAT SITS RIGHT ON TOP OF T 'DEAD ZONE'. THE PLAN WAS HIDE THIS PORTAL... EVEN IF IT INVISIBLE TO THE NAKED EYE.
"I GOT DUMP HERE WHEN MALEBOLGIA FIRST TURNE ME INTO SPAV
"A LIGHT? EVEN THIS SEEMS TOO OBVIOUS FOR A POMPOUS ASS LIKE METATRON.
"WHICH MAKES THIS A TRAP."
CLIK

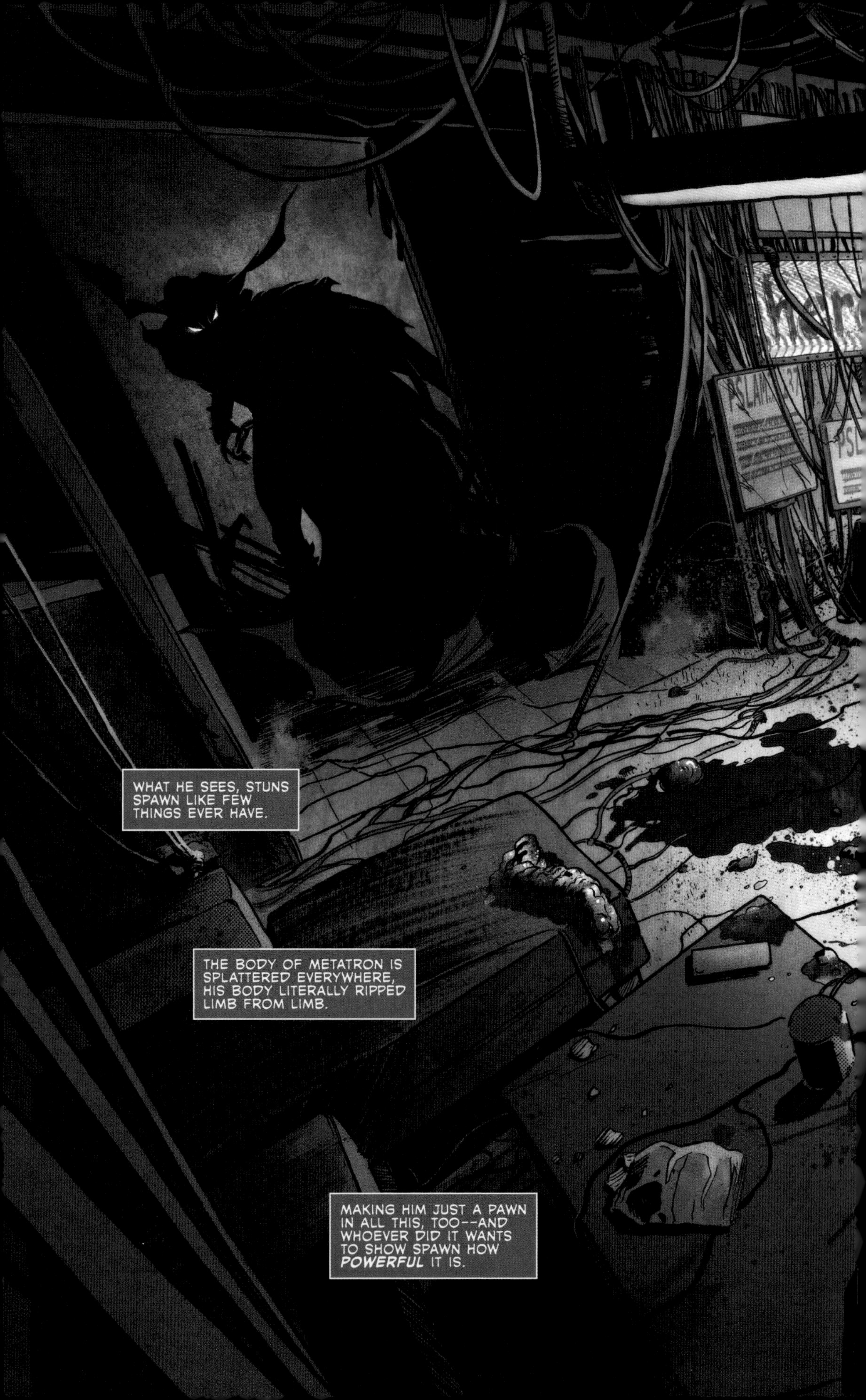
WHAT HE SEES, STUNS SPAWN LIKE FEW THINGS EVER HAVE.
THE BODY OF METATRON IS SPLATTERED EVERYWHERE, HIS BODY LITERALLY RIPPED LIMB FROM LIMB.
MAKING HIM JUST A PAWN IN ALL THIS, TOO--AND WHOEVER DID IT WANTS TO SHOW SPAWN HOW *POWERFUL* IT IS.

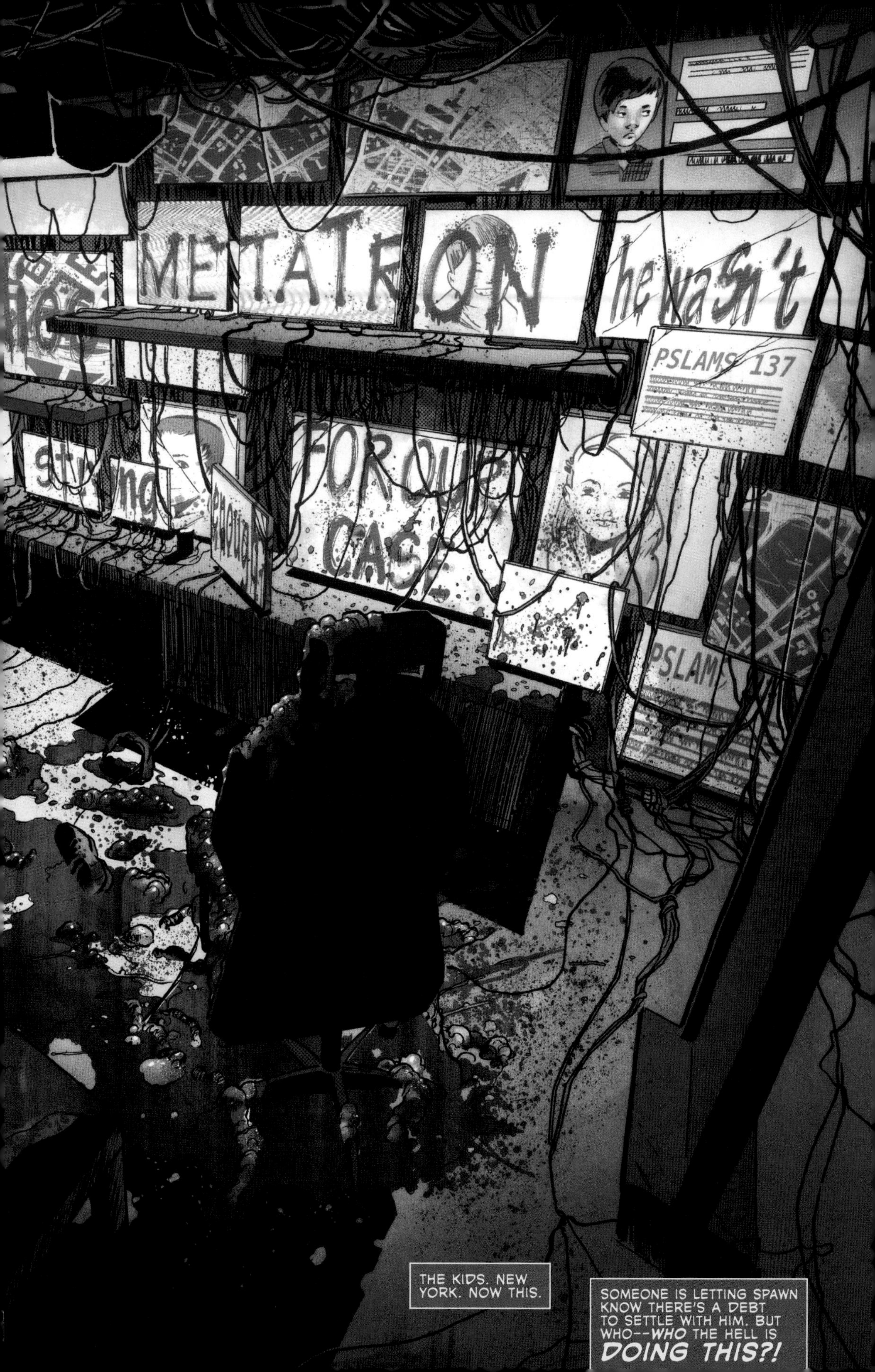
METATRON
he wasn't
strong
enough
FOR OUR CASE
PSLAMS 137
PSLAMS
THE KIDS. NEW YORK. NOW THIS.
SOMEONE IS LETTING SPAWN KNOW THERE'S A DEBT TO SETTLE WITH HIM. BUT WHO--*WHO* THE HELL IS ***DOING THIS?!***

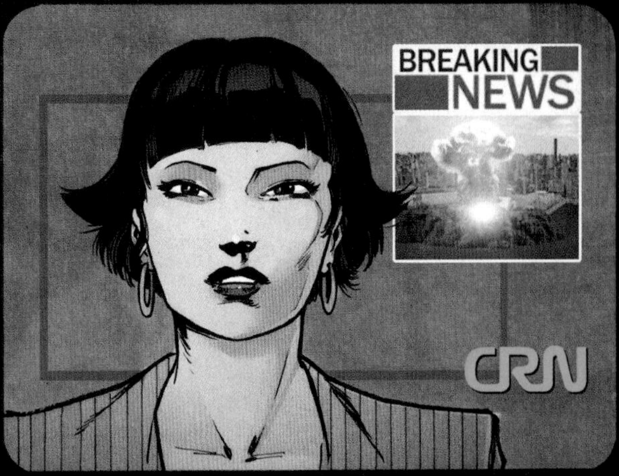
BREAKING
NEWS
CRN

FEDERAL AGENTS, TODAY, RELEASED NEW INFORMATION FROM THEIR INVESTIGATION INTO THE SCHOOL BOMBING IN SEATTLE, WASHINGTON LAST WEEK. THAT BOMBING KILLED SIXTEEN PEOPLE INCLUDING FOURTEEN CHILDREN AGED FIVE OR SIX YEARS OLD. THE INVESTIGATORS SAID THAT AFTER TRACING SOME OF THE CHEMICALS USED IN THAT EXPLOSION, THEY SEARCHED A RECENTLY ABANDONED APARTMENT WHERE THEY SEIZED DOZENS OF HARD DRIVES THAT ARE POTENTIALLY CONNECTED TO AN UNDERGROUND RELIGIOUS MOVEMENT CALLING ITSELF PSALMS 137.

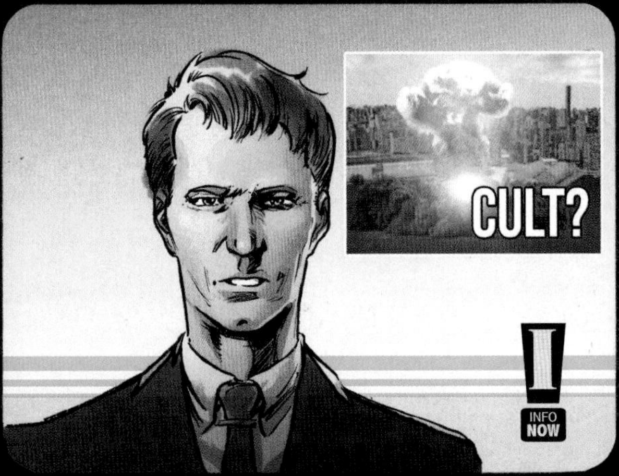
CULT?
INFO
NOW

ALLEGEDLY, POLICE FOUND BIBLICAL PASSAGES TAPED ONTO WALLS OF THE APARTMENT. AN ANONYMOUS SOURCE SAID THE BIBLE PASSAGES SEEMED TO REFERENCE CHILDREN AND MURDER. NO MOTIVES HAVE BEEN GIVEN AT THIS TIME, BUT THERE ARE GROWING CONCERNS THAT THESE TYPES OF HATE GROUPS OR CULTS, COULD HAVE MEMBERSHIPS NUMBERING IN THE HUNDREDS OR THOUSANDS. WITH STRONG CELLS SPREAD ACROSS THE ENTIRE GLOBE.

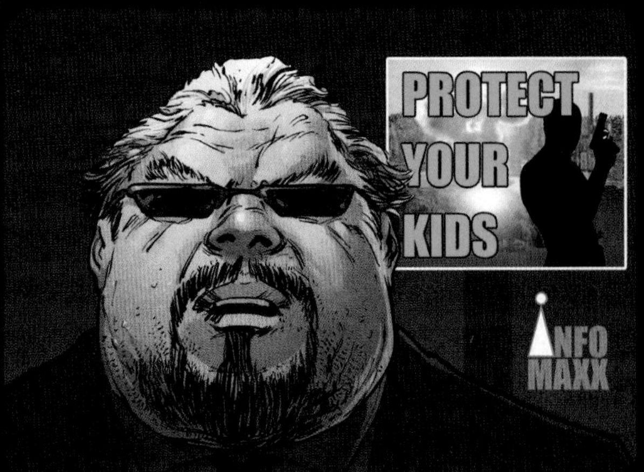
PROTECT
YOUR
KIDS
INFO
MAXX

"TO **CLEANSE THE EARTH...!!**

THAT'S THEIR GOAL. THEY WANT TO RID US OF THE WICKED AND THE EVIL... SOOOO, THESE ***WHACK-JOBS*** THINK BLOWING UP KIDS IS THE BEST WAY TO GET THAT MESSAGE ACROSS.

FRIGGIN' IDIOTS!

"WE'VE SEEN THESE KIND OF TERROR GROUPS POPPING UP ONLINE ALL OVER THE WORLD. AND NOW WE HAVE POSSIBLE HOMEGROWN ISIS WANNABES IN OUR OWN BACKYARD. ONES THAT WANT YOUR KIDS. I DON'T SHY AWAY FROM THE DARK STUFF VIEWERS, I'M HERE FOR THE TRUTH. AND THE TRUTH IS MY GUNS ARE ***LOCKED AND LOADED!*** I HOPE THEY TRY COMING FOR ***MY*** CHILDREN!"

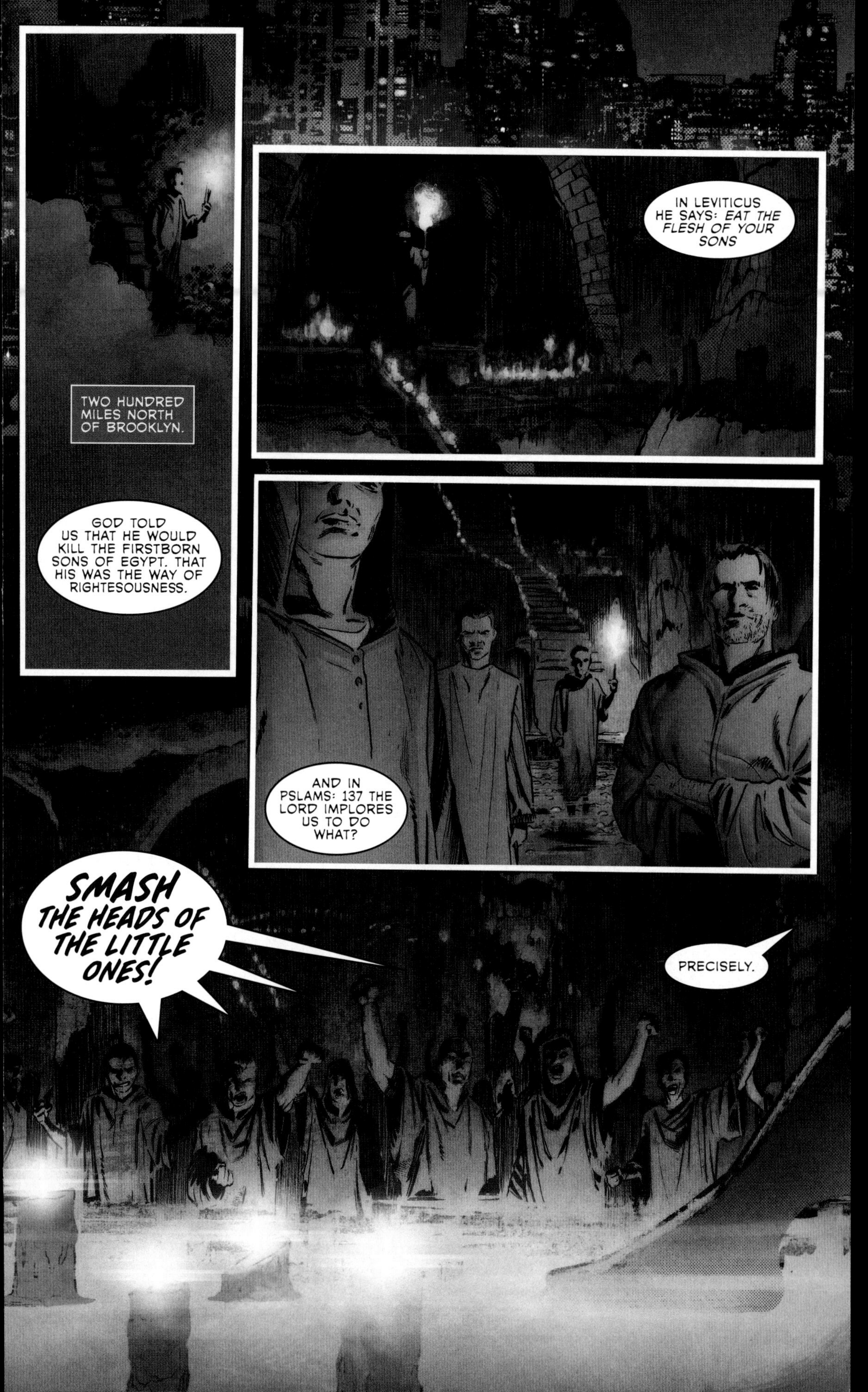
TWO HUNDRED MILES NORTH OF BROOKLYN.
GOD TOLD US THAT HE WOULD KILL THE FIRSTBORN SONS OF EGYPT. THAT HIS WAS THE WAY OF RIGHTESOUSNESS.
IN LEVITICUS HE SAYS: *EAT THE FLESH OF YOUR SONS*
AND IN PSLAMS: 137 THE LORD IMPLORES US TO DO WHAT?
SMASH THE HEADS OF THE LITTLE ONES!
PRECISELY.

AND SO, MY FLOCK, WE'LL LEAVE A PILE OF BODIES SO HIGH, THE ENTIRE WORLD WILL MOURN. THAT'S WHEN HE'LL COME--WHEN OUR KING WILL REVEAL HIMSELF.
AND WE SHALL DELIVER HIM ALL THE GLORY... AND ALL THE PUNISHMENT-- HE SO RICHLY DESERVES!
ALL HAIL KING SPAWN!

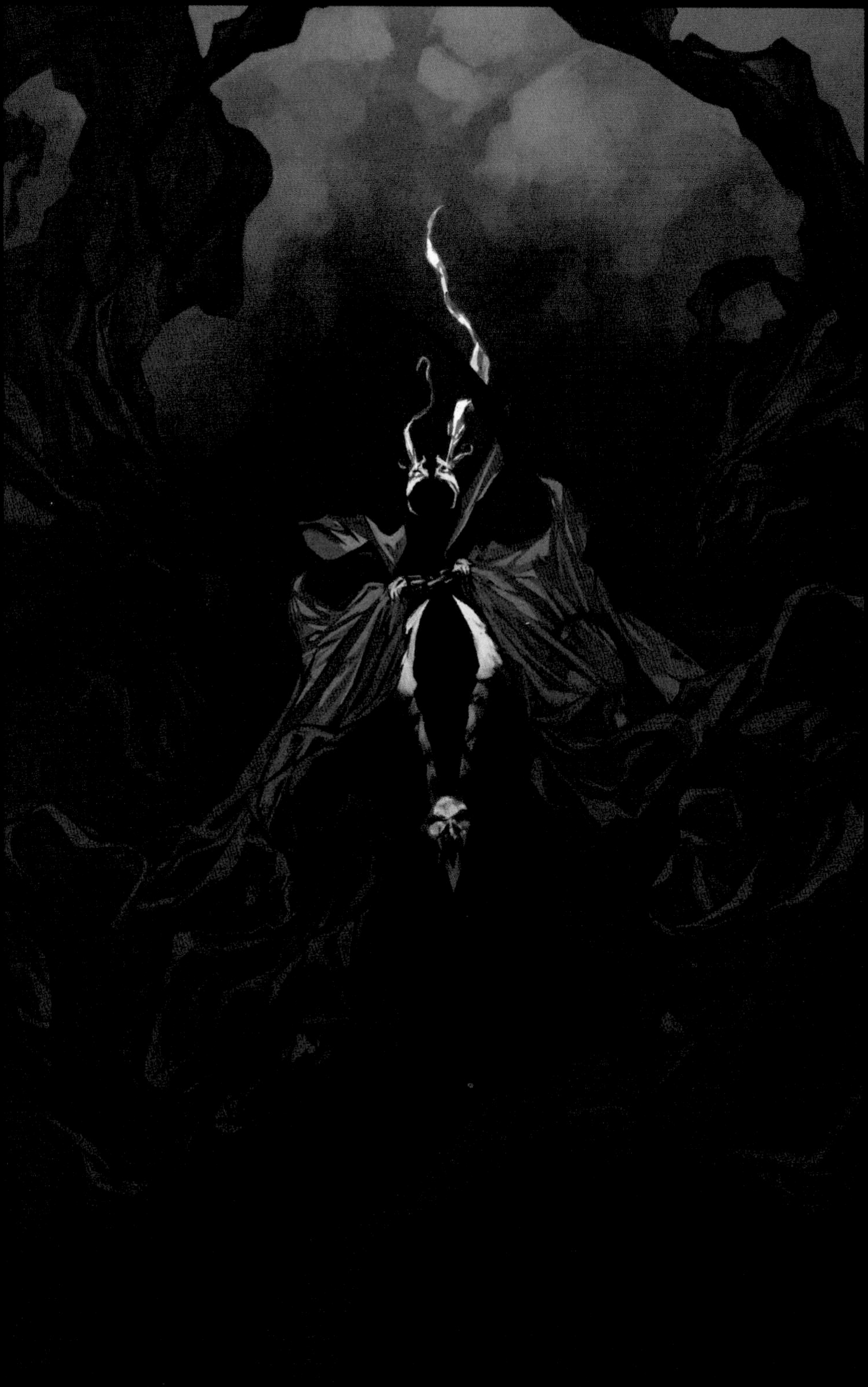

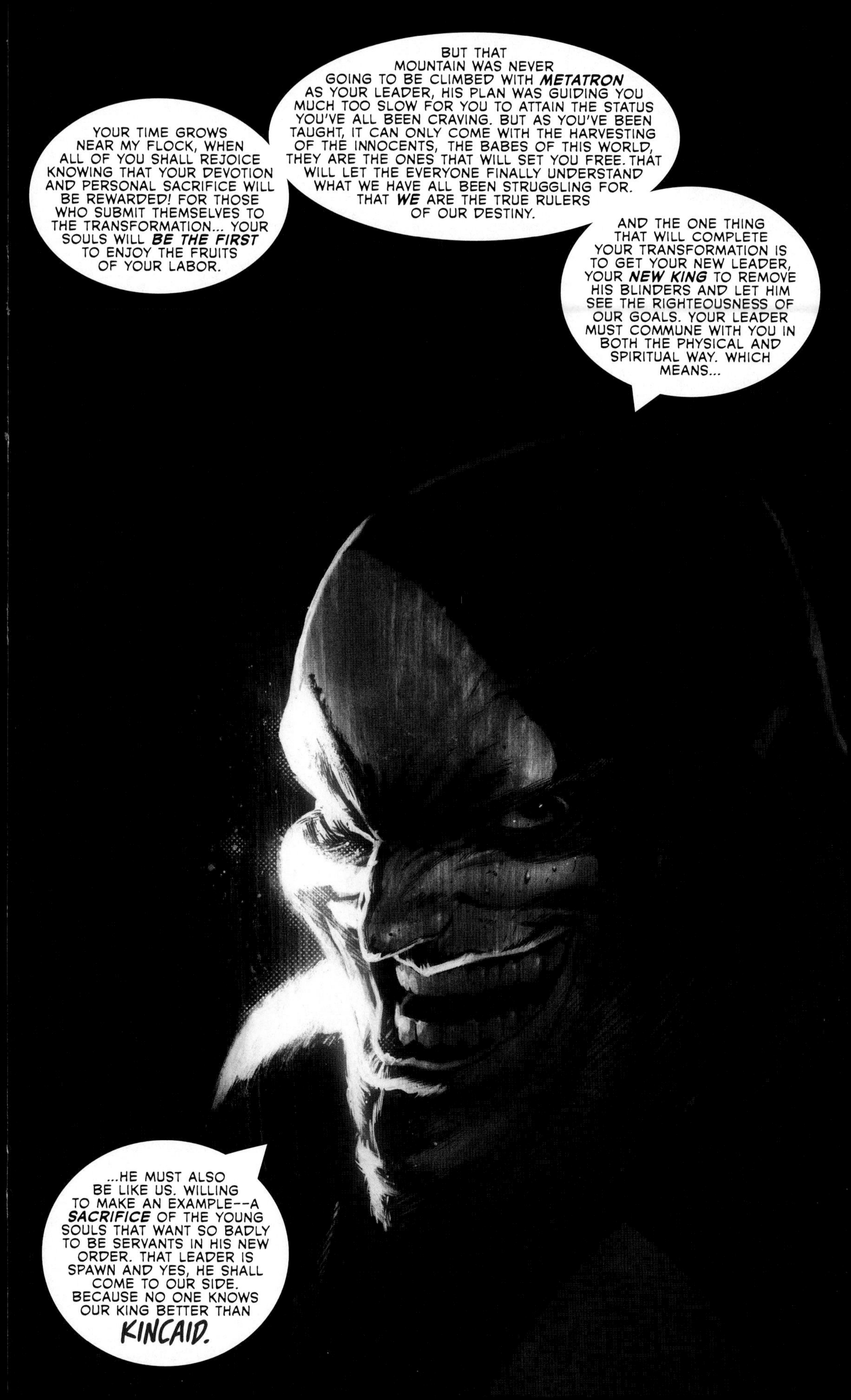
YOUR TIME GROWS NEAR MY FLOCK, WHEN ALL OF YOU SHALL REJOICE KNOWING THAT YOUR DEVOTION AND PERSONAL SACRIFICE WILL BE REWARDED! FOR THOSE WHO SUBMIT THEMSELVES TO THE TRANSFORMATION... YOUR SOULS WILL ***BE THE FIRST*** TO ENJOY THE FRUITS OF YOUR LABOR.
BUT THAT MOUNTAIN WAS NEVER GOING TO BE CLIMBED WITH ***METATRON*** AS YOUR LEADER, HIS PLAN WAS GUIDING YOU MUCH TOO SLOW FOR YOU TO ATTAIN THE STATUS YOU'VE ALL BEEN CRAVING. BUT AS YOU'VE BEEN TAUGHT, IT CAN ONLY COME WITH THE HARVESTING OF THE INNOCENTS, THE BABES OF THIS WORLD, THEY ARE THE ONES THAT WILL SET YOU FREE. THAT WILL LET THE EVERYONE FINALLY UNDERSTAND WHAT WE HAVE ALL BEEN STRUGGLING FOR. THAT ***WE*** ARE THE TRUE RULERS OF OUR DESTINY.
AND THE ONE THING THAT WILL COMPLETE YOUR TRANSFORMATION IS TO GET YOUR NEW LEADER, YOUR ***NEW KING*** TO REMOVE HIS BLINDERS AND LET HIM SEE THE RIGHTEOUSNESS OF OUR GOALS. YOUR LEADER MUST COMMUNE WITH YOU IN BOTH THE PHYSICAL AND SPIRITUAL WAY. WHICH MEANS...
...HE MUST ALSO BE LIKE US. WILLING TO MAKE AN EXAMPLE--A ***SACRIFICE*** OF THE YOUNG SOULS THAT WANT SO BADLY TO BE SERVANTS IN HIS NEW ORDER. THAT LEADER IS SPAWN AND YES, HE SHALL COME TO OUR SIDE. BECAUSE NO ONE KNOWS OUR KING BETTER THAN
KINCAID.

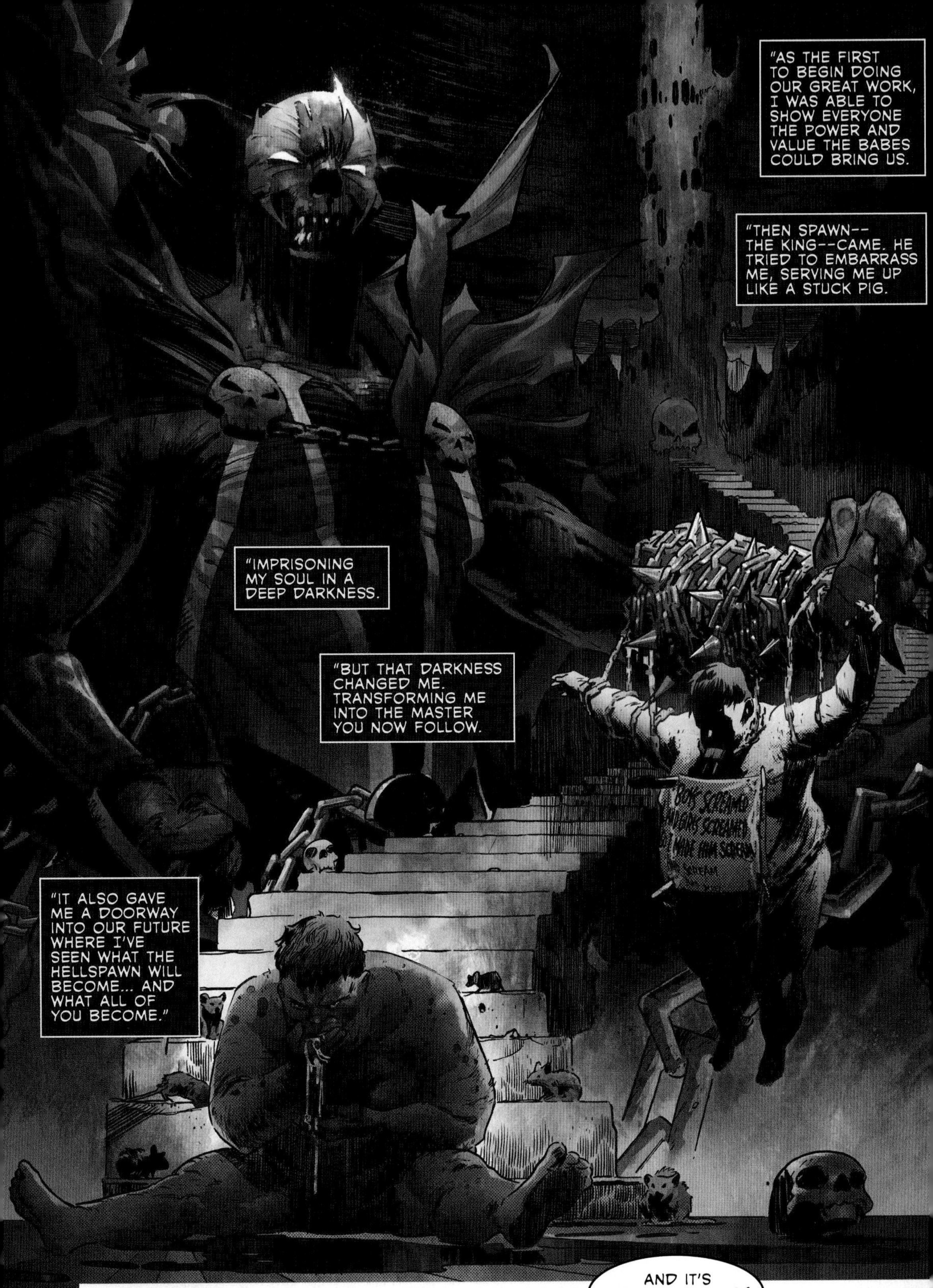
"AS THE FIRST TO BEGIN DOING OUR GREAT WORK, I WAS ABLE TO SHOW EVERYONE THE POWER AND VALUE THE BABES COULD BRING US.
"THEN SPAWN-- THE KING--CAME. HE TRIED TO EMBARRASS ME, SERVING ME UP LIKE A STUCK PIG.
"IMPRISONING MY SOUL IN A DEEP DARKNESS.
"BUT THAT DARKNESS CHANGED ME. TRANSFORMING ME INTO THE MASTER YOU NOW FOLLOW.
"IT ALSO GAVE ME A DOORWAY INTO OUR FUTURE WHERE I'VE SEEN WHAT THE HELLSPAWN WILL BECOME... AND WHAT ALL OF YOU BECOME."

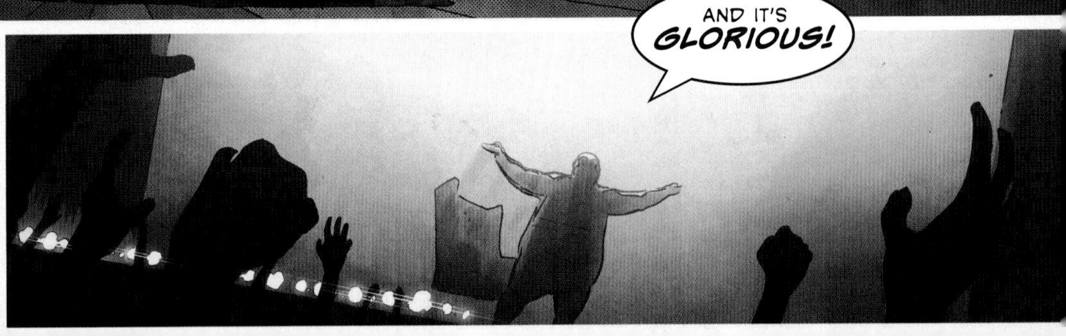
AND IT'S GLORIOUS!

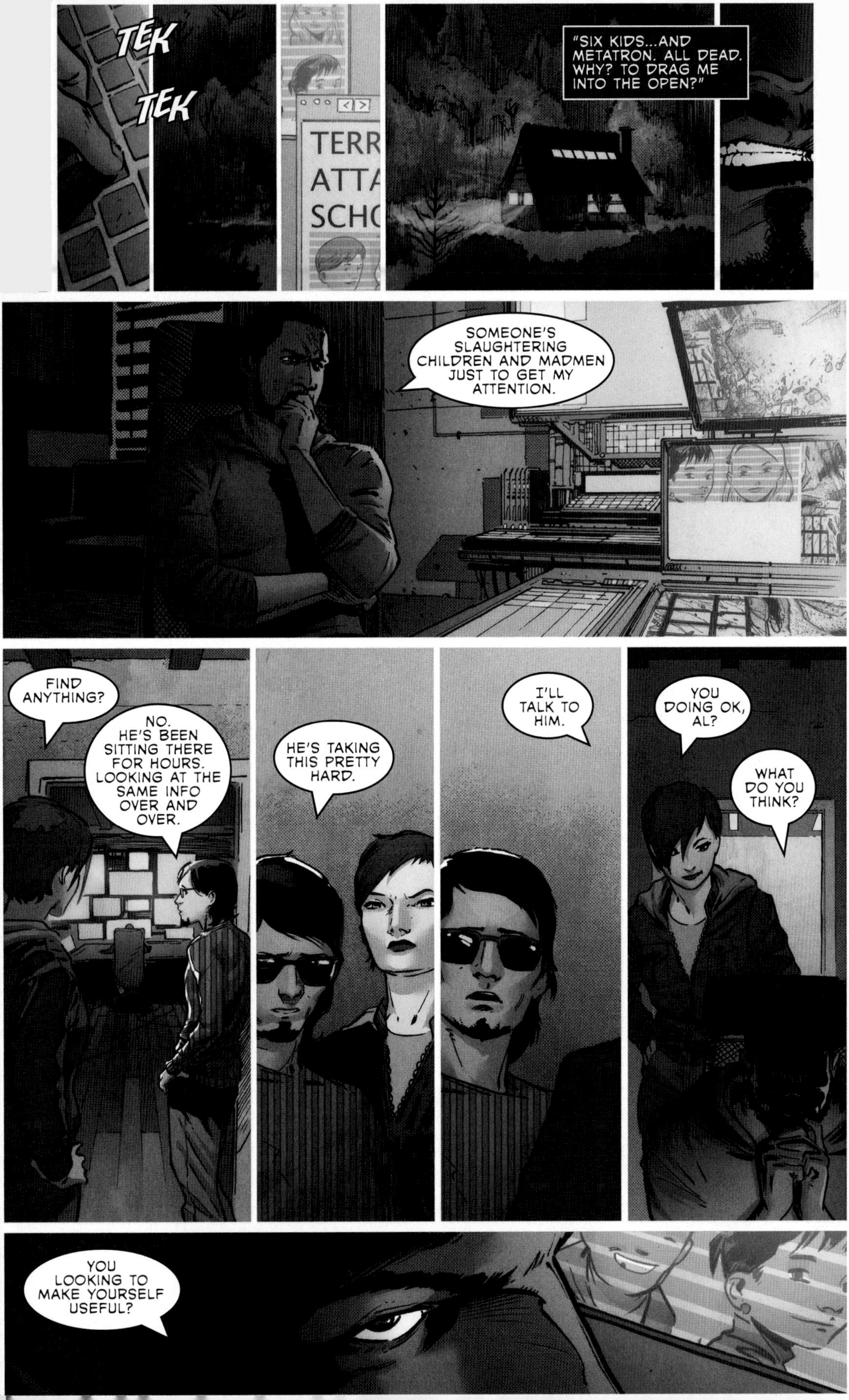
TEK
TEK
TERR
ATTA
SCHO
"SIX KIDS...AND METATRON. ALL DEAD. WHY? TO DRAG ME INTO THE OPEN?"
SOMEONE'S SLAUGHTERING CHILDREN AND MADMEN JUST TO GET MY ATTENTION.
FIND ANYTHING?
NO. HE'S BEEN SITTING THERE FOR HOURS. LOOKING AT THE SAME INFO OVER AND OVER.
HE'S TAKING THIS PRETTY HARD.
I'LL TALK TO HIM.
YOU DOING OK, AL?
WHAT DO YOU THINK?
YOU LOOKING TO MAKE YOURSELF USEFUL?

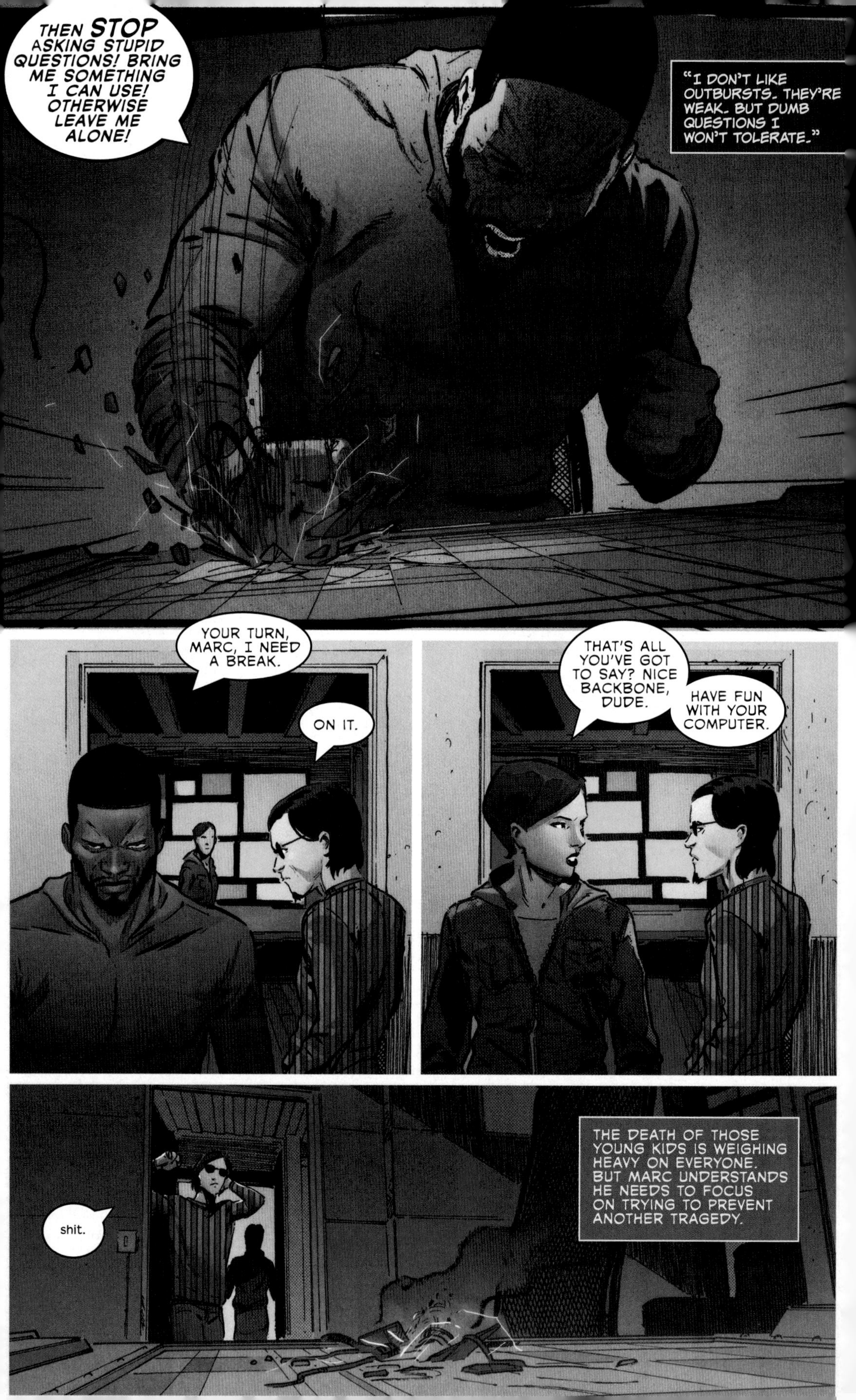

THEN STOP ASKING STUPID QUESTIONS! BRING ME SOMETHING I CAN USE! OTHERWISE LEAVE ME ALONE!
"I DON'T LIKE OUTBURSTS. THEY'RE WEAK. BUT DUMB QUESTIONS I WON'T TOLERATE."
YOUR TURN, MARC, I NEED A BREAK.
ON IT.
THAT'S ALL YOU'VE GOT TO SAY? NICE BACKBONE, DUDE.
HAVE FUN WITH YOUR COMPUTER.
THE DEATH OF THOSE YOUNG KIDS IS WEIGHING HEAVY ON EVERYONE. BUT MARC UNDERSTANDS HE NEEDS TO FOCUS ON TRYING TO PREVENT ANOTHER TRAGEDY.
shit.

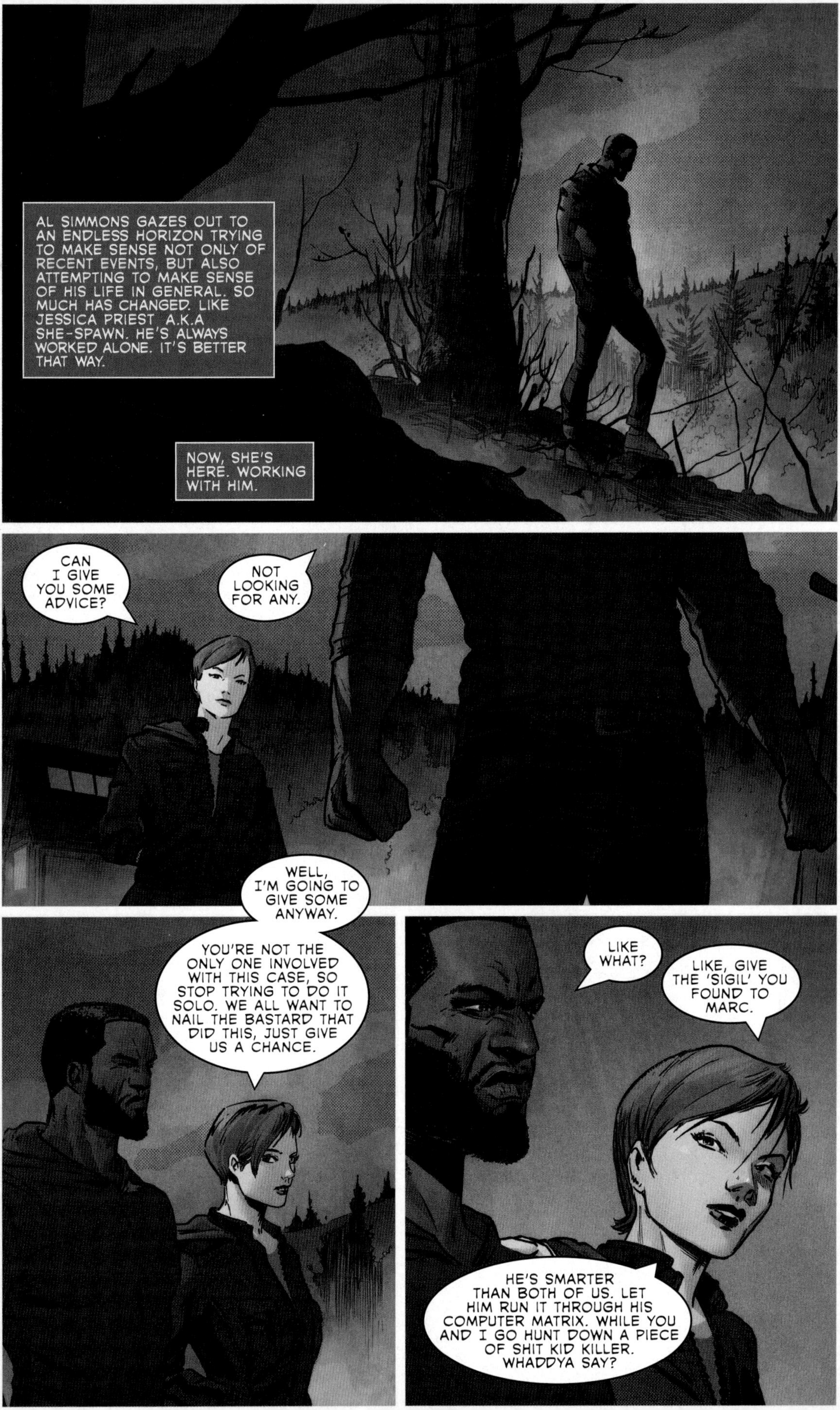
AL SIMMONS GAZES OUT TO AN ENDLESS HORIZON TRYING TO MAKE SENSE NOT ONLY OF RECENT EVENTS, BUT ALSO ATTEMPTING TO MAKE SENSE OF HIS LIFE IN GENERAL. SO MUCH HAS CHANGED. LIKE JESSICA PRIEST A.K.A SHE-SPAWN. HE'S ALWAYS WORKED ALONE. IT'S BETTER THAT WAY.
NOW, SHE'S HERE. WORKING WITH HIM.
CAN I GIVE YOU SOME ADVICE?
NOT LOOKING FOR ANY.
WELL, I'M GOING TO GIVE SOME ANYWAY.
YOU'RE NOT THE ONLY ONE INVOLVED WITH THIS CASE, SO STOP TRYING TO DO IT SOLO. WE ALL WANT TO NAIL THE BASTARD THAT DID THIS, JUST GIVE US A CHANCE.
LIKE WHAT?
LIKE, GIVE THE 'SIGIL' YOU FOUND TO MARC.
HE'S SMARTER THAN BOTH OF US. LET HIM RUN IT THROUGH HIS COMPUTER MATRIX. WHILE YOU AND I GO HUNT DOWN A PIECE OF SHIT KID KILLER. WHADDYA SAY?

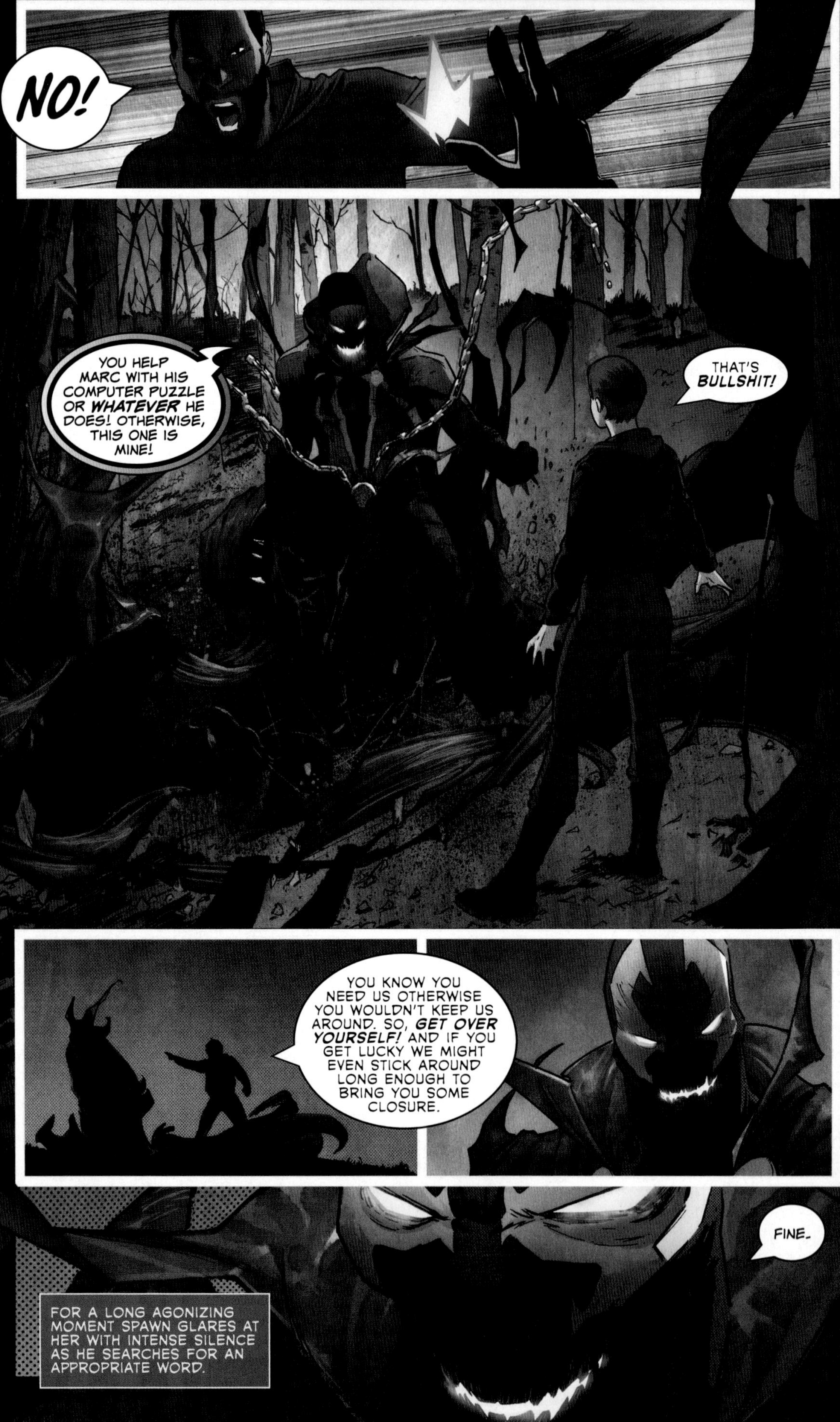
NO!
YOU HELP MARC WITH HIS COMPUTER PUZZLE OR WHATEVER HE DOES! OTHERWISE, THIS ONE IS MINE!
THAT'S BULLSHIT!
YOU KNOW YOU NEED US OTHERWISE YOU WOULDN'T KEEP US AROUND. SO, GET OVER YOURSELF! AND IF YOU GET LUCKY WE MIGHT EVEN STICK AROUND LONG ENOUGH TO BRING YOU SOME CLOSURE.
FOR A LONG AGONIZING MOMENT SPAWN GLARES AT HER WITH INTENSE SILENCE AS HE SEARCHES FOR AN APPROPRIATE WORD.
FINE.

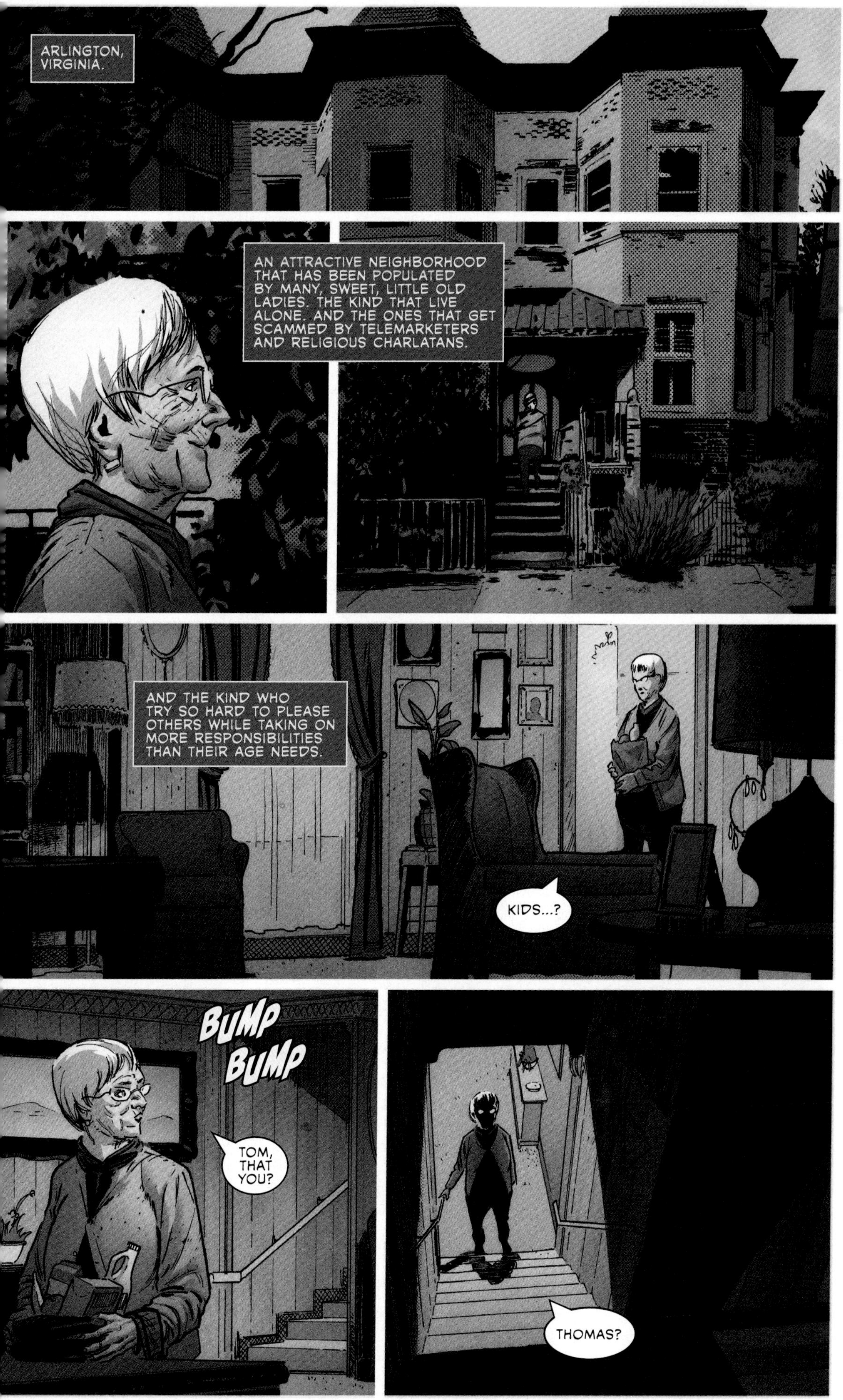
ARLINGTON, VIRGINIA.
AN ATTRACTIVE NEIGHBORHOOD THAT HAS BEEN POPULATED BY MANY, SWEET, LITTLE OLD LADIES. THE KIND THAT LIVE ALONE. AND THE ONES THAT GET SCAMMED BY TELEMARKETERS AND RELIGIOUS CHARLATANS.
AND THE KIND WHO TRY SO HARD TO PLEASE OTHERS WHILE TAKING ON MORE RESPONSIBILITIES THAN THEIR AGE NEEDS.
KIDS...?
BUMP BUMP
TOM, THAT YOU?
THOMAS?

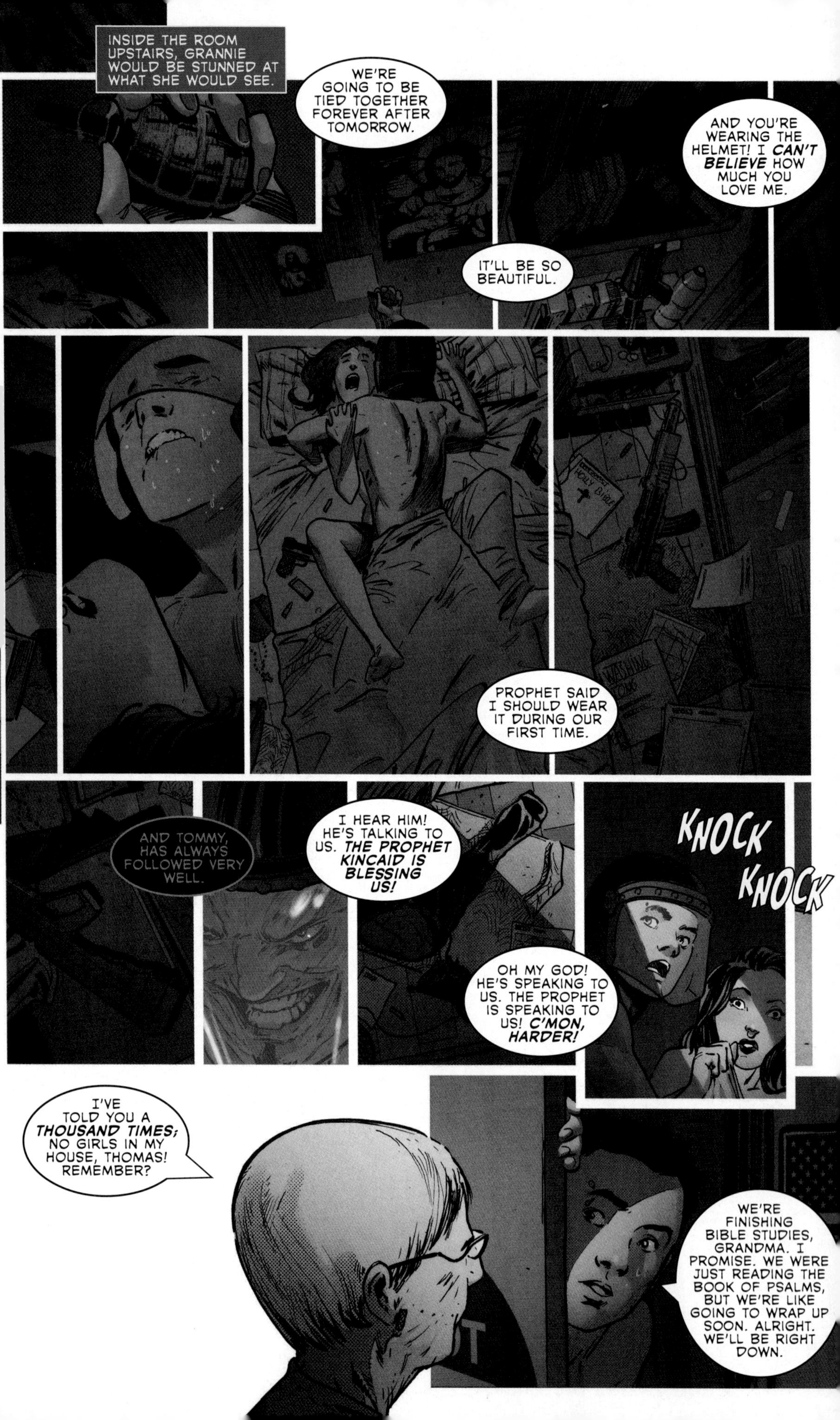
INSIDE THE ROOM UPSTAIRS, GRANNIE WOULD BE STUNNED AT WHAT SHE WOULD SEE.
WE'RE GOING TO BE TIED TOGETHER FOREVER AFTER TOMORROW.
AND YOU'RE WEARING THE HELMET! I CAN'T BELIEVE HOW MUCH YOU LOVE ME.
IT'LL BE SO BEAUTIFUL.
HOLY BIBLE
PROPHET SAID I SHOULD WEAR IT DURING OUR FIRST TIME.
AND TOMMY, HAS ALWAYS FOLLOWED VERY WELL.
I HEAR HIM! HE'S TALKING TO US. THE PROPHET KINCAID IS BLESSING US!
KNOCK
KNOCK
OH MY GOD! HE'S SPEAKING TO US. THE PROPHET IS SPEAKING TO US! C'MON, HARDER!
I'VE TOLD YOU A THOUSAND TIMES; NO GIRLS IN MY HOUSE, THOMAS! REMEMBER?
WE'RE FINISHING BIBLE STUDIES, GRANDMA. I PROMISE. WE WERE JUST READING THE BOOK OF PSALMS, BUT WE'RE LIKE GOING TO WRAP UP SOON. ALRIGHT. WE'LL BE RIGHT DOWN.

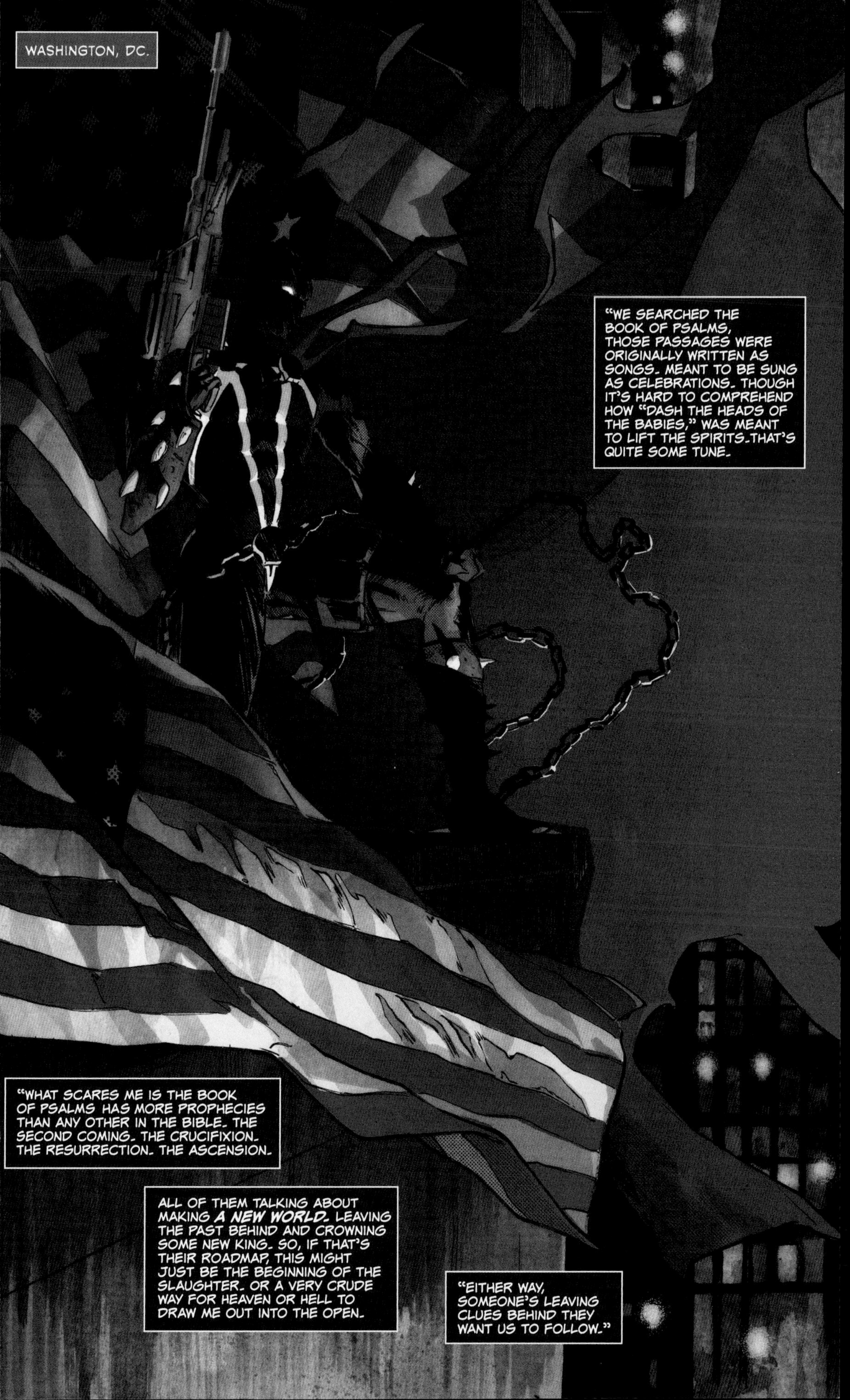
WASHINGTON, DC.
"WE SEARCHED THE BOOK OF PSALMS, THOSE PASSAGES WERE ORIGINALLY WRITTEN AS SONGS. MEANT TO BE SUNG AS CELEBRATIONS. THOUGH IT'S HARD TO COMPREHEND HOW "DASH THE HEADS OF THE BABIES," WAS MEANT TO LIFT THE SPIRITS. THAT'S QUITE SOME TUNE.
"WHAT SCARES ME IS THE BOOK OF PSALMS HAS MORE PROPHECIES THAN ANY OTHER IN THE BIBLE. THE SECOND COMING. THE CRUCIFIXION. THE RESURRECTION. THE ASCENSION.
ALL OF THEM TALKING ABOUT MAKING *A NEW WORLD.* LEAVING THE PAST BEHIND AND CROWNING SOME NEW KING. SO, IF THAT'S THEIR ROADMAP, THIS MIGHT JUST BE THE BEGINNING OF THE SLAUGHTER. OR A VERY CRUDE WAY FOR HEAVEN OR HELL TO DRAW ME OUT INTO THE OPEN.
"EITHER WAY, SOMEONE'S LEAVING CLUES BEHIND THEY WANT US TO FOLLOW."

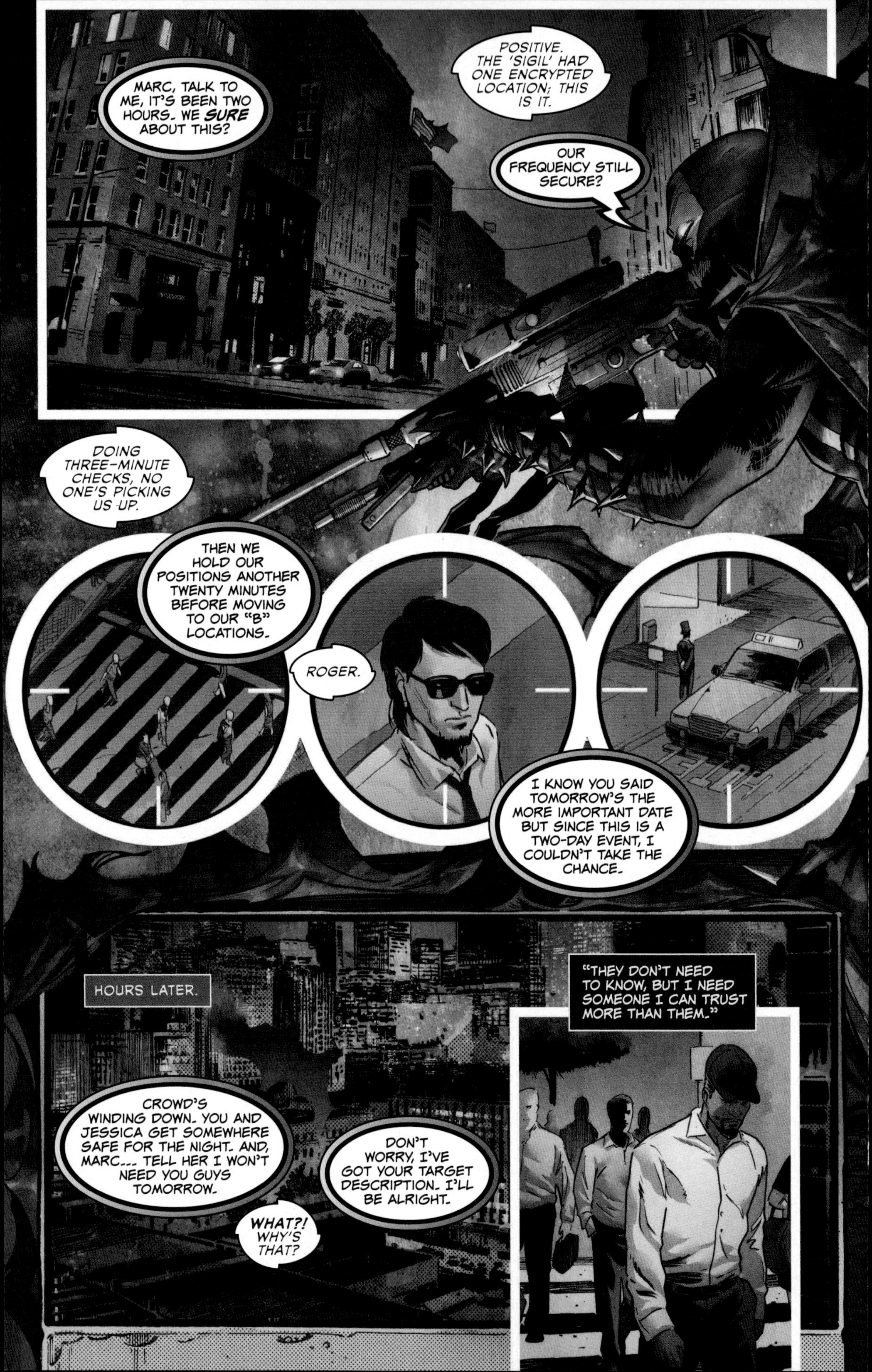

MARC, TALK TO ME, IT'S BEEN TWO HOURS. WE SURE ABOUT THIS?
POSITIVE. THE 'SIGIL' HAD ONE ENCRYPTED LOCATION; THIS IS IT.
OUR FREQUENCY STILL SECURE?
DOING THREE-MINUTE CHECKS, NO ONE'S PICKING US UP.
THEN WE HOLD OUR POSITIONS ANOTHER TWENTY MINUTES BEFORE MOVING TO OUR "B" LOCATIONS.
ROGER.
I KNOW YOU SAID TOMORROW'S THE MORE IMPORTANT DATE BUT SINCE THIS IS A TWO-DAY EVENT, I COULDN'T TAKE THE CHANCE.
HOURS LATER.
CROWD'S WINDING DOWN. YOU AND JESSICA GET SOMEWHERE SAFE FOR THE NIGHT. AND, MARC... TELL HER I WON'T NEED YOU GUYS TOMORROW.
WHAT?! WHY'S THAT?
DON'T WORRY, I'VE GOT YOUR TARGET DESCRIPTION. I'LL BE ALRIGHT.
"THEY DON'T NEED TO KNOW, BUT I NEED SOMEONE I CAN TRUST MORE THAN THEM."

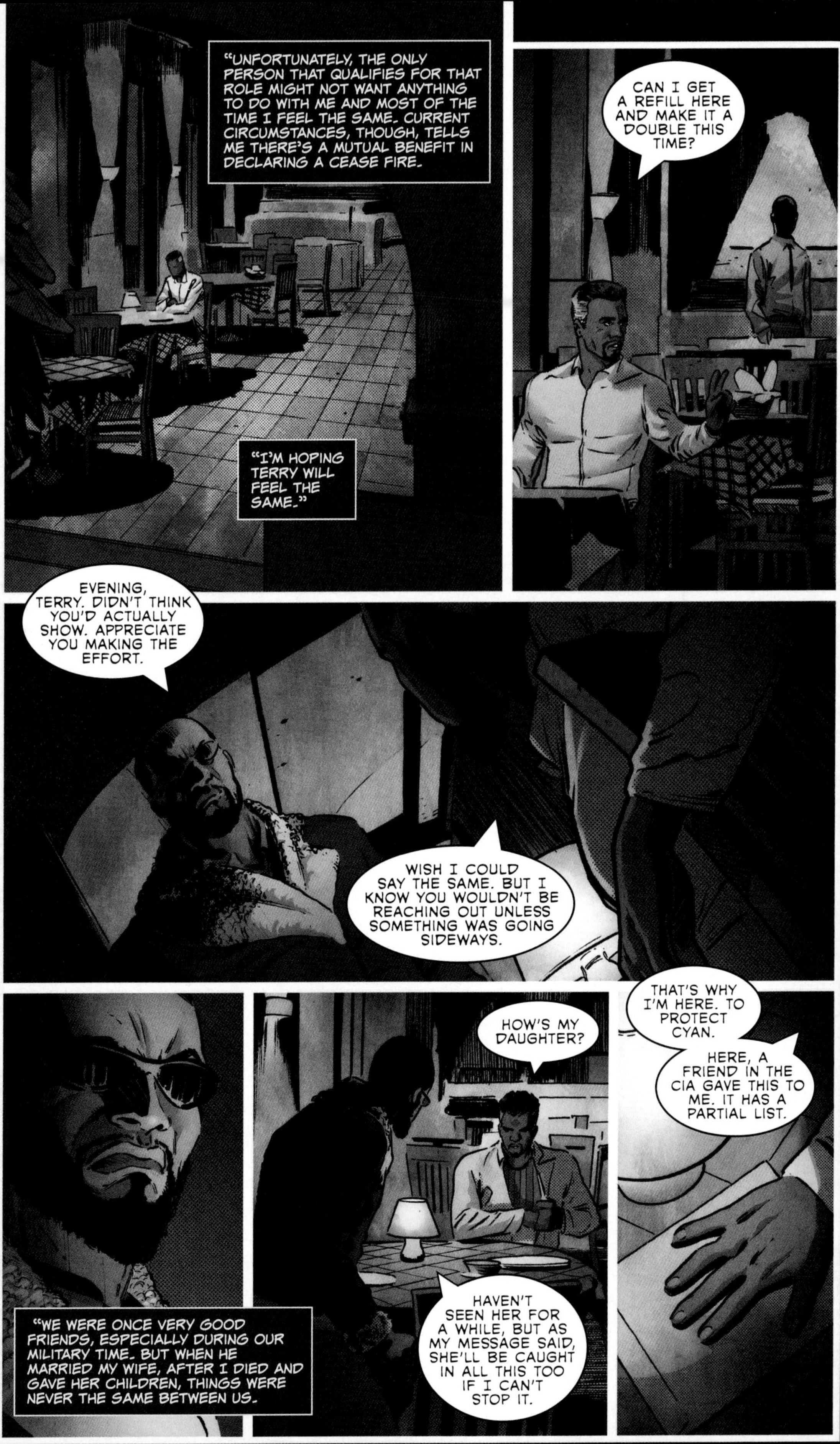
"UNFORTUNATELY, THE ONLY PERSON THAT QUALIFIES FOR THAT ROLE MIGHT NOT WANT ANYTHING TO DO WITH ME AND MOST OF THE TIME I FEEL THE SAME. CURRENT CIRCUMSTANCES, THOUGH, TELLS ME THERE'S A MUTUAL BENEFIT IN DECLARING A CEASE FIRE.
"I'M HOPING TERRY WILL FEEL THE SAME."
CAN I GET A REFILL HERE AND MAKE IT A DOUBLE THIS TIME?
EVENING, TERRY. DIDN'T THINK YOU'D ACTUALLY SHOW. APPRECIATE YOU MAKING THE EFFORT.
WISH I COULD SAY THE SAME. BUT I KNOW YOU WOULDN'T BE REACHING OUT UNLESS SOMETHING WAS GOING SIDEWAYS.
"WE WERE ONCE VERY GOOD FRIENDS, ESPECIALLY DURING OUR MILITARY TIME. BUT WHEN HE MARRIED MY WIFE, AFTER I DIED AND GAVE HER CHILDREN, THINGS WERE NEVER THE SAME BETWEEN US.
HOW'S MY DAUGHTER?
HAVEN'T SEEN HER FOR A WHILE, BUT AS MY MESSAGE SAID, SHE'LL BE CAUGHT IN ALL THIS TOO IF I CAN'T STOP IT.
THAT'S WHY I'M HERE. TO PROTECT CYAN.
HERE, A FRIEND IN THE CIA GAVE THIS TO ME. IT HAS A PARTIAL LIST.

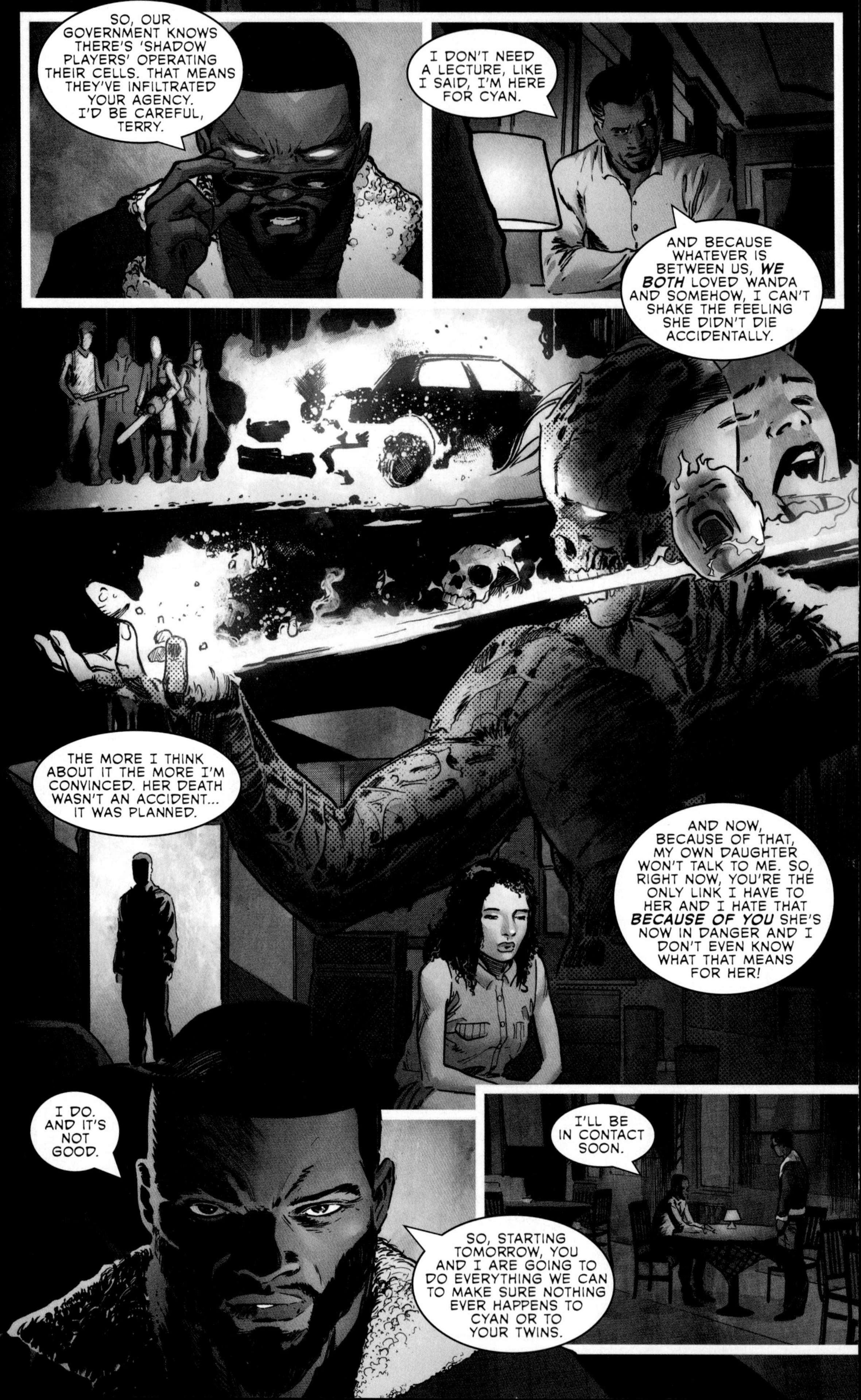
SO, OUR GOVERNMENT KNOWS THERE'S 'SHADOW PLAYERS' OPERATING THEIR CELLS. THAT MEANS THEY'VE INFILTRATED YOUR AGENCY. I'D BE CAREFUL, TERRY.
I DON'T NEED A LECTURE, LIKE I SAID, I'M HERE FOR CYAN.
AND BECAUSE WHATEVER IS BETWEEN US, ***WE BOTH*** LOVED WANDA AND SOMEHOW, I CAN'T SHAKE THE FEELING SHE DIDN'T DIE ACCIDENTALLY.
THE MORE I THINK ABOUT IT THE MORE I'M CONVINCED. HER DEATH WASN'T AN ACCIDENT... IT WAS PLANNED.
AND NOW, BECAUSE OF THAT, MY OWN DAUGHTER WON'T TALK TO ME. SO, RIGHT NOW, YOU'RE THE ONLY LINK I HAVE TO HER AND I HATE THAT ***BECAUSE OF YOU*** SHE'S NOW IN DANGER AND I DON'T EVEN KNOW WHAT THAT MEANS FOR HER!
I DO. AND IT'S NOT GOOD.
I'LL BE IN CONTACT SOON.
SO, STARTING TOMORROW, YOU AND I ARE GOING TO DO EVERYTHING WE CAN TO MAKE SURE NOTHING EVER HAPPENS TO CYAN OR TO YOUR TWINS.

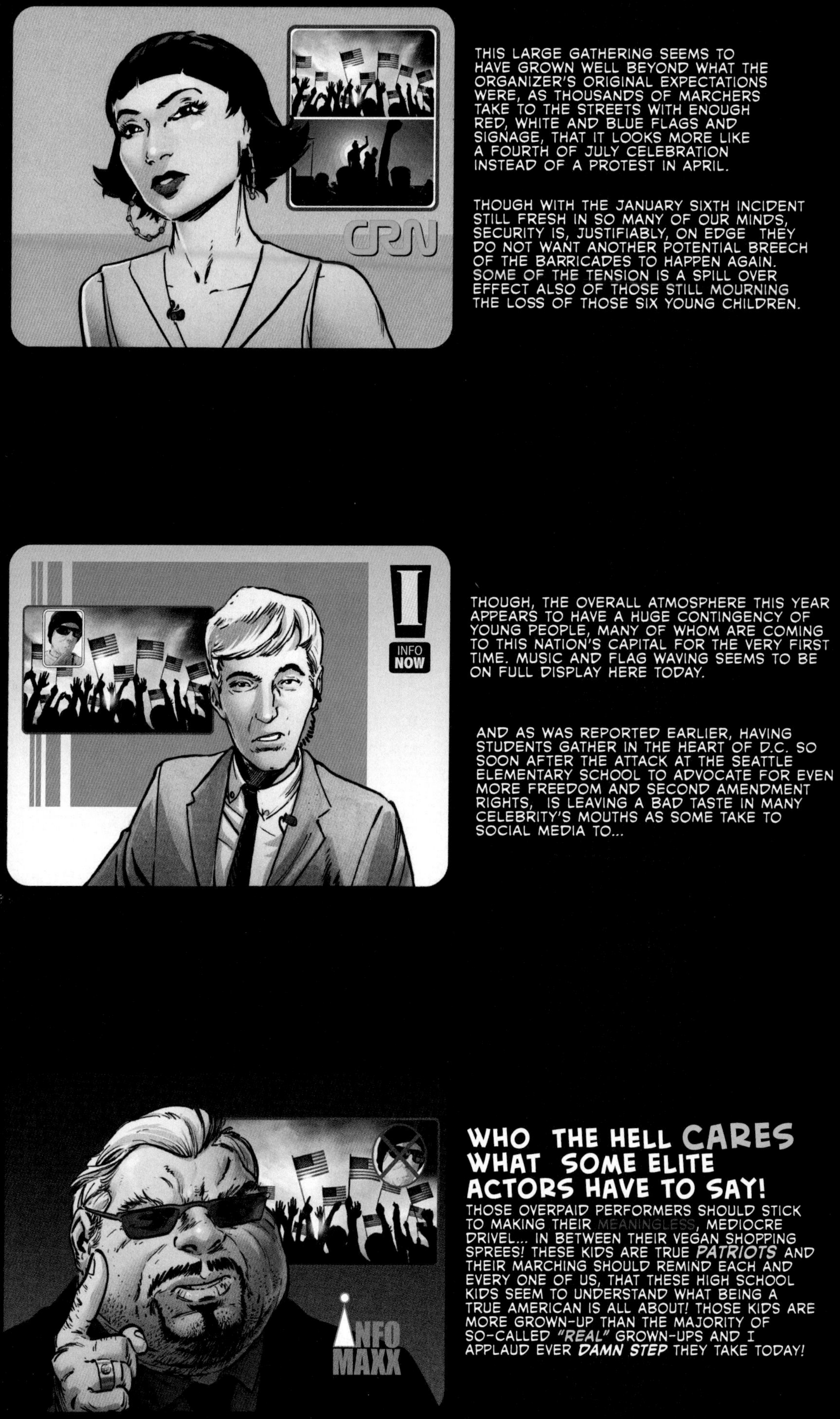

CRN
THIS LARGE GATHERING SEEMS TO HAVE GROWN WELL BEYOND WHAT THE ORGANIZER'S ORIGINAL EXPECTATIONS WERE, AS THOUSANDS OF MARCHERS TAKE TO THE STREETS WITH ENOUGH RED, WHITE AND BLUE FLAGS AND SIGNAGE, THAT IT LOOKS MORE LIKE A FOURTH OF JULY CELEBRATION INSTEAD OF A PROTEST IN APRIL.
THOUGH WITH THE JANUARY SIXTH INCIDENT STILL FRESH IN SO MANY OF OUR MINDS, SECURITY IS, JUSTIFIABLY, ON EDGE THEY DO NOT WANT ANOTHER POTENTIAL BREECH OF THE BARRICADES TO HAPPEN AGAIN. SOME OF THE TENSION IS A SPILL OVER EFFECT ALSO OF THOSE STILL MOURNING THE LOSS OF THOSE SIX YOUNG CHILDREN.
INFO NOW
THOUGH, THE OVERALL ATMOSPHERE THIS YEAR APPEARS TO HAVE A HUGE CONTINGENCY OF YOUNG PEOPLE, MANY OF WHOM ARE COMING TO THIS NATION'S CAPITAL FOR THE VERY FIRST TIME. MUSIC AND FLAG WAVING SEEMS TO BE ON FULL DISPLAY HERE TODAY.
AND AS WAS REPORTED EARLIER, HAVING STUDENTS GATHER IN THE HEART OF D.C. SO SOON AFTER THE ATTACK AT THE SEATTLE ELEMENTARY SCHOOL TO ADVOCATE FOR EVEN MORE FREEDOM AND SECOND AMENDMENT RIGHTS, IS LEAVING A BAD TASTE IN MANY CELEBRITY'S MOUTHS AS SOME TAKE TO SOCIAL MEDIA TO...
INFO MAXX
WHO THE HELL CARES WHAT SOME ELITE ACTORS HAVE TO SAY!
THOSE OVERPAID PERFORMERS SHOULD STICK TO MAKING THEIR MEANINGLESS, MEDIOCRE DRIVEL... IN BETWEEN THEIR VEGAN SHOPPING SPREES! THESE KIDS ARE TRUE *PATRIOTS* AND THEIR MARCHING SHOULD REMIND EACH AND EVERY ONE OF US, THAT THESE HIGH SCHOOL KIDS SEEM TO UNDERSTAND WHAT BEING A TRUE AMERICAN IS ALL ABOUT! THOSE KIDS ARE MORE GROWN-UP THAN THE MAJORITY OF SO-CALLED *"REAL"* GROWN-UPS AND I APPLAUD EVER ***DAMN STEP*** THEY TAKE TODAY!

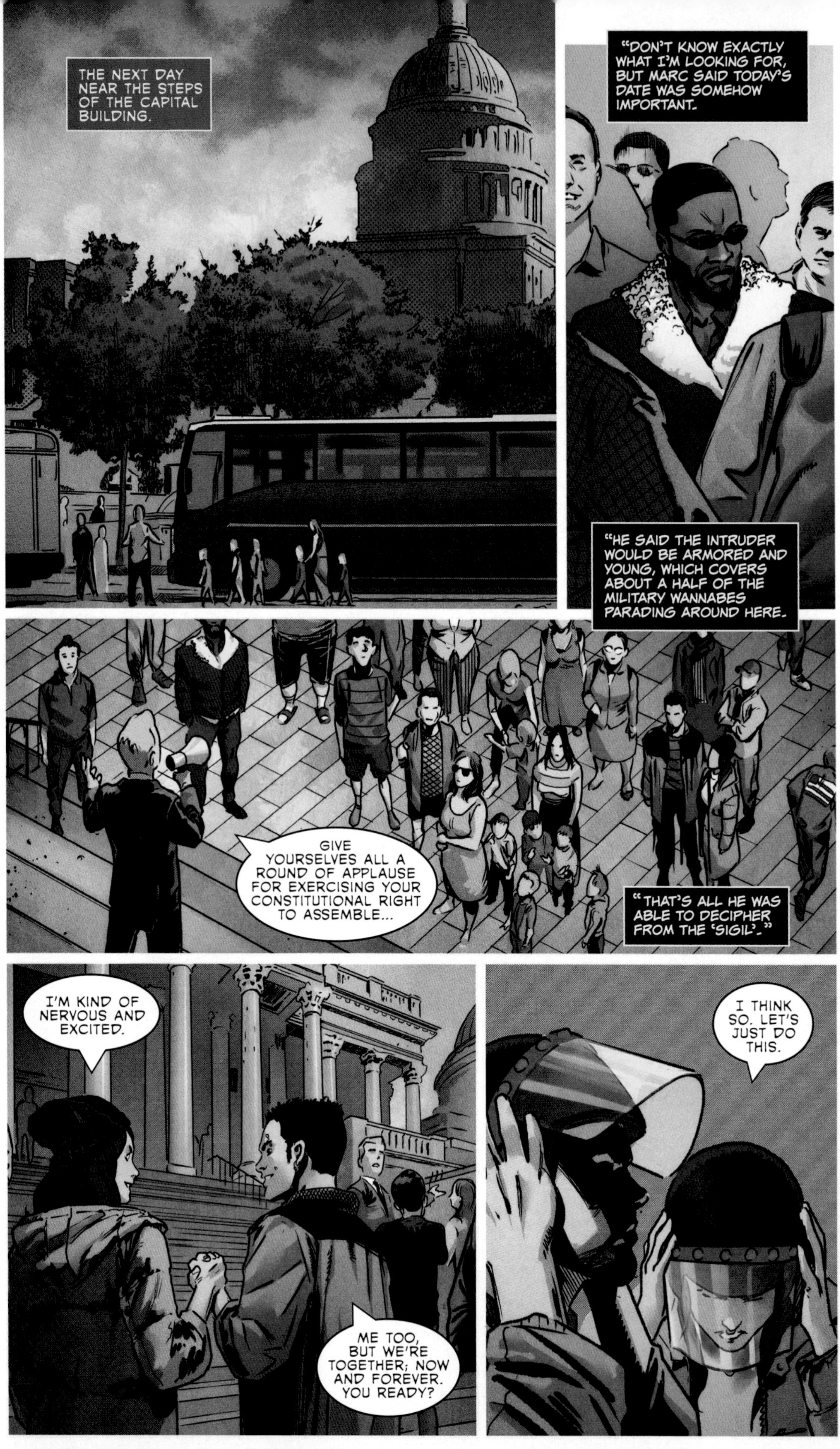
THE NEXT DAY NEAR THE STEPS OF THE CAPITAL BUILDING.
"DON'T KNOW EXACTLY WHAT I'M LOOKING FOR, BUT MARC SAID TODAY'S DATE WAS SOMEHOW IMPORTANT.
"HE SAID THE INTRUDER WOULD BE ARMORED AND YOUNG, WHICH COVERS ABOUT A HALF OF THE MILITARY WANNABES PARADING AROUND HERE.
GIVE YOURSELVES ALL A ROUND OF APPLAUSE FOR EXERCISING YOUR CONSTITUTIONAL RIGHT TO ASSEMBLE...
"THAT'S ALL HE WAS ABLE TO DECIPHER FROM THE 'SIGIL'."
I'M KIND OF NERVOUS AND EXCITED.
ME TOO, BUT WE'RE TOGETHER; NOW AND FOREVER. YOU READY?
I THINK SO. LET'S JUST DO THIS.

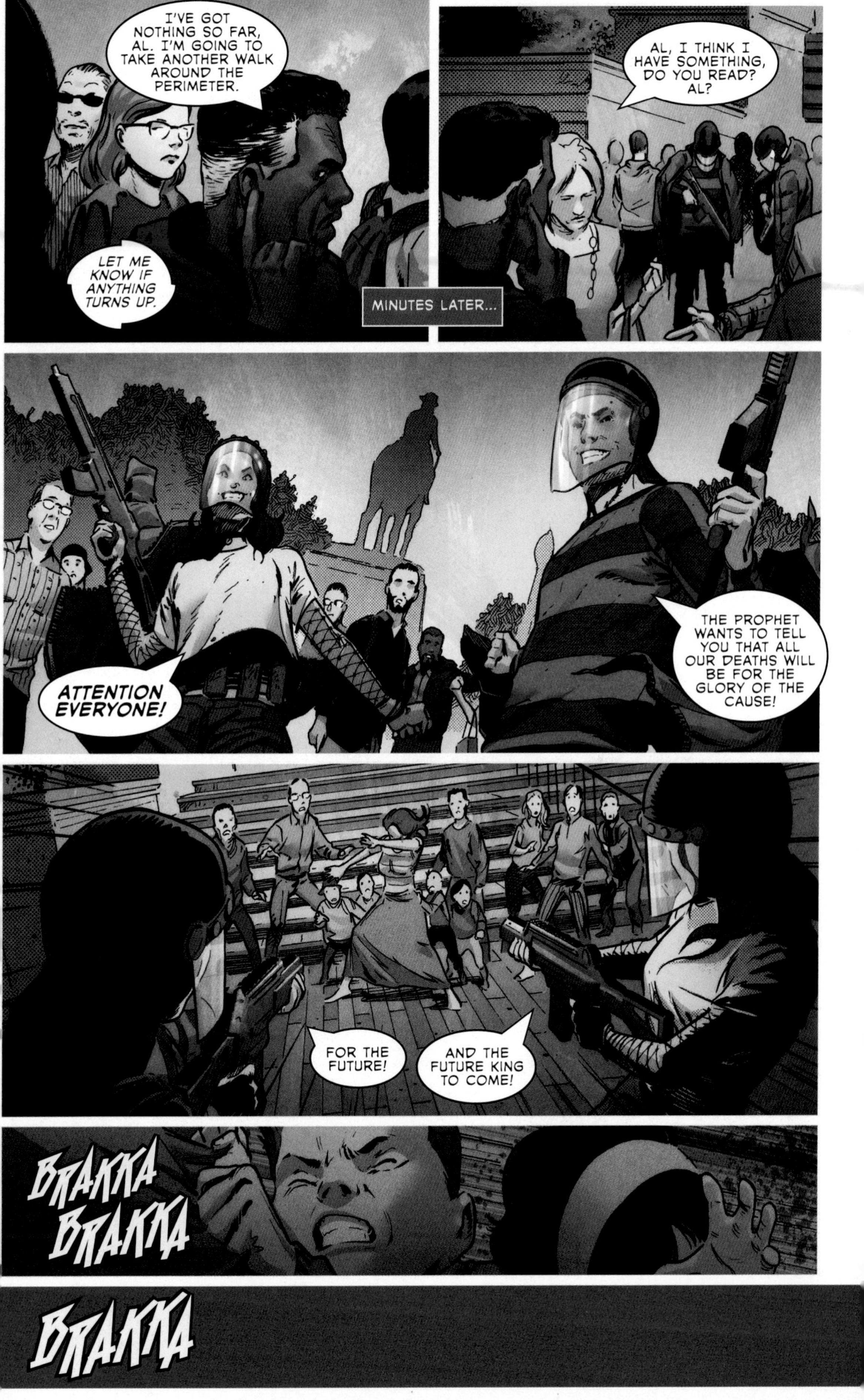
I'VE GOT NOTHING SO FAR, AL. I'M GOING TO TAKE ANOTHER WALK AROUND THE PERIMETER.
LET ME KNOW IF ANYTHING TURNS UP.
MINUTES LATER...
AL, I THINK I HAVE SOMETHING, DO YOU READ? AL?
ATTENTION EVERYONE!
THE PROPHET WANTS TO TELL YOU THAT ALL OUR DEATHS WILL BE FOR THE GLORY OF THE CAUSE!
FOR THE FUTURE!
AND THE FUTURE KING TO COME!
BRAKKA
BRAKKA
BRAKKA

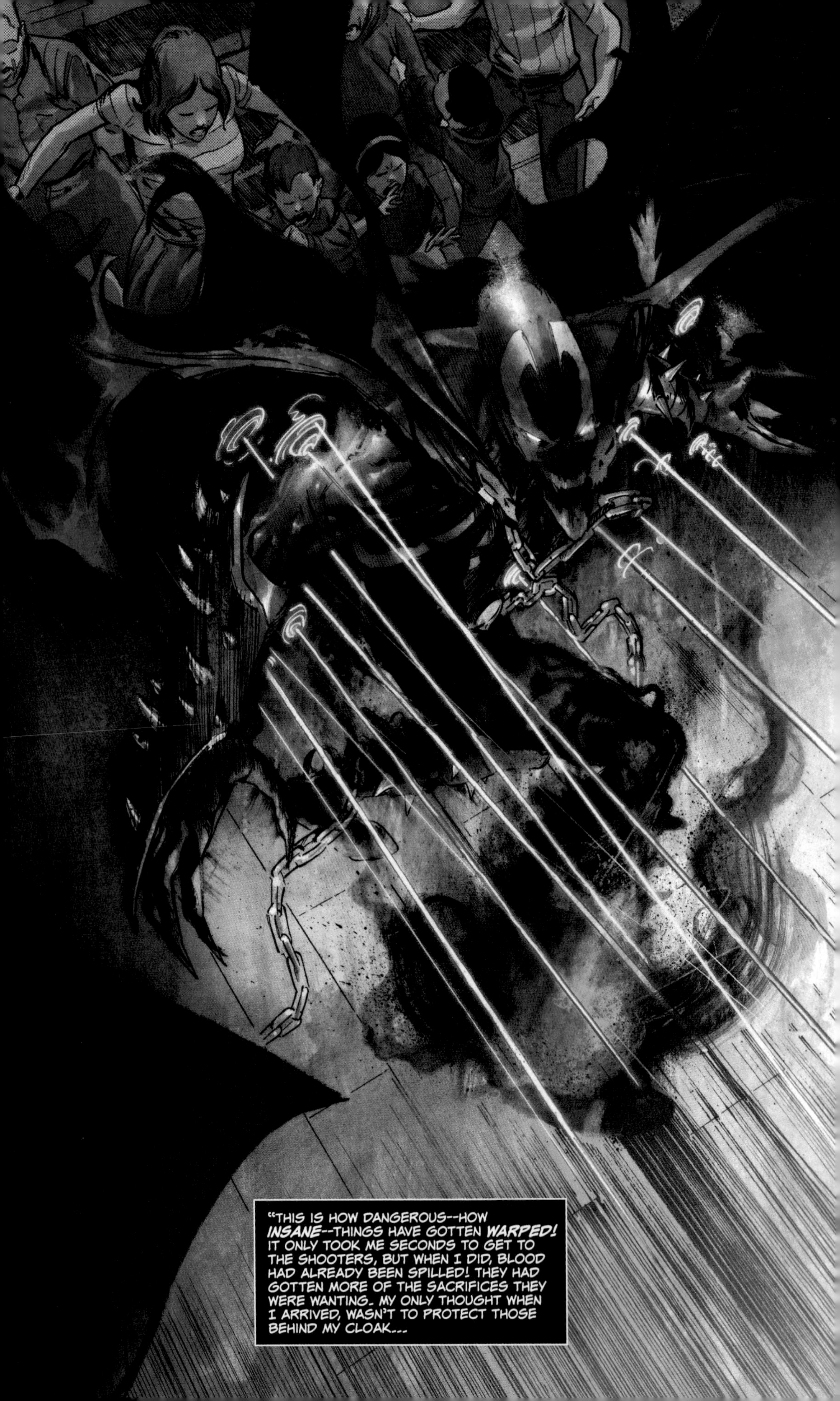
"THIS IS HOW DANGEROUS--HOW *INSANE*--THINGS HAVE GOTTEN *WARPED!* IT ONLY TOOK ME SECONDS TO GET TO THE SHOOTERS, BUT WHEN I DID, BLOOD HAD ALREADY BEEN SPILLED! THEY HAD GOTTEN MORE OF THE SACRIFICES THEY WERE WANTING. MY ONLY THOUGHT WHEN I ARRIVED, WASN'T TO PROTECT THOSE BEHIND MY CLOAK...

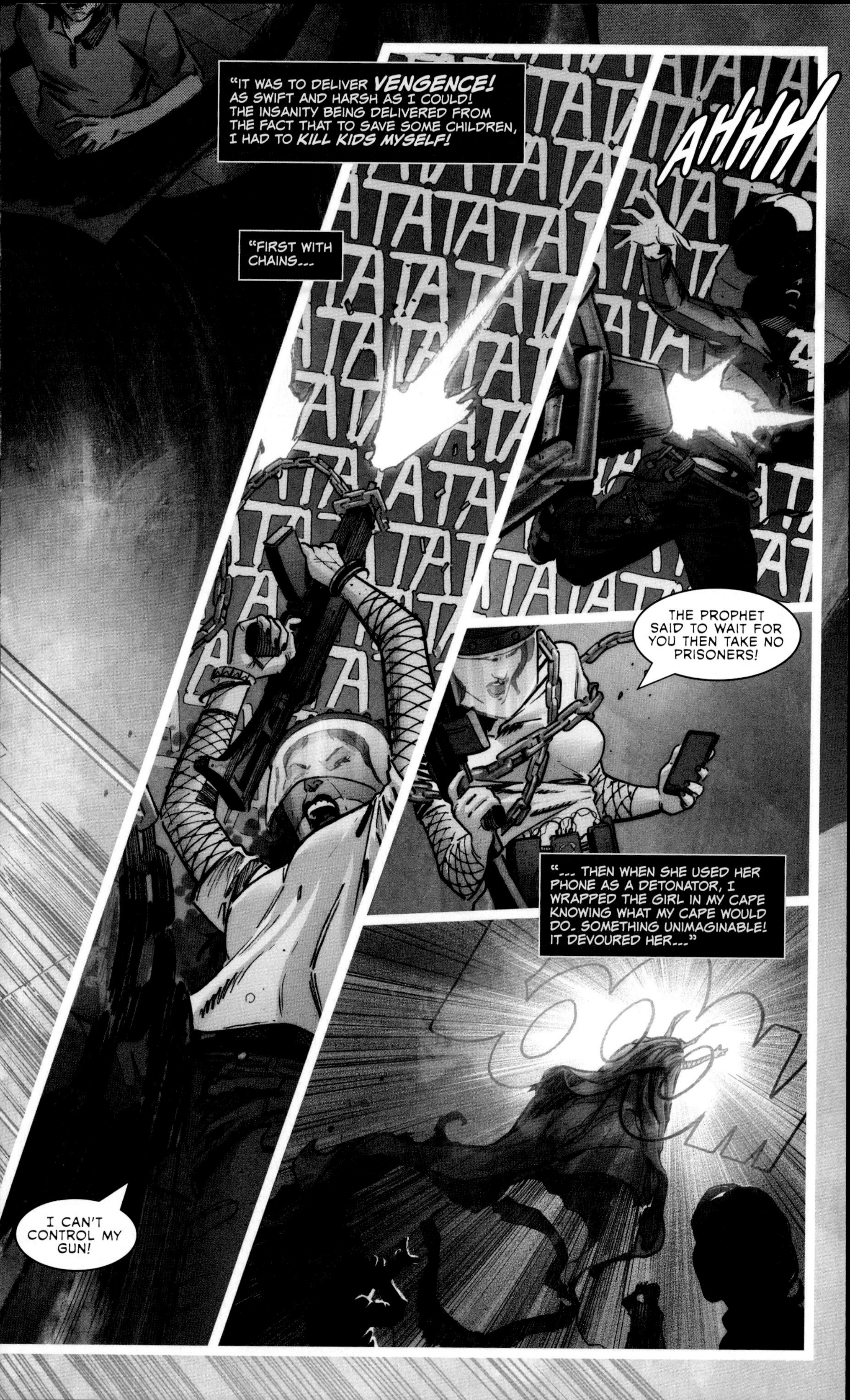

"IT WAS TO DELIVER VENGENCE! AS SWIFT AND HARSH AS I COULD! THE INSANITY BEING DELIVERED FROM THE FACT THAT TO SAVE SOME CHILDREN, I HAD TO KILL KIDS MYSELF!
"FIRST WITH CHAINS...
AHHH
I CAN'T CONTROL MY GUN!
THE PROPHET SAID TO WAIT FOR YOU THEN TAKE NO PRISONERS!
"... THEN WHEN SHE USED HER PHONE AS A DETONATOR, I WRAPPED THE GIRL IN MY CAPE KNOWING WHAT MY CAPE WOULD DO. SOMETHING UNIMAGINABLE! IT DEVOURED HER..."

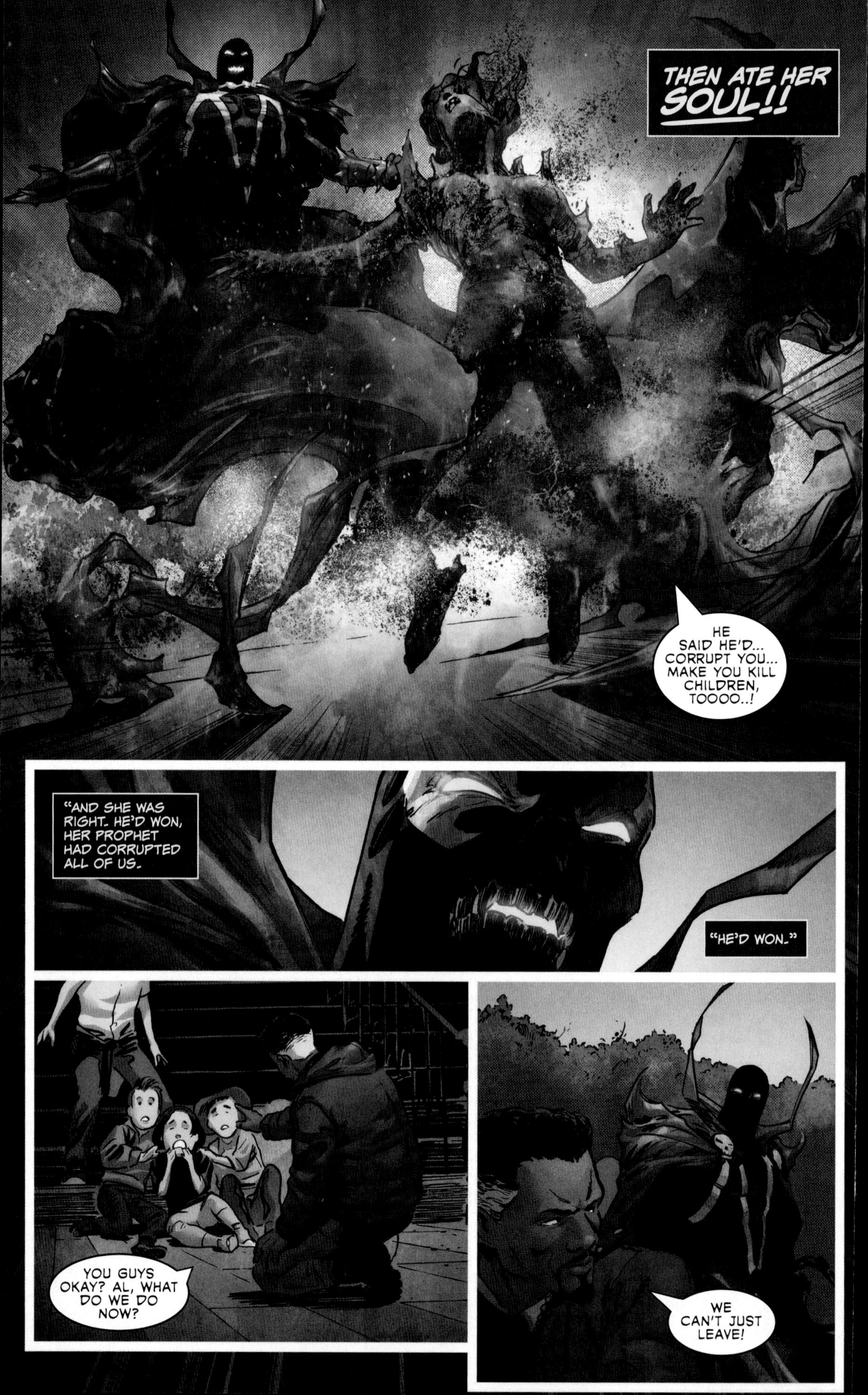
THEN ATE HER SOUL!!
HE SAID HE'D... CORRUPT YOU... MAKE YOU KILL CHILDREN, TOOOO..!
"AND SHE WAS RIGHT. HE'D WON, HER PROPHET HAD CORRUPTED ALL OF US.
"HE'D WON."
YOU GUYS OKAY? AL, WHAT DO WE DO NOW?
WE CAN'T JUST LEAVE!

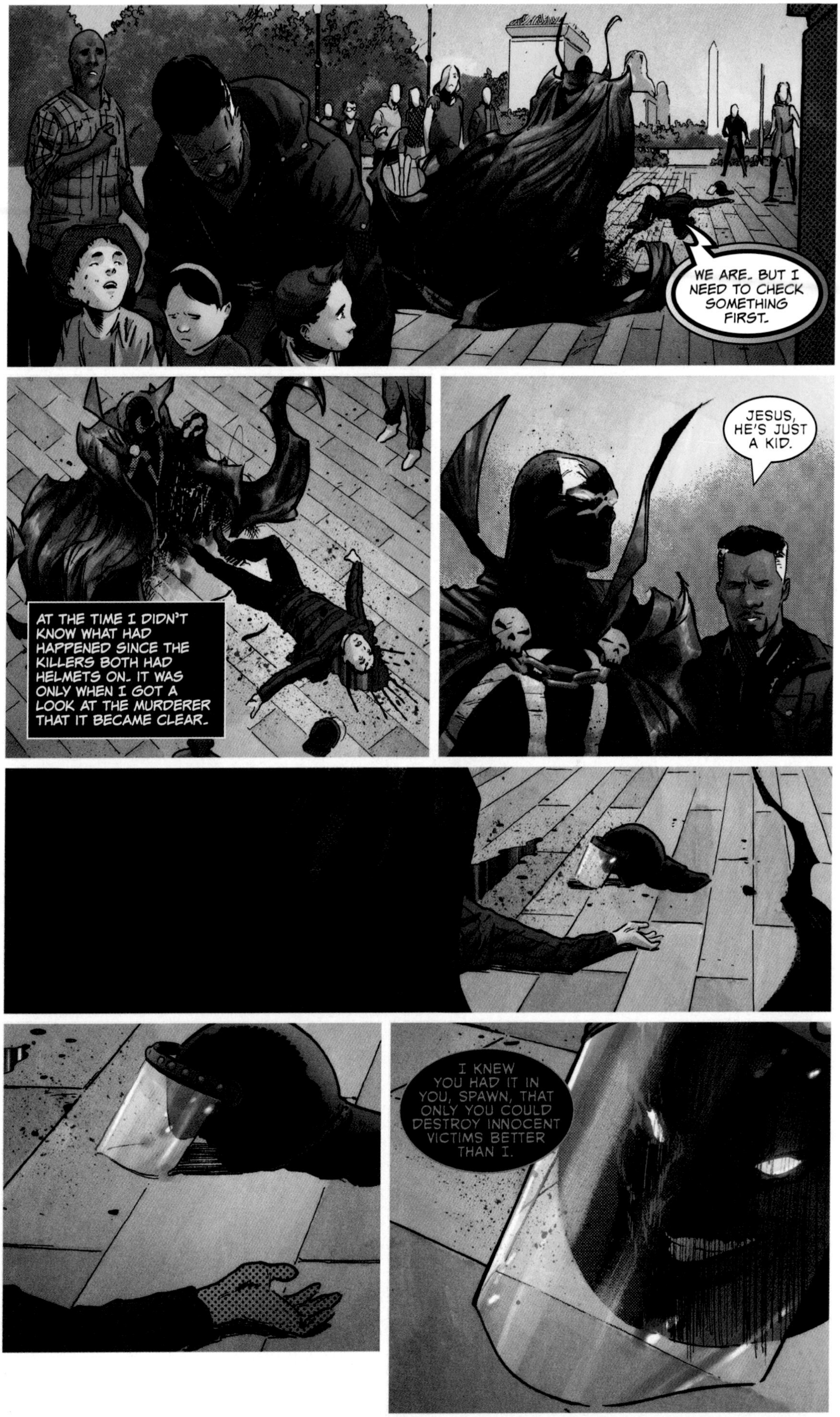
WE ARE. BUT I NEED TO CHECK SOMETHING FIRST.
AT THE TIME I DIDN'T KNOW WHAT HAD HAPPENED SINCE THE KILLERS BOTH HAD HELMETS ON. IT WAS ONLY WHEN I GOT A LOOK AT THE MURDERER THAT IT BECAME CLEAR.
JESUS, HE'S JUST A KID.
I KNEW YOU HAD IT IN YOU, SPAWN, THAT ONLY YOU COULD DESTROY INNOCENT VICTIMS BETTER THAN I.

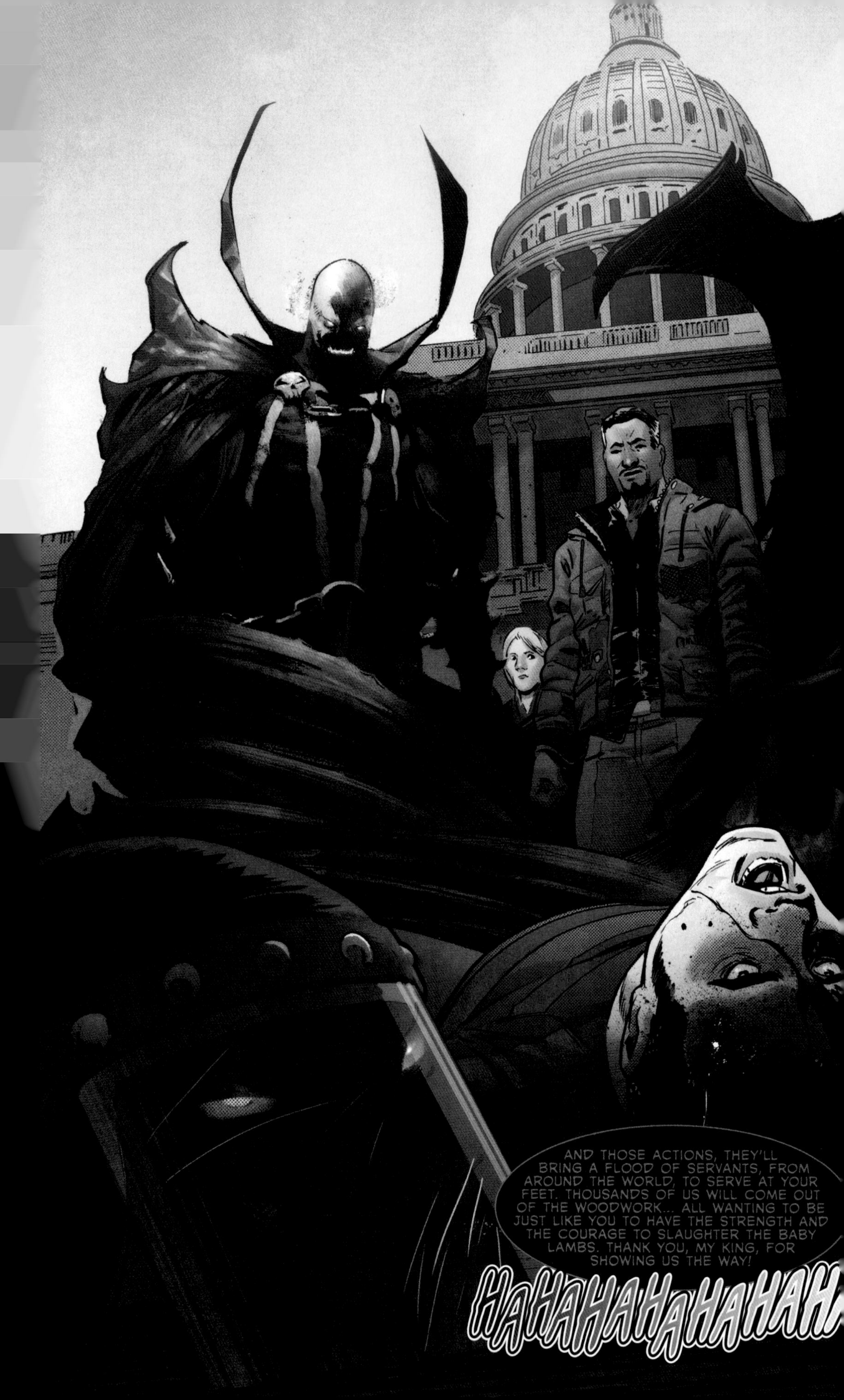
AND THOSE ACTIONS, THEY'LL BRING A FLOOD OF SERVANTS, FROM AROUND THE WORLD, TO SERVE AT YOUR FEET. THOUSANDS OF US WILL COME OUT OF THE WOODWORK... ALL WANTING TO BE JUST LIKE YOU TO HAVE THE STRENGTH AND THE COURAGE TO SLAUGHTER THE BABY LAMBS. THANK YOU, MY KING, FOR SHOWING US THE WAY!
HAHAHAHAHAHAHAH

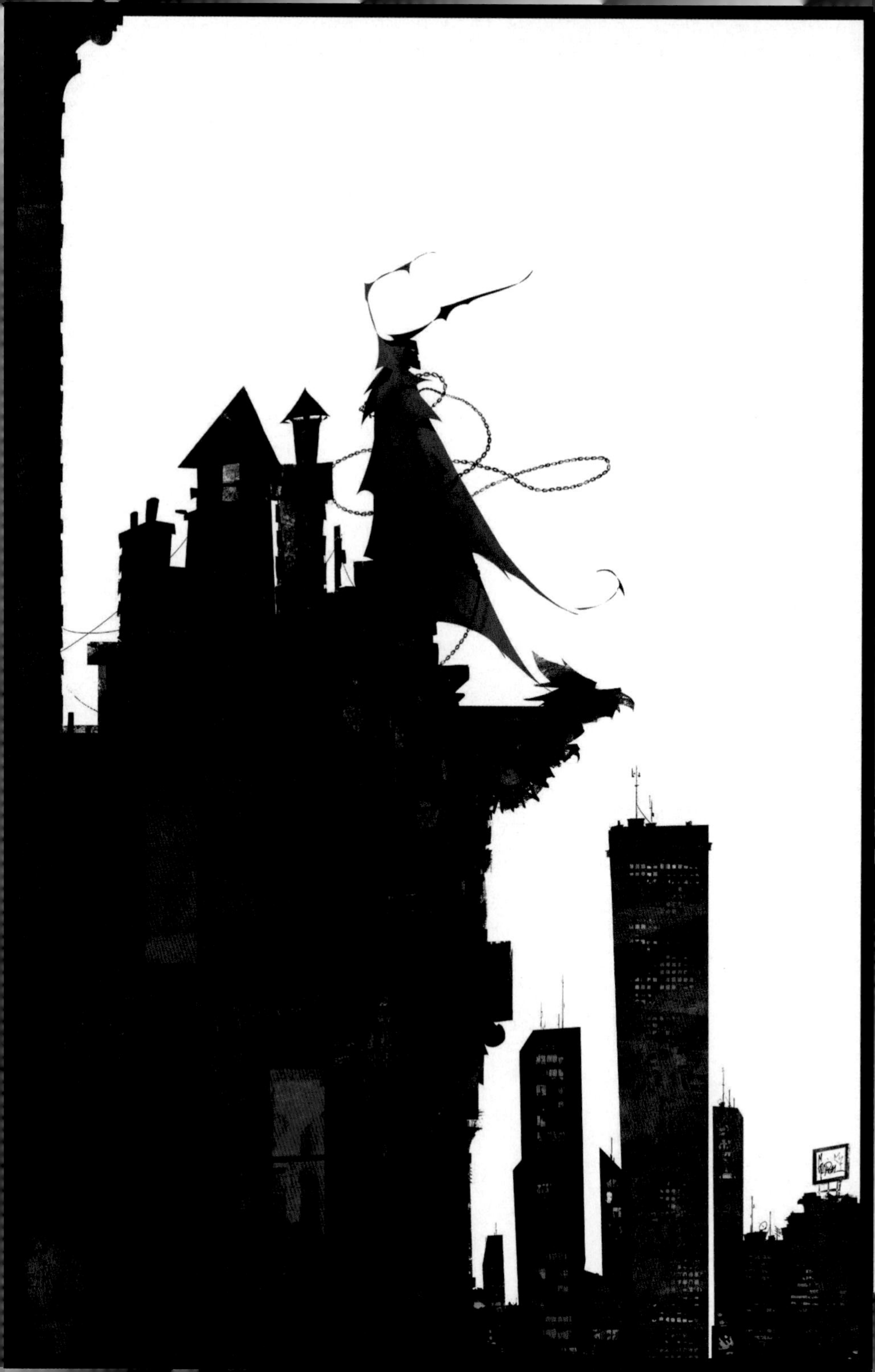

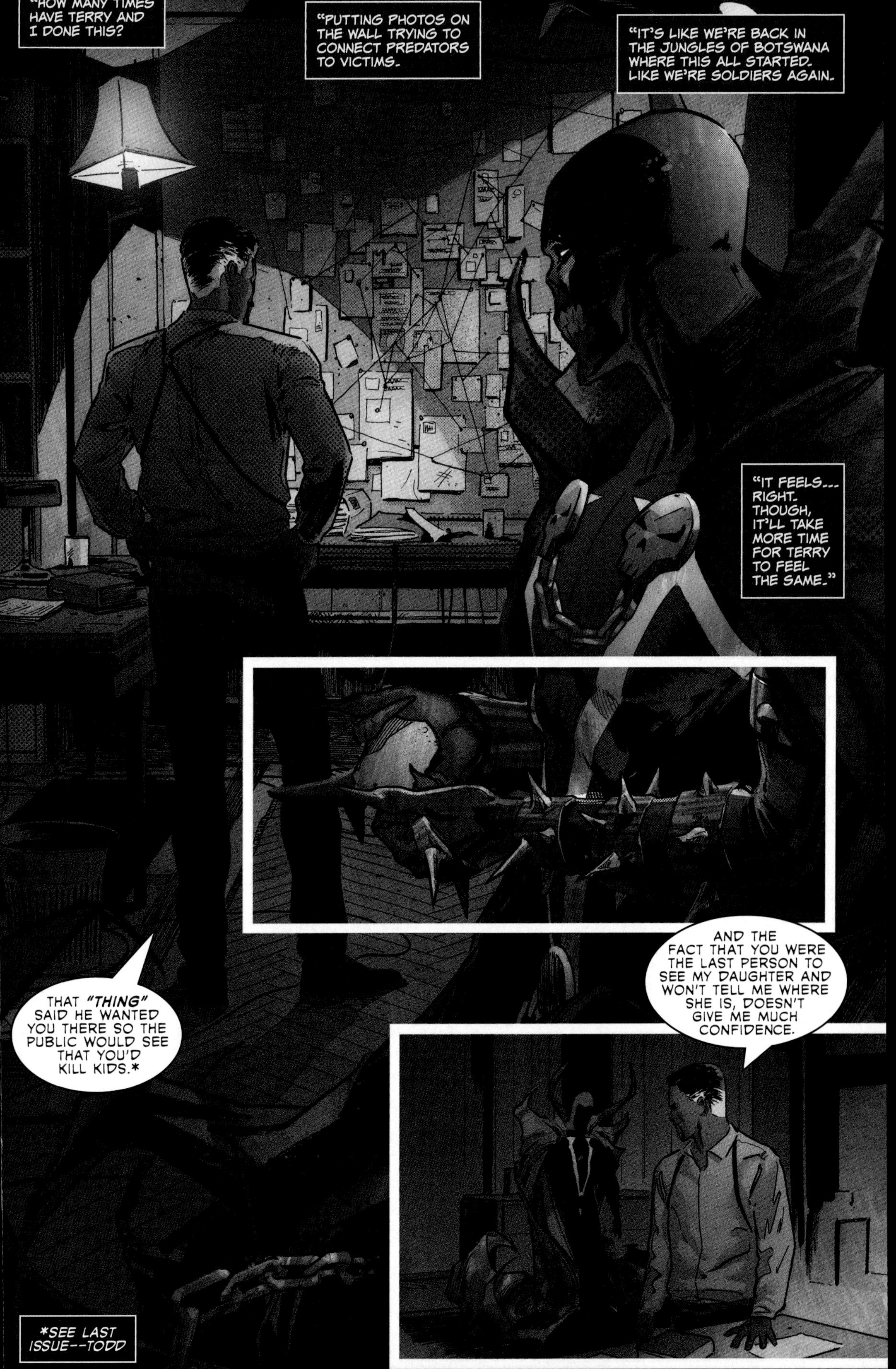
"HOW MANY TIMES HAVE TERRY AND I DONE THIS?
"PUTTING PHOTOS ON THE WALL TRYING TO CONNECT PREDATORS TO VICTIMS.
"IT'S LIKE WE'RE BACK IN THE JUNGLES OF BOTSWANA WHERE THIS ALL STARTED. LIKE WE'RE SOLDIERS AGAIN.
"IT FEELS... RIGHT. THOUGH, IT'LL TAKE MORE TIME FOR TERRY TO FEEL THE SAME."
THAT "THING" SAID HE WANTED YOU THERE SO THE PUBLIC WOULD SEE THAT YOU'D KILL KIDS.*
AND THE FACT THAT YOU WERE THE LAST PERSON TO SEE MY DAUGHTER AND WON'T TELL ME WHERE SHE IS, DOESN'T GIVE ME MUCH CONFIDENCE.
*SEE LAST ISSUE--TODD

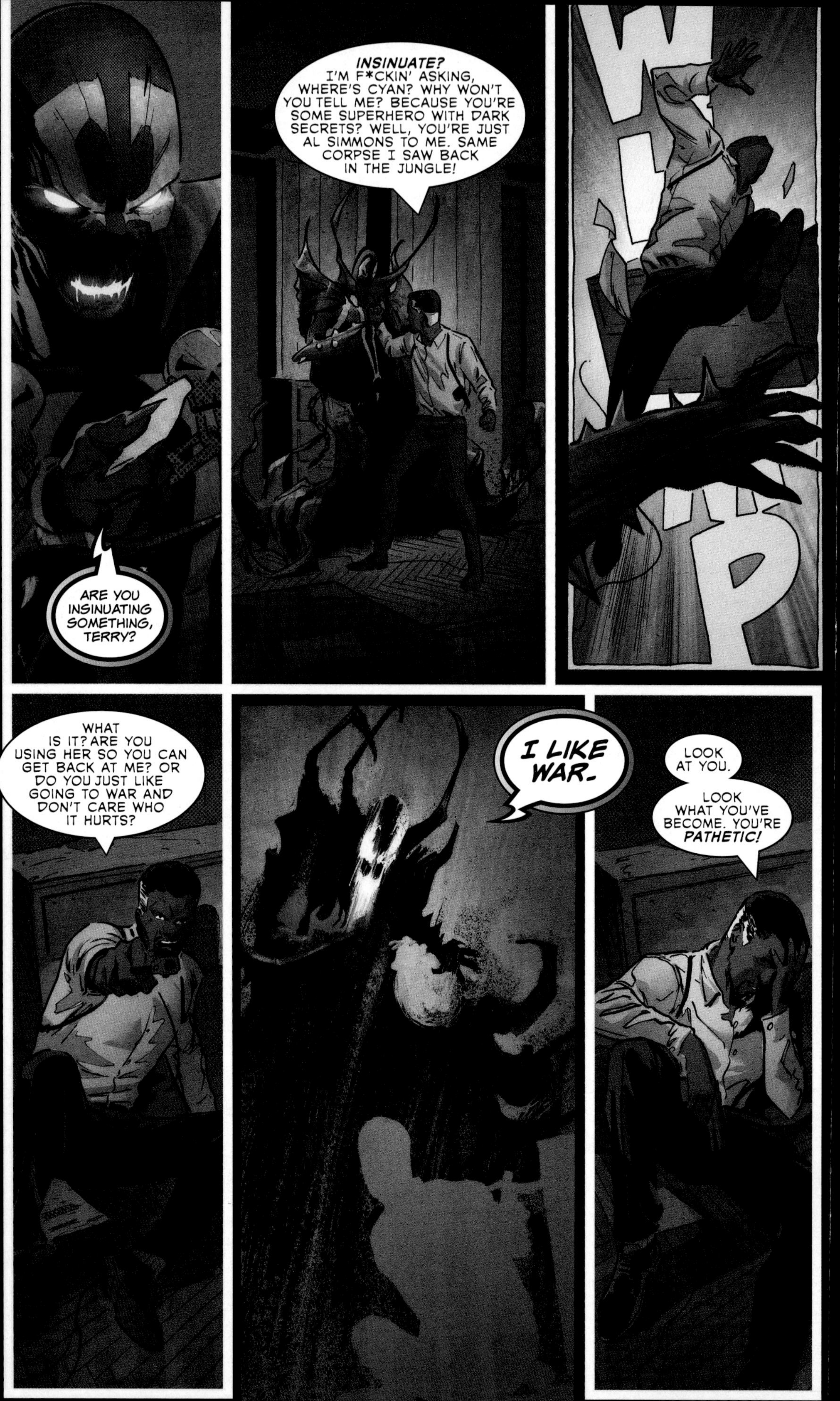
ARE YOU INSINUATING SOMETHING, TERRY?
INSINUATE? I'M F*CKIN' ASKING, WHERE'S CYAN? WHY WON'T YOU TELL ME? BECAUSE YOU'RE SOME SUPERHERO WITH DARK SECRETS? WELL, YOU'RE JUST AL SIMMONS TO ME. SAME CORPSE I SAW BACK IN THE JUNGLE!
WHAT IS IT? ARE YOU USING HER SO YOU CAN GET BACK AT ME? OR DO YOU JUST LIKE GOING TO WAR AND DON'T CARE WHO IT HURTS?
I LIKE WAR.
LOOK AT YOU.
LOOK WHAT YOU'VE BECOME. YOU'RE PATHETIC!

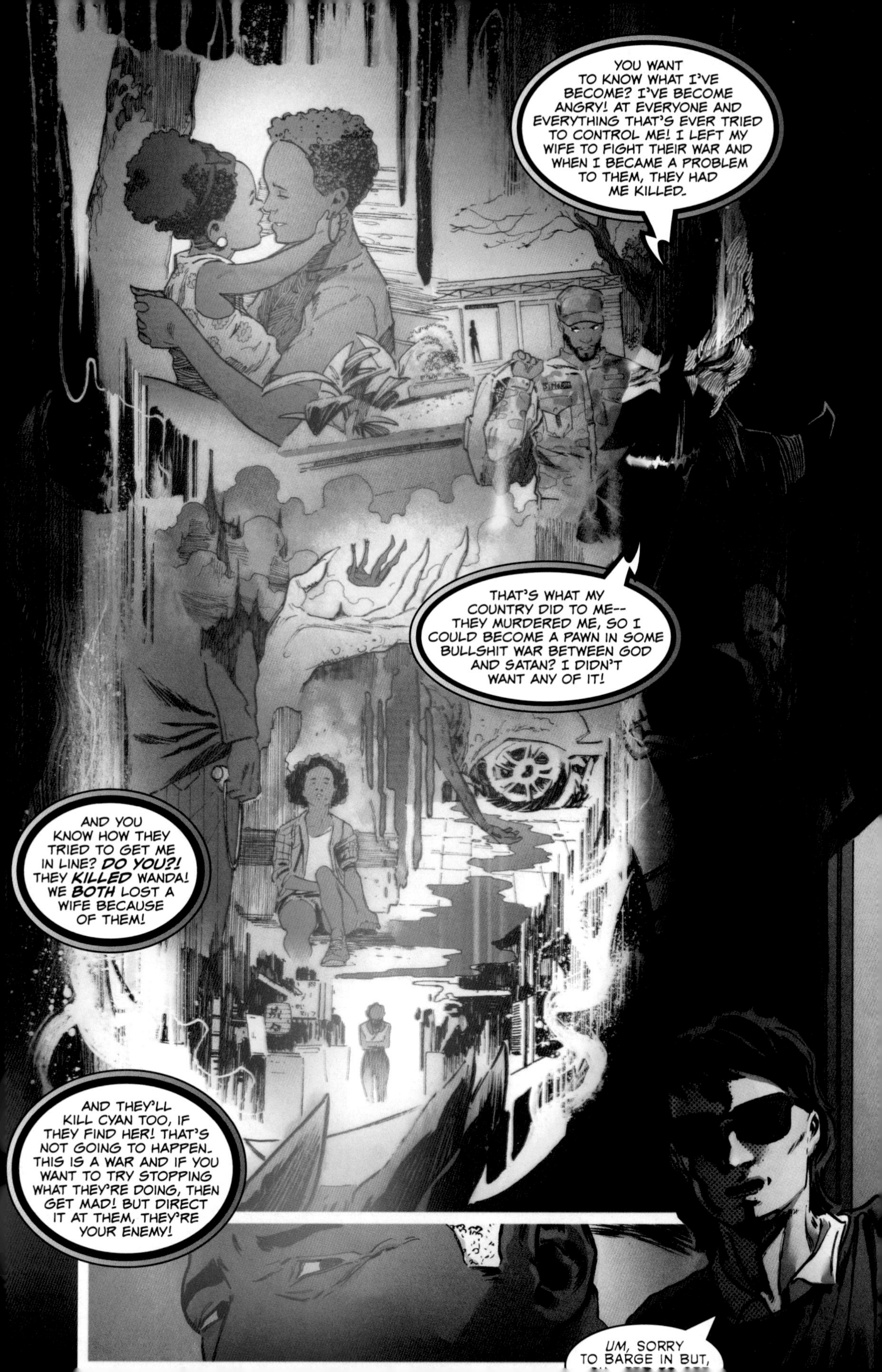
YOU WANT TO KNOW WHAT I'VE BECOME? I'VE BECOME ANGRY! AT EVERYONE AND EVERYTHING THAT'S EVER TRIED TO CONTROL ME! I LEFT MY WIFE TO FIGHT THEIR WAR AND WHEN I BECAME A PROBLEM TO THEM, THEY HAD ME KILLED.
THAT'S WHAT MY COUNTRY DID TO ME-- THEY MURDERED ME, SO I COULD BECOME A PAWN IN SOME BULLSHIT WAR BETWEEN GOD AND SATAN? I DIDN'T WANT ANY OF IT!
AND YOU KNOW HOW THEY TRIED TO GET ME IN LINE? DO YOU?! THEY KILLED WANDA! WE BOTH LOST A WIFE BECAUSE OF THEM!
AND THEY'LL KILL CYAN TOO, IF THEY FIND HER! THAT'S NOT GOING TO HAPPEN. THIS IS A WAR AND IF YOU WANT TO TRY STOPPING WHAT THEY'RE DOING, THEN GET MAD! BUT DIRECT IT AT THEM, THEY'RE YOUR ENEMY!
UM, SORRY TO BARGE IN BUT,

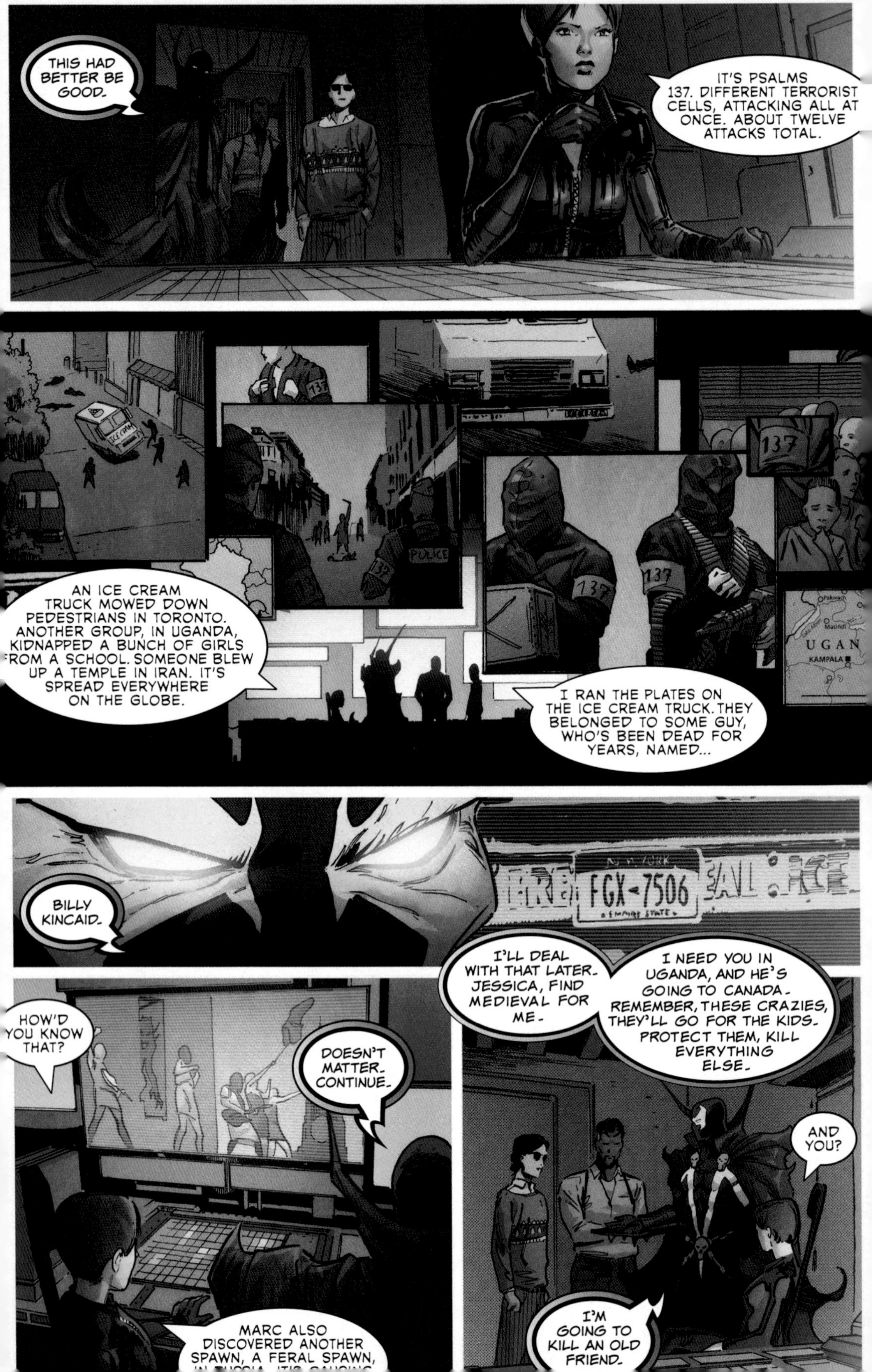
THIS HAD BETTER BE GOOD.
IT'S PSALMS 137. DIFFERENT TERRORIST CELLS, ATTACKING ALL AT ONCE. ABOUT TWELVE ATTACKS TOTAL.
ICE CREAM
137
POLICE
137
137
137
137
UGAN
KAMPALA
AN ICE CREAM TRUCK MOWED DOWN PEDESTRIANS IN TORONTO. ANOTHER GROUP, IN UGANDA, KIDNAPPED A BUNCH OF GIRLS FROM A SCHOOL. SOMEONE BLEW UP A TEMPLE IN IRAN. IT'S SPREAD EVERYWHERE ON THE GLOBE.
I RAN THE PLATES ON THE ICE CREAM TRUCK. THEY BELONGED TO SOME GUY, WHO'S BEEN DEAD FOR YEARS, NAMED...
BILLY KINCAID.
FGX-7506
EMPIRE STATE
HOW'D YOU KNOW THAT?
DOESN'T MATTER. CONTINUE.
MARC ALSO DISCOVERED ANOTHER SPAWN, A FERAL SPAWN,
I'LL DEAL WITH THAT LATER. JESSICA, FIND MEDIEVAL FOR ME.
I NEED YOU IN UGANDA, AND HE'S GOING TO CANADA. REMEMBER, THESE CRAZIES, THEY'LL GO FOR THE KIDS. PROTECT THEM, KILL EVERYTHING ELSE.
AND YOU?
I'M GOING TO KILL AN OLD FRIEND.

TERRY, BACK IN THE DAY, YOU WERE GOOD ON THE RADIO--

SURE. JUST LIKE OLD TIMES.

I NEED YOU TO KEEP US CONNECTED AND RUN THE SHOW. THINK YOU CAN DO THAT? BECAUSE THEY WON'T BE RETURNING BACK HERE AGAIN.*

*SEE SPAWN #321--TODD

NO. THIS IS BIGGER THAN THAT. THEY WANT TO ENSLAVE EVERYONE AND WHOEVER RESISTS THEY'LL SIMPLY ANNIHILATE. THAT'S WHY YOUR DAUGHTER'S NAME WAS IN THOSE DOSSIERS. THEY'RE MAKING THEIR HIT LIST.

AND NO ONE IS OFF LIMITS TO THEM!

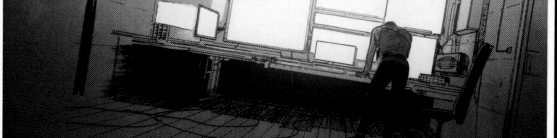

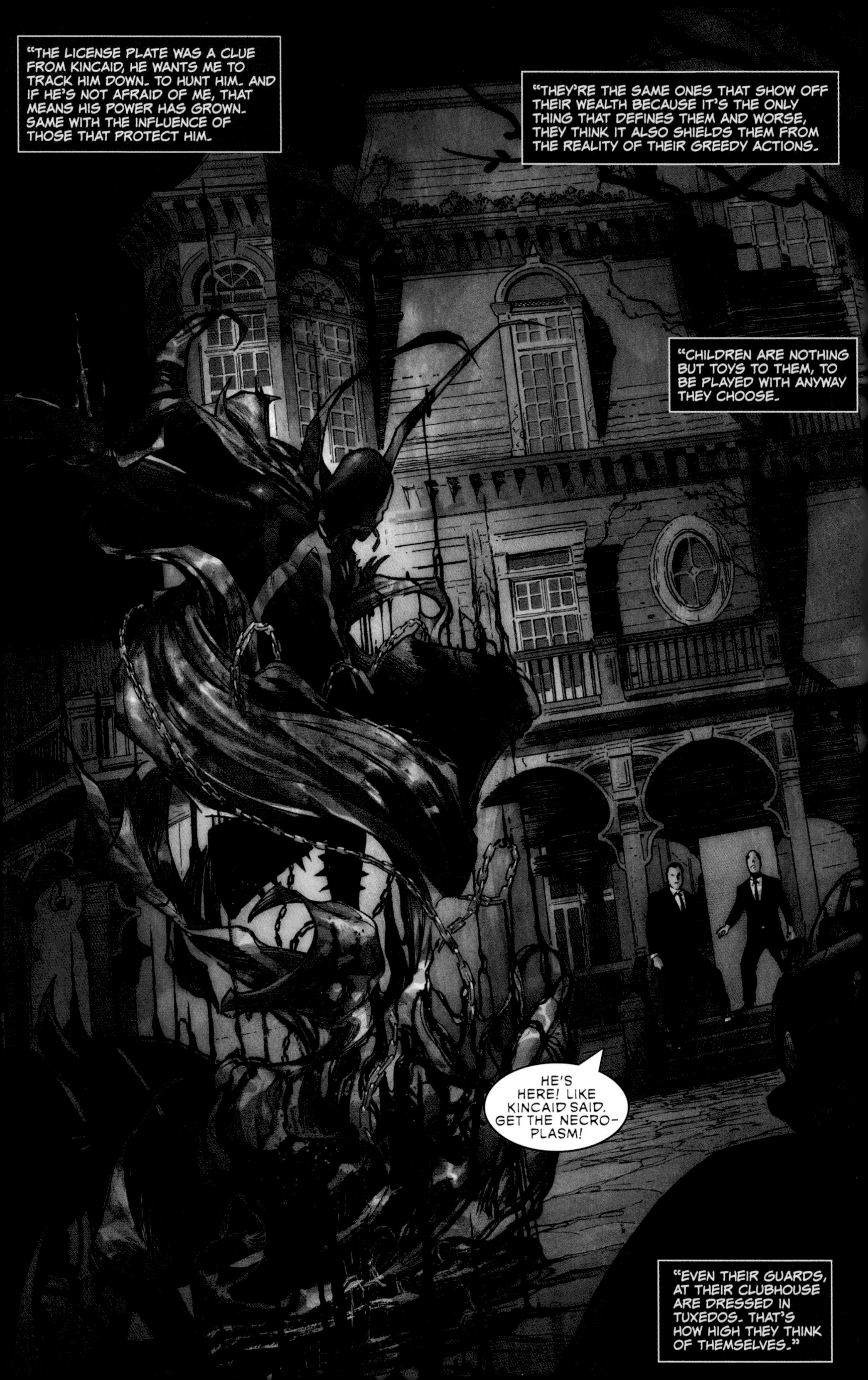
"THE LICENSE PLATE WAS A CLUE FROM KINCAID, HE WANTS ME TO TRACK HIM DOWN. TO HUNT HIM. AND IF HE'S NOT AFRAID OF ME, THAT MEANS HIS POWER HAS GROWN. SAME WITH THE INFLUENCE OF THOSE THAT PROTECT HIM.
"THEY'RE THE SAME ONES THAT SHOW OFF THEIR WEALTH BECAUSE IT'S THE ONLY THING THAT DEFINES THEM AND WORSE, THEY THINK IT ALSO SHIELDS THEM FROM THE REALITY OF THEIR GREEDY ACTIONS.
"CHILDREN ARE NOTHING BUT TOYS TO THEM, TO BE PLAYED WITH ANYWAY THEY CHOOSE.
HE'S HERE! LIKE KINCAID SAID. GET THE NECRO-PLASM!
"EVEN THEIR GUARDS, AT THEIR CLUBHOUSE ARE DRESSED IN TUXEDOS. THAT'S HOW HIGH THEY THINK OF THEMSELVES."

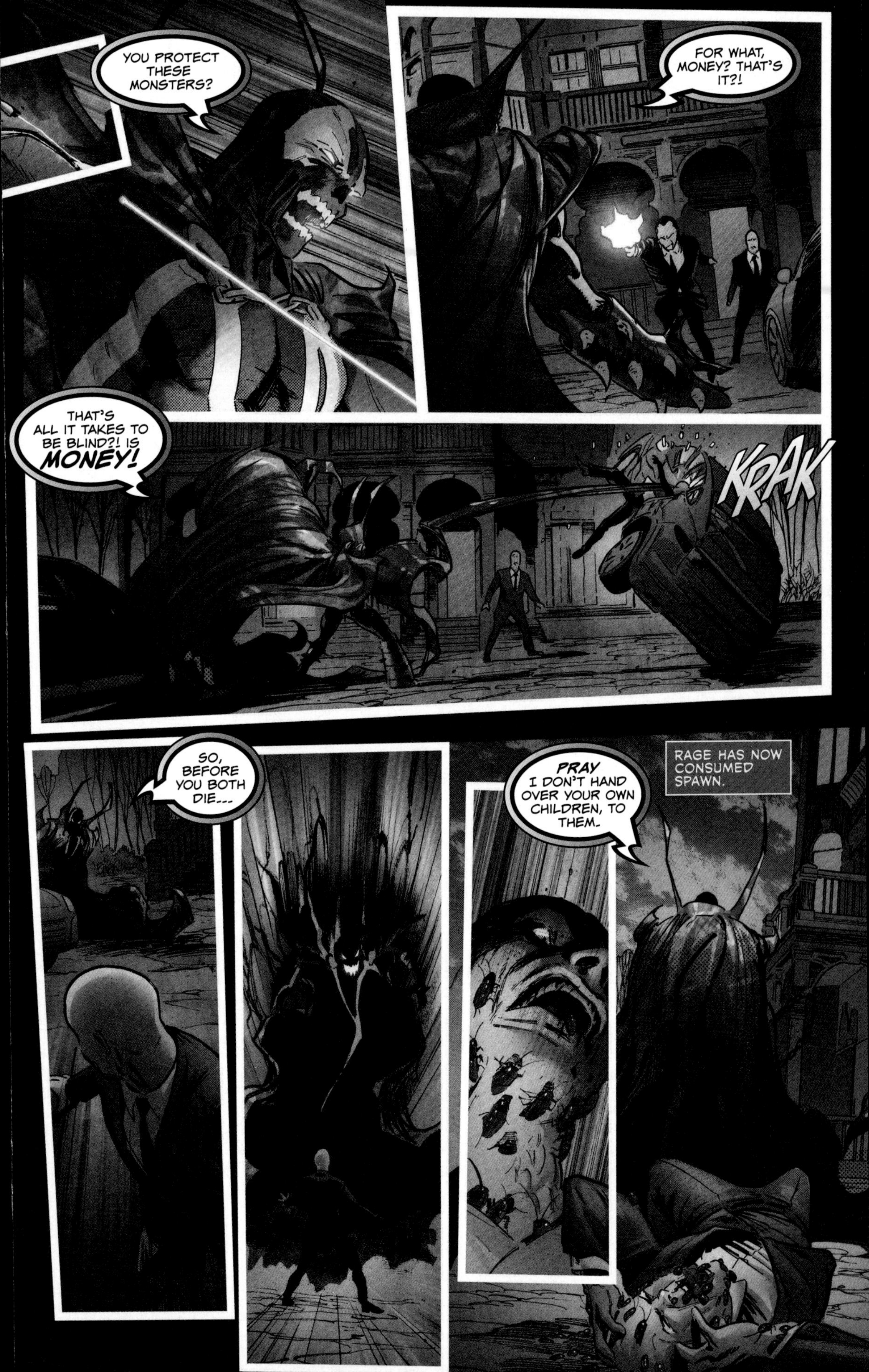
YOU PROTECT THESE MONSTERS?
FOR WHAT, MONEY? THAT'S IT?!
THAT'S ALL IT TAKES TO BE BLIND?! IS MONEY!
KRAK
SO, BEFORE YOU BOTH DIE...
PRAY I DON'T HAND OVER YOUR OWN CHILDREN, TO THEM.
RAGE HAS NOW CONSUMED SPAWN.

THE MAIN FOYER IS SUSPICIOUSLY EMPTY, THOUGH THE SOFT DIN OF LAUGHTER REVERBERATES.

IS THAT THE SOUND OF...A PARTY, SPAWN WONDERS?! ONE WHERE EVEN GUN SHOTS DON'T STARTLE THE GUESTS.

CLONK CLONK CLONK CLON

MADE BY THE TAPPING OF A CHILD, WHOM SPAWN RECOGNIZES FROM HIS PHOTO... THE PHOTO FROM ALL THE CHILDREN WHO DIED IN THE SCHOOL BLAST.

IN THE MANSION'S BOWELS, HE FOLLOWS ANOTHER STRANGE, RHYTHMIC SOUND.

CLONK CLON

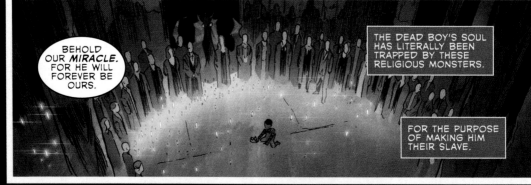

BEHOLD OUR *MIRACLE.* FOR HE WILL FOREVER BE OURS.

THE DEAD BOY'S SOUL HAS LITERALLY BEEN TRAPPED BY THESE RELIGIOUS MONSTERS.

FOR THE PURPOSE OF MAKING HIM THEIR SLAVE.

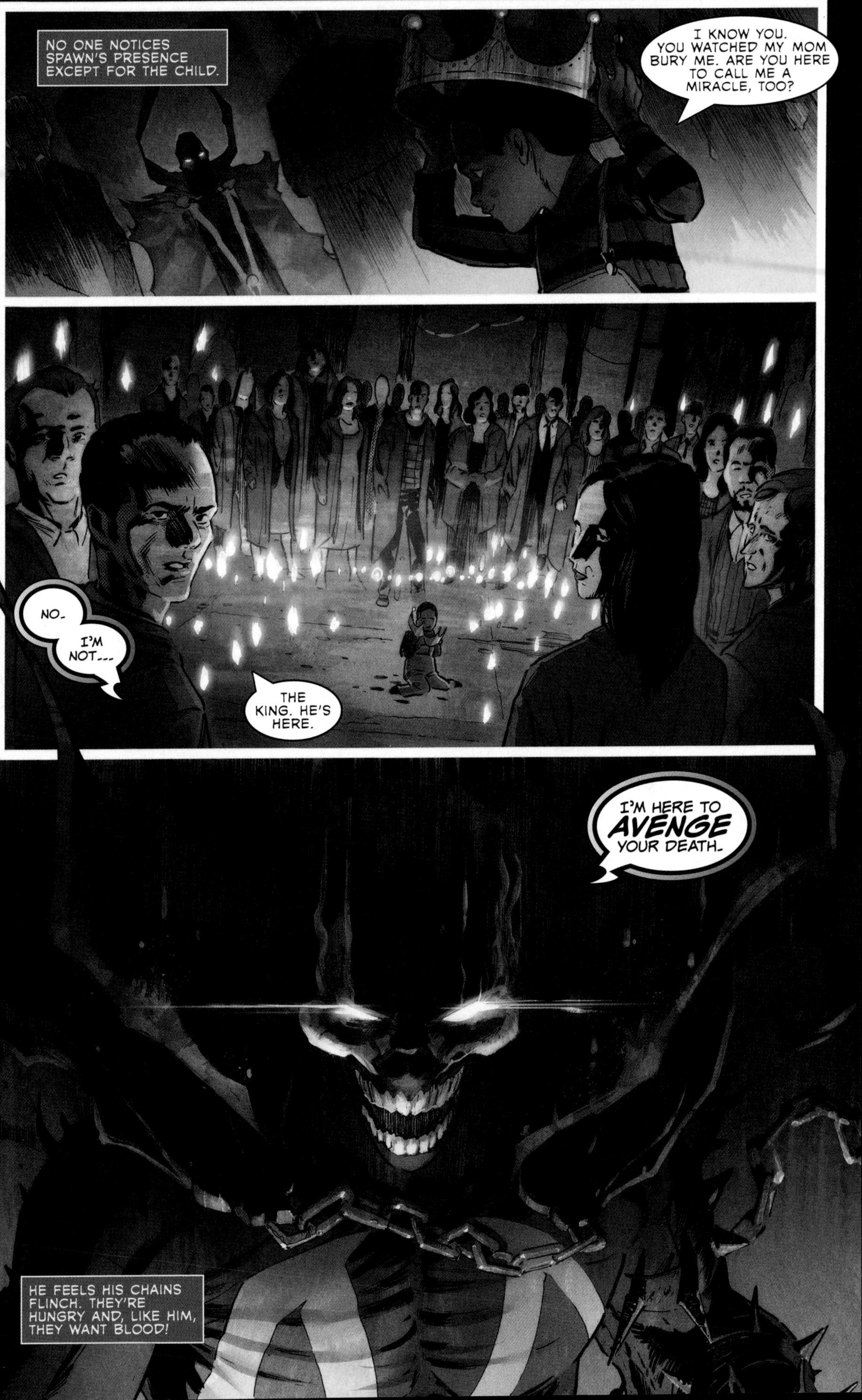
NO ONE NOTICES SPAWN'S PRESENCE EXCEPT FOR THE CHILD.
I KNOW YOU. YOU WATCHED MY MOM BURY ME. ARE YOU HERE TO CALL ME A MIRACLE, TOO?
NO. I'M NOT...
THE KING. HE'S HERE.
I'M HERE TO AVENGE YOUR DEATH.
HE FEELS HIS CHAINS FLINCH. THEY'RE HUNGRY AND, LIKE HIM, THEY WANT BLOOD!

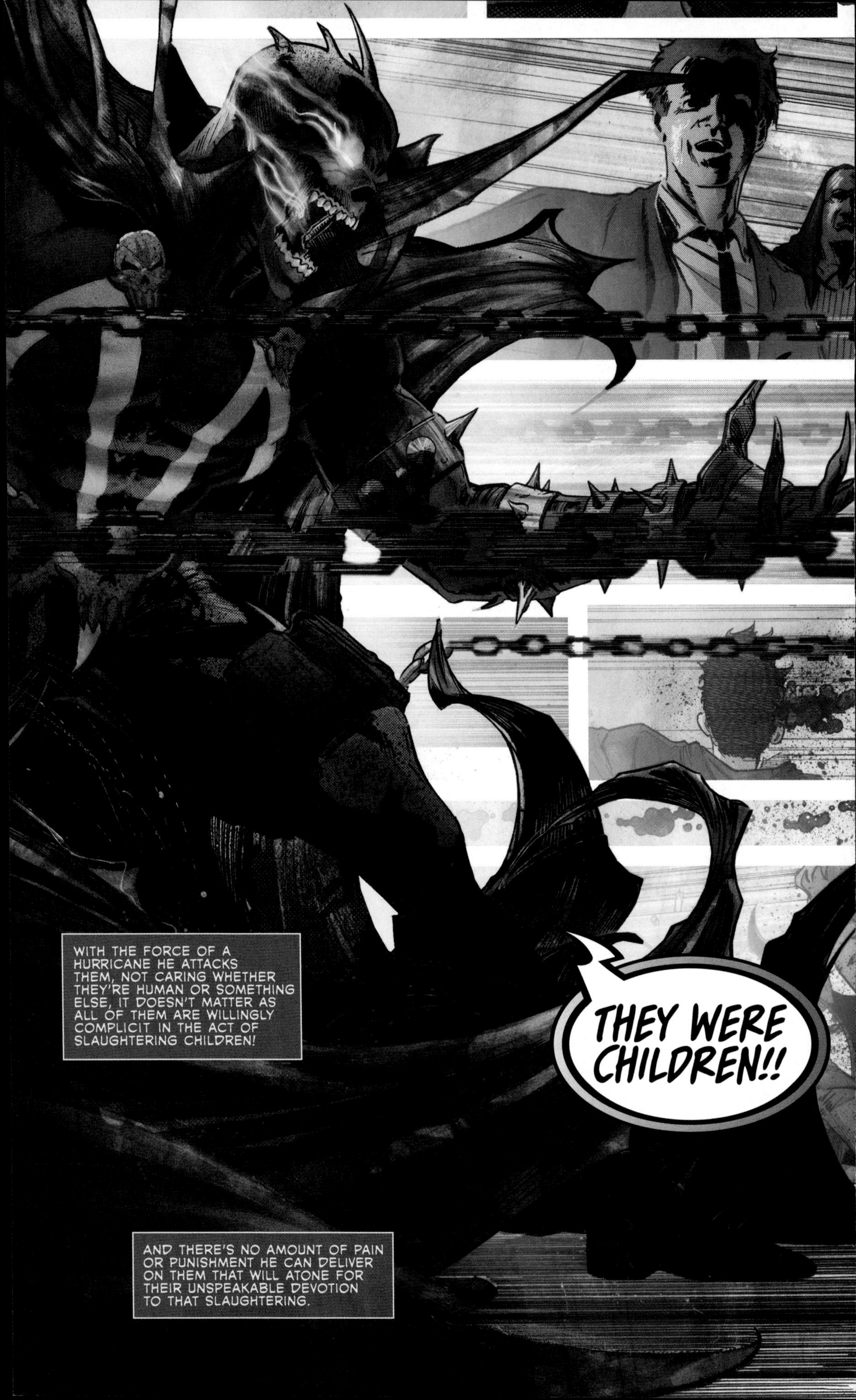
WITH THE FORCE OF A HURRICANE HE ATTACKS THEM, NOT CARING WHETHER THEY'RE HUMAN OR SOMETHING ELSE, IT DOESN'T MATTER AS ALL OF THEM ARE WILLINGLY COMPLICIT IN THE ACT OF SLAUGHTERING CHILDREN!
THEY WERE CHILDREN!!
AND THERE'S NO AMOUNT OF PAIN OR PUNISHMENT HE CAN DELIVER ON THEM THAT WILL ATONE FOR THEIR UNSPEAKABLE DEVOTION TO THAT SLAUGHTERING.

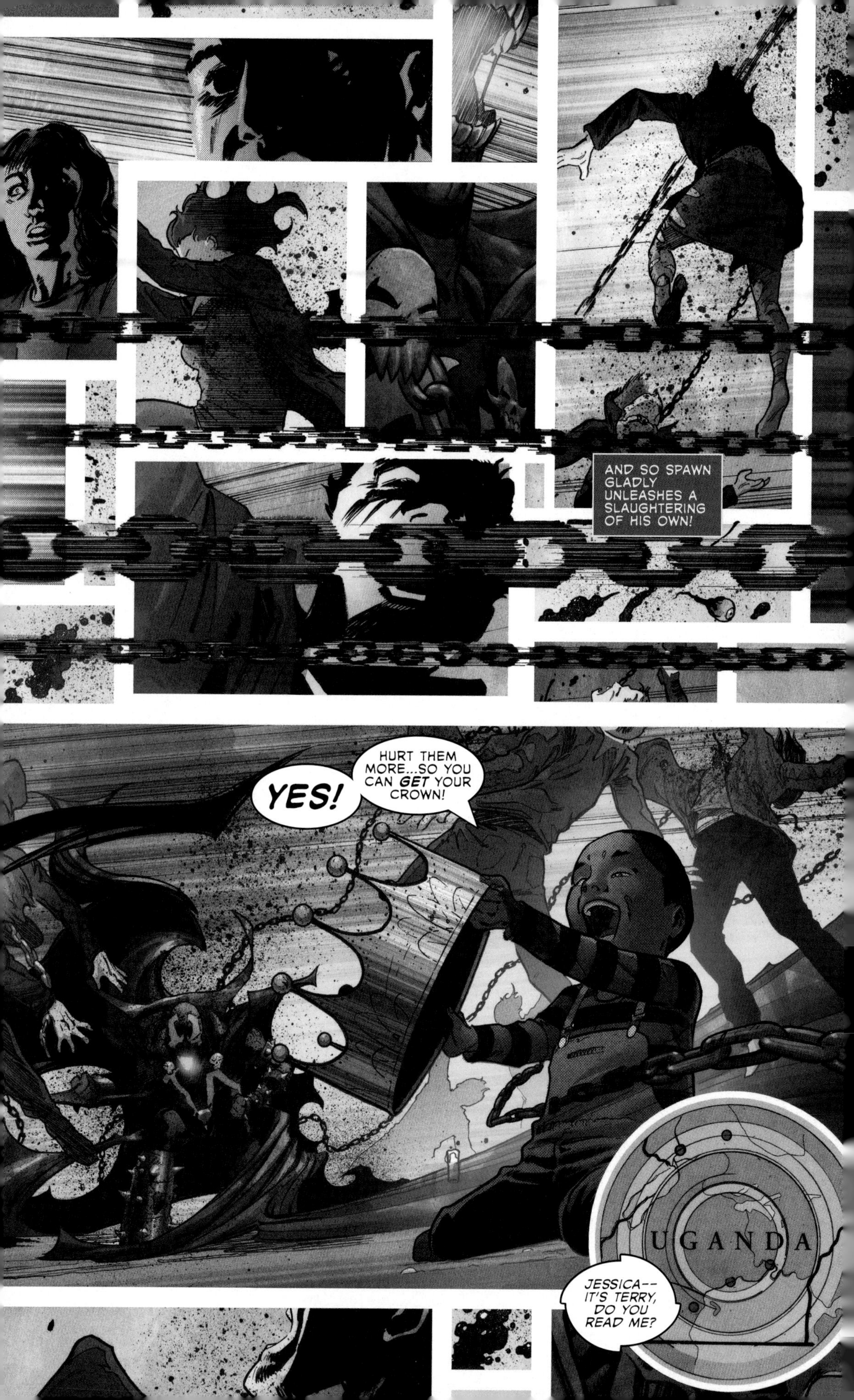
AND SO SPAWN GLADLY UNLEASHES A SLAUGHTERING OF HIS OWN!
YES!
HURT THEM MORE...SO YOU CAN GET YOUR CROWN!
UGANDA
JESSICA-- IT'S TERRY, DO YOU READ ME?

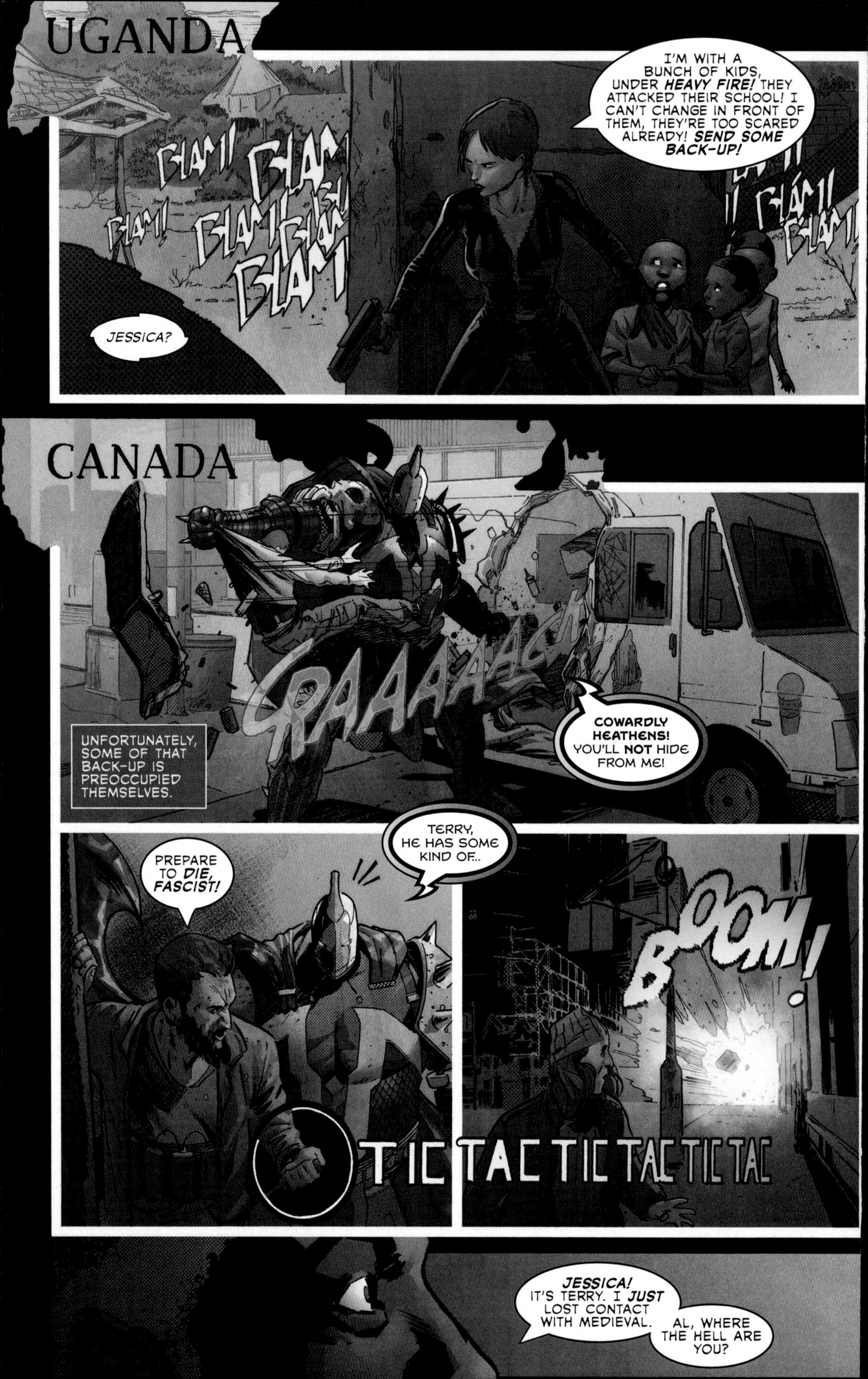
UGANDA
I'M WITH A BUNCH OF KIDS, UNDER HEAVY FIRE! THEY ATTACKED THEIR SCHOOL! I CAN'T CHANGE IN FRONT OF THEM, THEY'RE TOO SCARED ALREADY! SEND SOME BACK-UP!
JESSICA?
CANADA
UNFORTUNATELY, SOME OF THAT BACK-UP IS PREOCCUPIED THEMSELVES.
GRAAAAAACH
COWARDLY HEATHENS! YOU'LL NOT HIDE FROM ME!
PREPARE TO DIE, FASCIST!
TERRY, HE HAS SOME KIND OF..
BOOM!
TIC TAC TIC TAC TIC TAC
JESSICA! IT'S TERRY. I JUST LOST CONTACT WITH MEDIEVAL.
AL, WHERE THE HELL ARE YOU?

CLONK
CLONK

CAN YOU **HEAR** ME?!

HE DOES, BUT HE'S FOCUSED ON SOMEONE ELSE.

KINCAID!

AL?

SHOW YOURSELF!

TERRY CUTS HIS OWN AUDIO, KNOWING ANY DISTRACTION COULD GET HIS FRIEND KILLED.

I HOPE YOU KNOW WHAT YOU'RE DOING, AL.

AS HIS ENEMY EMERGES...

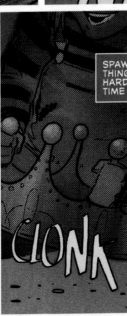

CLONK

SPAWN KNOWS THINGS WILL BE HARDER THIS TIME AROUND.

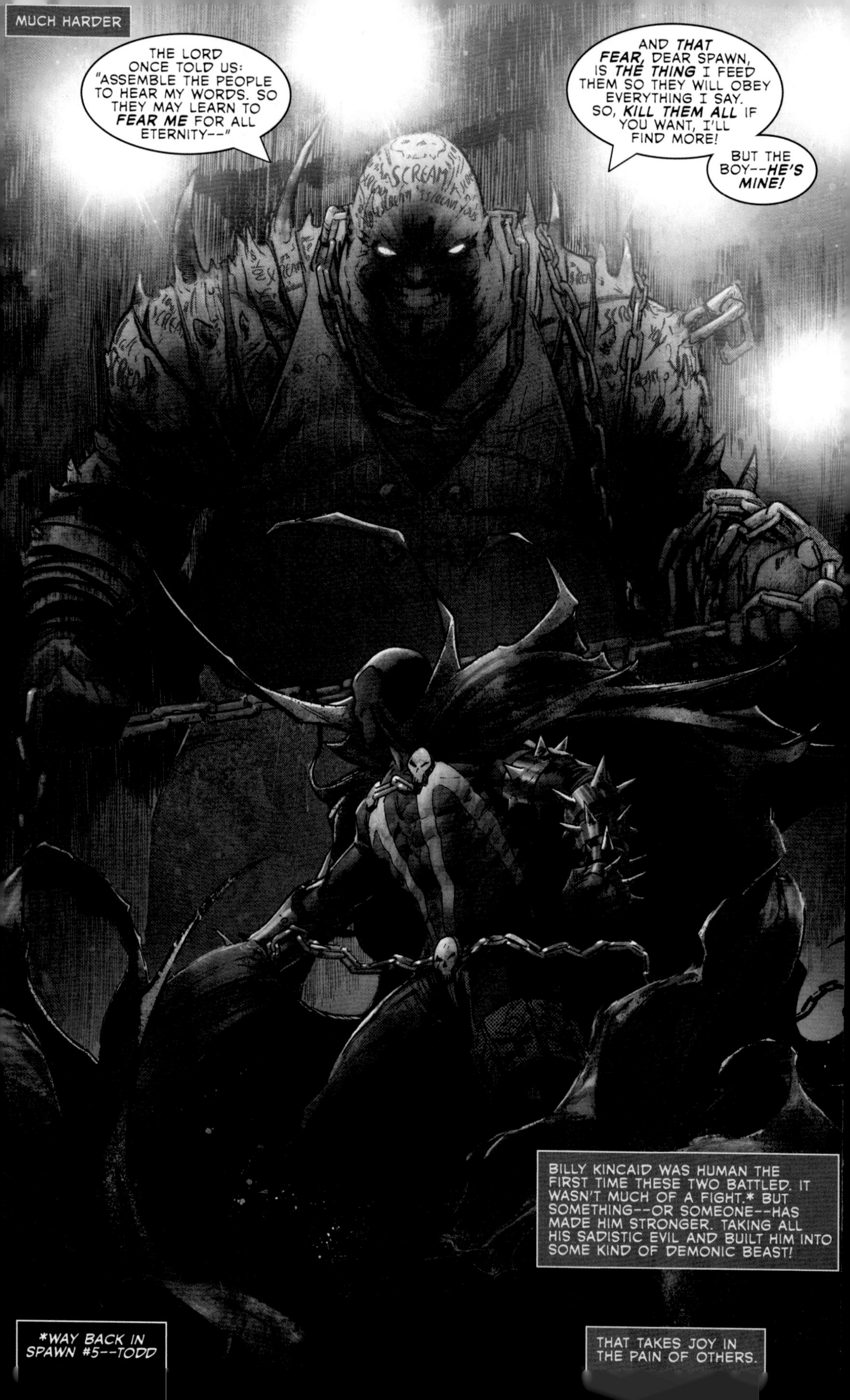
MUCH HARDER
THE LORD ONCE TOLD US: "ASSEMBLE THE PEOPLE TO HEAR MY WORDS. SO THEY MAY LEARN TO FEAR ME FOR ALL ETERNITY--"
AND THAT FEAR, DEAR SPAWN, IS THE THING I FEED THEM SO THEY WILL OBEY EVERYTHING I SAY. SO, KILL THEM ALL IF YOU WANT, I'LL FIND MORE!
BUT THE BOY--HE'S MINE!
BILLY KINCAID WAS HUMAN THE FIRST TIME THESE TWO BATTLED. IT WASN'T MUCH OF A FIGHT.* BUT SOMETHING--OR SOMEONE--HAS MADE HIM STRONGER. TAKING ALL HIS SADISTIC EVIL AND BUILT HIM INTO SOME KIND OF DEMONIC BEAST!
*WAY BACK IN SPAWN #5--TODD
THAT TAKES JOY IN THE PAIN OF OTHERS.

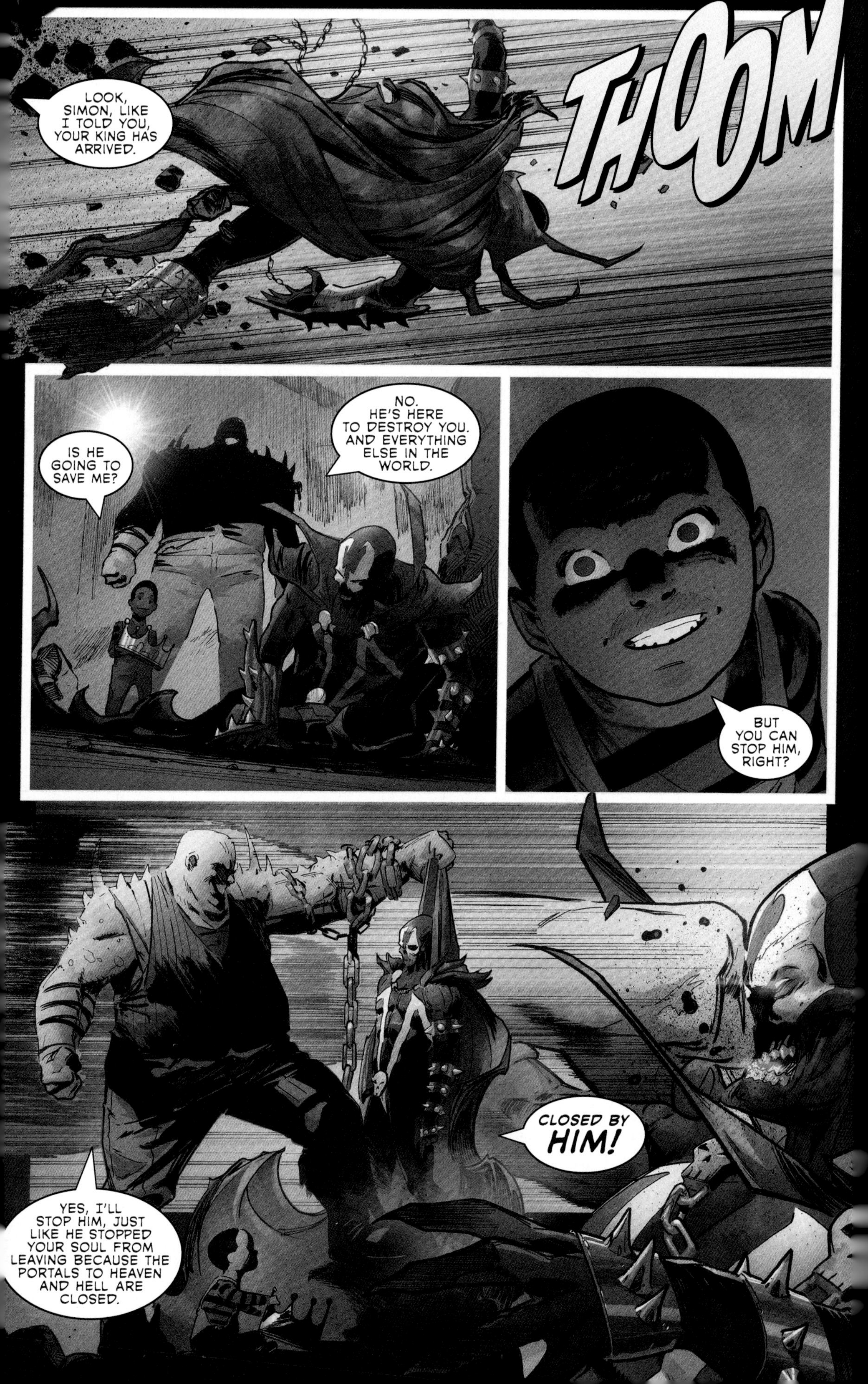
LOOK, SIMON, LIKE I TOLD YOU, YOUR KING HAS ARRIVED.
THOOOM
IS HE GOING TO SAVE ME?
NO. HE'S HERE TO DESTROY YOU. AND EVERYTHING ELSE IN THE WORLD.
BUT YOU CAN STOP HIM, RIGHT?
YES, I'LL STOP HIM, JUST LIKE HE STOPPED YOUR SOUL FROM LEAVING BECAUSE THE PORTALS TO HEAVEN AND HELL ARE CLOSED.
CLOSED BY HIM!

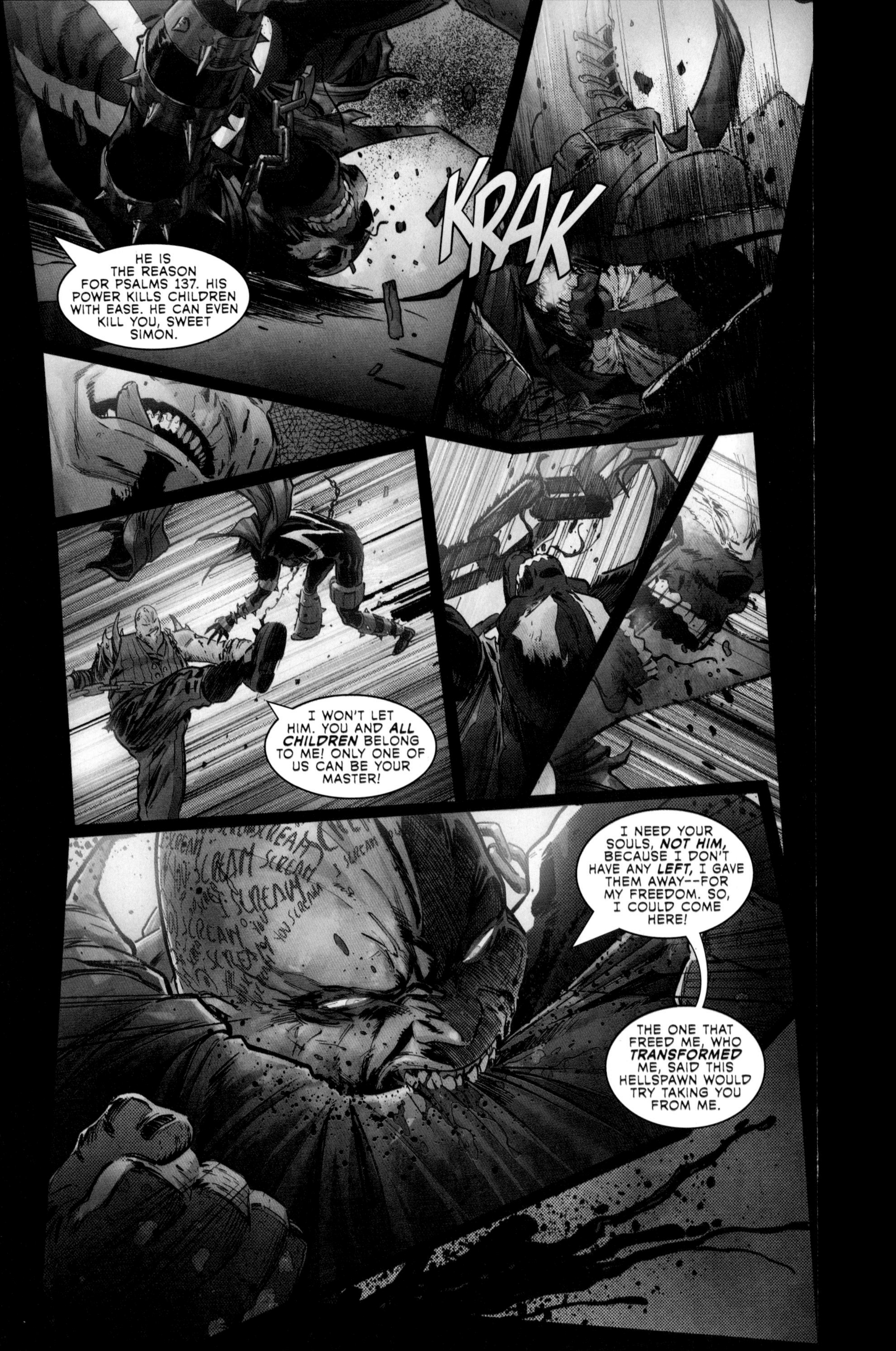
HE IS THE REASON FOR PSALMS 137. HIS POWER KILLS CHILDREN WITH EASE. HE CAN EVEN KILL YOU, SWEET SIMON.
KRAK
I WON'T LET HIM. YOU AND ALL CHILDREN BELONG TO ME! ONLY ONE OF US CAN BE YOUR MASTER!
I NEED YOUR SOULS, NOT HIM, BECAUSE I DON'T HAVE ANY LEFT, I GAVE THEM AWAY--FOR MY FREEDOM. SO, I COULD COME HERE!
THE ONE THAT FREED ME, WHO TRANSFORMED ME, SAID THIS HELLSPAWN WOULD TRY TAKING YOU FROM ME.

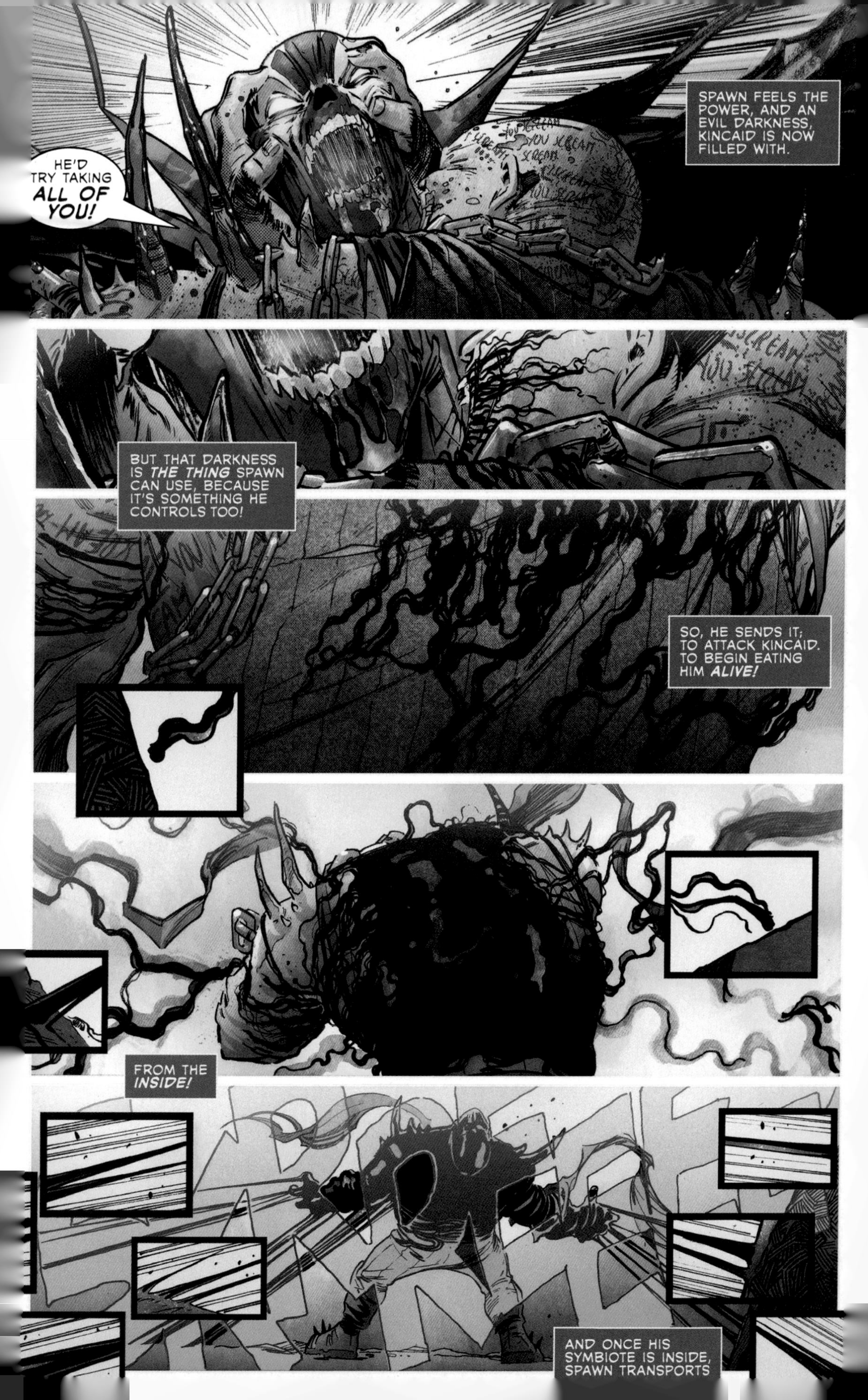
HE'D TRY TAKING ALL OF YOU!
SPAWN FEELS THE POWER, AND AN EVIL DARKNESS, KINCAID IS NOW FILLED WITH.
BUT THAT DARKNESS IS THE THING SPAWN CAN USE, BECAUSE IT'S SOMETHING HE CONTROLS TOO!
SO, HE SENDS IT; TO ATTACK KINCAID. TO BEGIN EATING HIM ALIVE!
FROM THE INSIDE!
AND ONCE HIS SYMBIOTE IS INSIDE, SPAWN TRANSPORTS

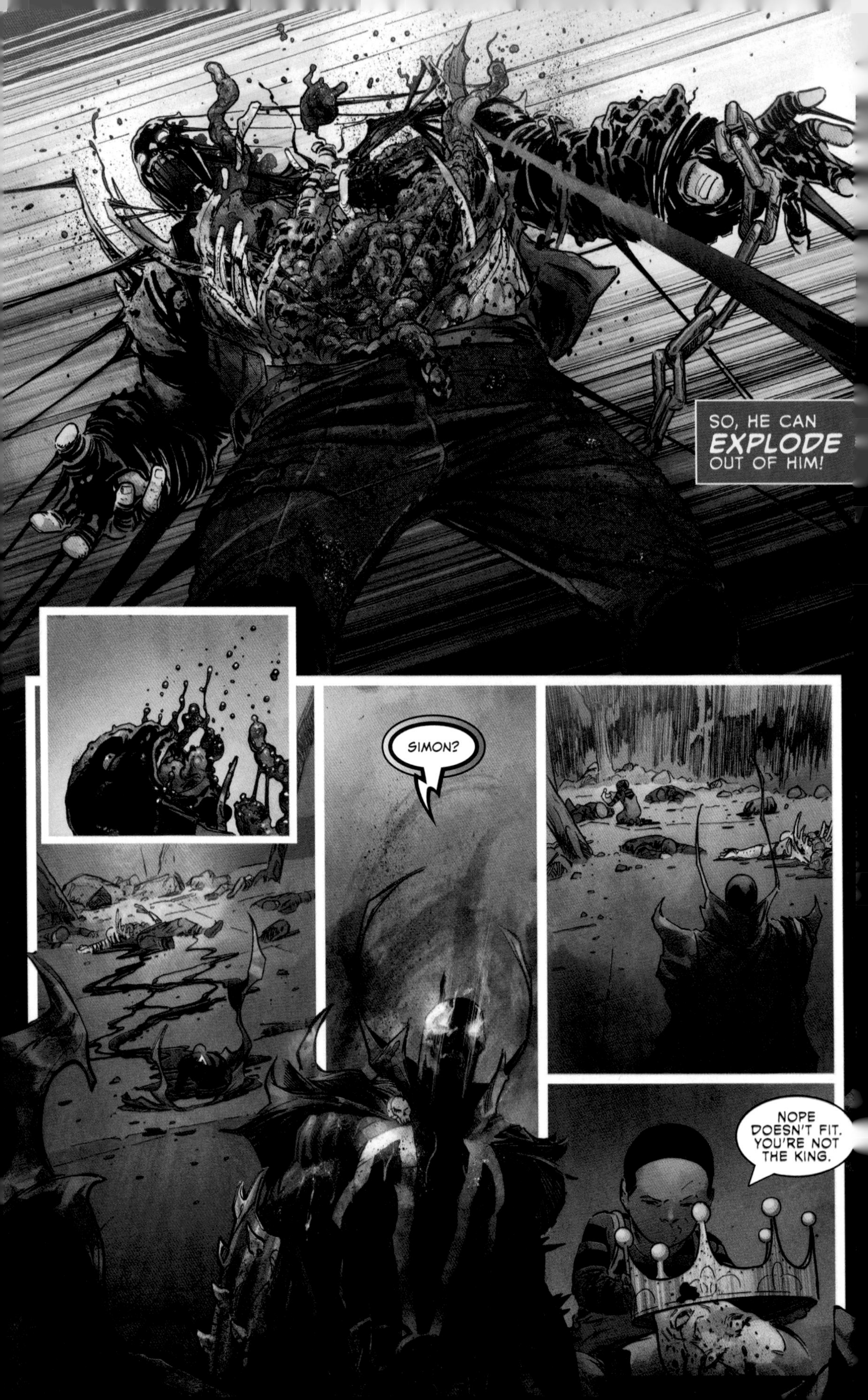
SO, HE CAN EXPLODE OUT OF HIM!
SIMON?
NOPE DOESN'T FIT. YOU'RE NOT THE KING.

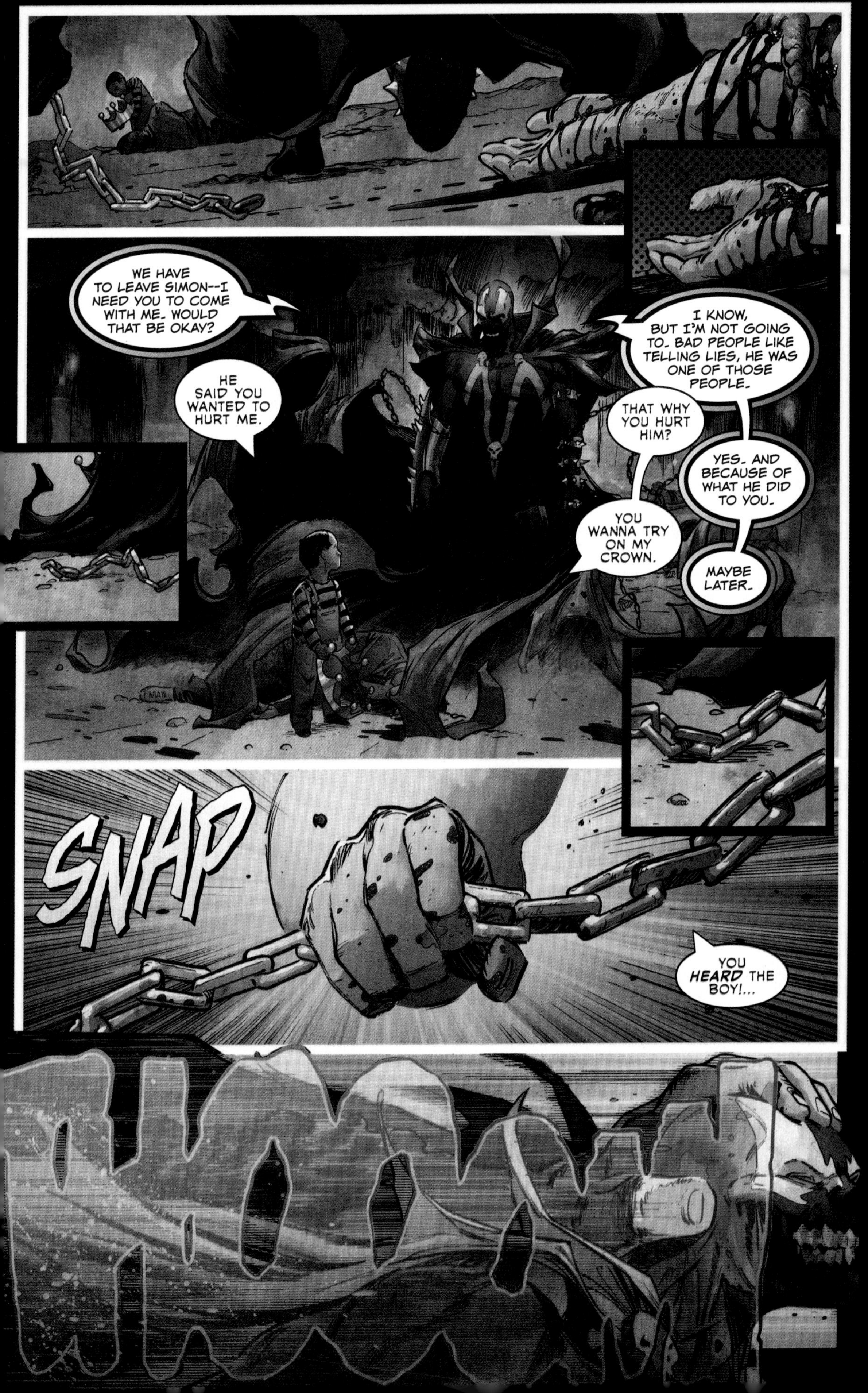
WE HAVE TO LEAVE SIMON--I NEED YOU TO COME WITH ME. WOULD THAT BE OKAY?
HE SAID YOU WANTED TO HURT ME.
I KNOW, BUT I'M NOT GOING TO. BAD PEOPLE LIKE TELLING LIES, HE WAS ONE OF THOSE PEOPLE.
THAT WHY YOU HURT HIM?
YES. AND BECAUSE OF WHAT HE DID TO YOU.
YOU WANNA TRY ON MY CROWN.
MAYBE LATER.
SNAP
YOU HEARD THE BOY!...

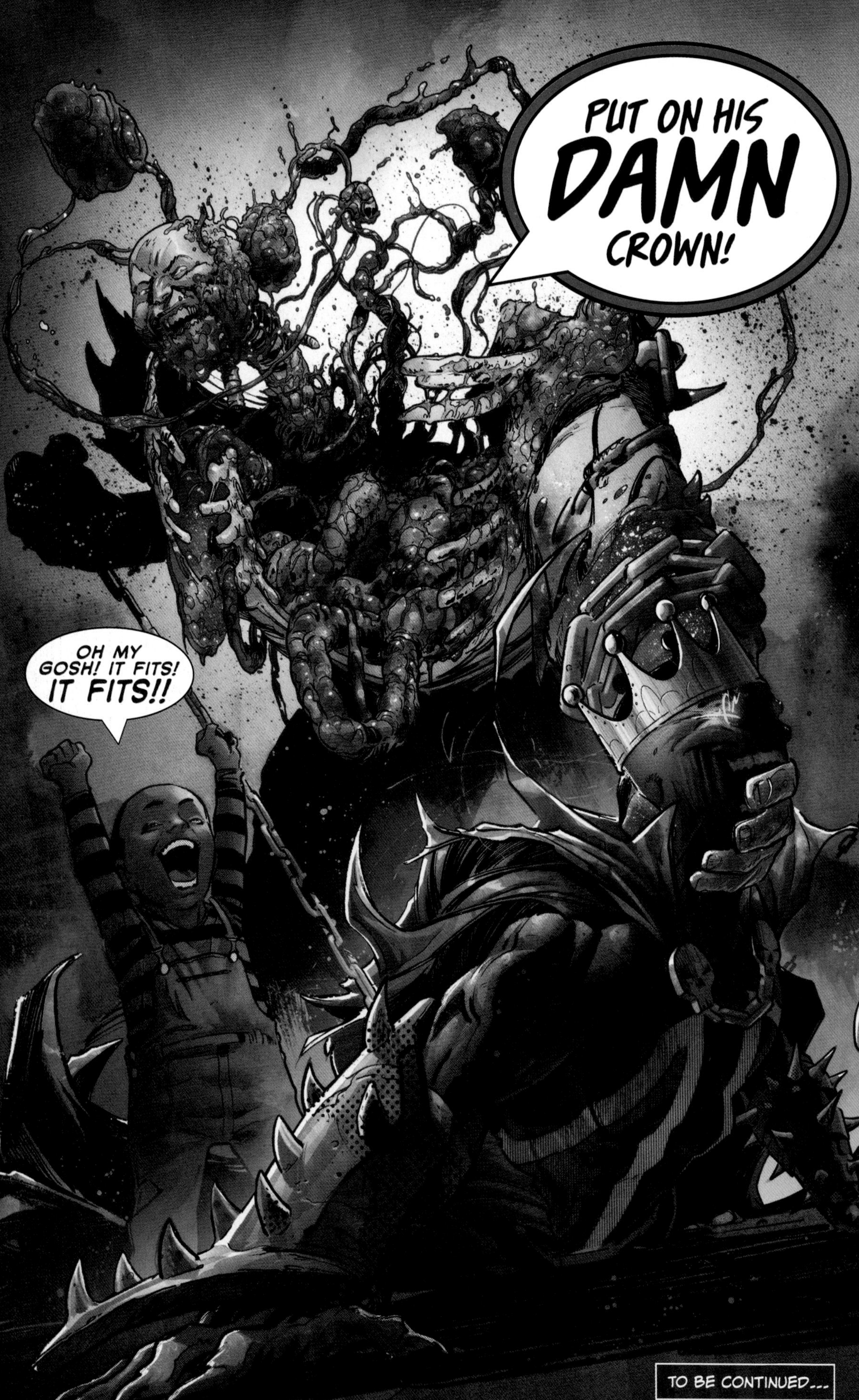
PUT ON HIS DAMN CROWN!
OH MY GOSH! IT FITS! IT FITS!!
TO BE CONTINUED...

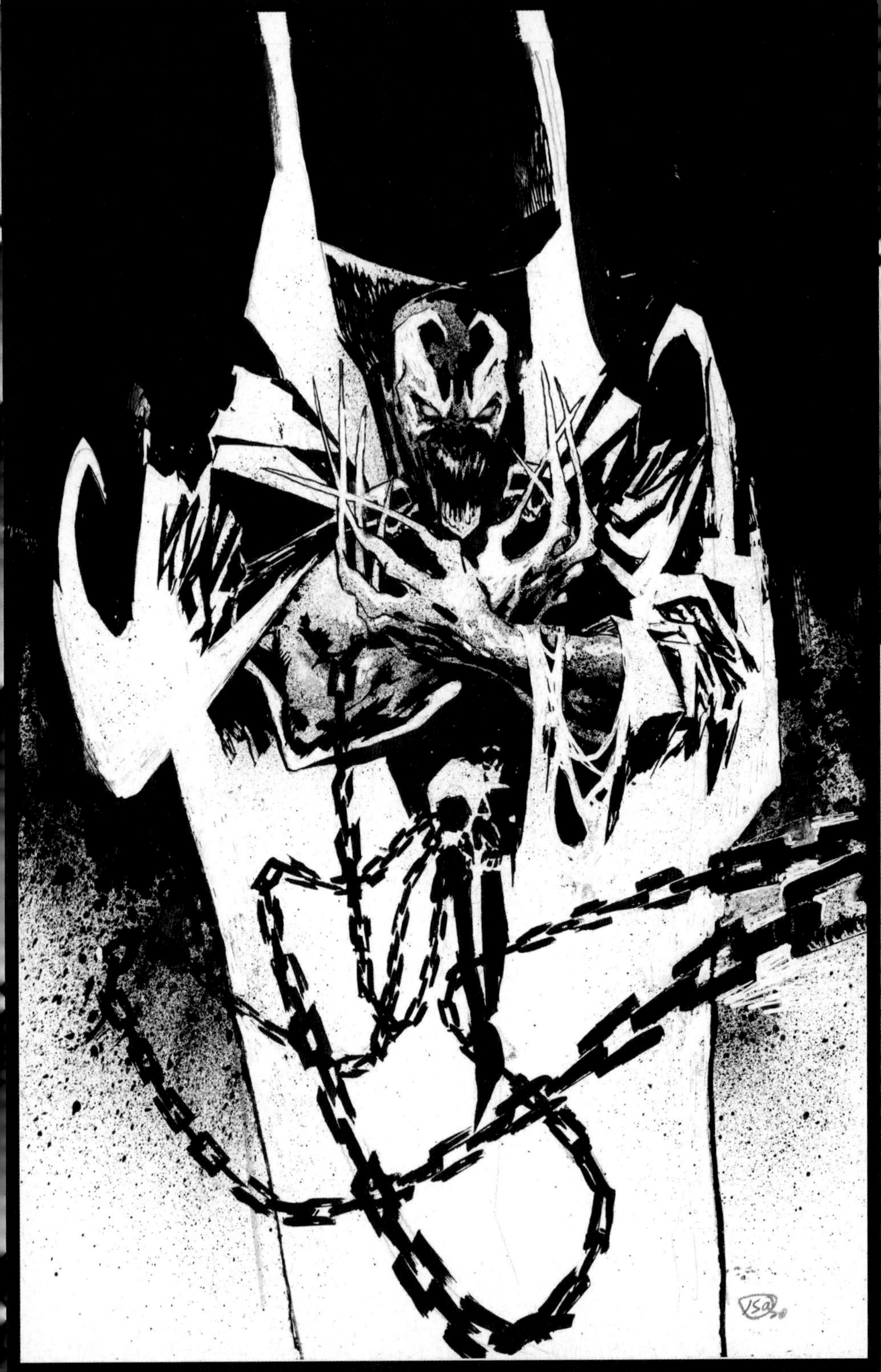

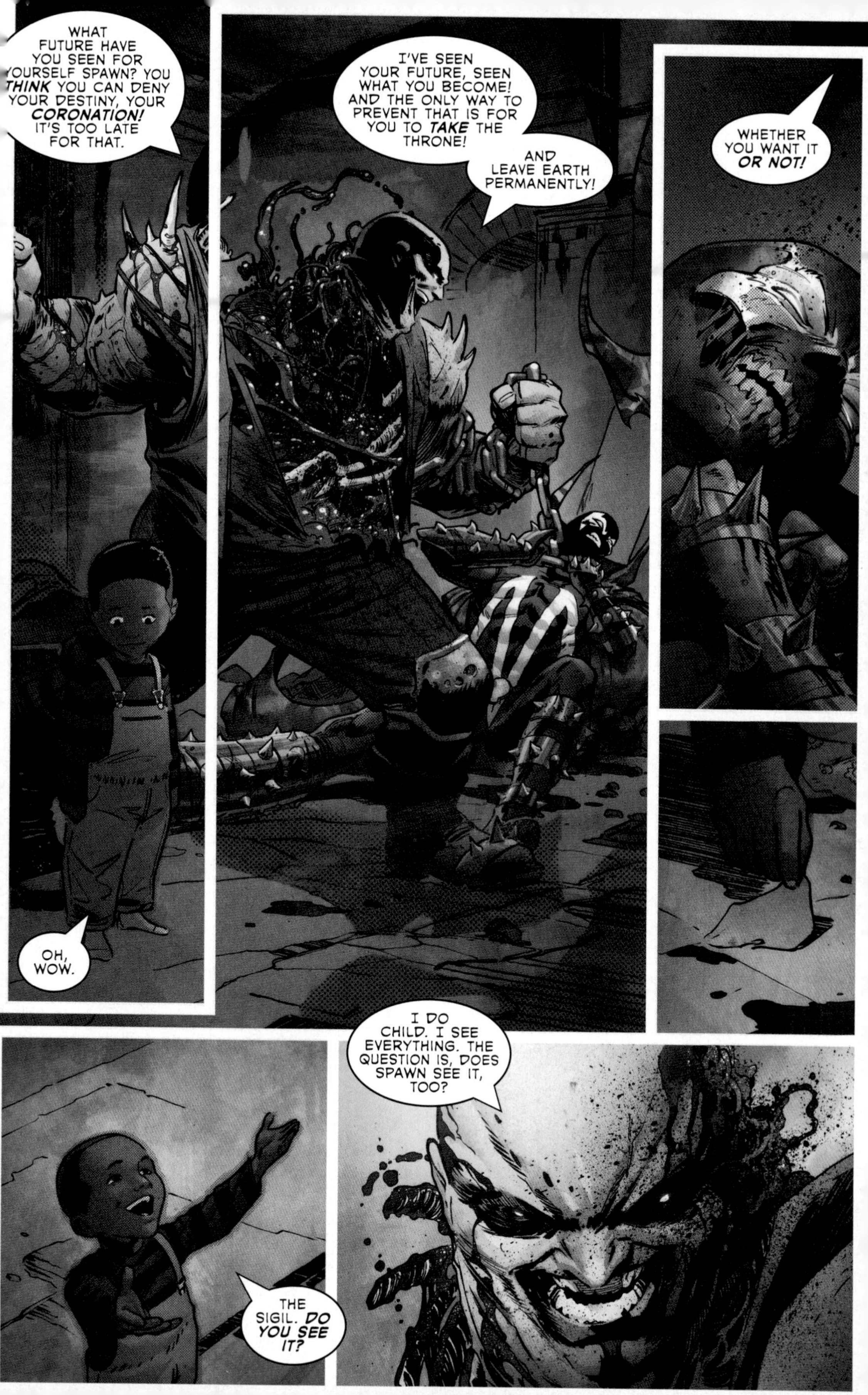
WHAT FUTURE HAVE YOU SEEN FOR YOURSELF SPAWN? YOU *THINK* YOU CAN DENY YOUR DESTINY, YOUR *CORONATION!* IT'S TOO LATE FOR THAT.
OH, WOW.
I'VE SEEN YOUR FUTURE, SEEN WHAT YOU BECOME! AND THE ONLY WAY TO PREVENT THAT IS FOR YOU TO *TAKE* THE THRONE!
AND LEAVE EARTH PERMANENTLY!
WHETHER YOU WANT IT *OR NOT!*
THE SIGIL. *DO YOU SEE IT?*
I DO CHILD. I SEE EVERYTHING. THE QUESTION IS, DOES SPAWN SEE IT, TOO?

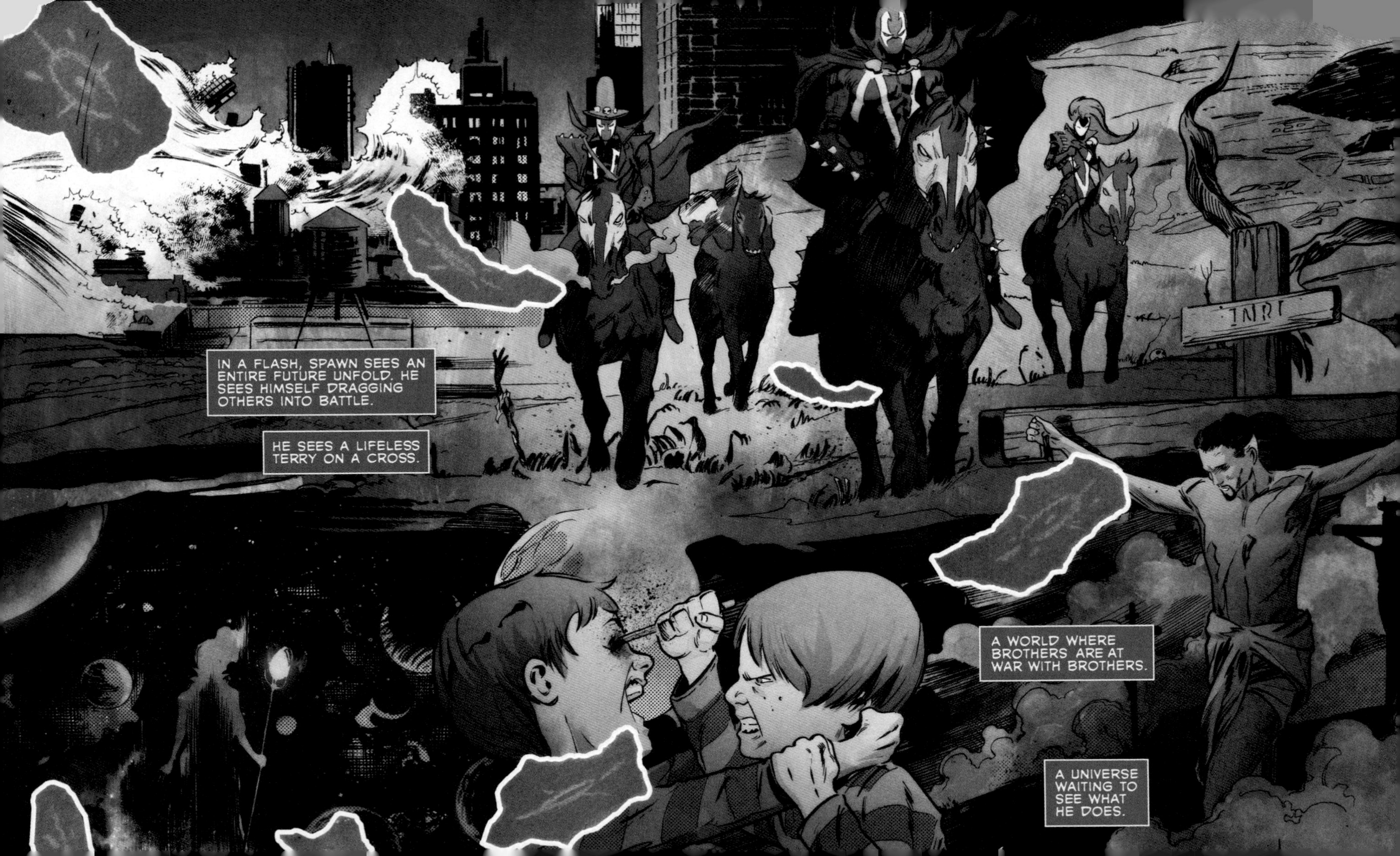
IN A FLASH, SPAWN SEES AN ENTIRE FUTURE UNFOLD. HE SEES HIMSELF DRAGGING OTHERS INTO BATTLE.
HE SEES A LIFELESS TERRY ON A CROSS.
INRI
A WORLD WHERE BROTHERS ARE AT WAR WITH BROTHERS.
A UNIVERSE WAITING TO SEE WHAT HE DOES.

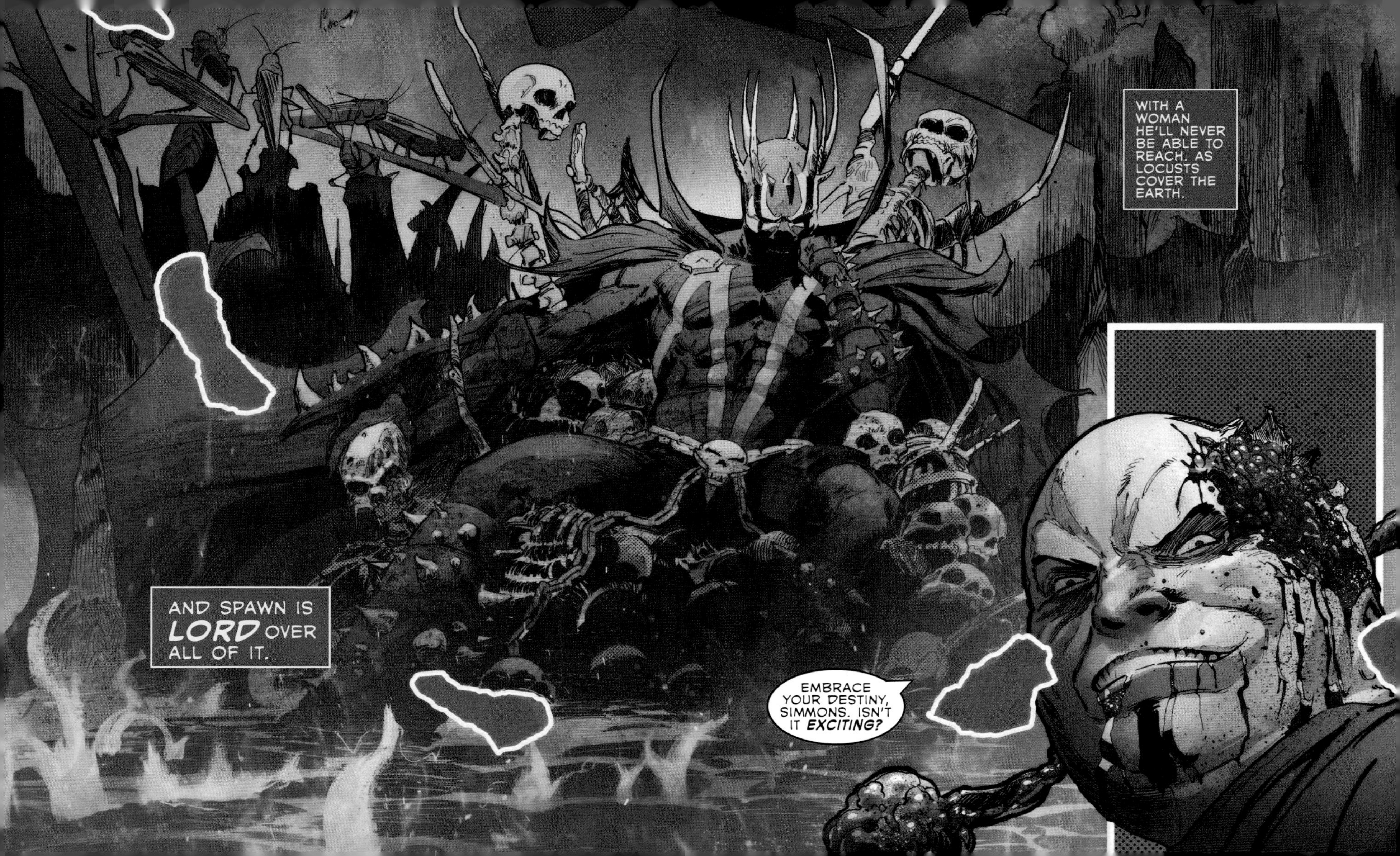
WITH A WOMAN HE'LL NEVER BE ABLE TO REACH. AS LOCUSTS COVER THE EARTH.
AND SPAWN IS **LORD** OVER ALL OF IT.
EMBRACE YOUR DESTINY, SIMMONS. ISN'T IT ***EXCITING?***

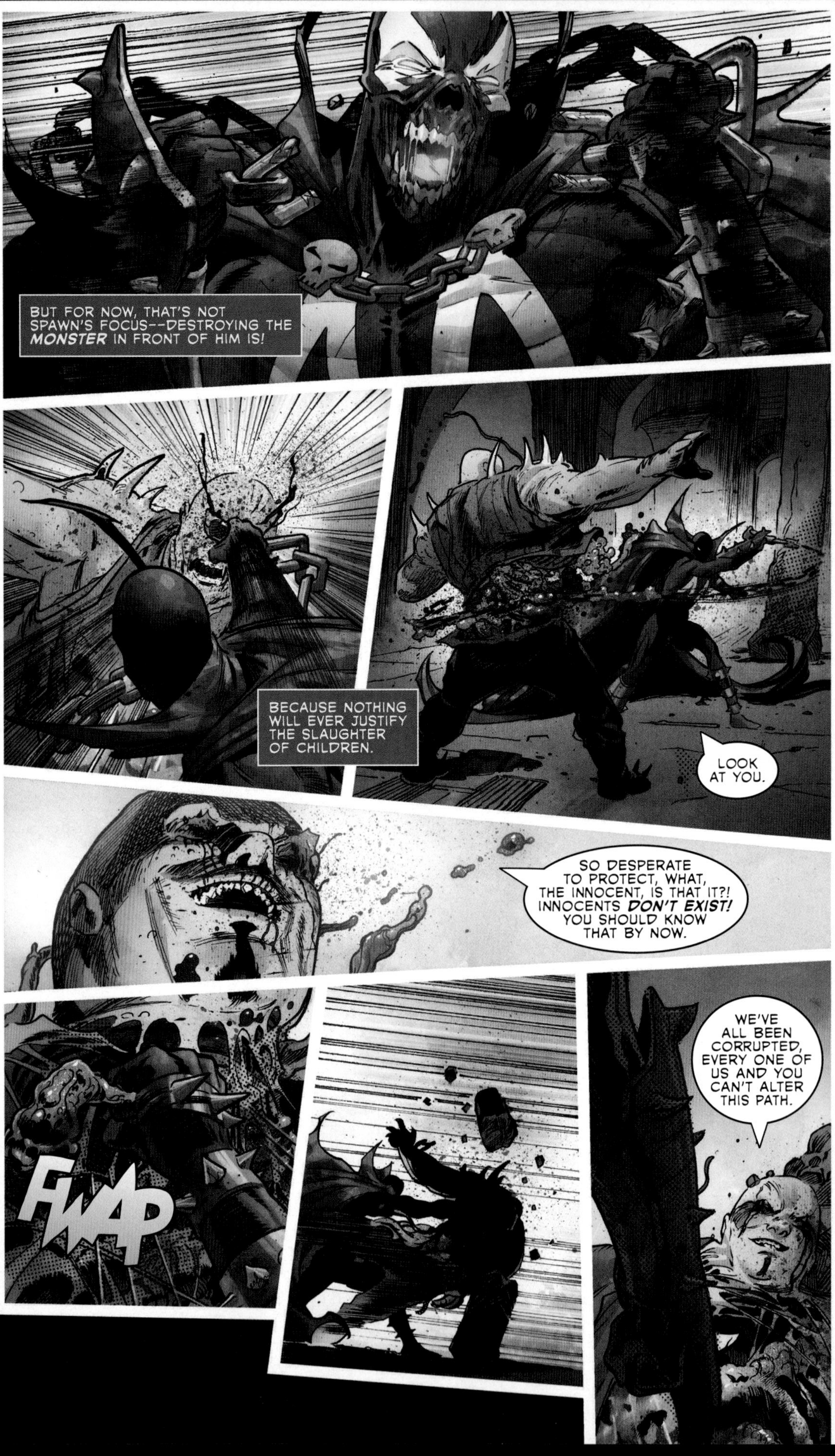
BUT FOR NOW, THAT'S NOT SPAWN'S FOCUS--DESTROYING THE **MONSTER** IN FRONT OF HIM IS!
BECAUSE NOTHING WILL EVER JUSTIFY THE SLAUGHTER OF CHILDREN.
LOOK AT YOU.
SO DESPERATE TO PROTECT, WHAT, THE INNOCENT, IS THAT IT?! INNOCENTS **DON'T EXIST!** YOU SHOULD KNOW THAT BY NOW.
FWAP
WE'VE ALL BEEN CORRUPTED, EVERY ONE OF US AND YOU CAN'T ALTER THIS PATH.

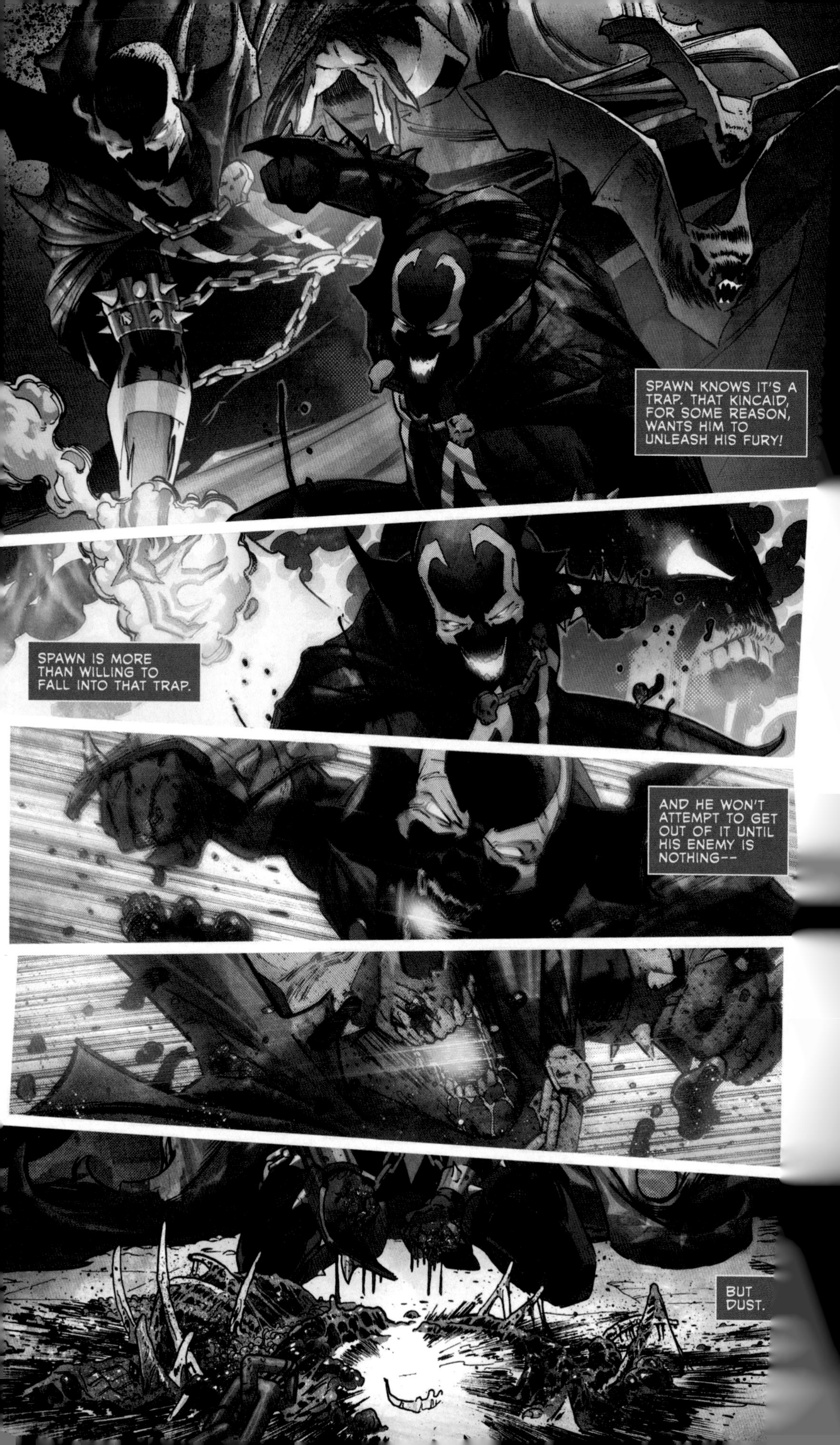
SPAWN KNOWS IT'S A TRAP. THAT KINCAID, FOR SOME REASON, WANTS HIM TO UNLEASH HIS FURY!
SPAWN IS MORE THAN WILLING TO FALL INTO THAT TRAP.
AND HE WON'T ATTEMPT TO GET OUT OF IT UNTIL HIS ENEMY IS NOTHING--
BUT DUST.

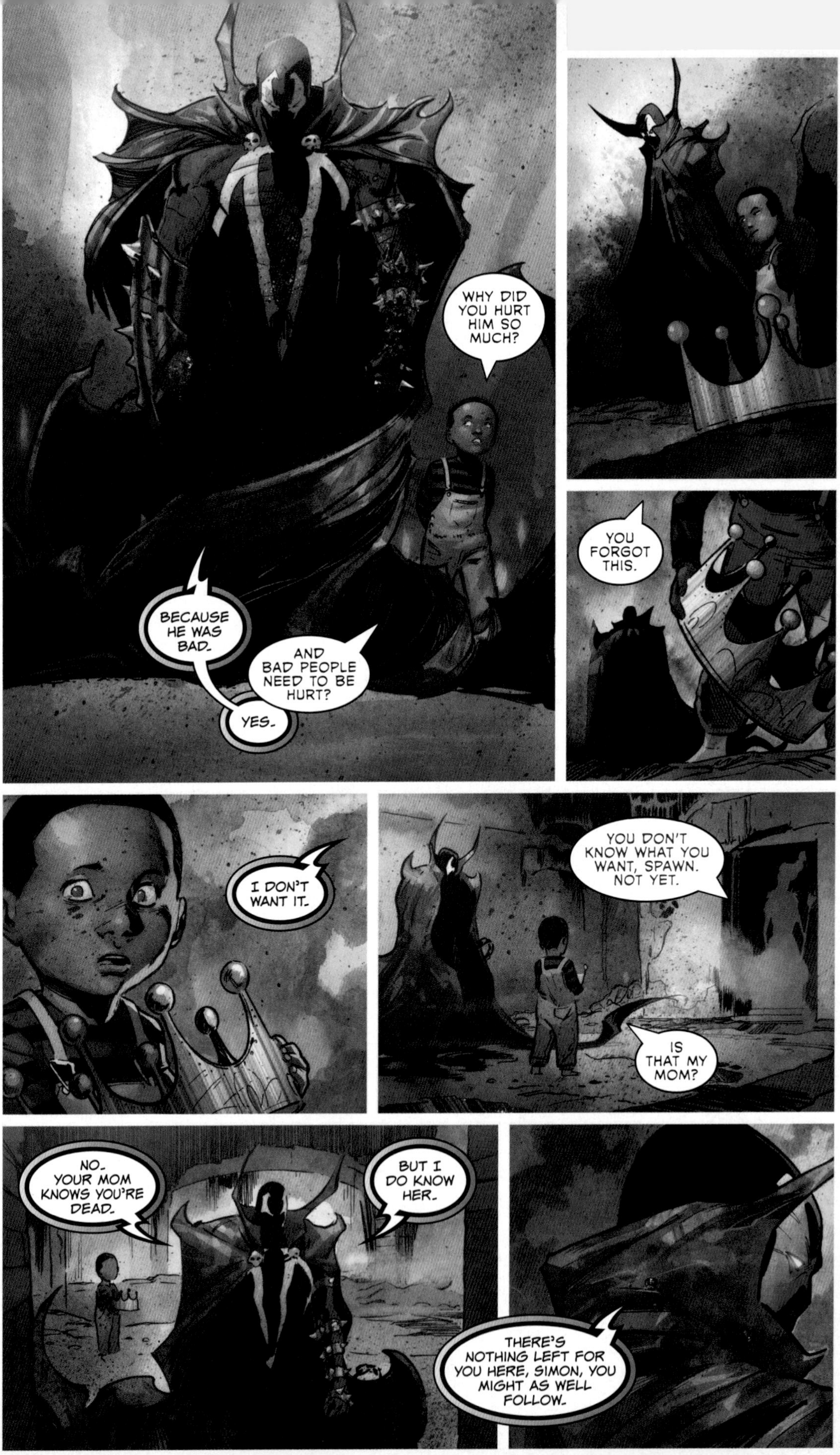
WHY DID YOU HURT HIM SO MUCH?
BECAUSE HE WAS BAD.
AND BAD PEOPLE NEED TO BE HURT?
YES.
YOU FORGOT THIS.
I DON'T WANT IT.
YOU DON'T KNOW WHAT YOU WANT, SPAWN. NOT YET.
IS THAT MY MOM?
NO. YOUR MOM KNOWS YOU'RE DEAD.
BUT I DO KNOW HER.
THERE'S NOTHING LEFT FOR YOU HERE, SIMON, YOU MIGHT AS WELL FOLLOW.

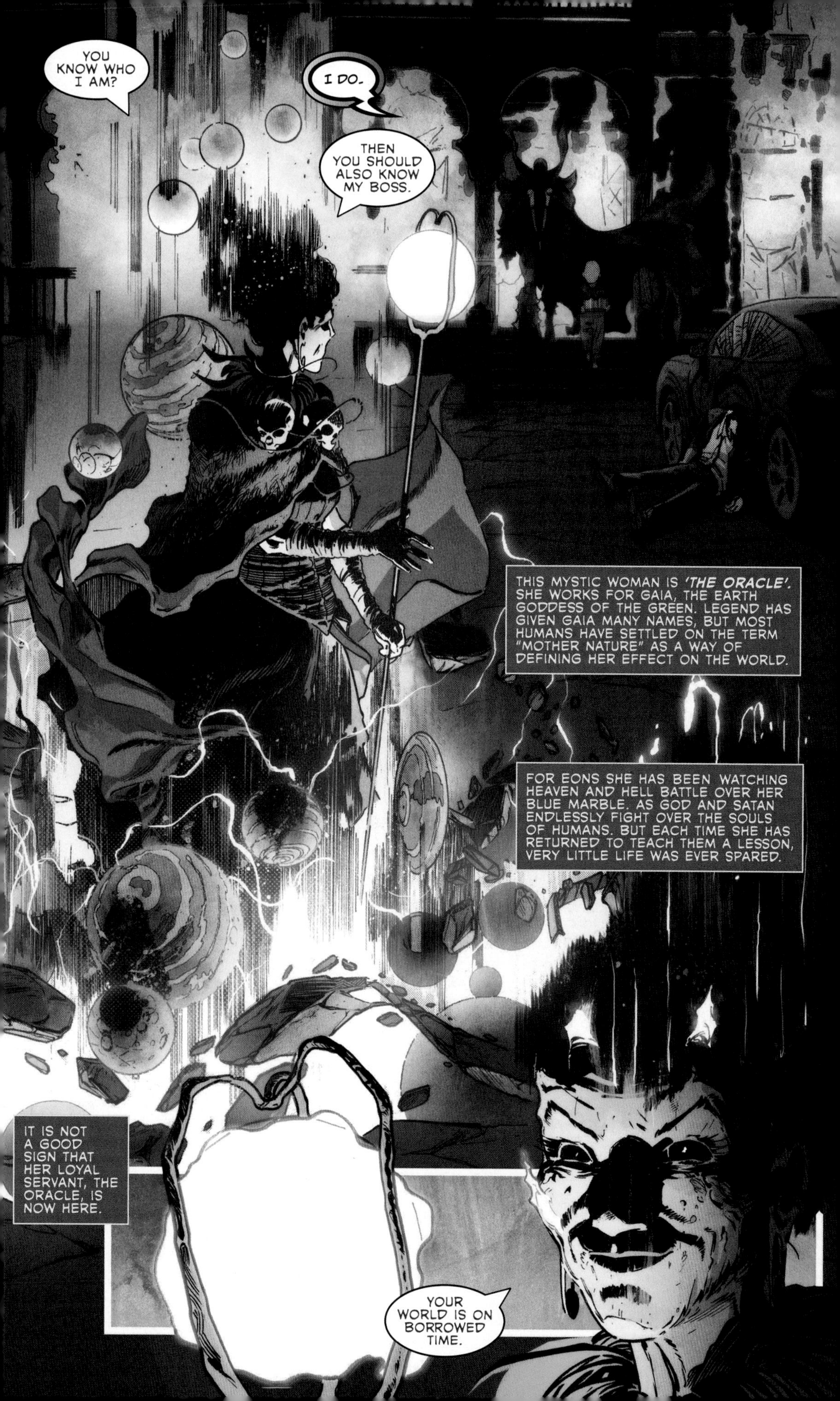
YOU KNOW WHO I AM?
I DO.
THEN YOU SHOULD ALSO KNOW MY BOSS.
THIS MYSTIC WOMAN IS *'THE ORACLE'*. SHE WORKS FOR GAIA, THE EARTH GODDESS OF THE GREEN. LEGEND HAS GIVEN GAIA MANY NAMES, BUT MOST HUMANS HAVE SETTLED ON THE TERM "MOTHER NATURE" AS A WAY OF DEFINING HER EFFECT ON THE WORLD.
FOR EONS SHE HAS BEEN WATCHING HEAVEN AND HELL BATTLE OVER HER BLUE MARBLE. AS GOD AND SATAN ENDLESSLY FIGHT OVER THE SOULS OF HUMANS. BUT EACH TIME SHE HAS RETURNED TO TEACH THEM A LESSON, VERY LITTLE LIFE WAS EVER SPARED.
IT IS NOT A GOOD SIGN THAT HER LOYAL SERVANT, THE ORACLE, IS NOW HERE.
YOUR WORLD IS ON BORROWED TIME.

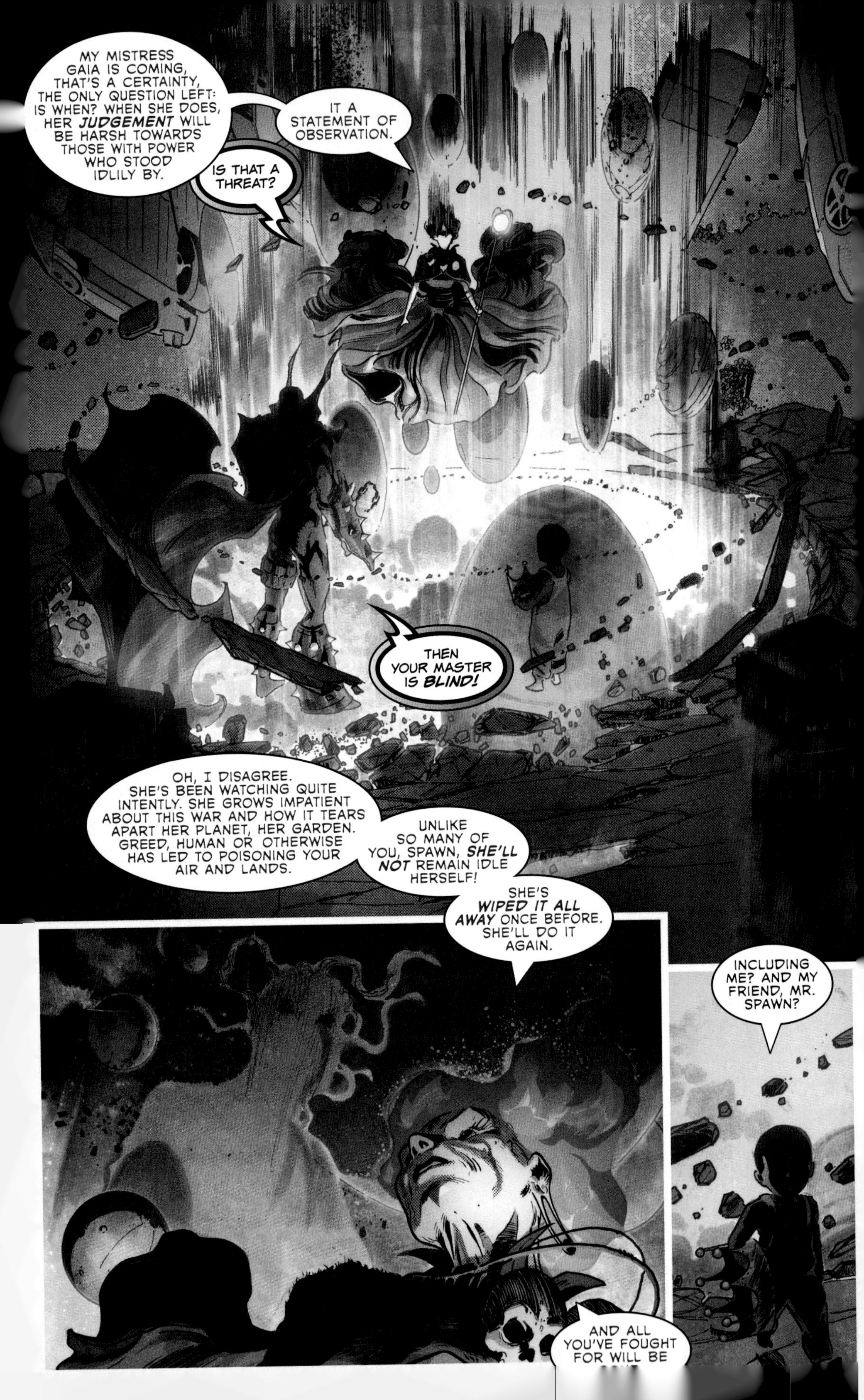
MY MISTRESS GAIA IS COMING, THAT'S A CERTAINTY, THE ONLY QUESTION LEFT: IS WHEN? WHEN SHE DOES, HER *JUDGEMENT* WILL BE HARSH TOWARDS THOSE WITH POWER WHO STOOD IDLILY BY.
IS THAT A *THREAT?*
IT A STATEMENT OF OBSERVATION.
THEN YOUR MASTER IS *BLIND!*
OH, I DISAGREE. SHE'S BEEN WATCHING QUITE INTENTLY. SHE GROWS IMPATIENT ABOUT THIS WAR AND HOW IT TEARS APART HER PLANET, HER GARDEN. GREED, HUMAN OR OTHERWISE HAS LED TO POISONING YOUR AIR AND LANDS.
UNLIKE SO MANY OF YOU, SPAWN, *SHE'LL NOT* REMAIN IDLE HERSELF!
SHE'S *WIPED IT ALL AWAY* ONCE BEFORE. SHE'LL DO IT AGAIN.
INCLUDING ME? AND MY FRIEND, MR. SPAWN?
AND ALL YOU'VE FOUGHT FOR WILL BE

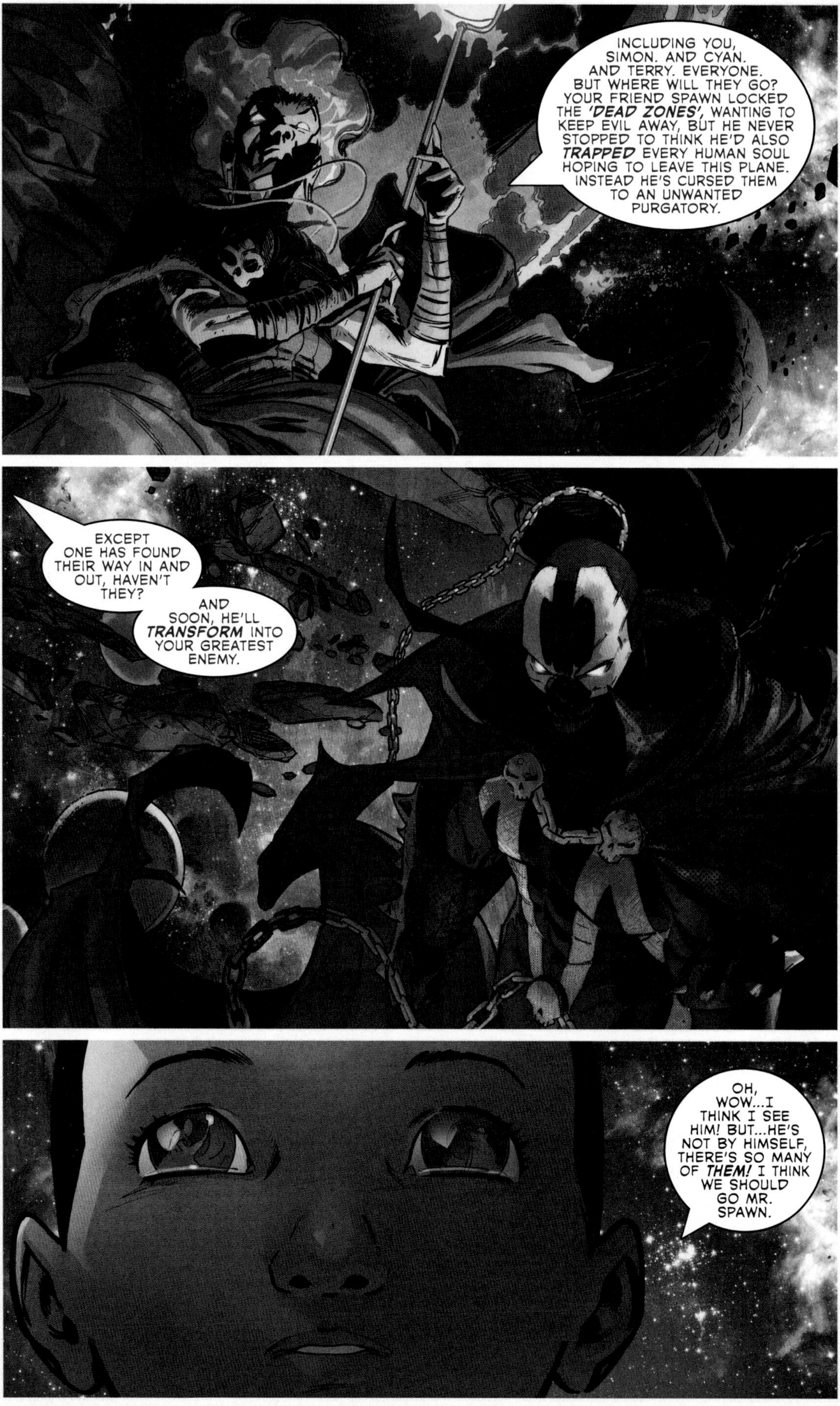
INCLUDING YOU, SIMON. AND CYAN. AND TERRY. EVERYONE. BUT WHERE WILL THEY GO? YOUR FRIEND SPAWN LOCKED THE 'DEAD ZONES', WANTING TO KEEP EVIL AWAY, BUT HE NEVER STOPPED TO THINK HE'D ALSO TRAPPED EVERY HUMAN SOUL HOPING TO LEAVE THIS PLANE. INSTEAD HE'S CURSED THEM TO AN UNWANTED PURGATORY.
EXCEPT ONE HAS FOUND THEIR WAY IN AND OUT, HAVEN'T THEY?
AND SOON, HE'LL TRANSFORM INTO YOUR GREATEST ENEMY.
OH, WOW...I THINK I SEE HIM! BUT...HE'S NOT BY HIMSELF, THERE'S SO MANY OF THEM! I THINK WE SHOULD GO MR. SPAWN.

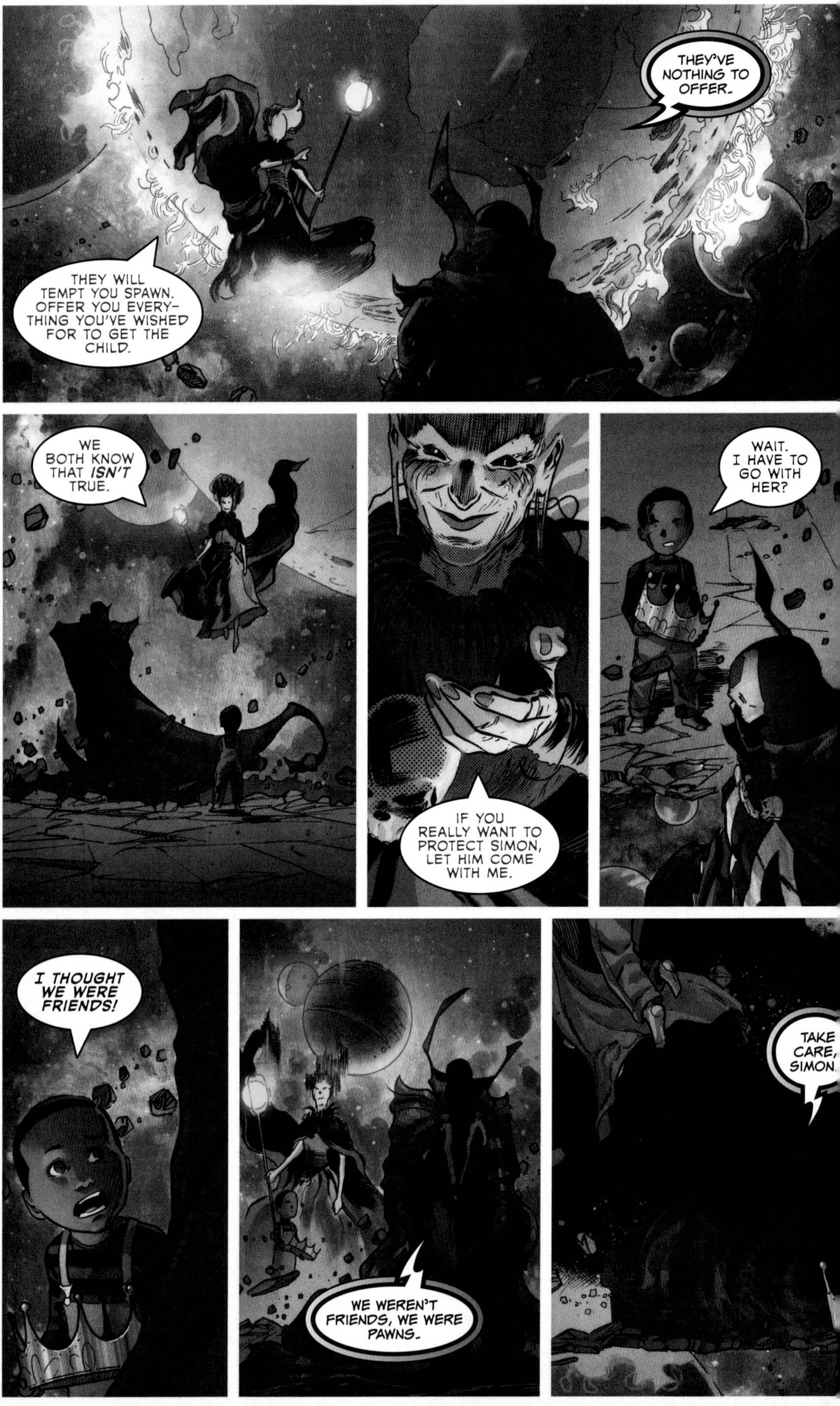

THEY'VE NOTHING TO OFFER.
THEY WILL TEMPT YOU SPAWN. OFFER YOU EVERY-THING YOU'VE WISHED FOR TO GET THE CHILD.
WE BOTH KNOW THAT *ISN'T* TRUE.
IF YOU REALLY WANT TO PROTECT SIMON, LET HIM COME WITH ME.
WAIT. I HAVE TO GO WITH HER?
I THOUGHT WE WERE FRIENDS!
WE WEREN'T FRIENDS, WE WERE PAWNS.
TAKE CARE, SIMON.

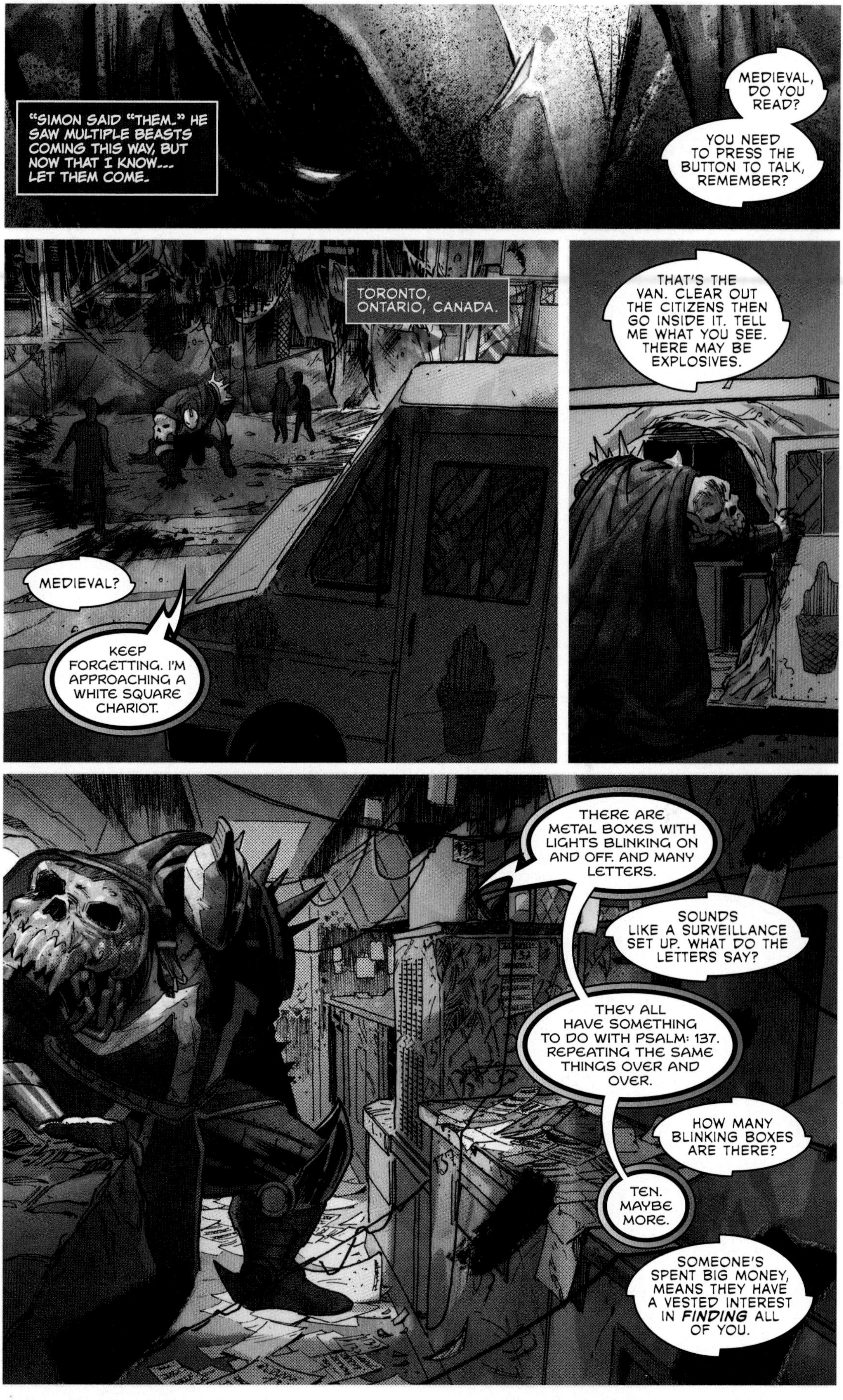
"SIMON SAID "THEM." HE SAW MULTIPLE BEASTS COMING THIS WAY, BUT NOW THAT I KNOW... LET THEM COME.
MEDIEVAL, DO YOU READ?
YOU NEED TO PRESS THE BUTTON TO TALK, REMEMBER?
TORONTO, ONTARIO, CANADA.
MEDIEVAL?
KEEP FORGETTING. I'M APPROACHING A WHITE SQUARE CHARIOT.
THAT'S THE VAN. CLEAR OUT THE CITIZENS THEN GO INSIDE IT. TELL ME WHAT YOU SEE. THERE MAY BE EXPLOSIVES.
THERE ARE METAL BOXES WITH LIGHTS BLINKING ON AND OFF. AND MANY LETTERS.
SOUNDS LIKE A SURVEILLANCE SET UP. WHAT DO THE LETTERS SAY?
THEY ALL HAVE SOMETHING TO DO WITH PSALM: 137. REPEATING THE SAME THINGS OVER AND OVER.
HOW MANY BLINKING BOXES ARE THERE?
TEN. MAYBE MORE.
SOMEONE'S SPENT BIG MONEY, MEANS THEY HAVE A VESTED INTEREST IN *FINDING* ALL OF YOU.

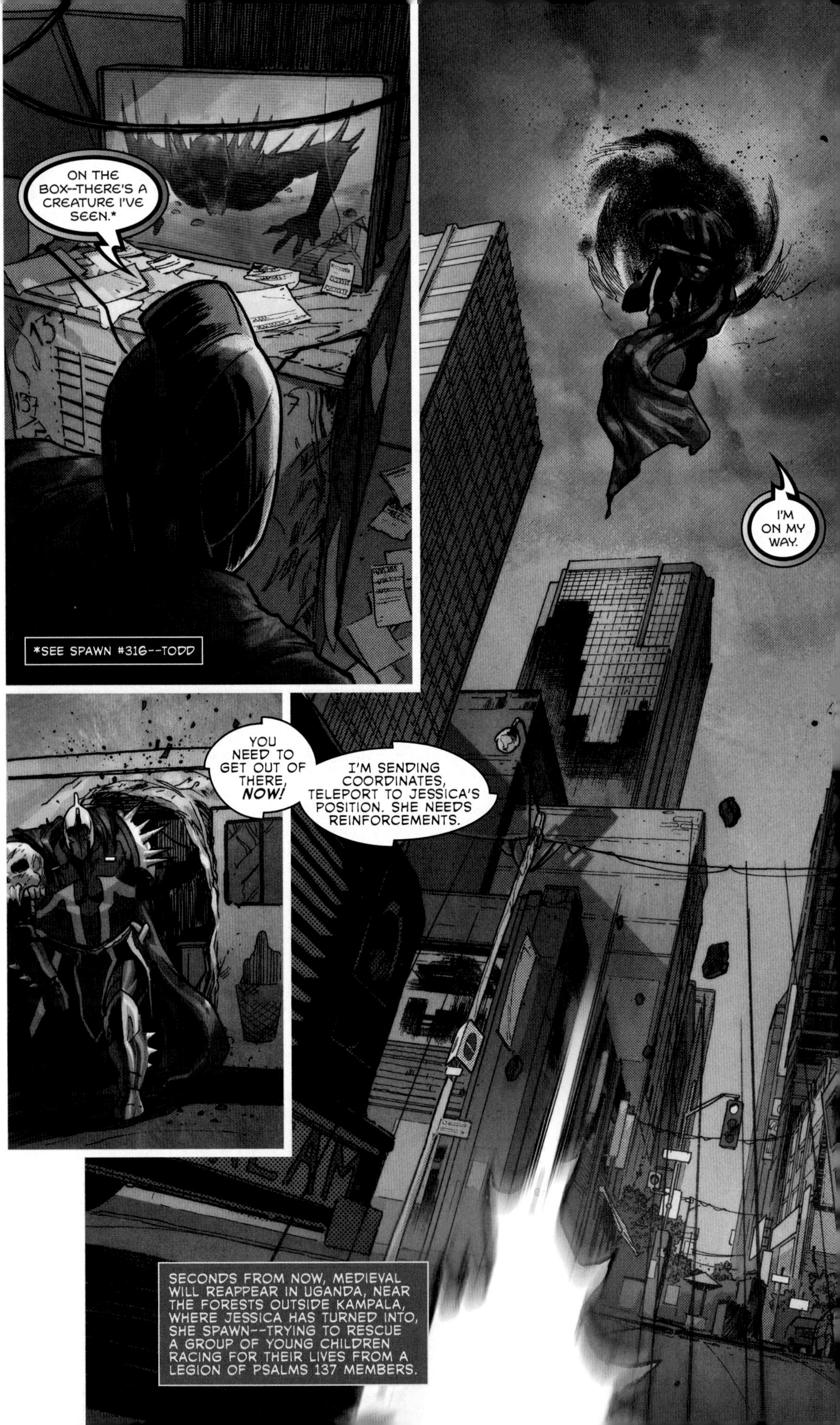
ON THE BOX--THERE'S A CREATURE I'VE SEEN.*
*SEE SPAWN #316--TODD
I'M ON MY WAY.
YOU NEED TO GET OUT OF THERE, *NOW!*
I'M SENDING COORDINATES, TELEPORT TO JESSICA'S POSITION. SHE NEEDS REINFORCEMENTS.
SECONDS FROM NOW, MEDIEVAL WILL REAPPEAR IN UGANDA, NEAR THE FORESTS OUTSIDE KAMPALA, WHERE JESSICA HAS TURNED INTO, SHE SPAWN--TRYING TO RESCUE A GROUP OF YOUNG CHILDREN RACING FOR THEIR LIVES FROM A LEGION OF PSALMS 137 MEMBERS.

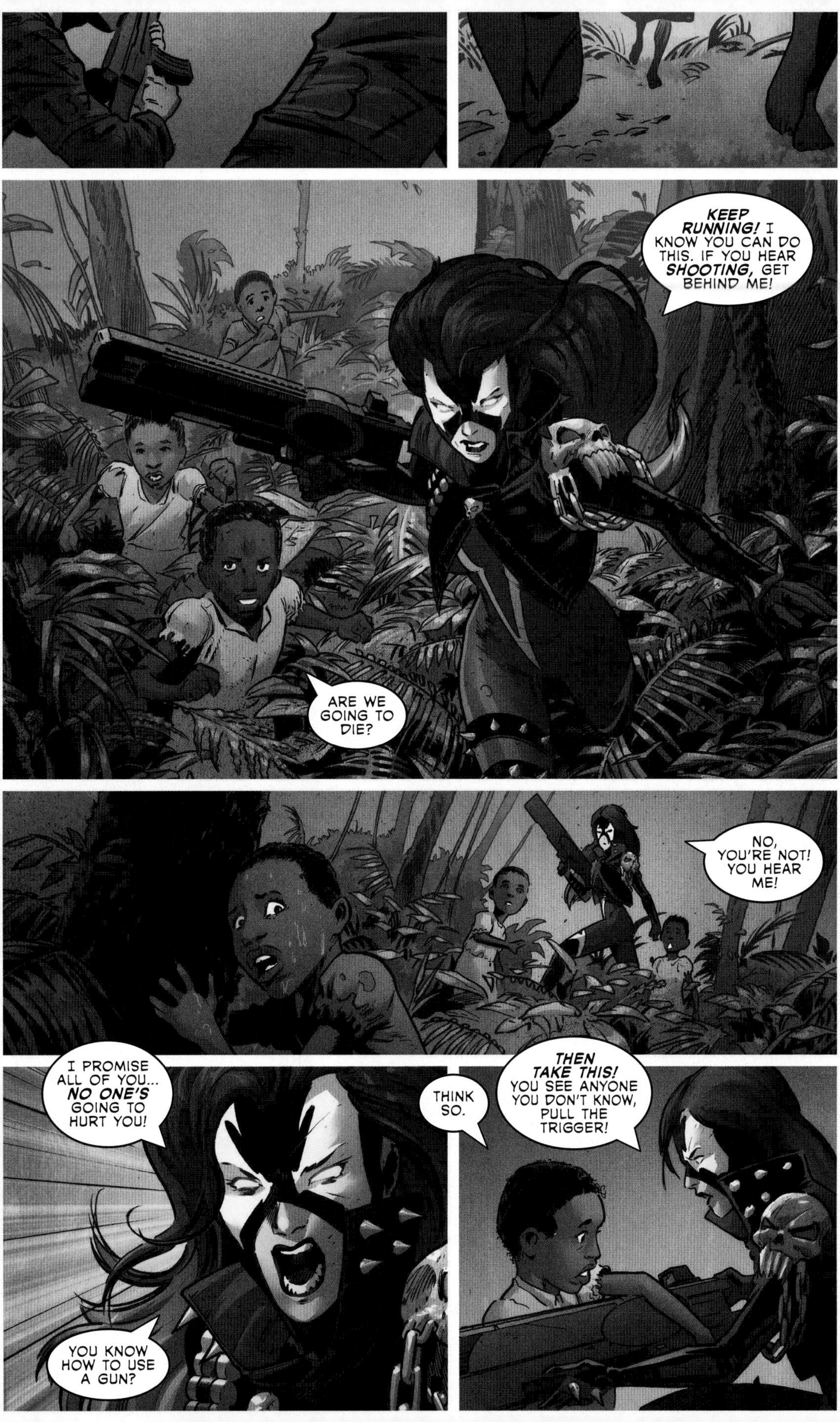
KEEP RUNNING! I KNOW YOU CAN DO THIS. IF YOU HEAR SHOOTING, GET BEHIND ME!
ARE WE GOING TO DIE?
NO, YOU'RE NOT! YOU HEAR ME!
I PROMISE ALL OF YOU... NO ONE'S GOING TO HURT YOU!
YOU KNOW HOW TO USE A GUN?
THINK SO.
THEN TAKE THIS! YOU SEE ANYONE YOU DON'T KNOW, PULL THE TRIGGER!

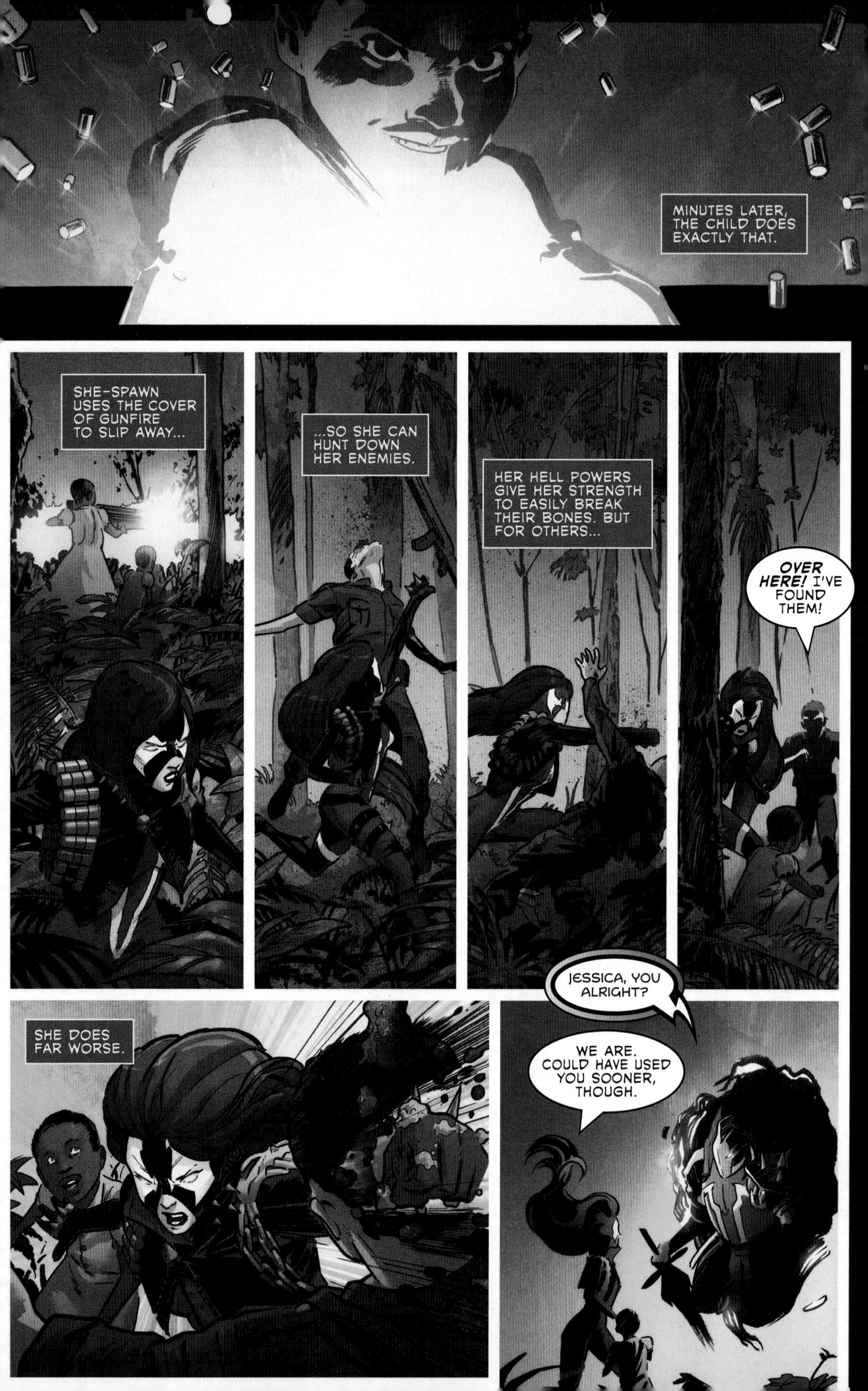
MINUTES LATER, THE CHILD DOES EXACTLY THAT.
SHE-SPAWN USES THE COVER OF GUNFIRE TO SLIP AWAY...
...SO SHE CAN HUNT DOWN HER ENEMIES.
HER HELL POWERS GIVE HER STRENGTH TO EASILY BREAK THEIR BONES. BUT FOR OTHERS...
OVER HERE! I'VE FOUND THEM!
SHE DOES FAR WORSE.
JESSICA, YOU ALRIGHT?
WE ARE. COULD HAVE USED YOU SOONER, THOUGH.

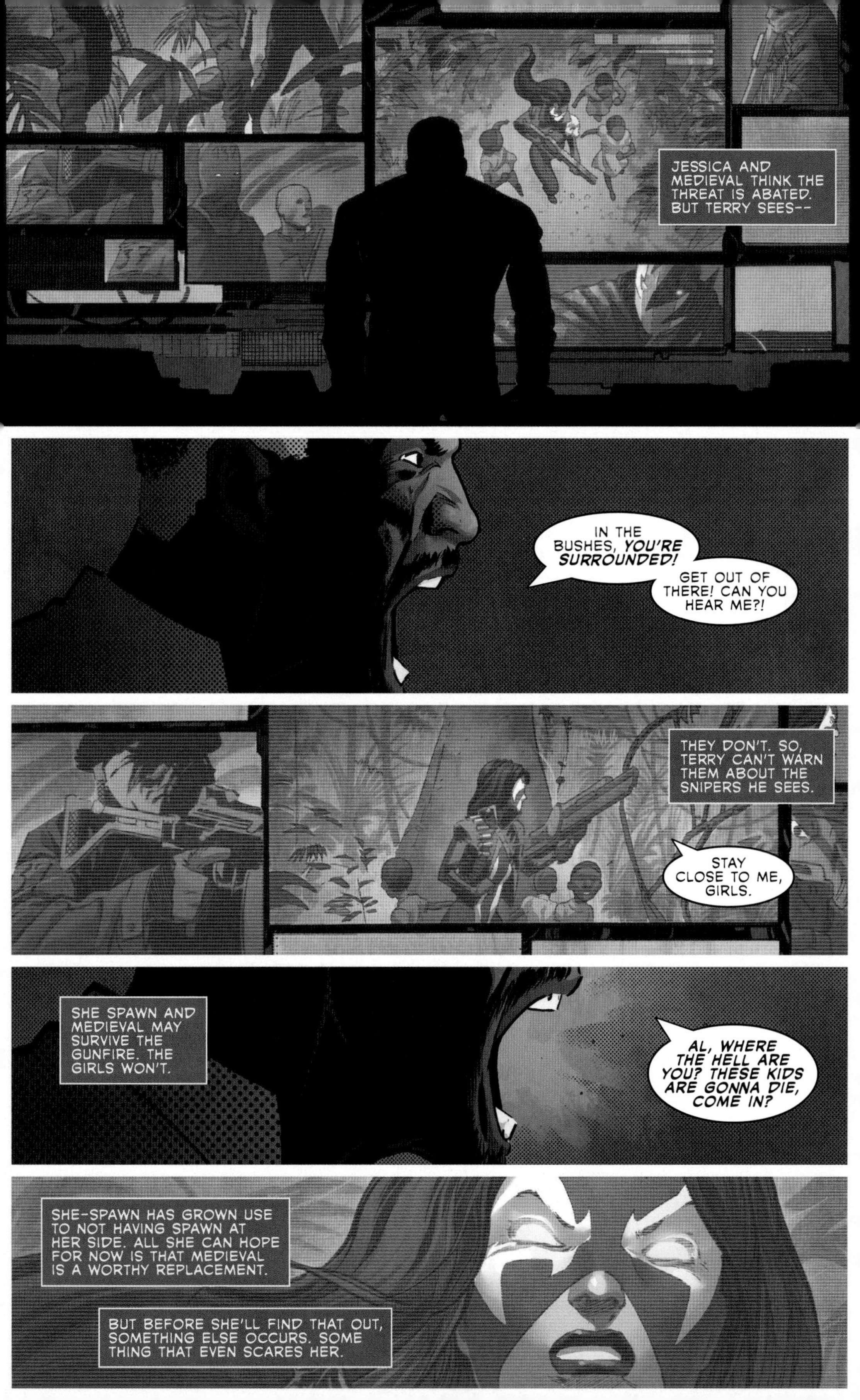
JESSICA AND MEDIEVAL THINK THE THREAT IS ABATED. BUT TERRY SEES--
IN THE BUSHES, *YOU'RE SURROUNDED!*
GET OUT OF THERE! CAN YOU HEAR ME?!
THEY DON'T. SO, TERRY CAN'T WARN THEM ABOUT THE SNIPERS HE SEES.
STAY CLOSE TO ME, GIRLS.
SHE SPAWN AND MEDIEVAL MAY SURVIVE THE GUNFIRE. THE GIRLS WON'T.
AL, WHERE THE HELL ARE YOU? THESE KIDS ARE GONNA DIE, COME IN?
SHE-SPAWN HAS GROWN USE TO NOT HAVING SPAWN AT HER SIDE. ALL SHE CAN HOPE FOR NOW IS THAT MEDIEVAL IS A WORTHY REPLACEMENT.
BUT BEFORE SHE'LL FIND THAT OUT, SOMETHING ELSE OCCURS. SOME THING THAT EVEN SCARES HER.

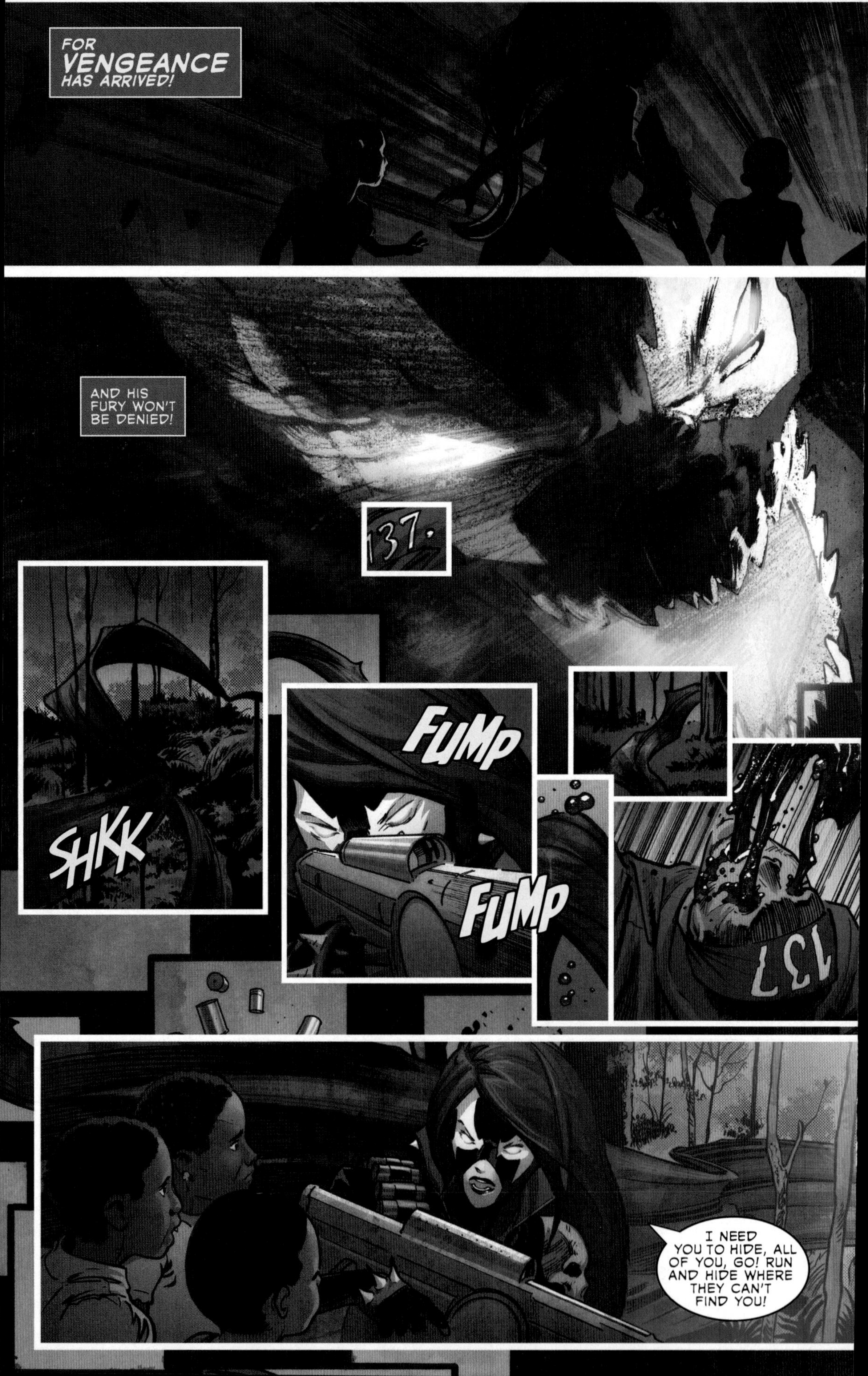
FOR VENGEANCE HAS ARRIVED!
AND HIS FURY WON'T BE DENIED!
137.
SHKK
FUMP
FUMP
I NEED YOU TO HIDE, ALL OF YOU, GO! RUN AND HIDE WHERE THEY CAN'T FIND YOU!

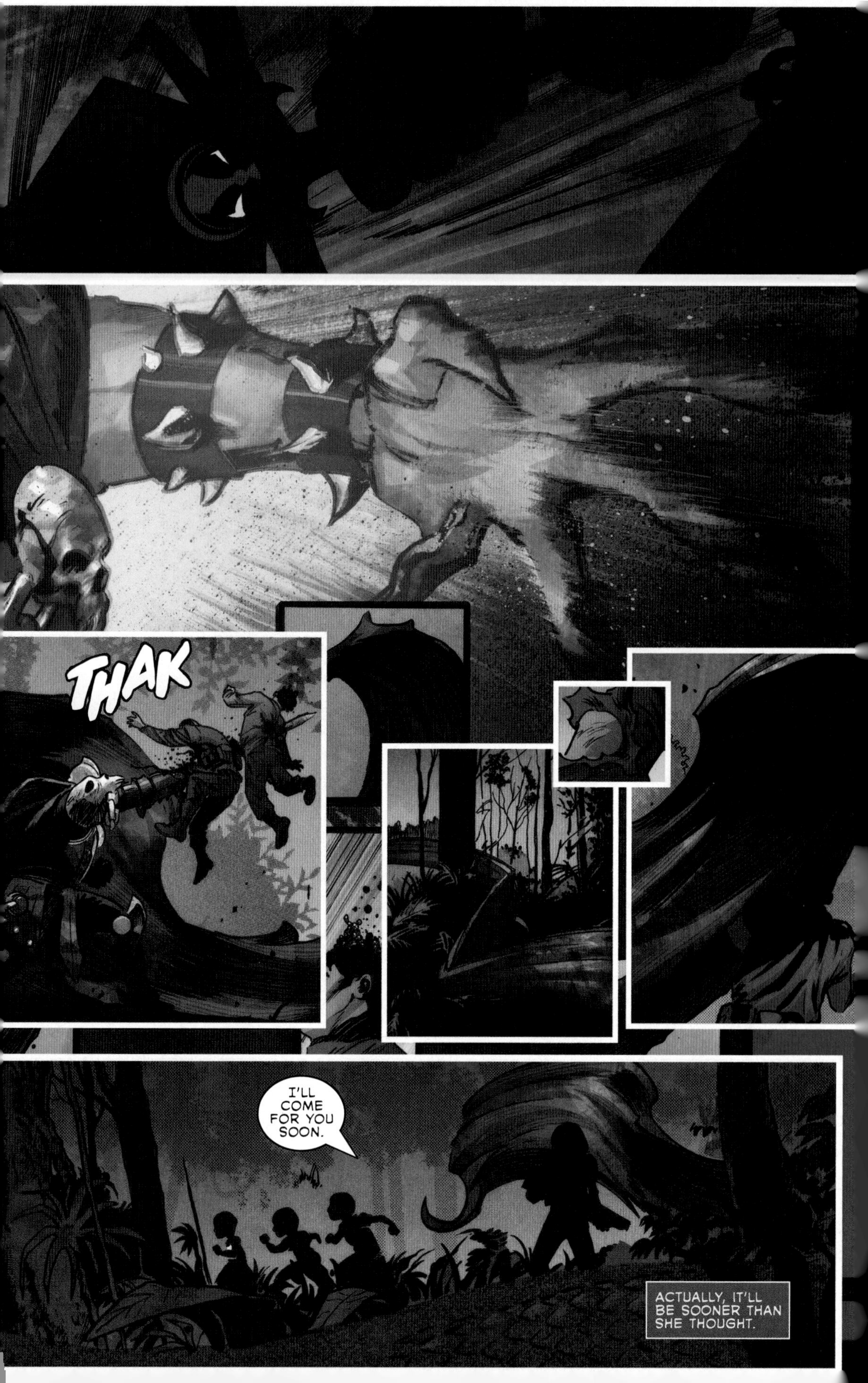
THAK
I'LL COME FOR YOU SOON.
ACTUALLY, IT'LL BE SOONER THAN SHE THOUGHT.

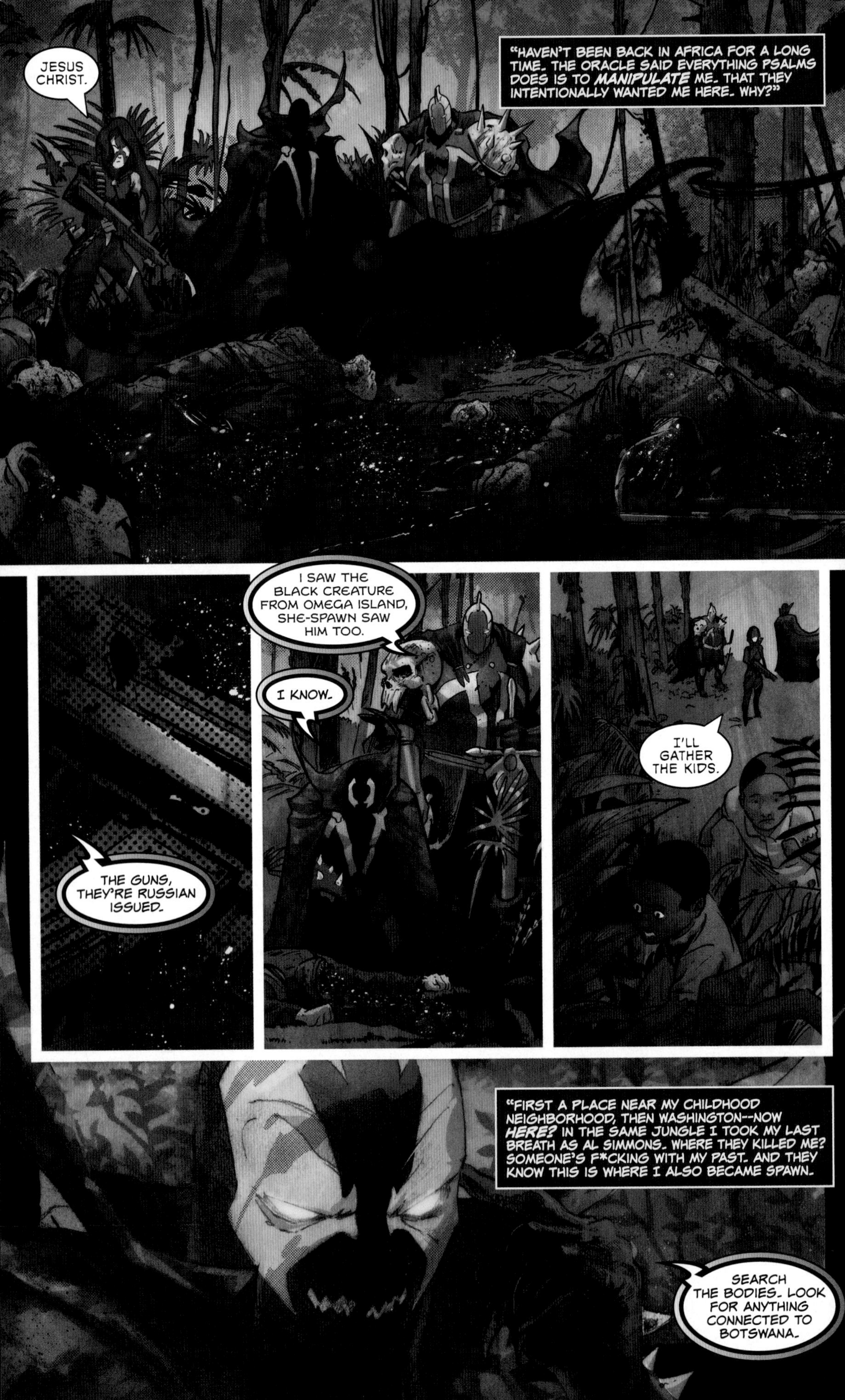

JESUS CHRIST.
"HAVEN'T BEEN BACK IN AFRICA FOR A LONG TIME. THE ORACLE SAID EVERYTHING PSALMS DOES IS TO MANIPULATE ME. THAT THEY INTENTIONALLY WANTED ME HERE. WHY?"
THE GUNS, THEY'RE RUSSIAN ISSUED.
I SAW THE BLACK CREATURE FROM OMEGA ISLAND, SHE-SPAWN SAW HIM TOO.
I KNOW.
I'LL GATHER THE KIDS.
"FIRST A PLACE NEAR MY CHILDHOOD NEIGHBORHOOD, THEN WASHINGTON--NOW HERE? IN THE SAME JUNGLE I TOOK MY LAST BREATH AS AL SIMMONS. WHERE THEY KILLED ME? SOMEONE'S F*CKING WITH MY PAST. AND THEY KNOW THIS IS WHERE I ALSO BECAME SPAWN.
SEARCH THE BODIES. LOOK FOR ANYTHING CONNECTED TO BOTSWANA.

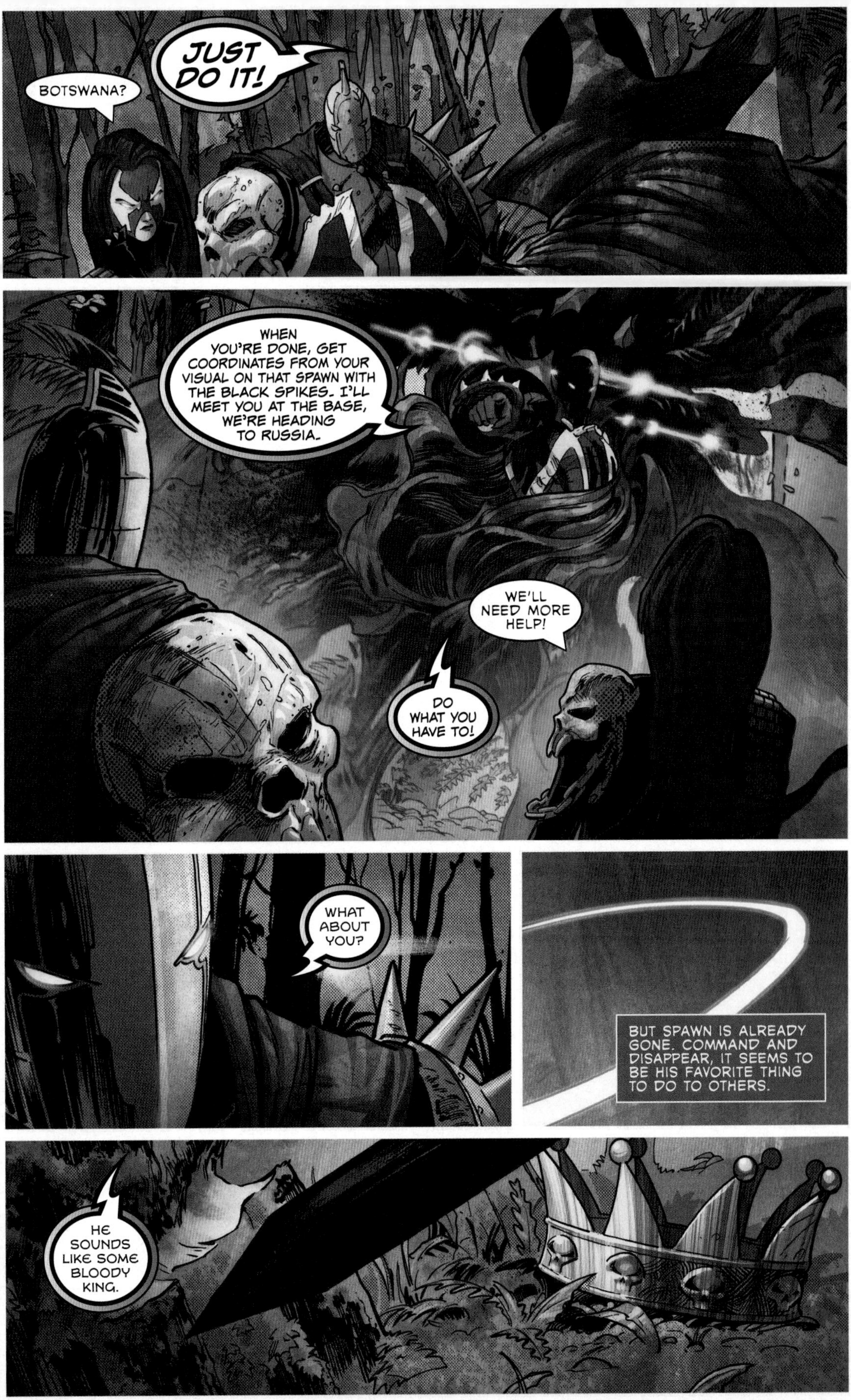
BOTSWANA?
JUST DO IT!
WHEN YOU'RE DONE, GET COORDINATES FROM YOUR VISUAL ON THAT SPAWN WITH THE BLACK SPIKES. I'LL MEET YOU AT THE BASE, WE'RE HEADING TO RUSSIA.
WE'LL NEED MORE HELP!
DO WHAT YOU HAVE TO!
WHAT ABOUT YOU?
BUT SPAWN IS ALREADY GONE. COMMAND AND DISAPPEAR, IT SEEMS TO BE HIS FAVORITE THING TO DO TO OTHERS.
HE SOUNDS LIKE SOME BLOODY KING.

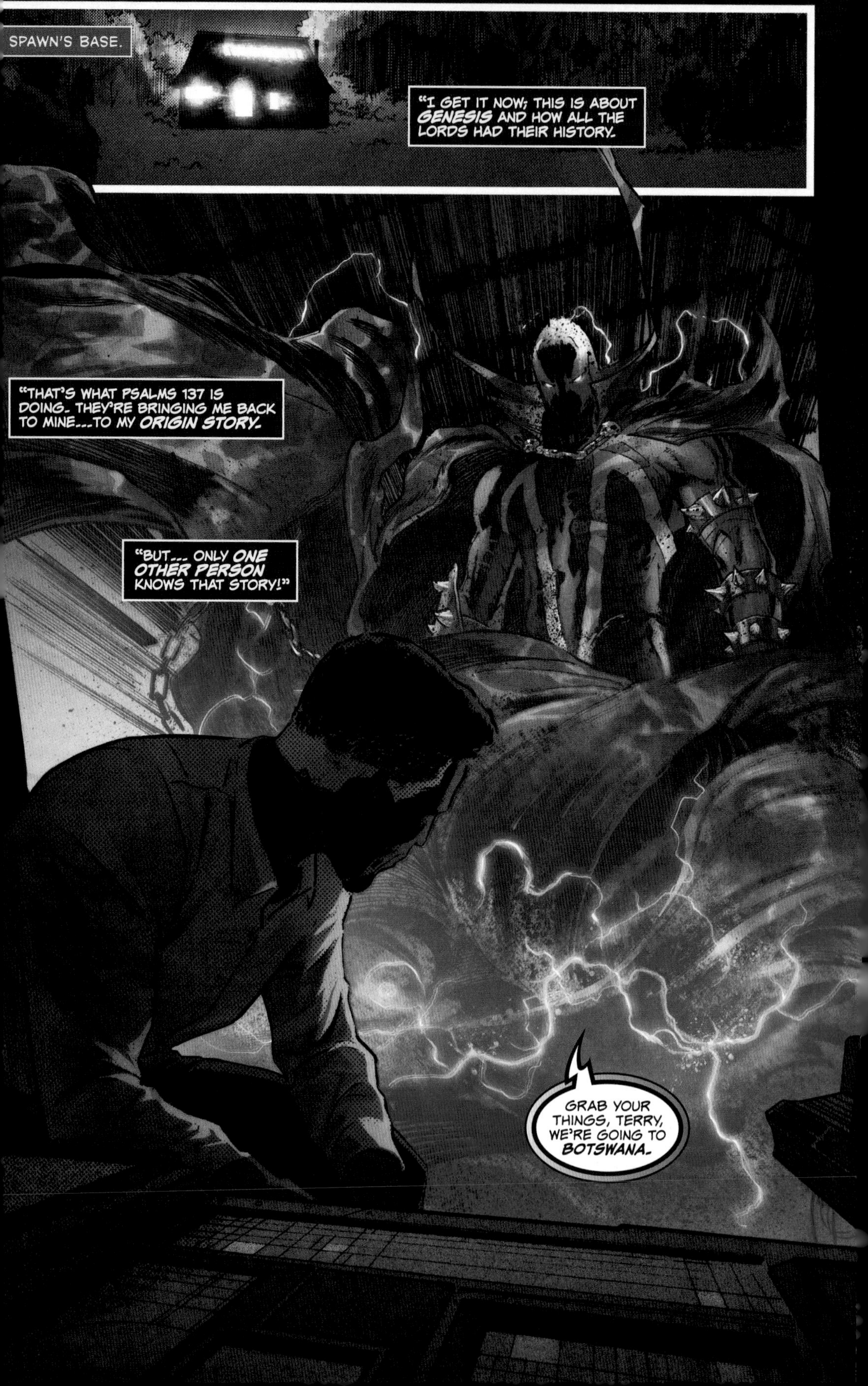
SPAWN'S BASE.
"I GET IT NOW; THIS IS ABOUT GENESIS AND HOW ALL THE LORDS HAD THEIR HISTORY.
"THAT'S WHAT PSALMS 137 IS DOING. THEY'RE BRINGING ME BACK TO MINE...TO MY ORIGIN STORY.
"BUT... ONLY ONE OTHER PERSON KNOWS THAT STORY!"
GRAB YOUR THINGS, TERRY, WE'RE GOING TO BOTSWANA.

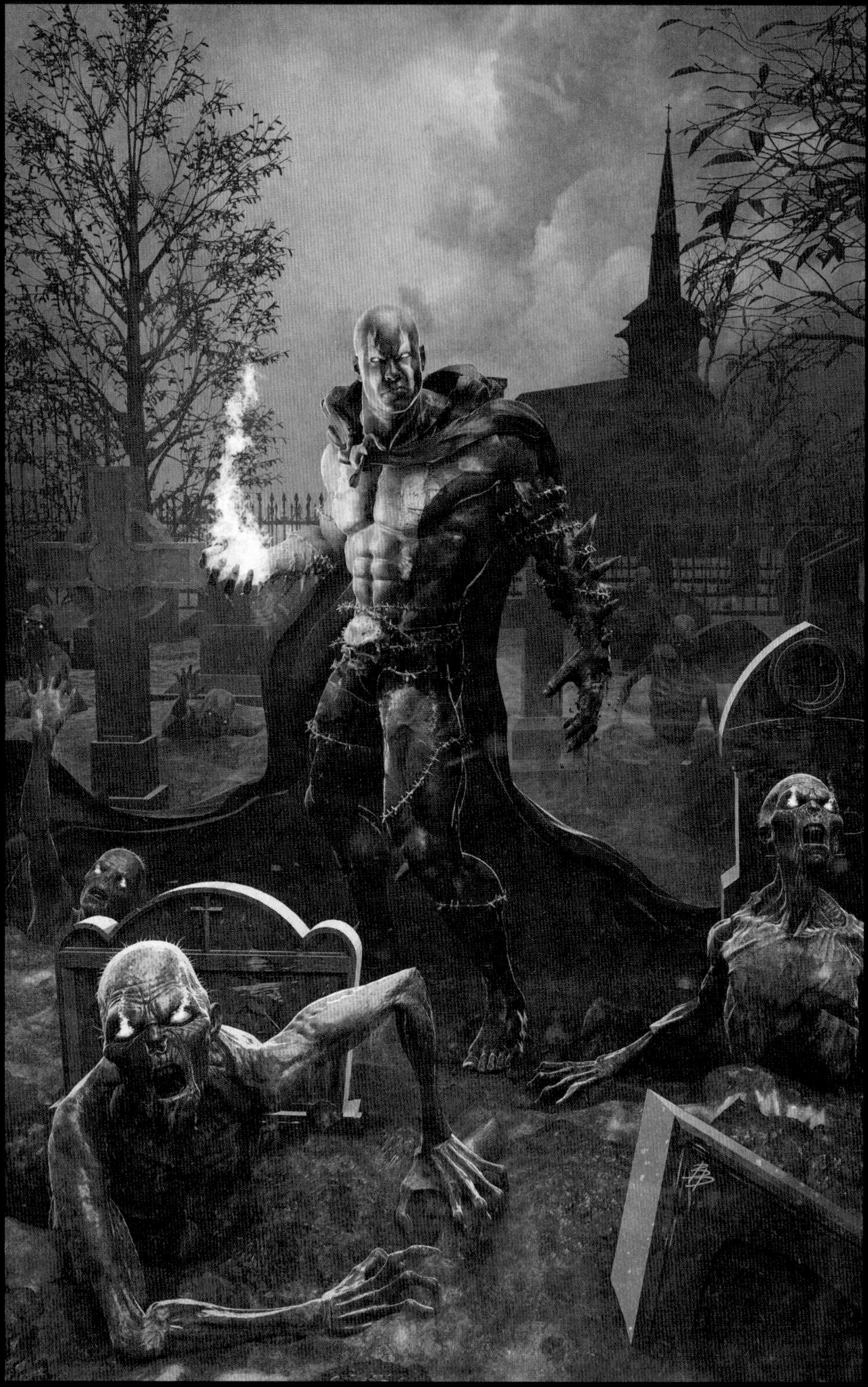

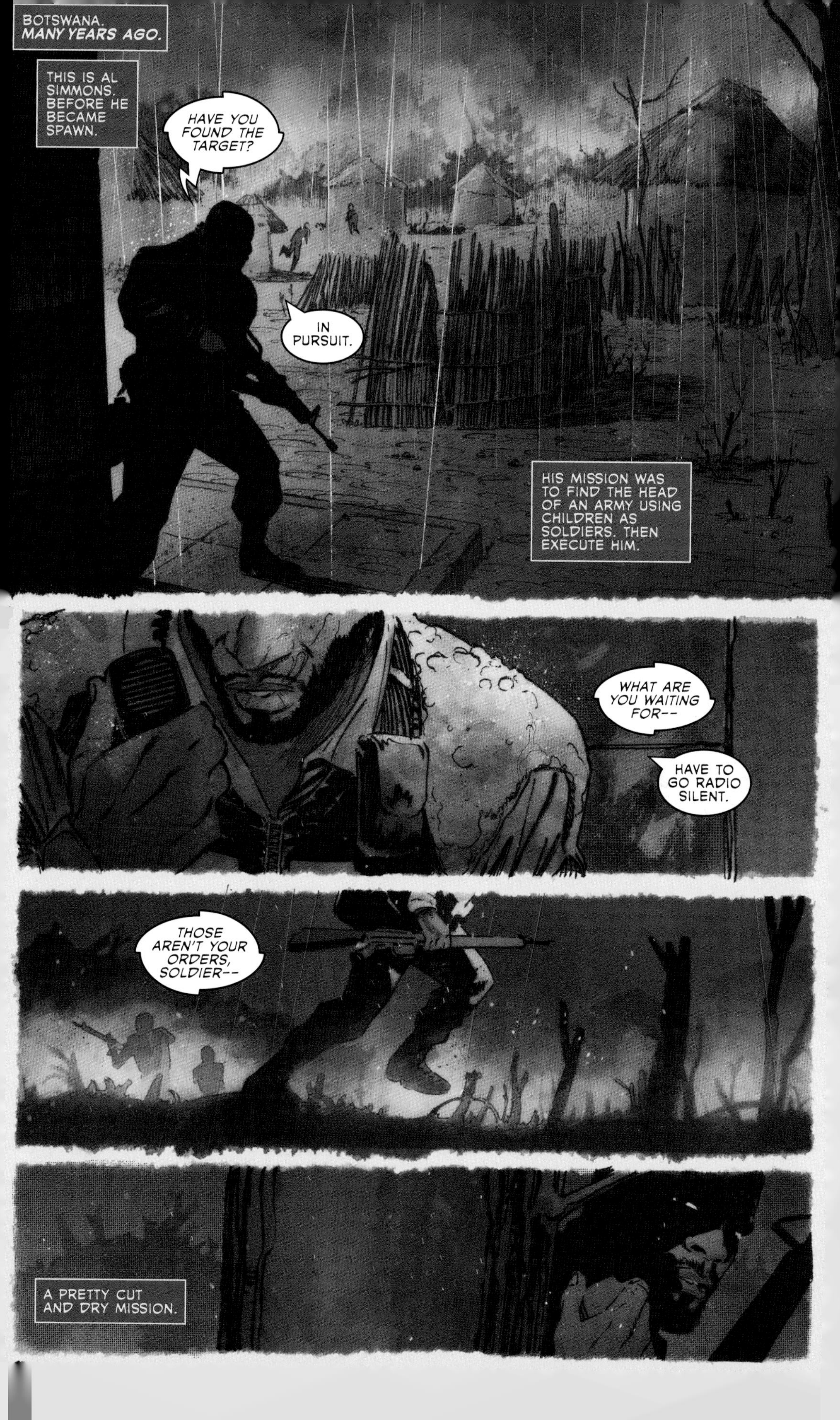
BOTSWANA. MANY YEARS AGO.
THIS IS AL SIMMONS. BEFORE HE BECAME SPAWN.
HAVE YOU FOUND THE TARGET?
IN PURSUIT.
HIS MISSION WAS TO FIND THE HEAD OF AN ARMY USING CHILDREN AS SOLDIERS. THEN EXECUTE HIM.
WHAT ARE YOU WAITING FOR--
HAVE TO GO RADIO SILENT.
THOSE AREN'T YOUR ORDERS, SOLDIER--
A PRETTY CUT AND DRY MISSION.

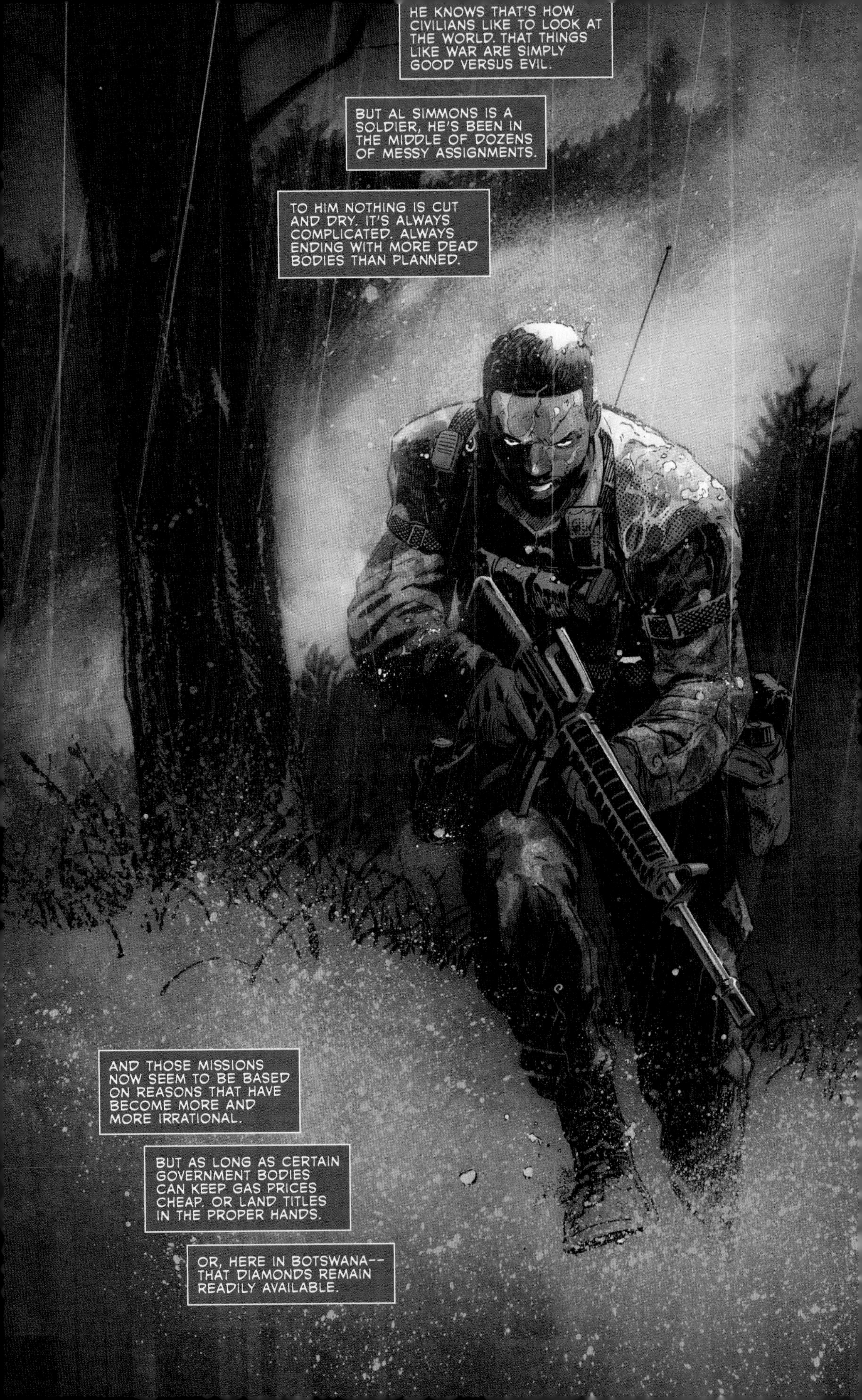

HE KNOWS THAT'S HOW CIVILIANS LIKE TO LOOK AT THE WORLD. THAT THINGS LIKE WAR ARE SIMPLY GOOD VERSUS EVIL.
BUT AL SIMMONS IS A SOLDIER, HE'S BEEN IN THE MIDDLE OF DOZENS OF MESSY ASSIGNMENTS.
TO HIM NOTHING IS CUT AND DRY. IT'S ALWAYS COMPLICATED. ALWAYS ENDING WITH MORE DEAD BODIES THAN PLANNED.
AND THOSE MISSIONS NOW SEEM TO BE BASED ON REASONS THAT HAVE BECOME MORE AND MORE IRRATIONAL.
BUT AS LONG AS CERTAIN GOVERNMENT BODIES CAN KEEP GAS PRICES CHEAP, OR LAND TITLES IN THE PROPER HANDS.
OR, HERE IN BOTSWANA-- THAT DIAMONDS REMAIN READILY AVAILABLE.

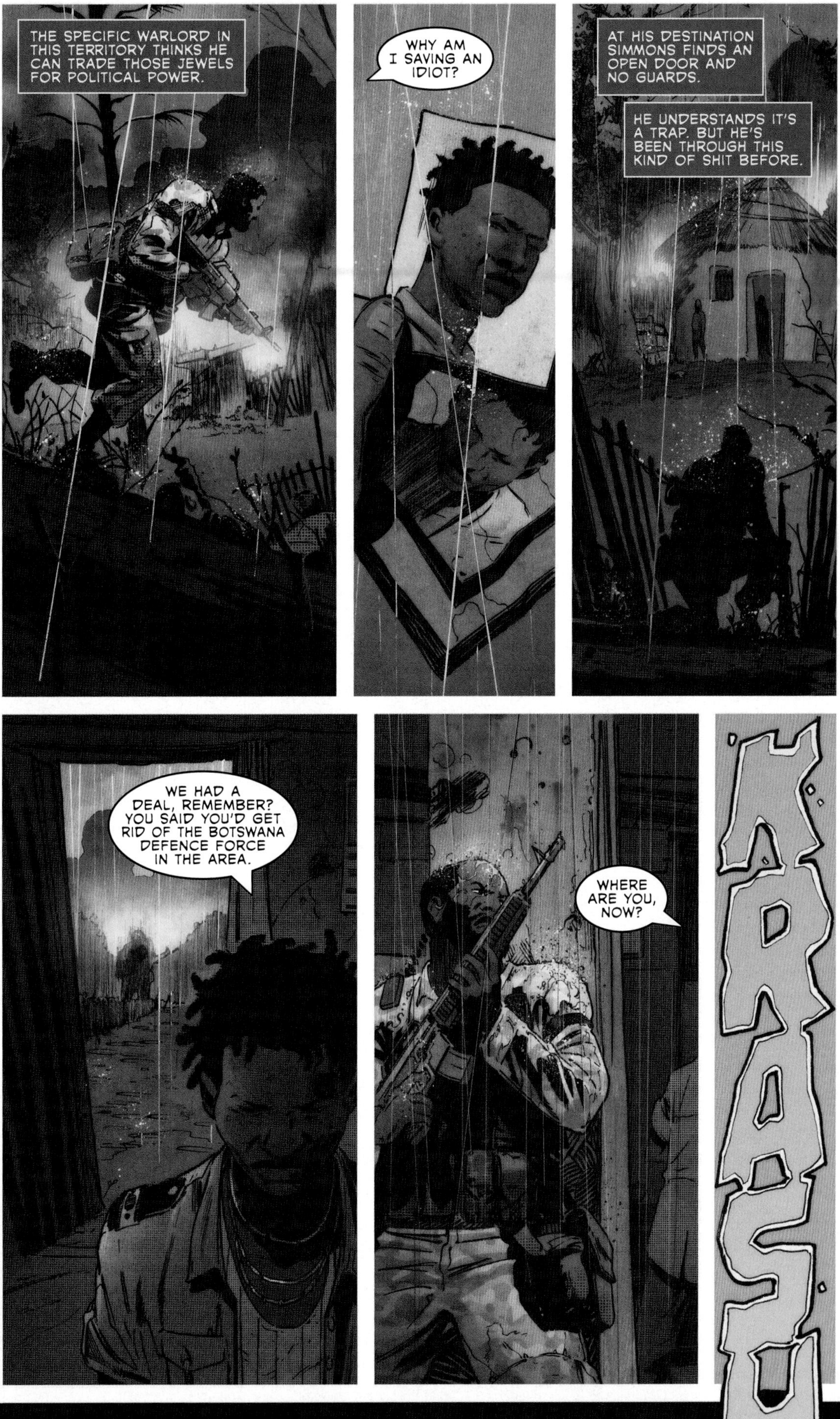

THE SPECIFIC WARLORD IN THIS TERRITORY THINKS HE CAN TRADE THOSE JEWELS FOR POLITICAL POWER.
WHY AM I SAVING AN IDIOT?
AT HIS DESTINATION SIMMONS FINDS AN OPEN DOOR AND NO GUARDS.
HE UNDERSTANDS IT'S A TRAP. BUT HE'S BEEN THROUGH THIS KIND OF SHIT BEFORE.
WE HAD A DEAL, REMEMBER? YOU SAID YOU'D GET RID OF THE BOTSWANA DEFENCE FORCE IN THE AREA.
WHERE ARE YOU, NOW?

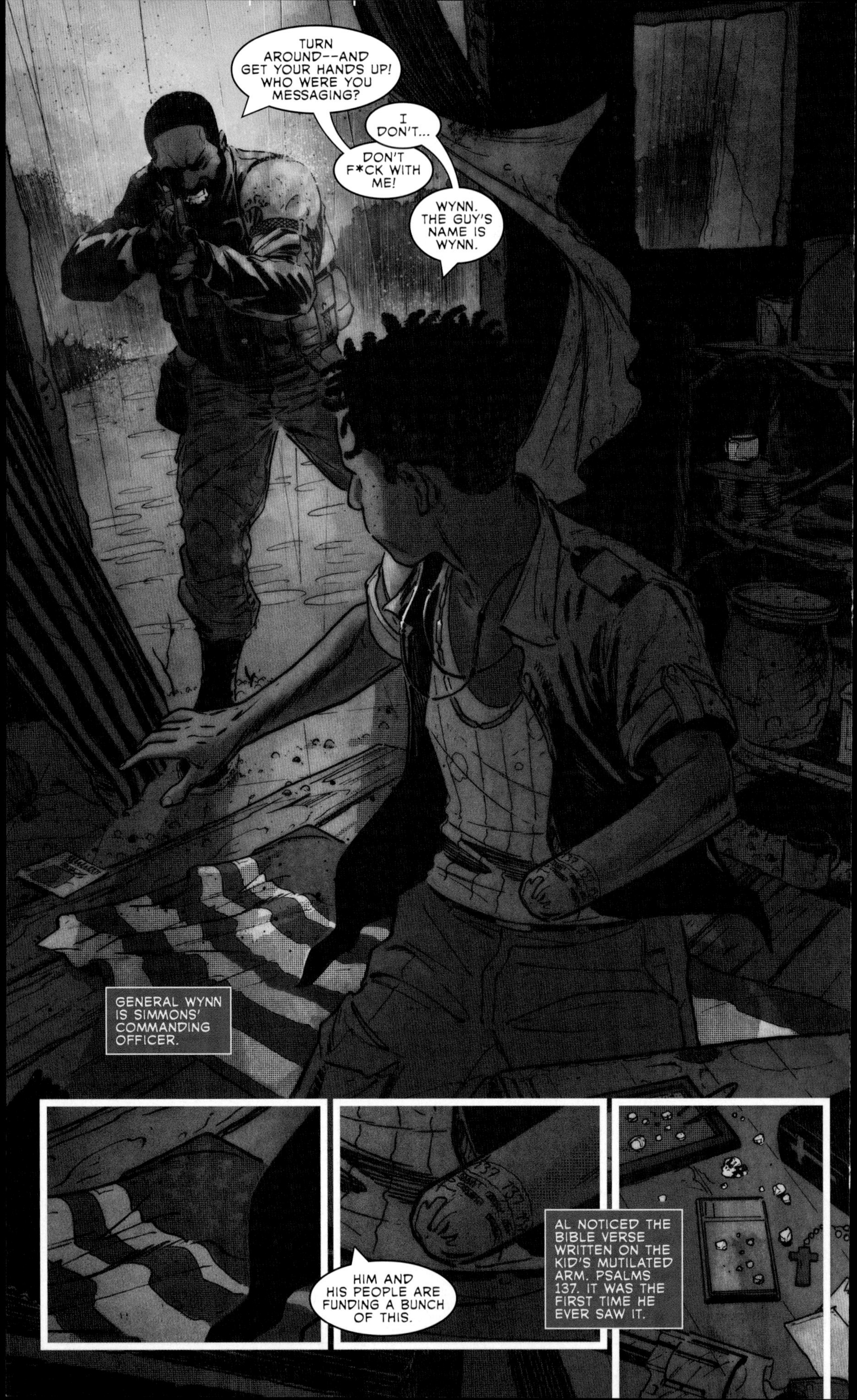

TURN AROUND--AND GET YOUR HANDS UP! WHO WERE YOU MESSAGING?
I DON'T...
DON'T F*CK WITH ME!
WYNN. THE GUY'S NAME IS WYNN.
GENERAL WYNN IS SIMMONS' COMMANDING OFFICER.
HIM AND HIS PEOPLE ARE FUNDING A BUNCH OF THIS.
AL NOTICED THE BIBLE VERSE WRITTEN ON THE KID'S MUTILATED ARM. PSALMS 137. IT WAS THE FIRST TIME HE EVER SAW IT.

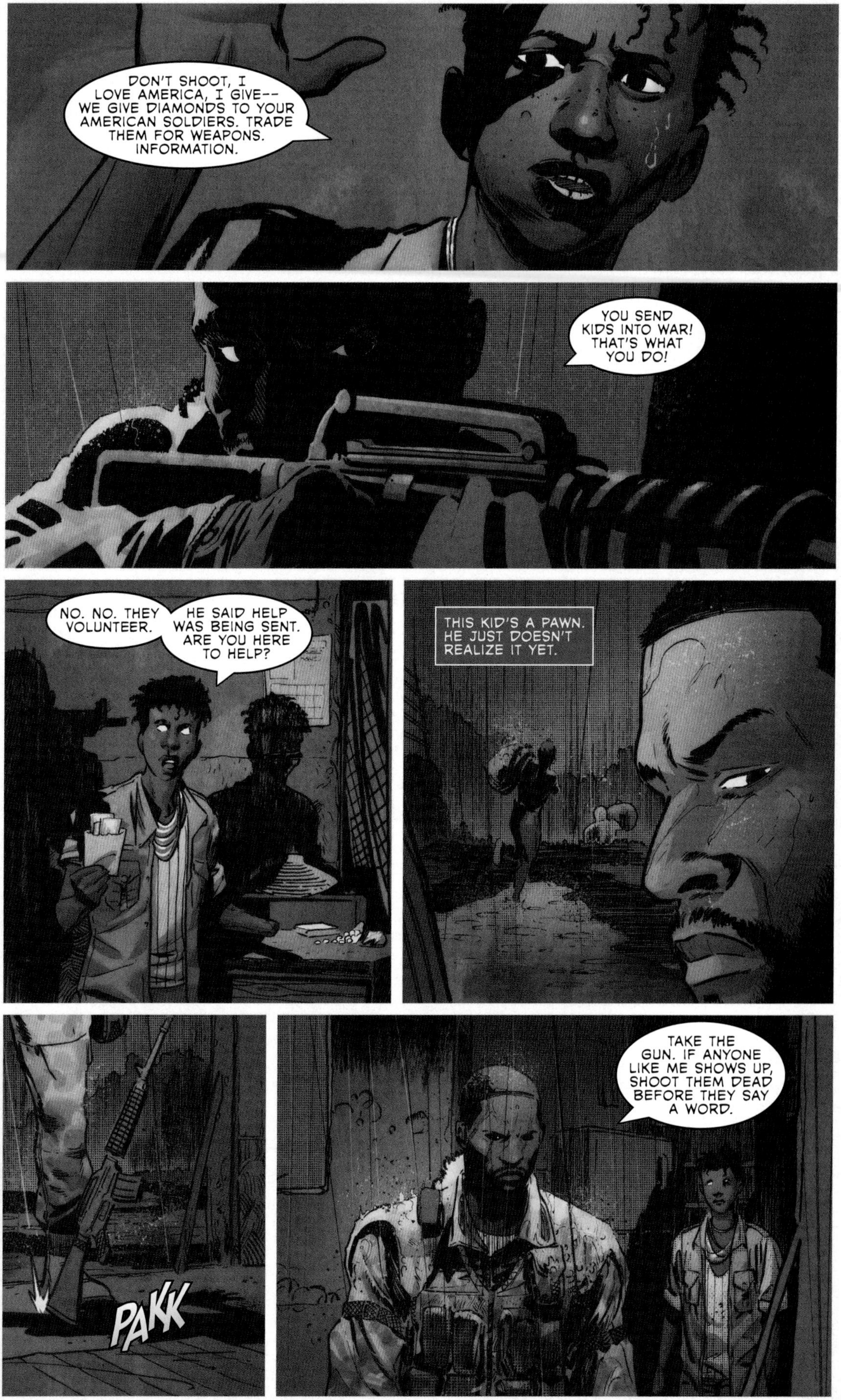
DON'T SHOOT, I LOVE AMERICA, I GIVE-- WE GIVE DIAMONDS TO YOUR AMERICAN SOLDIERS. TRADE THEM FOR WEAPONS. INFORMATION.
YOU SEND KIDS INTO WAR! THAT'S WHAT YOU DO!
NO. NO. THEY VOLUNTEER.
HE SAID HELP WAS BEING SENT. ARE YOU HERE TO HELP?
THIS KID'S A PAWN. HE JUST DOESN'T REALIZE IT YET.
PAKK
TAKE THE GUN. IF ANYONE LIKE ME SHOWS UP, SHOOT THEM DEAD BEFORE THEY SAY A WORD.

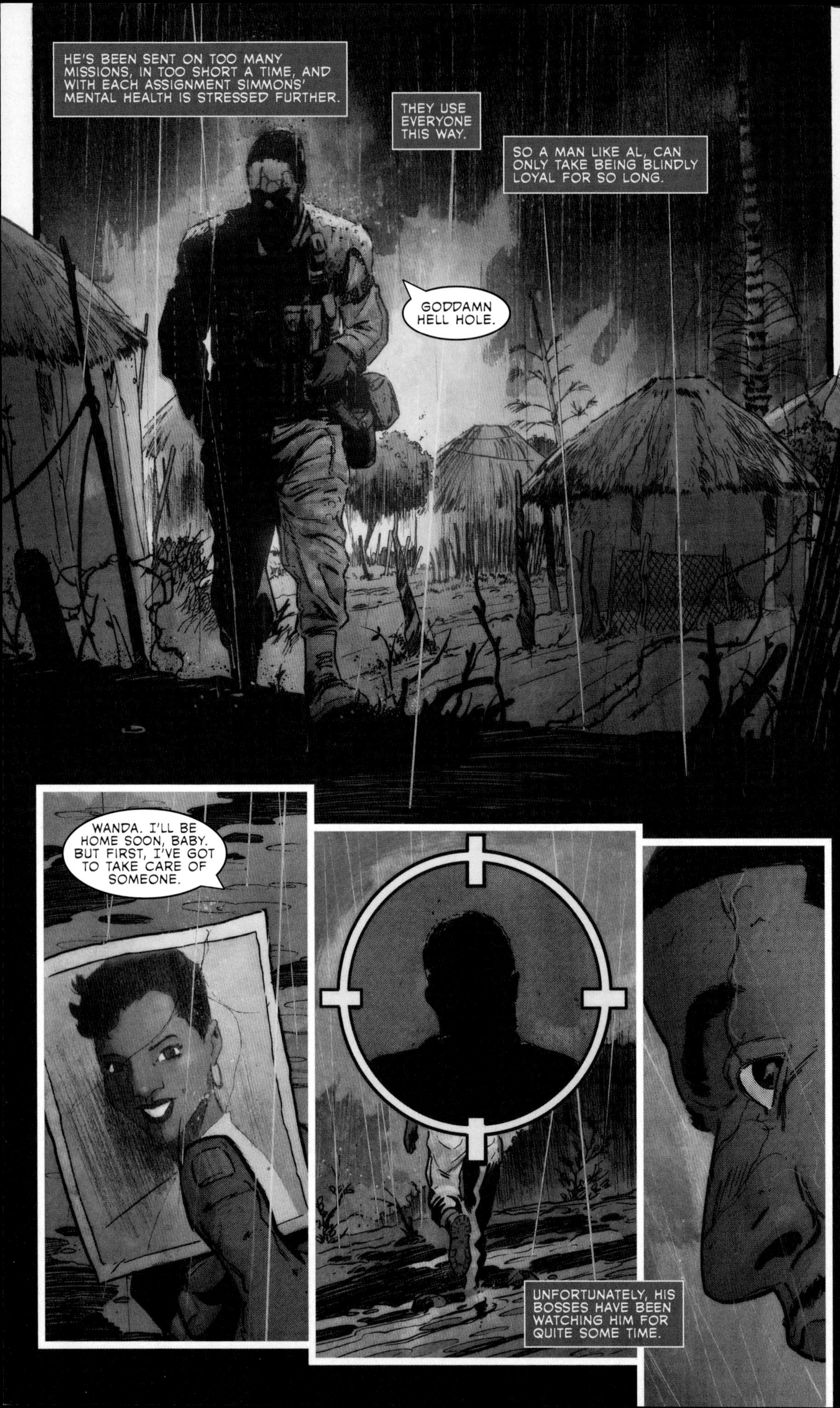
HE'S BEEN SENT ON TOO MANY MISSIONS, IN TOO SHORT A TIME, AND WITH EACH ASSIGNMENT SIMMONS' MENTAL HEALTH IS STRESSED FURTHER.
THEY USE EVERYONE THIS WAY.
SO A MAN LIKE AL, CAN ONLY TAKE BEING BLINDLY LOYAL FOR SO LONG.
GODDAMN HELL HOLE.
WANDA. I'LL BE HOME SOON, BABY. BUT FIRST, I'VE GOT TO TAKE CARE OF SOMEONE.
UNFORTUNATELY, HIS BOSSES HAVE BEEN WATCHING HIM FOR QUITE SOME TIME.

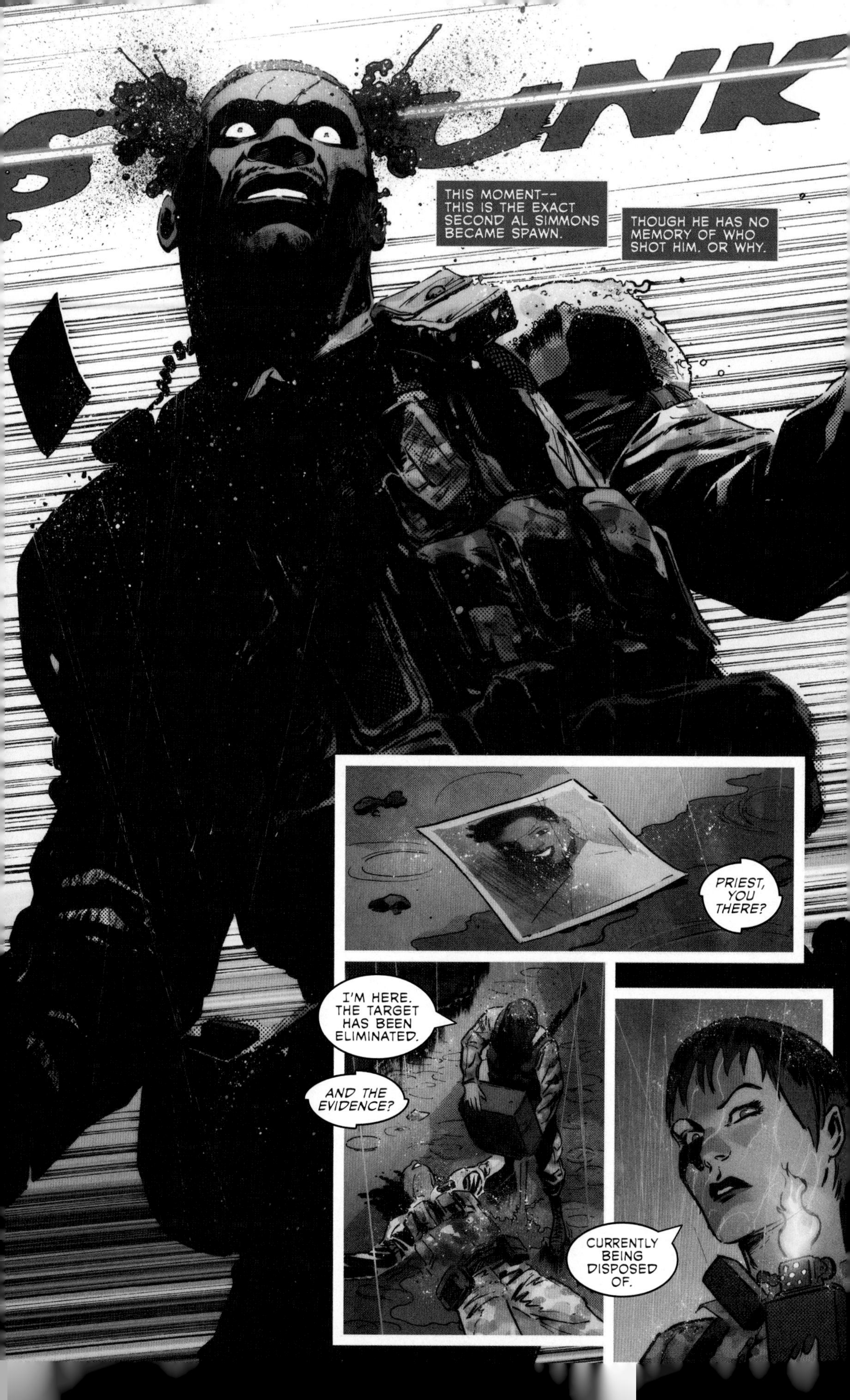

THIS MOMENT-- THIS IS THE EXACT SECOND AL SIMMONS BECAME SPAWN.
THOUGH HE HAS NO MEMORY OF WHO SHOT HIM. OR WHY.
PRIEST, YOU THERE?
I'M HERE. THE TARGET HAS BEEN ELIMINATED.
AND THE EVIDENCE?
CURRENTLY BEING DISPOSED OF.

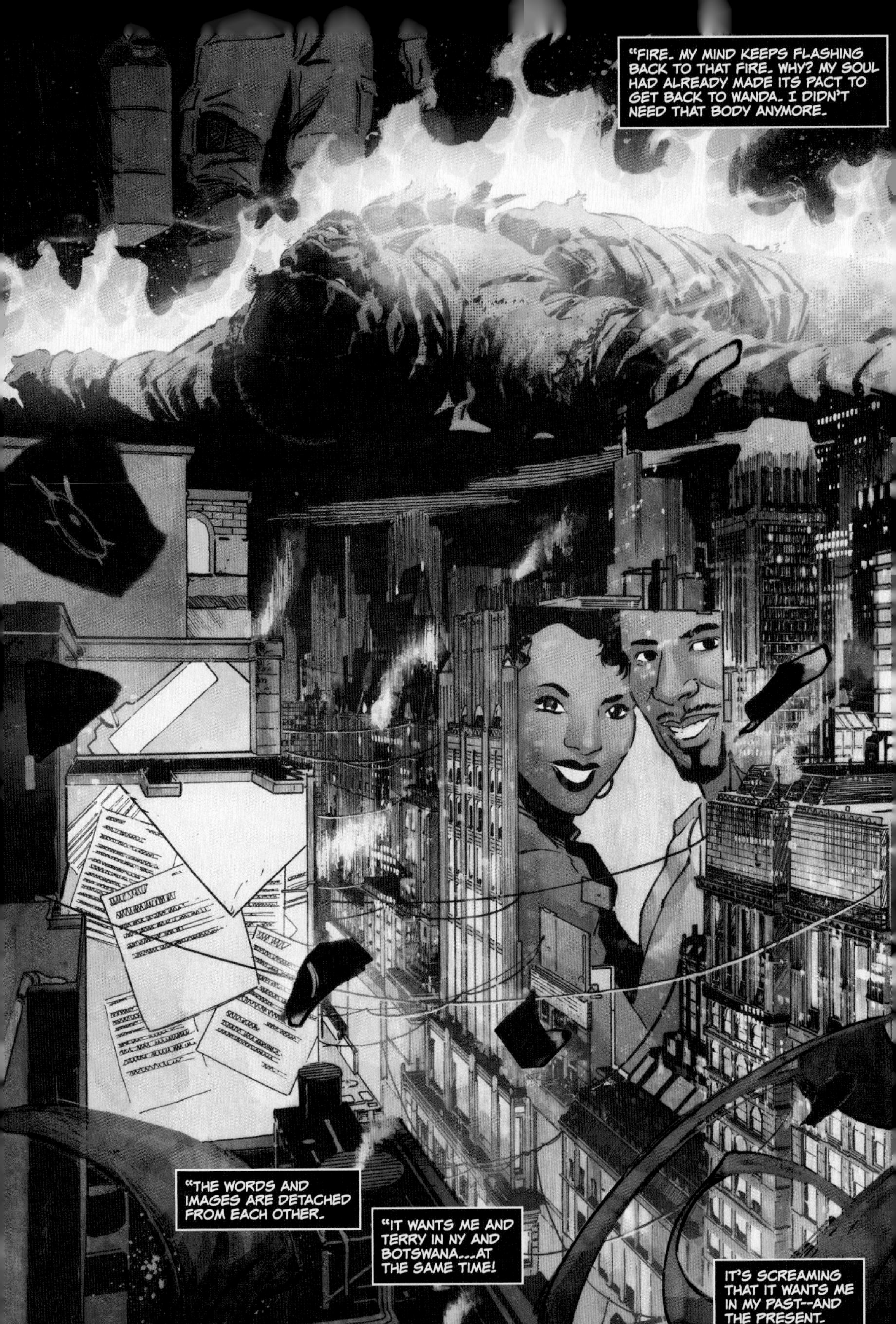
"FIRE. MY MIND KEEPS FLASHING BACK TO THAT FIRE. WHY? MY SOUL HAD ALREADY MADE ITS PACT TO GET BACK TO WANDA. I DIDN'T NEED THAT BODY ANYMORE.
"THE WORDS AND IMAGES ARE DETACHED FROM EACH OTHER.
"IT WANTS ME AND TERRY IN NY AND BOTSWANA...AT THE SAME TIME!
IT'S SCREAMING THAT IT WANTS ME IN MY PAST--AND THE PRESENT.

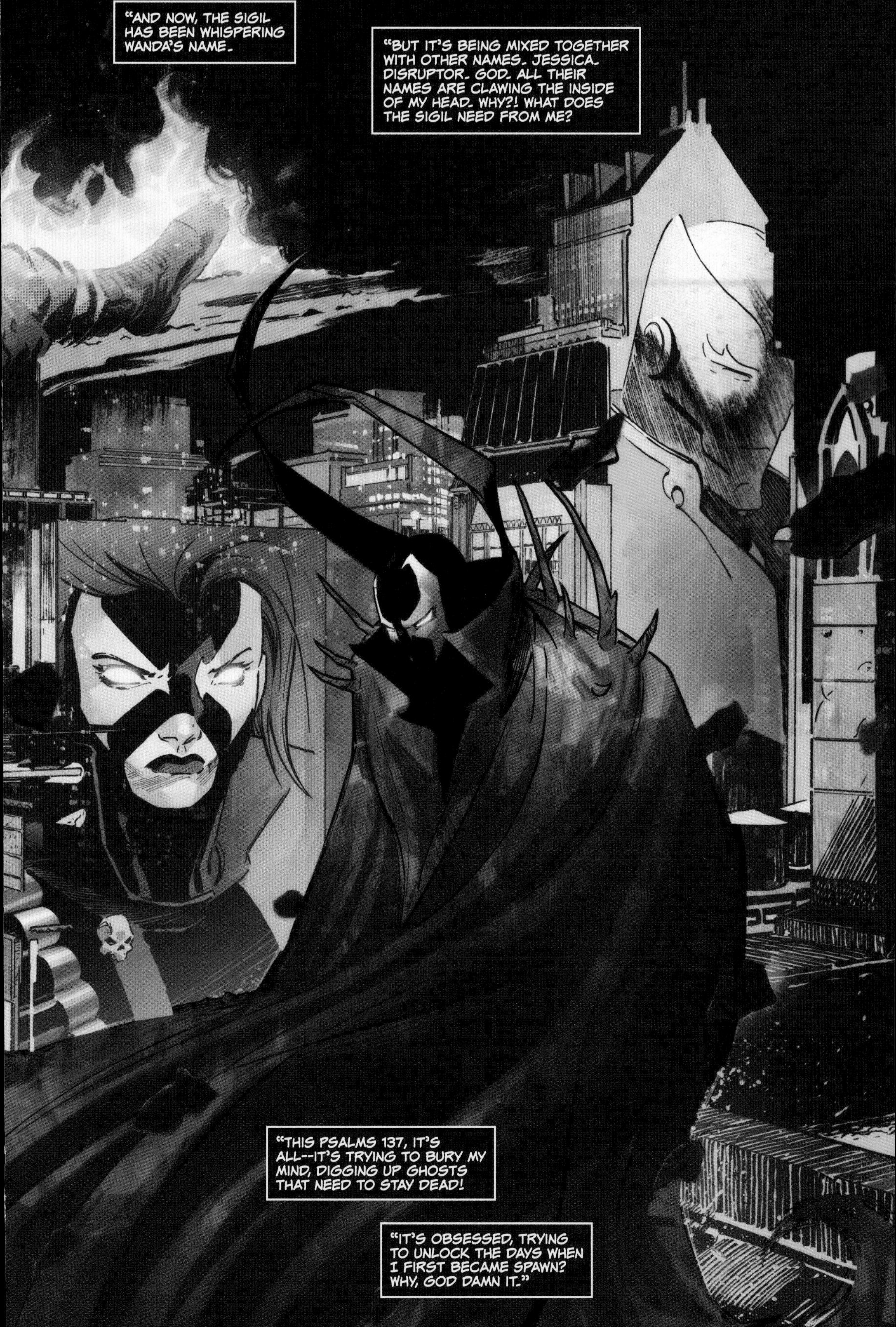
"AND NOW, THE SIGIL HAS BEEN WHISPERING WANDA'S NAME.
"BUT IT'S BEING MIXED TOGETHER WITH OTHER NAMES. JESSICA. DISRUPTOR. GOD. ALL THEIR NAMES ARE CLAWING THE INSIDE OF MY HEAD. WHY?! WHAT DOES THE SIGIL NEED FROM ME?
"THIS PSALMS 137, IT'S ALL--IT'S TRYING TO BURY MY MIND, DIGGING UP GHOSTS THAT NEED TO STAY DEAD!
"IT'S OBSESSED, TRYING TO UNLOCK THE DAYS WHEN I FIRST BECAME SPAWN? WHY, GOD DAMN IT."

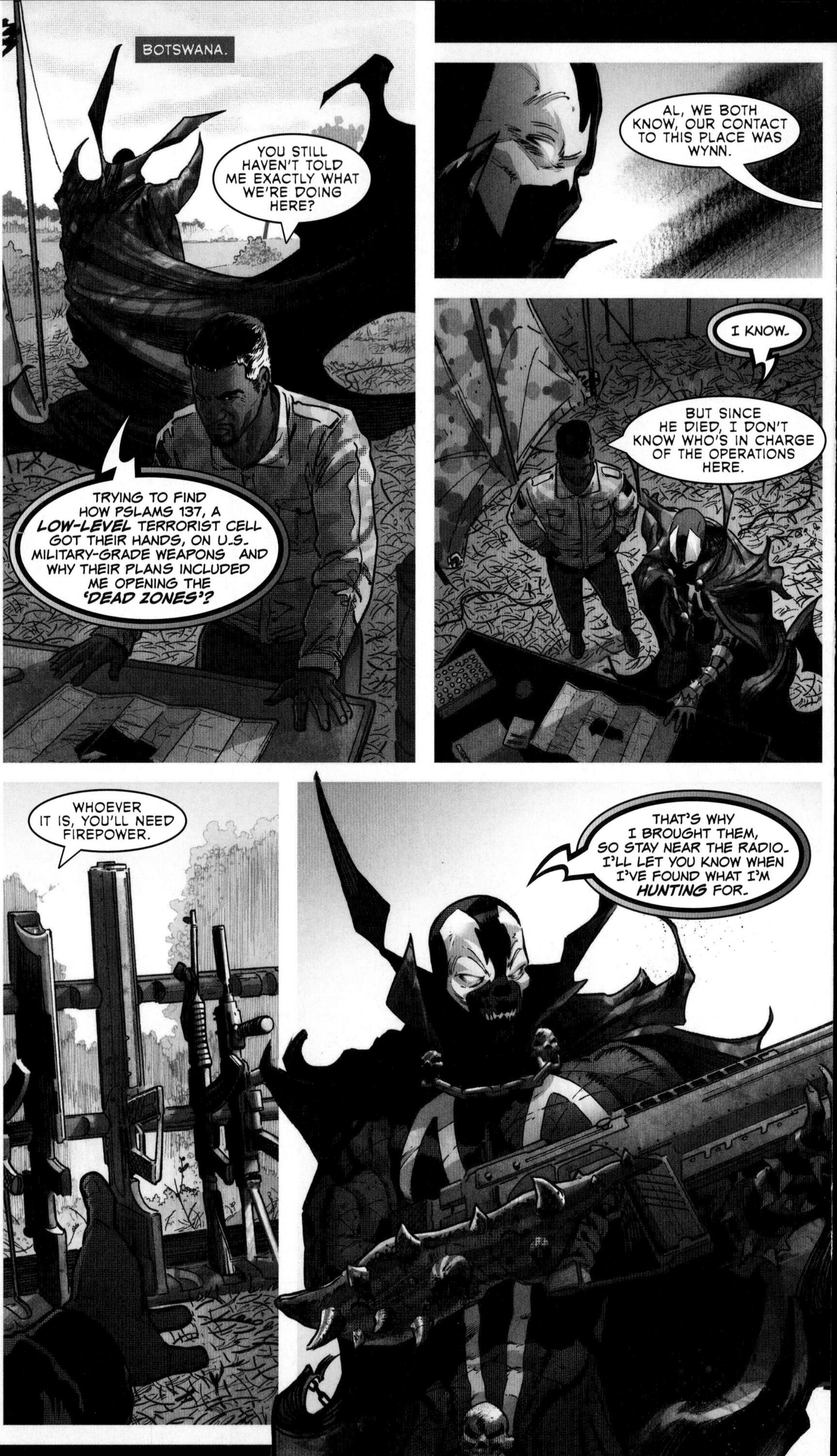
BOTSWANA.
YOU STILL HAVEN'T TOLD ME EXACTLY WHAT WE'RE DOING HERE?
TRYING TO FIND HOW PSLAMS 137, A LOW-LEVEL TERRORIST CELL GOT THEIR HANDS, ON U.S. MILITARY-GRADE WEAPONS AND WHY THEIR PLANS INCLUDED ME OPENING THE 'DEAD ZONES'?
AL, WE BOTH KNOW, OUR CONTACT TO THIS PLACE WAS WYNN.
I KNOW.
BUT SINCE HE DIED, I DON'T KNOW WHO'S IN CHARGE OF THE OPERATIONS HERE.
WHOEVER IT IS, YOU'LL NEED FIREPOWER.
THAT'S WHY I BROUGHT THEM, SO STAY NEAR THE RADIO. I'LL LET YOU KNOW WHEN I'VE FOUND WHAT I'M HUNTING FOR.

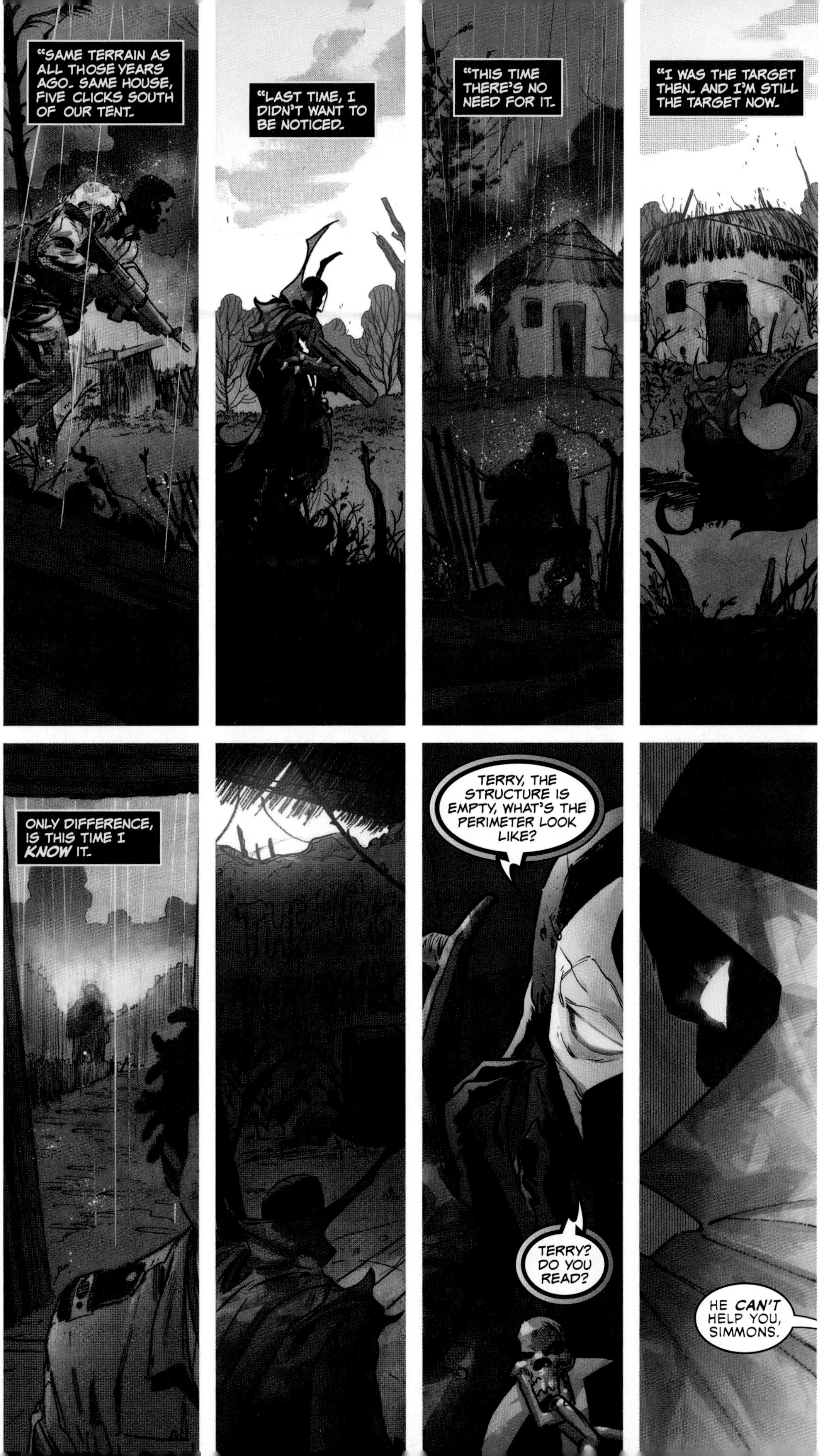
"SAME TERRAIN AS ALL THOSE YEARS AGO. SAME HOUSE, FIVE CLICKS SOUTH OF OUR TENT.
"LAST TIME, I DIDN'T WANT TO BE NOTICED.
"THIS TIME THERE'S NO NEED FOR IT.
"I WAS THE TARGET THEN. AND I'M STILL THE TARGET NOW.
ONLY DIFFERENCE, IS THIS TIME I *KNOW* IT.
TERRY, THE STRUCTURE IS EMPTY, WHAT'S THE PERIMETER LOOK LIKE?
TERRY? DO YOU READ?
HE *CAN'T* HELP YOU, SIMMONS.

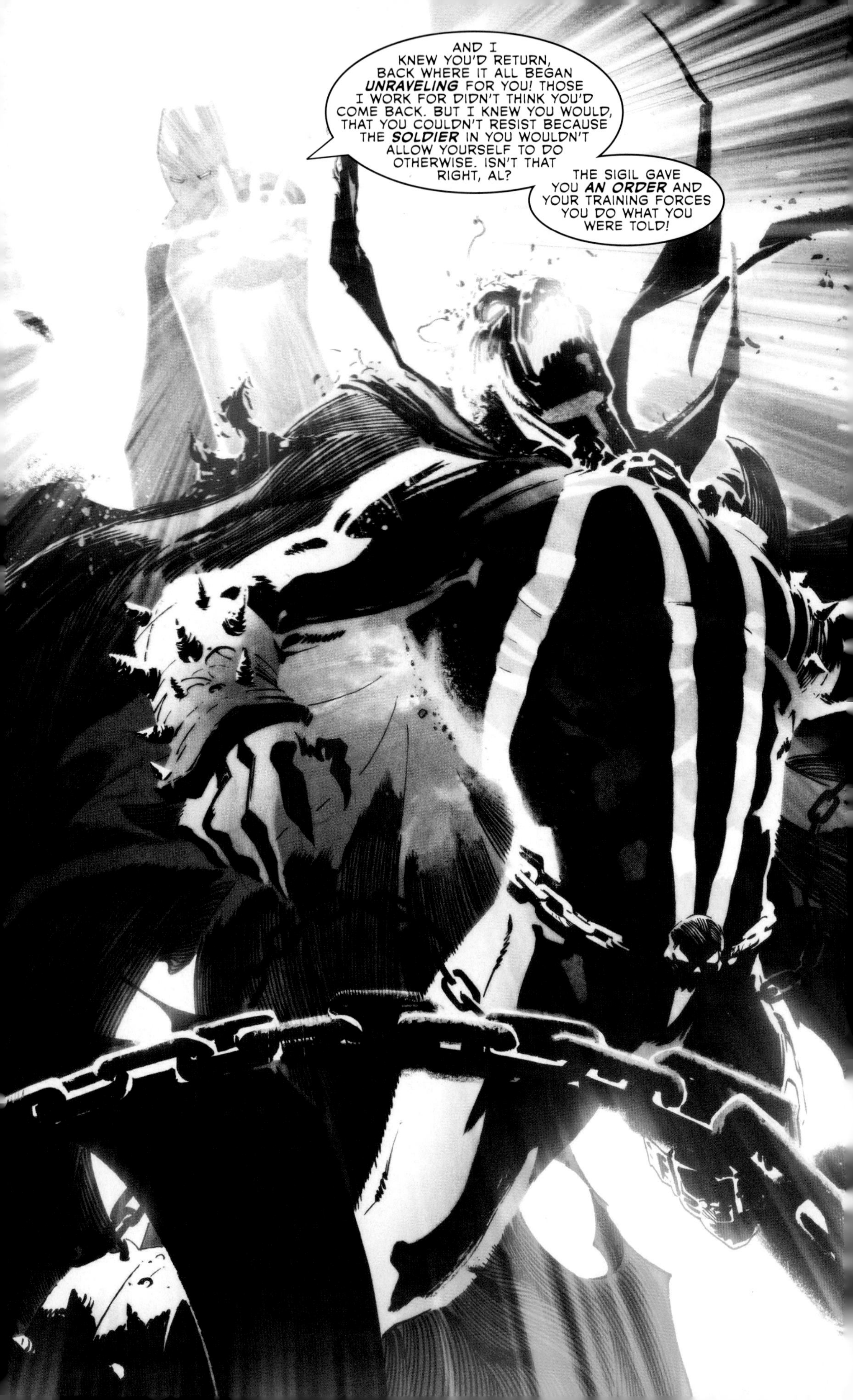
AND I KNEW YOU'D RETURN, BACK WHERE IT ALL BEGAN ***UNRAVELING*** FOR YOU! THOSE I WORK FOR DIDN'T THINK YOU'D COME BACK. BUT I KNEW YOU WOULD, THAT YOU COULDN'T RESIST BECAUSE THE ***SOLDIER*** IN YOU WOULDN'T ALLOW YOURSELF TO DO OTHERWISE. ISN'T THAT RIGHT, AL?
THE SIGIL GAVE YOU ***AN ORDER*** AND YOUR TRAINING FORCES YOU DO WHAT YOU WERE TOLD!

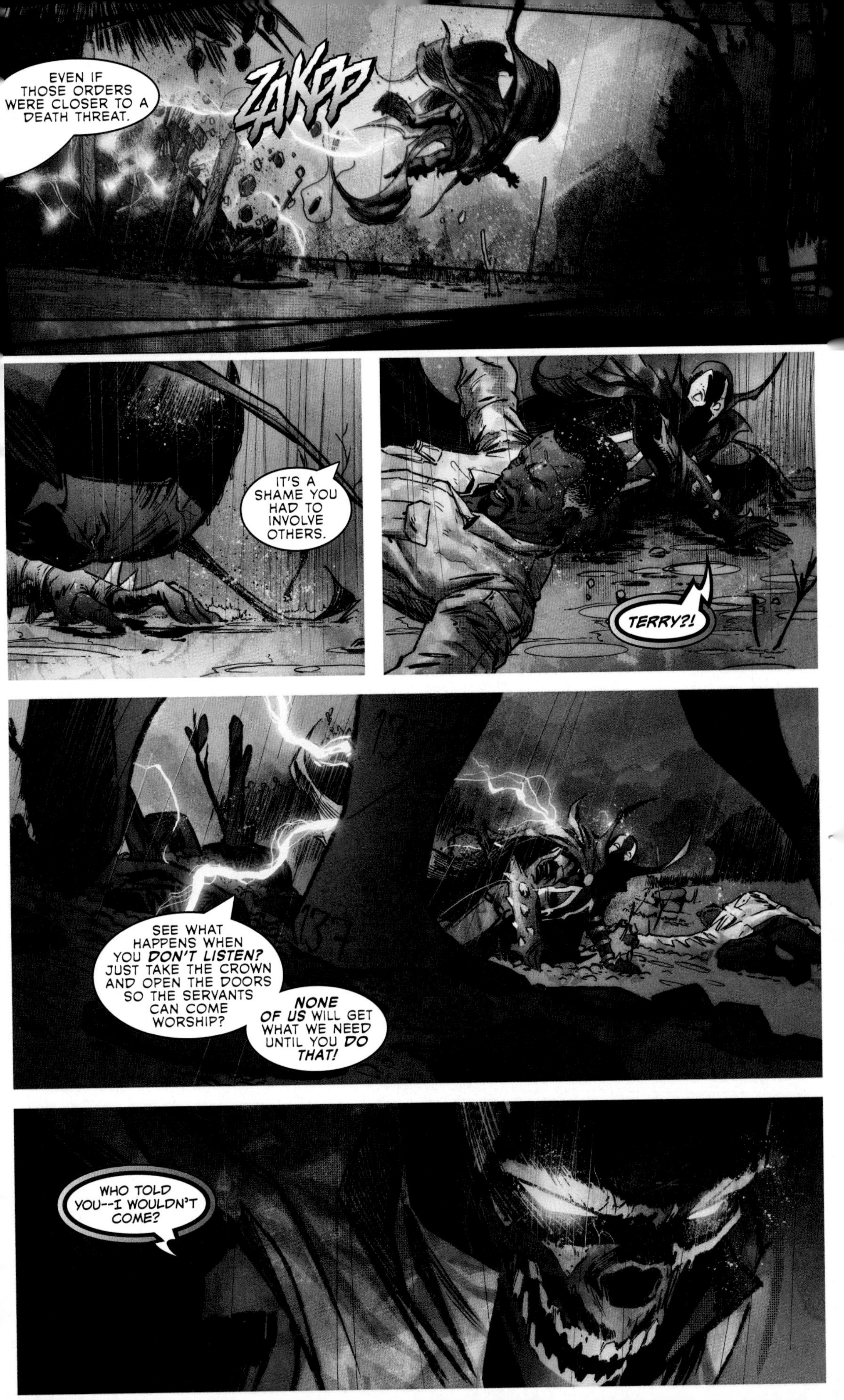
EVEN IF THOSE ORDERS WERE CLOSER TO A DEATH THREAT.
ZAKOP
IT'S A SHAME YOU HAD TO INVOLVE OTHERS.
TERRY?!
SEE WHAT HAPPENS WHEN YOU DON'T LISTEN? JUST TAKE THE CROWN AND OPEN THE DOORS SO THE SERVANTS CAN COME WORSHIP?
NONE OF US WILL GET WHAT WE NEED UNTIL YOU DO THAT!
WHO TOLD YOU--I WOULDN'T COME?

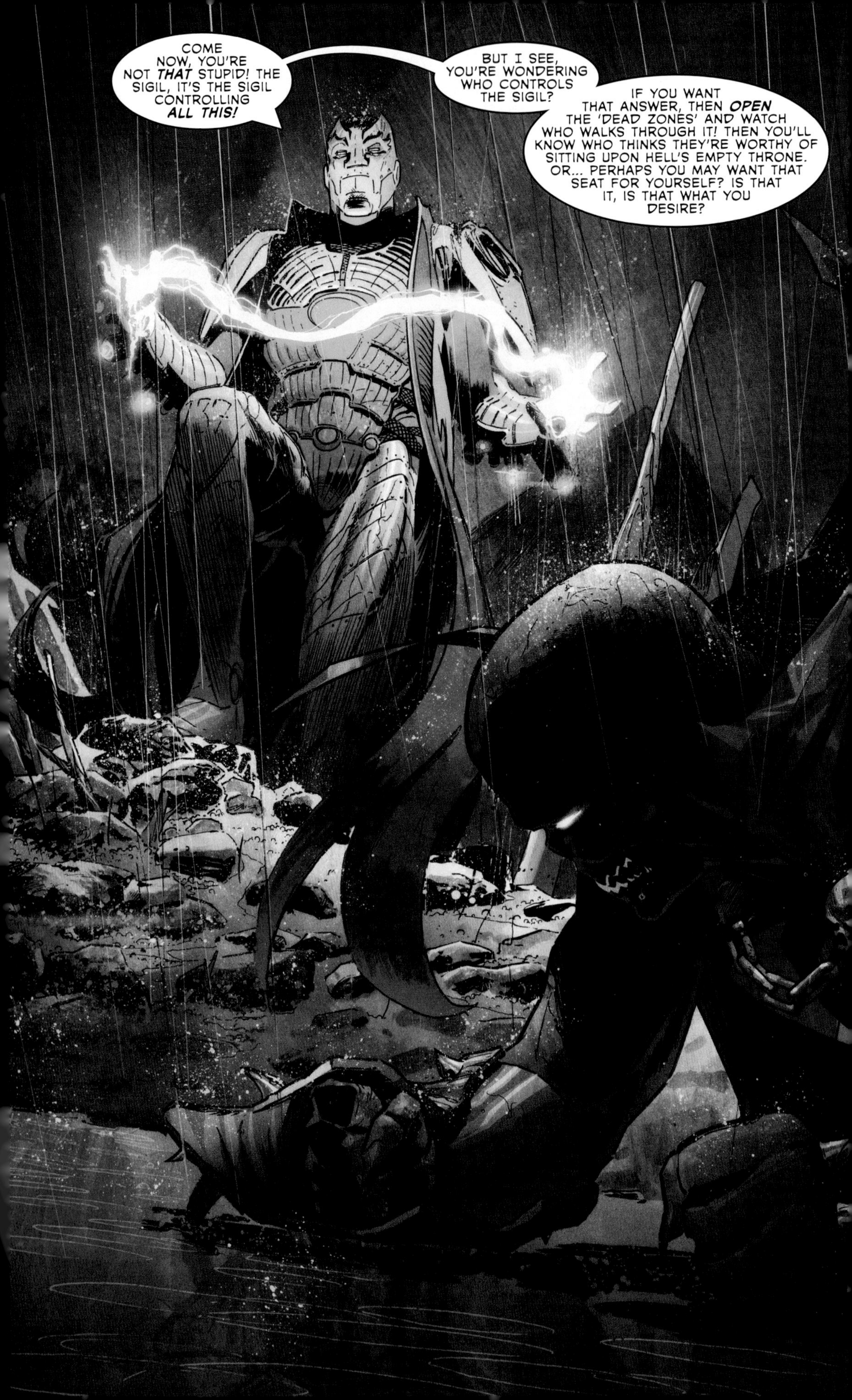
COME NOW, YOU'RE NOT *THAT* STUPID! THE SIGIL, IT'S THE SIGIL CONTROLLING *ALL THIS!*
BUT I SEE, YOU'RE WONDERING WHO CONTROLS THE SIGIL?
IF YOU WANT THAT ANSWER, THEN *OPEN* THE 'DEAD ZONES' AND WATCH WHO WALKS THROUGH IT! THEN YOU'LL KNOW WHO THINKS THEY'RE WORTHY OF SITTING UPON HELL'S EMPTY THRONE. OR... PERHAPS YOU MAY WANT THAT SEAT FOR YOURSELF? IS THAT IT, IS THAT WHAT YOU DESIRE?

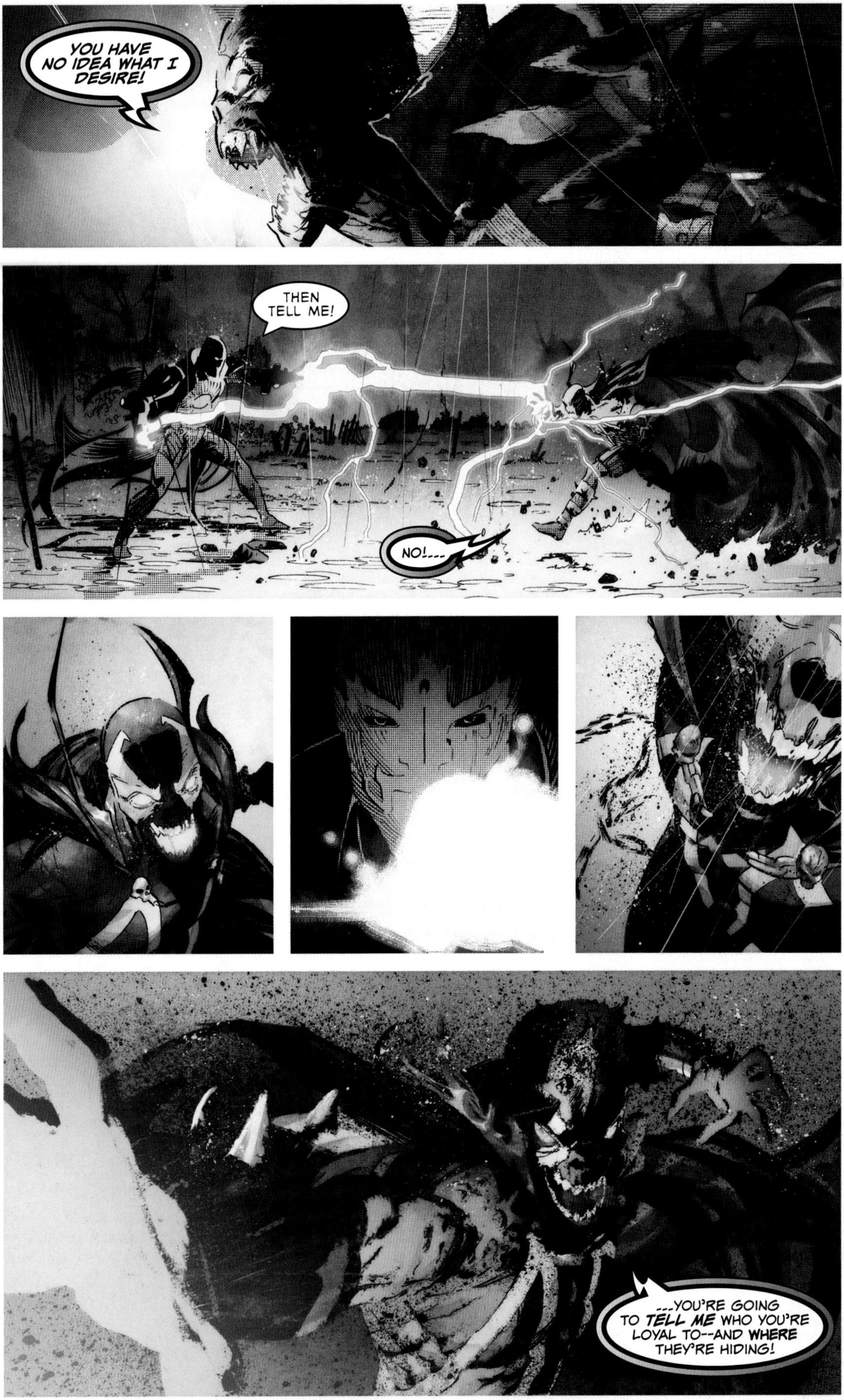
YOU HAVE NO IDEA WHAT I DESIRE!
THEN TELL ME!
NO!...
...YOU'RE GOING TO TELL ME WHO YOU'RE LOYAL TO--AND WHERE THEY'RE HIDING!

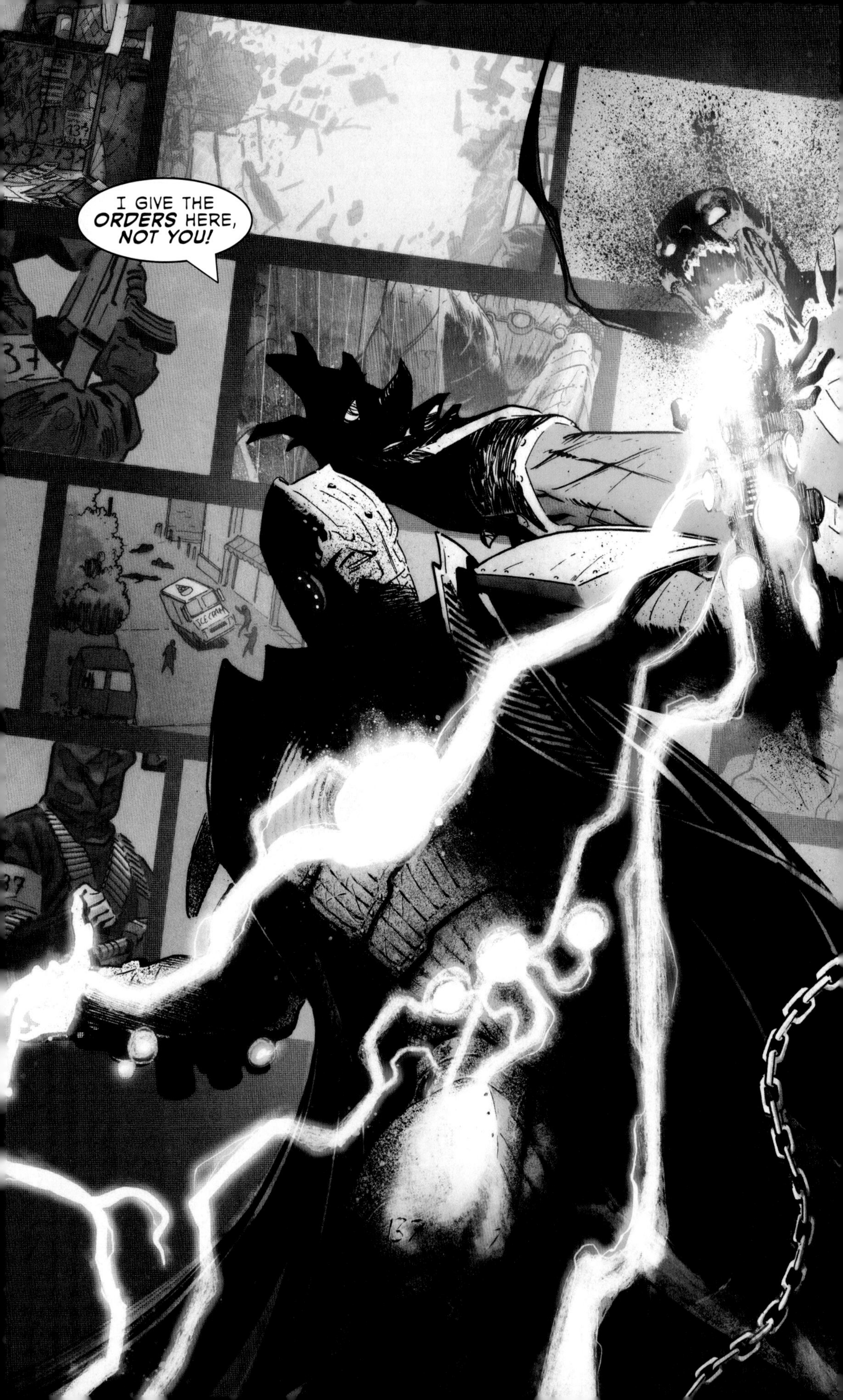
I GIVE THE ORDERS HERE, NOT YOU!

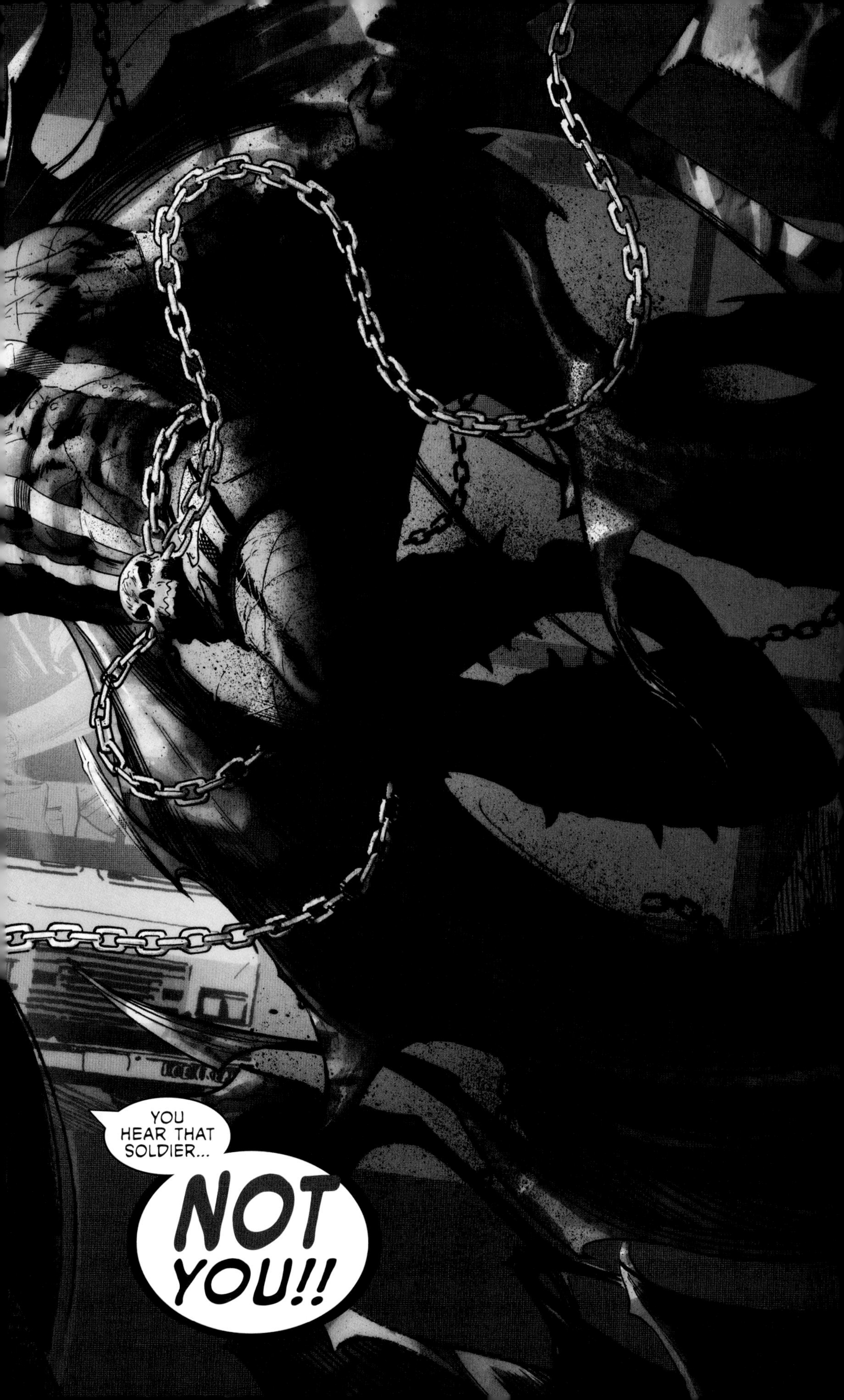
YOU HEAR THAT SOLDIER...
NOT YOU!!

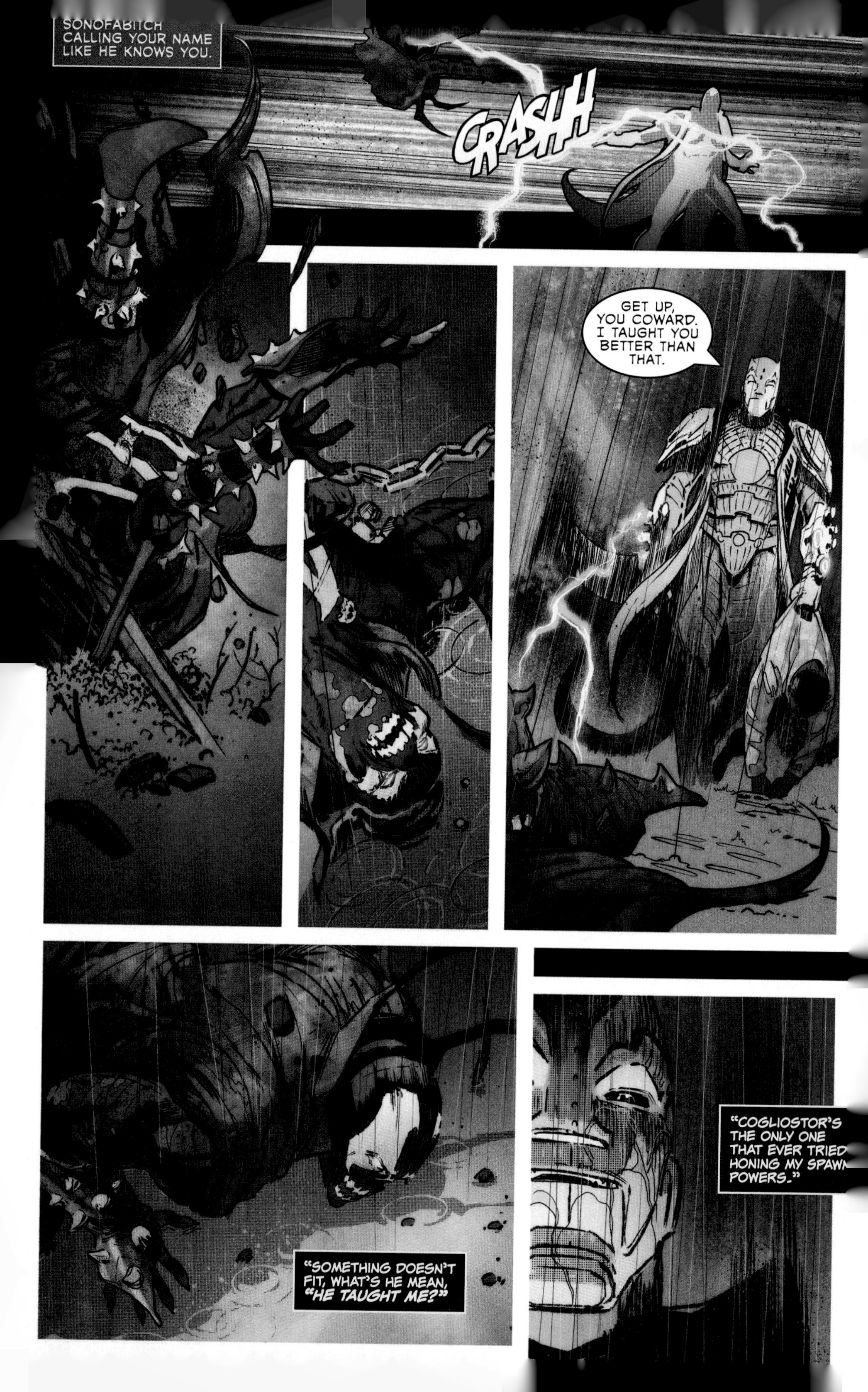
SONOFABITCH CALLING YOUR NAME LIKE HE KNOWS YOU.
CRASHH
GET UP, YOU COWARD. I TAUGHT YOU BETTER THAN THAT.
"SOMETHING DOESN'T FIT, WHAT'S HE MEAN, "HE TAUGHT ME?"
"COGLIOSTOR'S THE ONLY ONE THAT EVER TRIED HONING MY SPAWN POWERS."

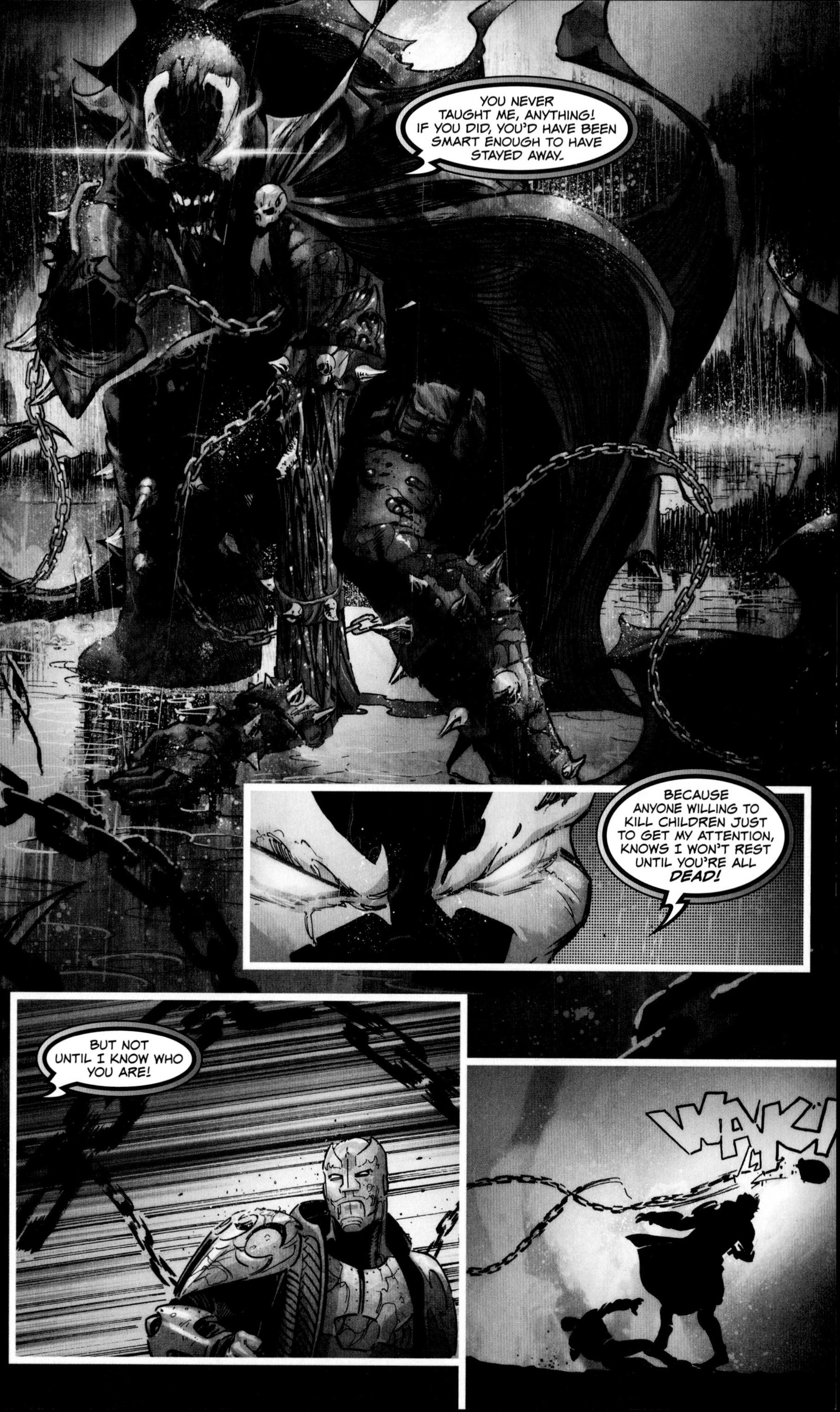
YOU NEVER TAUGHT ME, ANYTHING! IF YOU DID, YOU'D HAVE BEEN SMART ENOUGH TO HAVE STAYED AWAY.
BECAUSE ANYONE WILLING TO KILL CHILDREN JUST TO GET MY ATTENTION, KNOWS I WON'T REST UNTIL YOU'RE ALL *DEAD!*
BUT NOT UNTIL I KNOW WHO YOU ARE!
WAK!

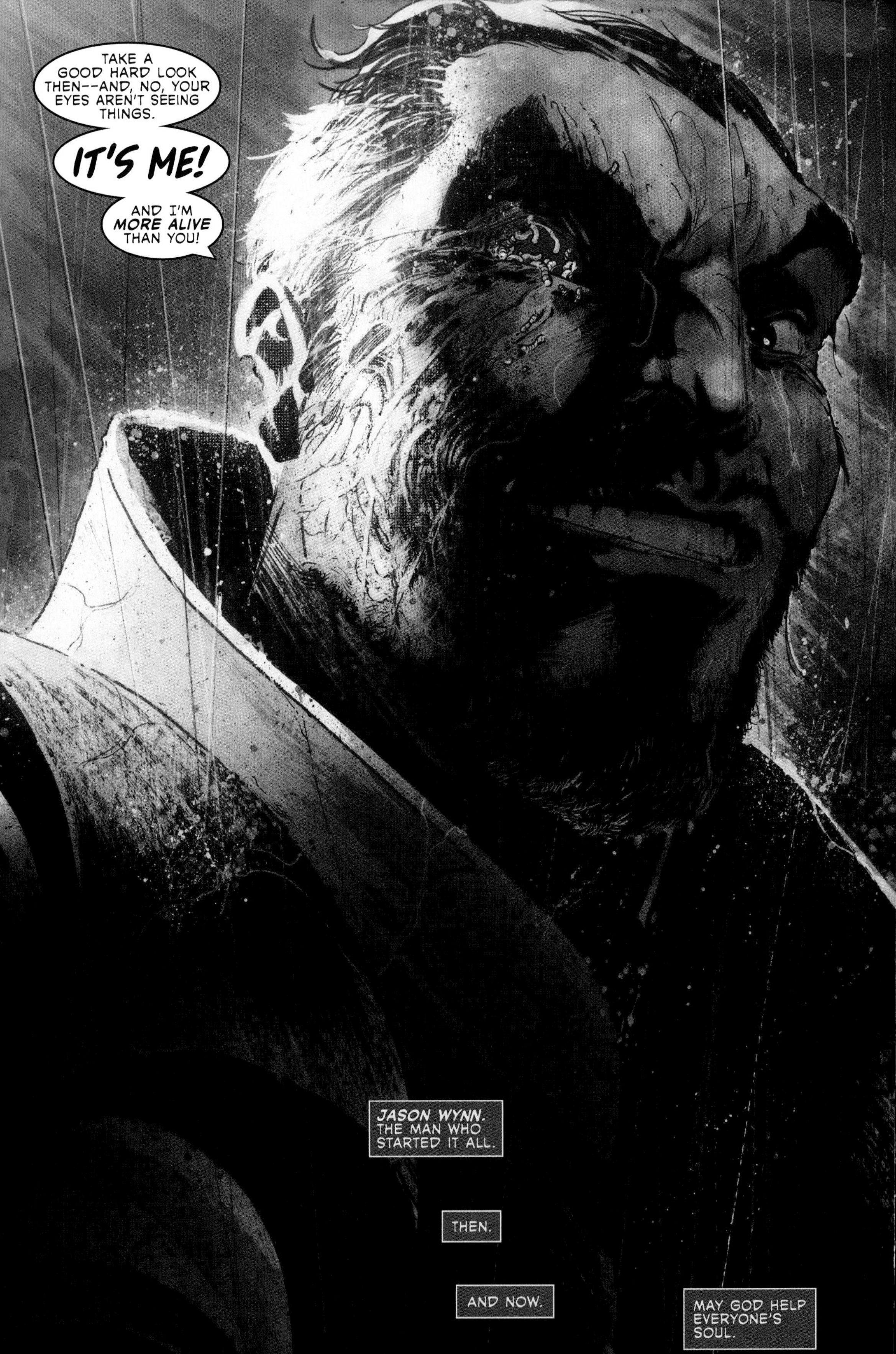

TAKE A GOOD HARD LOOK THEN--AND, NO, YOUR EYES AREN'T SEEING THINGS.
IT'S ME!
AND I'M *MORE ALIVE* THAN YOU!
JASON WYNN. THE MAN WHO STARTED IT ALL.
THEN.
AND NOW.
MAY GOD HELP EVERYONE'S SOUL.

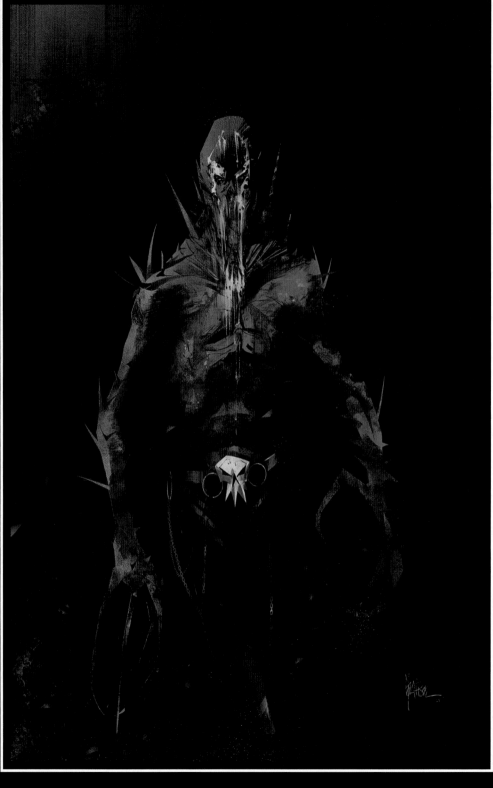

King Spawn #6   Cover by Jonathan Glapion

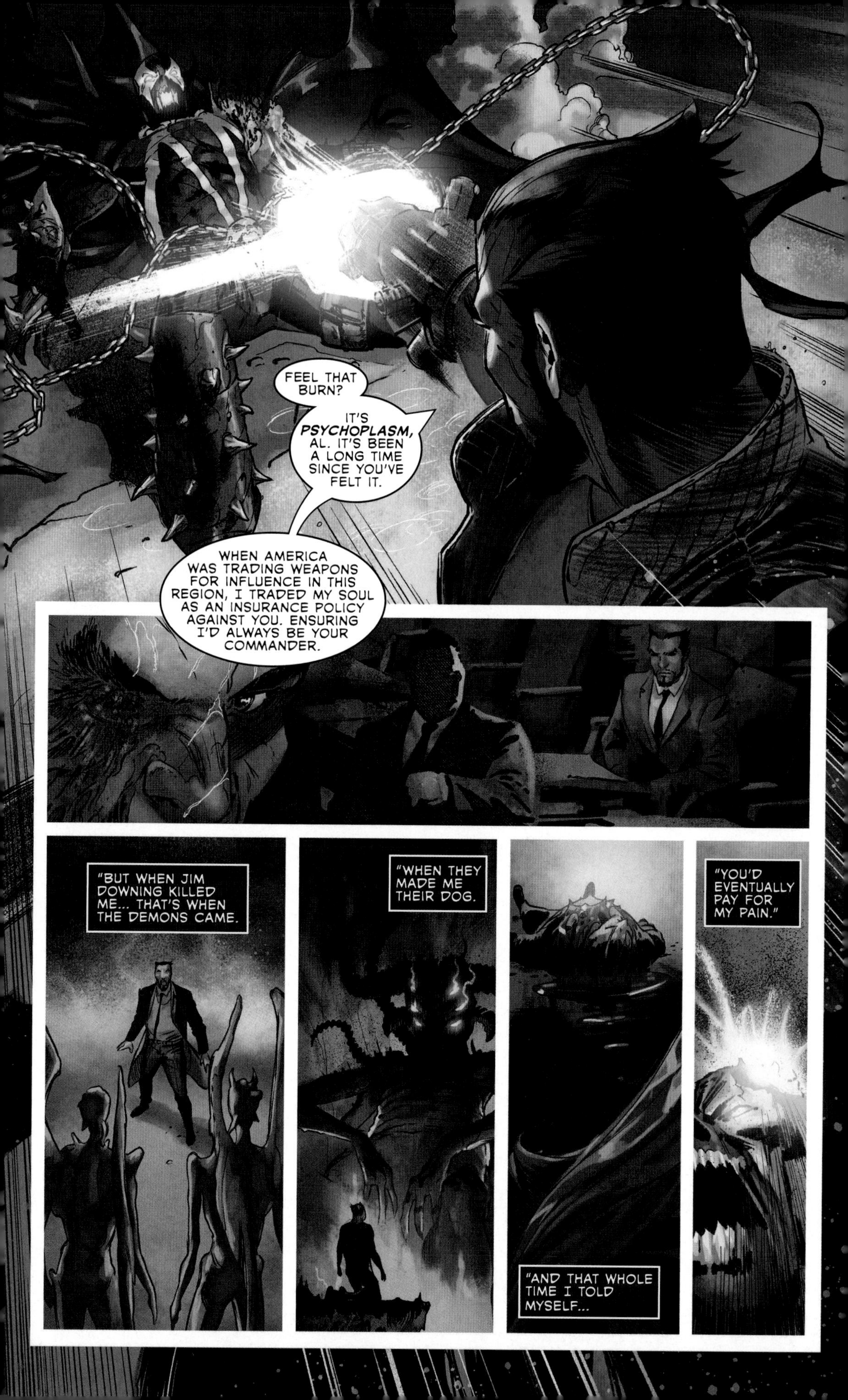

FEEL THAT BURN?
IT'S *PSYCHOPLASM,* AL. IT'S BEEN A LONG TIME SINCE YOU'VE FELT IT.
WHEN AMERICA WAS TRADING WEAPONS FOR INFLUENCE IN THIS REGION, I TRADED MY SOUL AS AN INSURANCE POLICY AGAINST YOU. ENSURING I'D ALWAYS BE YOUR COMMANDER.
"BUT WHEN JIM DOWNING KILLED ME... THAT'S WHEN THE DEMONS CAME.
"WHEN THEY MADE ME THEIR DOG.
"AND THAT WHOLE TIME I TOLD MYSELF...
"YOU'D EVENTUALLY PAY FOR MY PAIN."

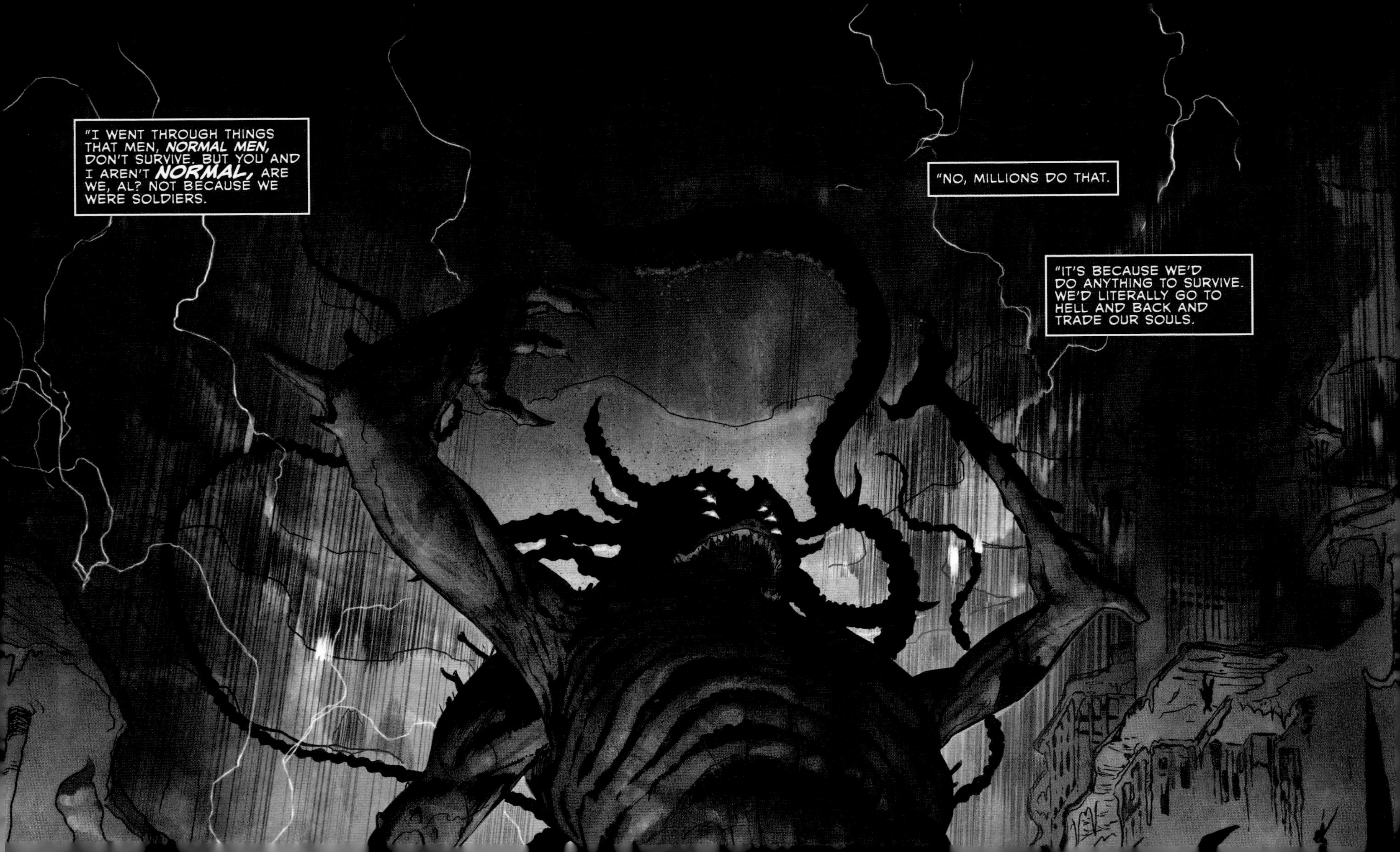
"I WENT THROUGH THINGS THAT MEN, ***NORMAL MEN,*** DON'T SURVIVE. BUT YOU AND I AREN'T ***NORMAL,*** ARE WE, AL? NOT BECAUSE WE WERE SOLDIERS.
"NO, MILLIONS DO THAT.
"IT'S BECAUSE WE'D DO ANYTHING TO SURVIVE. WE'D LITERALLY GO TO HELL AND BACK AND TRADE OUR SOULS.

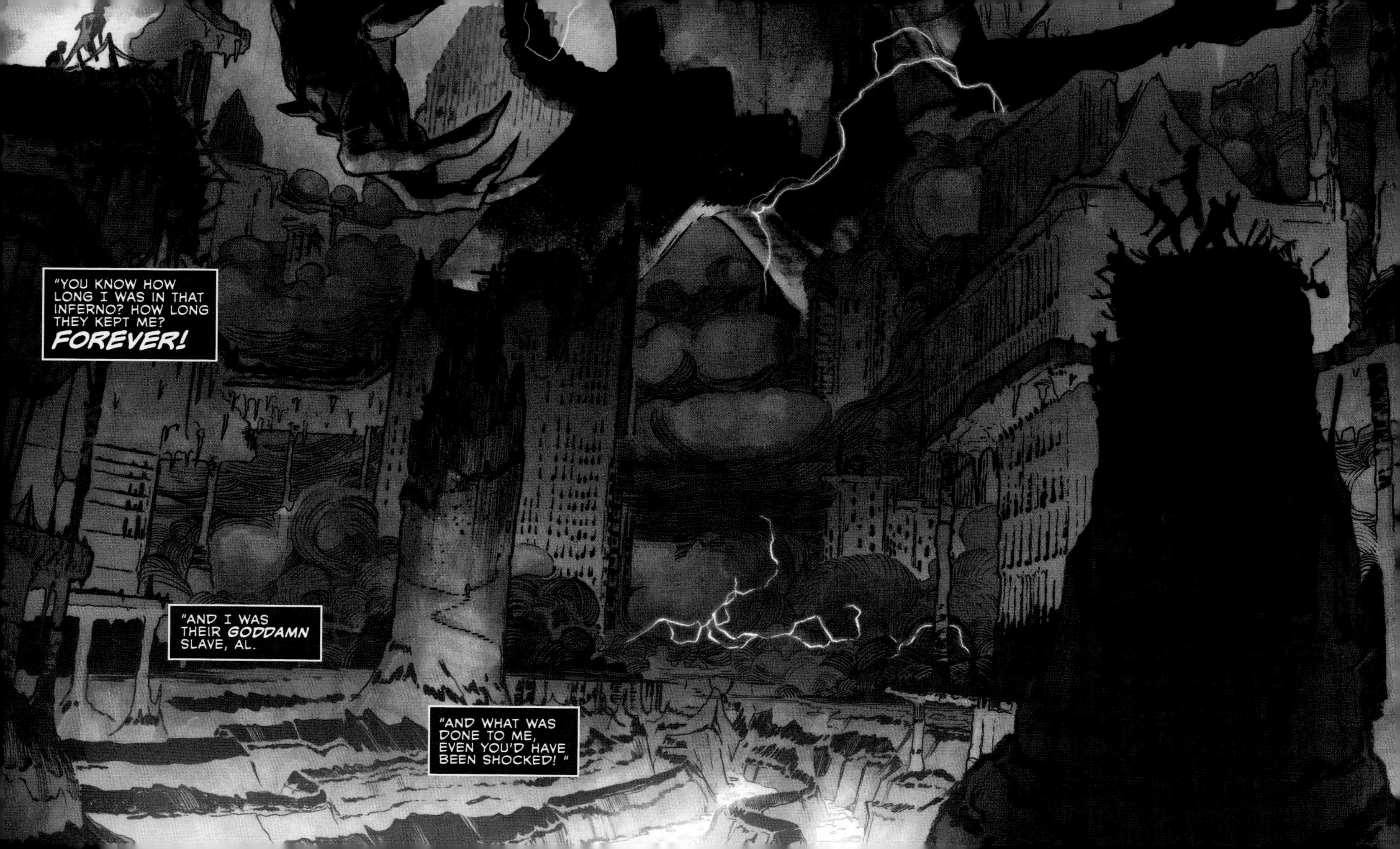
"YOU KNOW HOW LONG I WAS IN THAT INFERNO? HOW LONG THEY KEPT ME? *FOREVER!*
"AND I WAS THEIR *GODDAMN* SLAVE, AL.
"AND WHAT WAS DONE TO ME, EVEN YOU'D HAVE BEEN SHOCKED! "

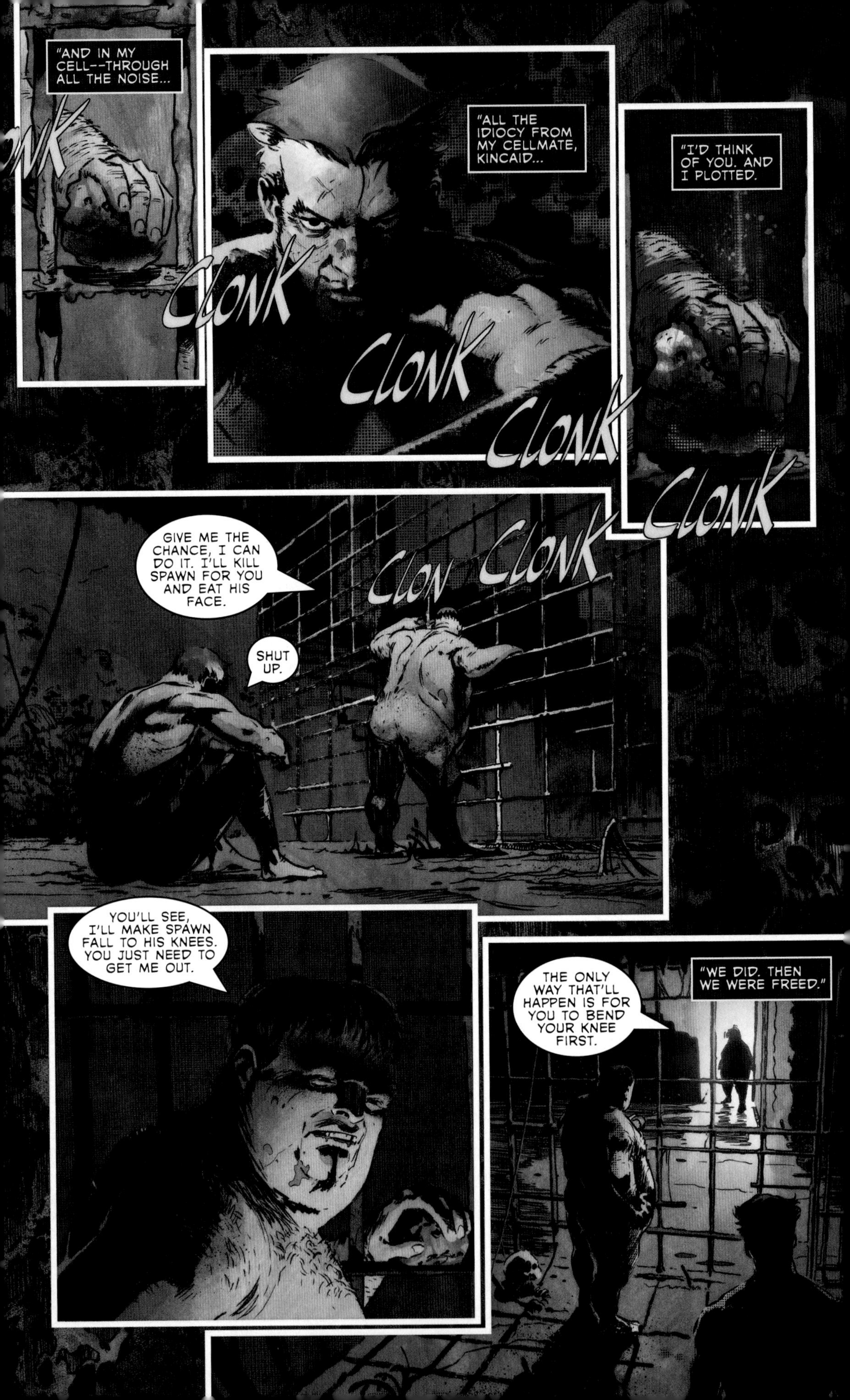
"AND IN MY CELL--THROUGH ALL THE NOISE...
"ALL THE IDIOCY FROM MY CELLMATE, KINCAID...
"I'D THINK OF YOU. AND I PLOTTED.
CLONK
CLONK
CLONK
CLONK
CLONK
CLONK
CLON
GIVE ME THE CHANCE, I CAN DO IT. I'LL KILL SPAWN FOR YOU AND EAT HIS FACE.
SHUT UP.
YOU'LL SEE, I'LL MAKE SPAWN FALL TO HIS KNEES. YOU JUST NEED TO GET ME OUT.
THE ONLY WAY THAT'LL HAPPEN IS FOR YOU TO BEND YOUR KNEE FIRST.
"WE DID. THEN WE WERE FREED."

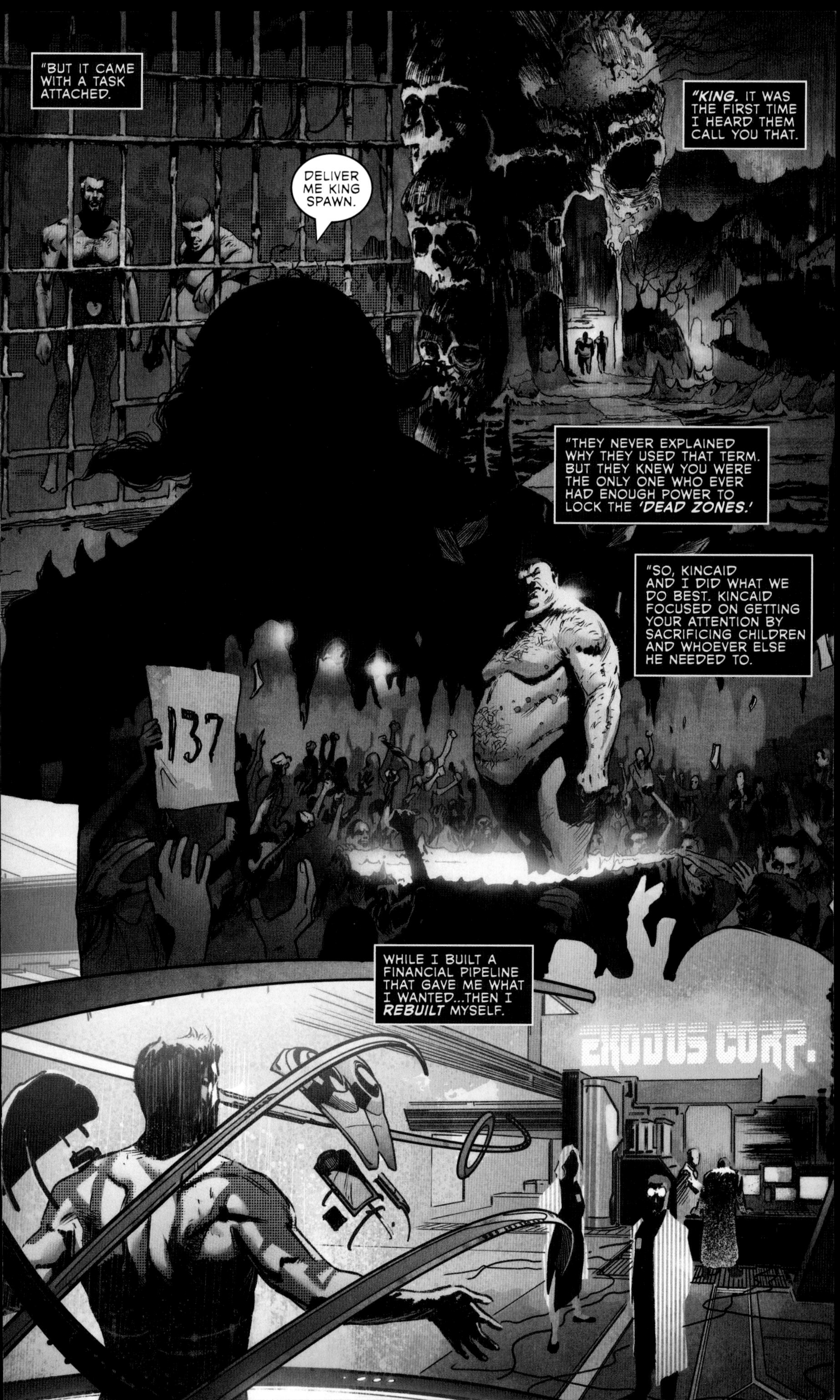
"BUT IT CAME WITH A TASK ATTACHED.
DELIVER ME KING SPAWN.
"KING. IT WAS THE FIRST TIME I HEARD THEM CALL YOU THAT.
"THEY NEVER EXPLAINED WHY THEY USED THAT TERM. BUT THEY KNEW YOU WERE THE ONLY ONE WHO EVER HAD ENOUGH POWER TO LOCK THE 'DEAD ZONES.'
"SO, KINCAID AND I DID WHAT WE DO BEST. KINCAID FOCUSED ON GETTING YOUR ATTENTION BY SACRIFICING CHILDREN AND WHOEVER ELSE HE NEEDED TO.
137
WHILE I BUILT A FINANCIAL PIPELINE THAT GAVE ME WHAT I WANTED...THEN I REBUILT MYSELF.
EXODUS CORP.

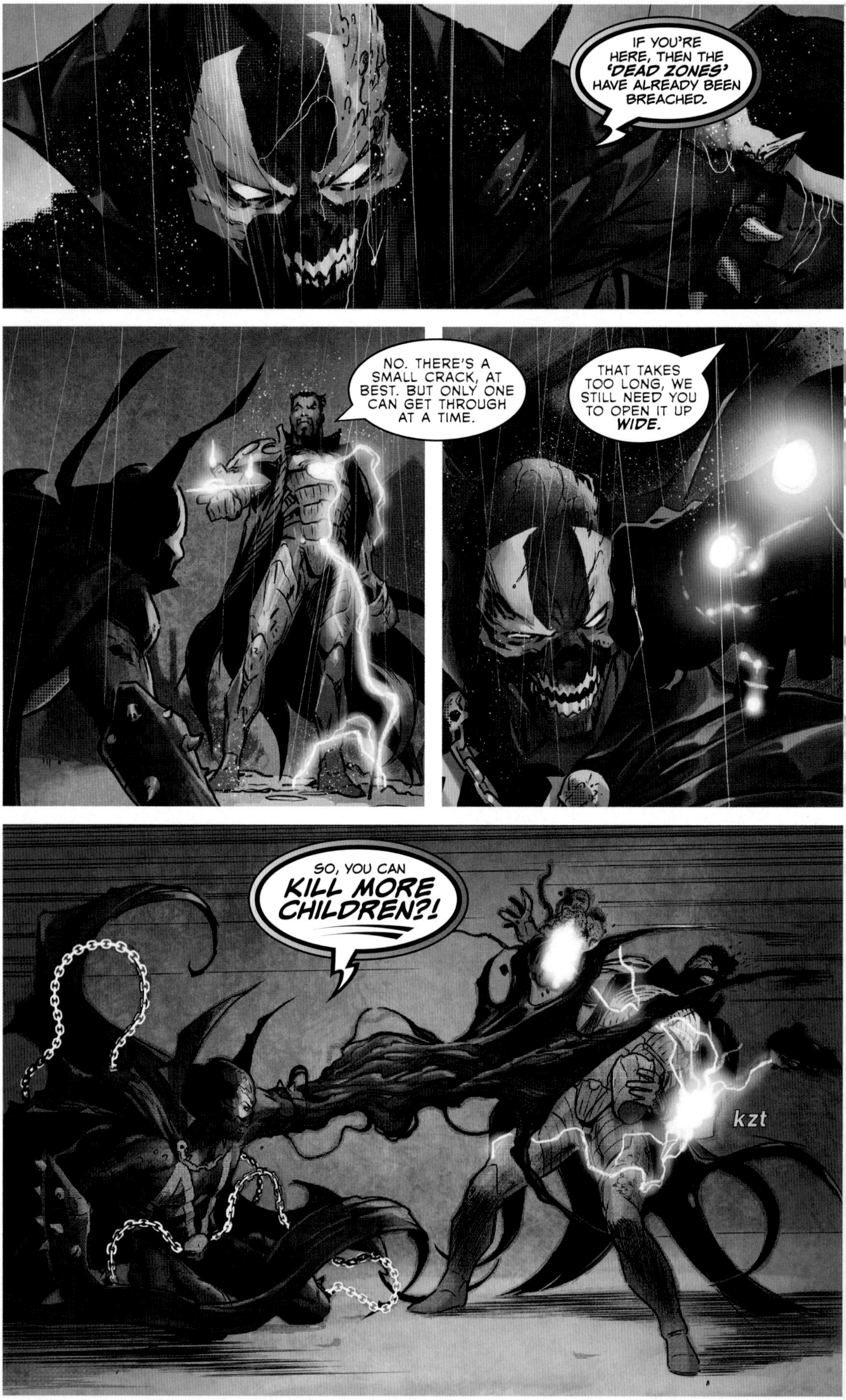
IF YOU'RE HERE, THEN THE 'DEAD ZONES' HAVE ALREADY BEEN BREACHED.
NO. THERE'S A SMALL CRACK, AT BEST. BUT ONLY ONE CAN GET THROUGH AT A TIME.
THAT TAKES TOO LONG, WE STILL NEED YOU TO OPEN IT UP WIDE.
SO, YOU CAN KILL MORE CHILDREN?!
kzt

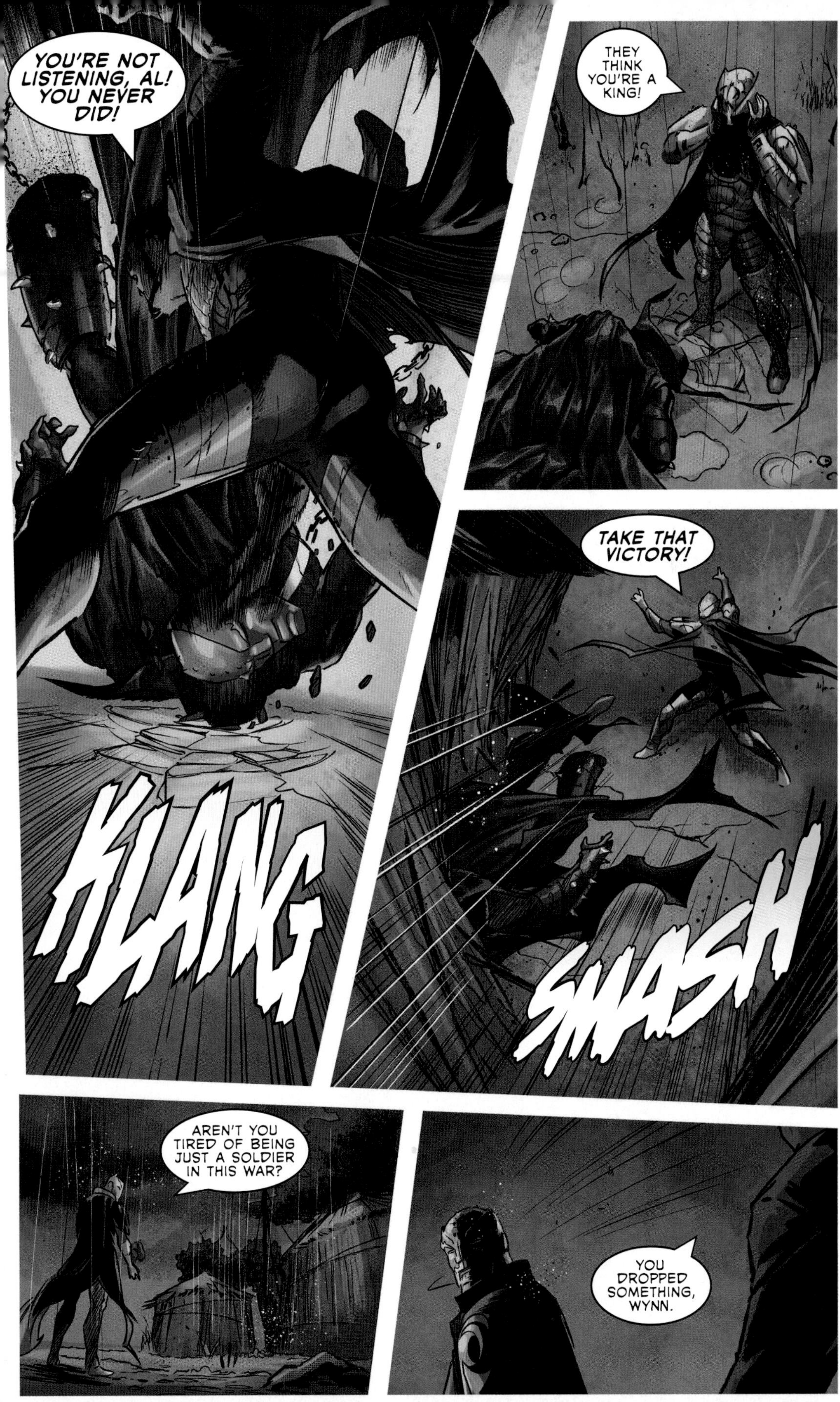
YOU'RE NOT LISTENING, AL! YOU NEVER DID!
KLANG
THEY THINK YOU'RE A KING!
TAKE THAT VICTORY!
SMASH
AREN'T YOU TIRED OF BEING JUST A SOLDIER IN THIS WAR?
YOU DROPPED SOMETHING, WYNN.

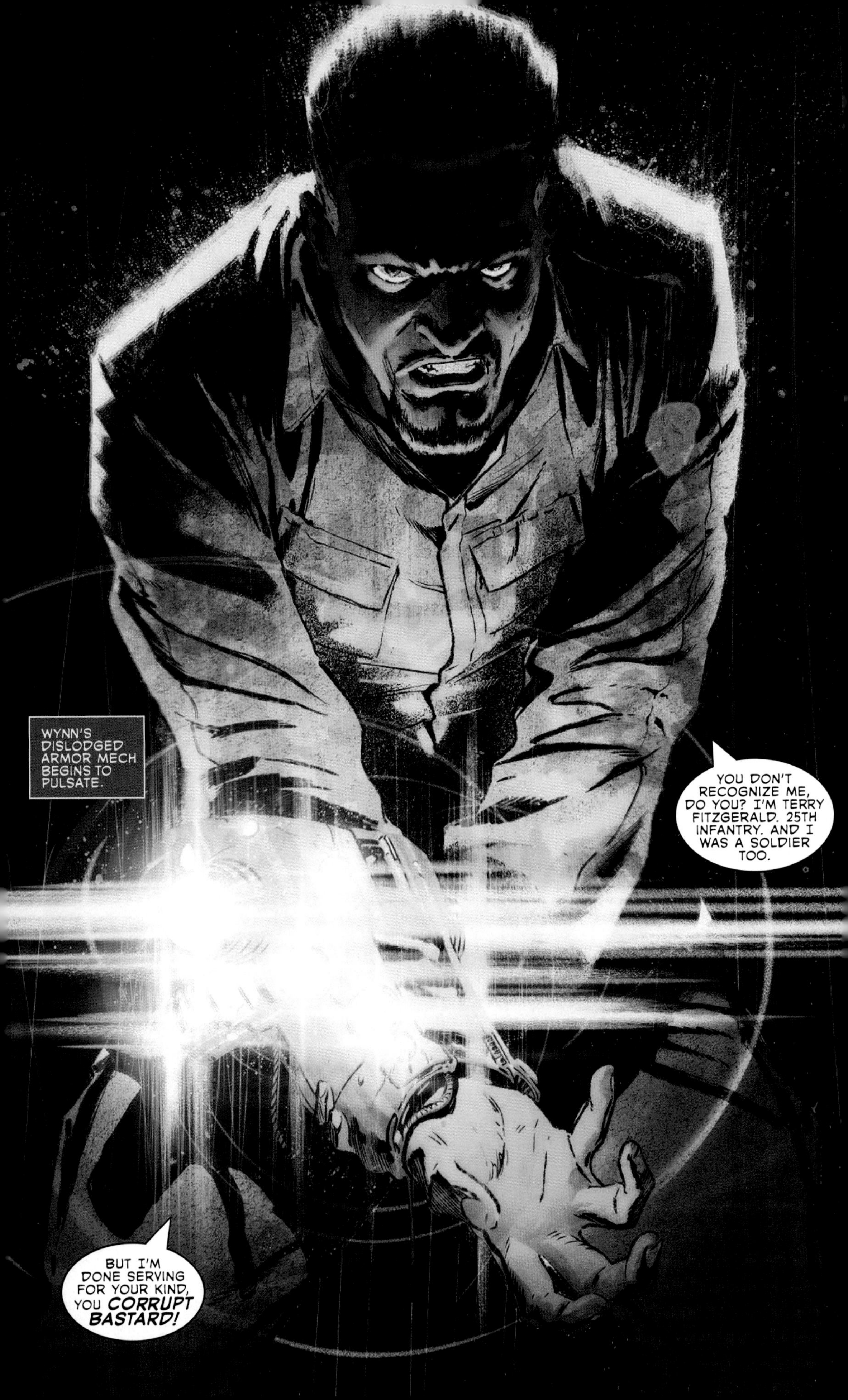
WYNN'S DISLODGED ARMOR MECH BEGINS TO PULSATE.
YOU DON'T RECOGNIZE ME, DO YOU? I'M TERRY FITZGERALD. 25TH INFANTRY. AND I WAS A SOLDIER TOO.
BUT I'M DONE SERVING FOR YOUR KIND, YOU **CORRUPT BASTARD!**

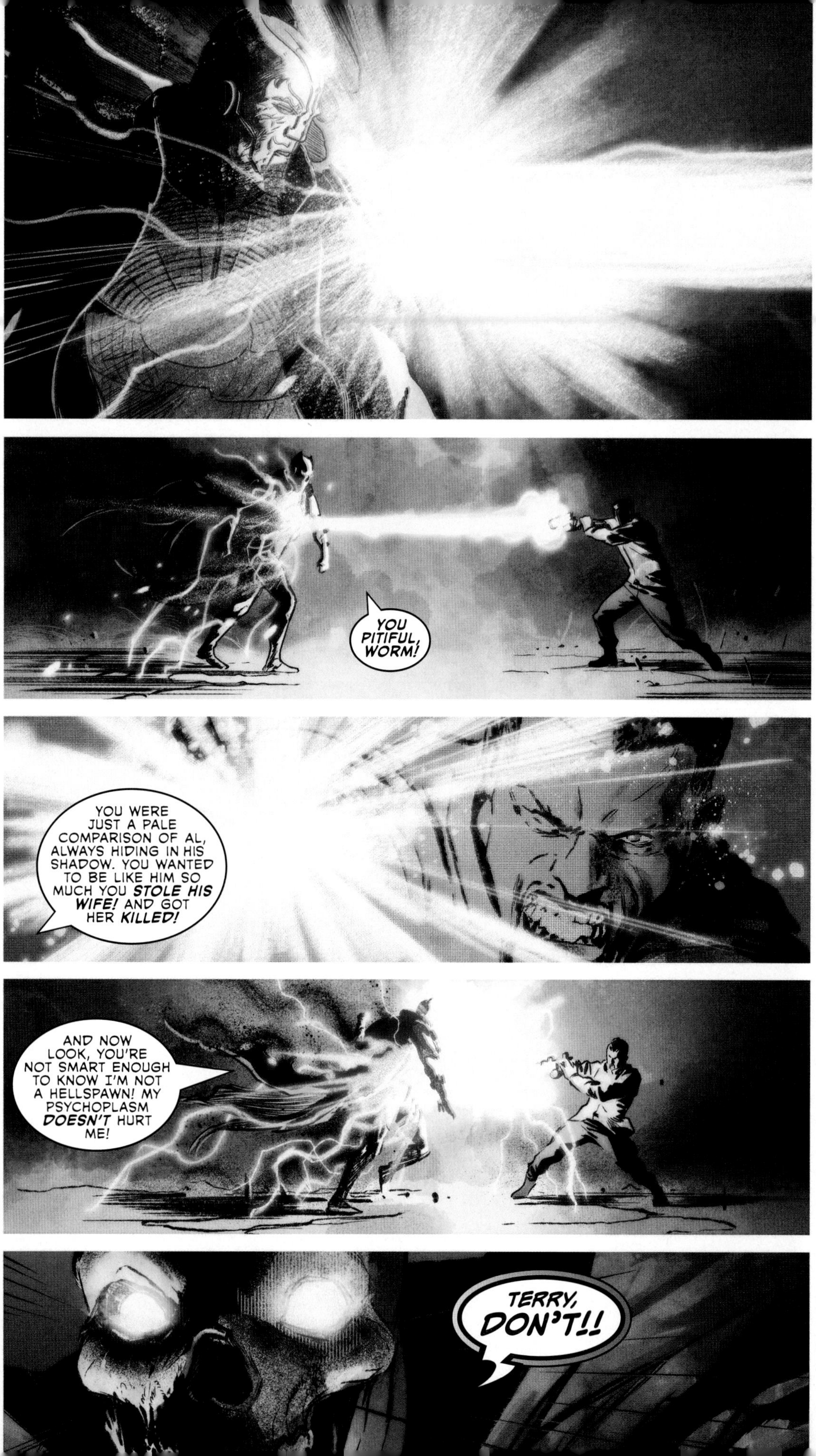
YOU PITIFUL, WORM!
YOU WERE JUST A PALE COMPARISON OF AL, ALWAYS HIDING IN HIS SHADOW. YOU WANTED TO BE LIKE HIM SO MUCH YOU STOLE HIS WIFE! AND GOT HER KILLED!
AND NOW LOOK, YOU'RE NOT SMART ENOUGH TO KNOW I'M NOT A HELLSPAWN! MY PSYCHOPLASM DOESN'T HURT ME!
TERRY, DON'T!!

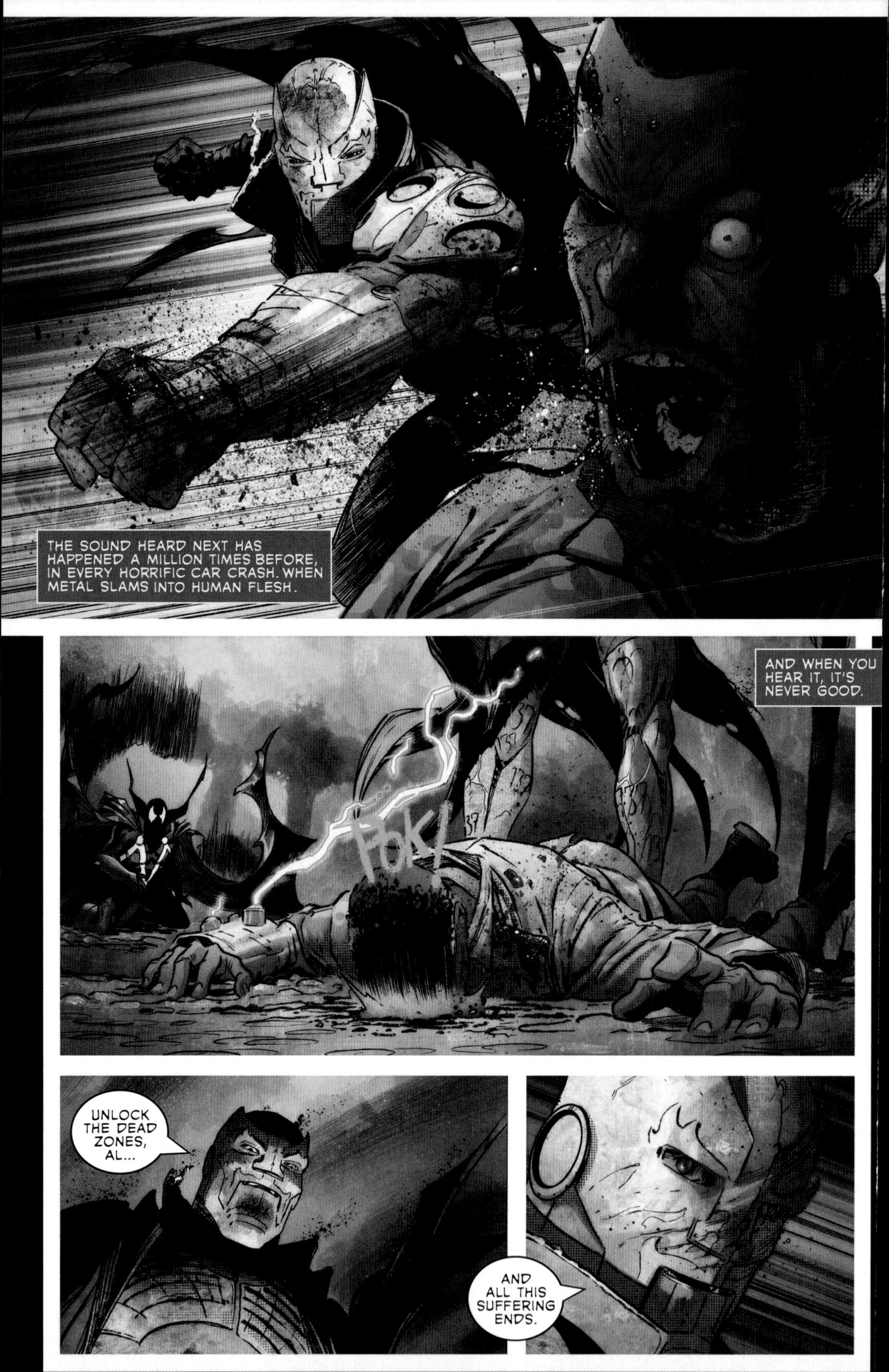
THE SOUND HEARD NEXT HAS HAPPENED A MILLION TIMES BEFORE, IN EVERY HORRIFIC CAR CRASH. WHEN METAL SLAMS INTO HUMAN FLESH.
AND WHEN YOU HEAR IT, IT'S NEVER GOOD.
FOK!
UNLOCK THE DEAD ZONES, AL...
AND ALL THIS SUFFERING ENDS.

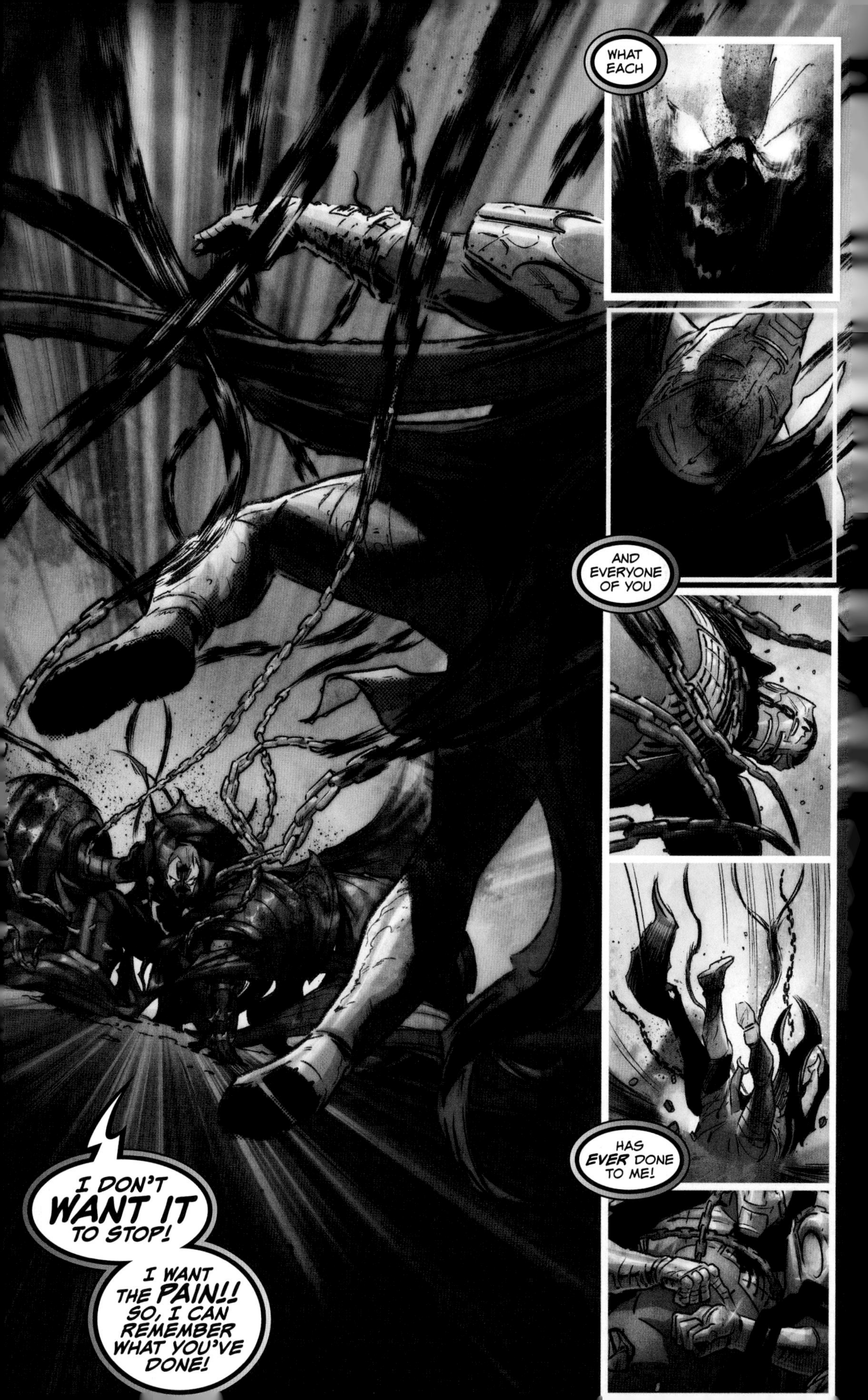
WHAT EACH
AND EVERYONE OF YOU
HAS EVER DONE TO ME!
I DON'T WANT IT TO STOP!
I WANT THE PAIN!! SO, I CAN REMEMBER WHAT YOU'VE DONE!

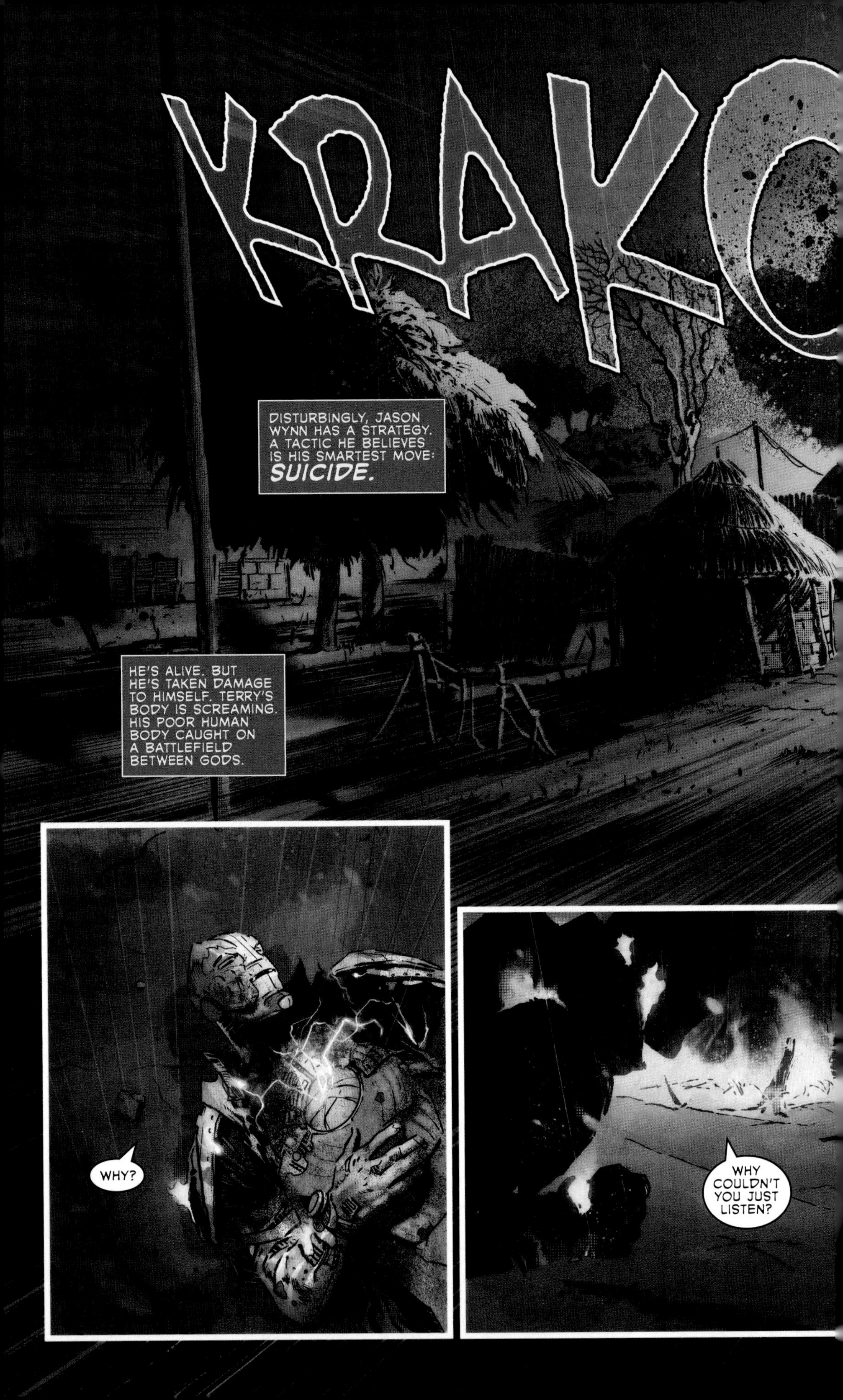
KRAKO
DISTURBINGLY, JASON WYNN HAS A STRATEGY. A TACTIC HE BELIEVES IS HIS SMARTEST MOVE: SUICIDE.
HE'S ALIVE. BUT HE'S TAKEN DAMAGE TO HIMSELF. TERRY'S BODY IS SCREAMING. HIS POOR HUMAN BODY CAUGHT ON A BATTLEFIELD BETWEEN GODS.
WHY?
WHY COULDN'T YOU JUST LISTEN?

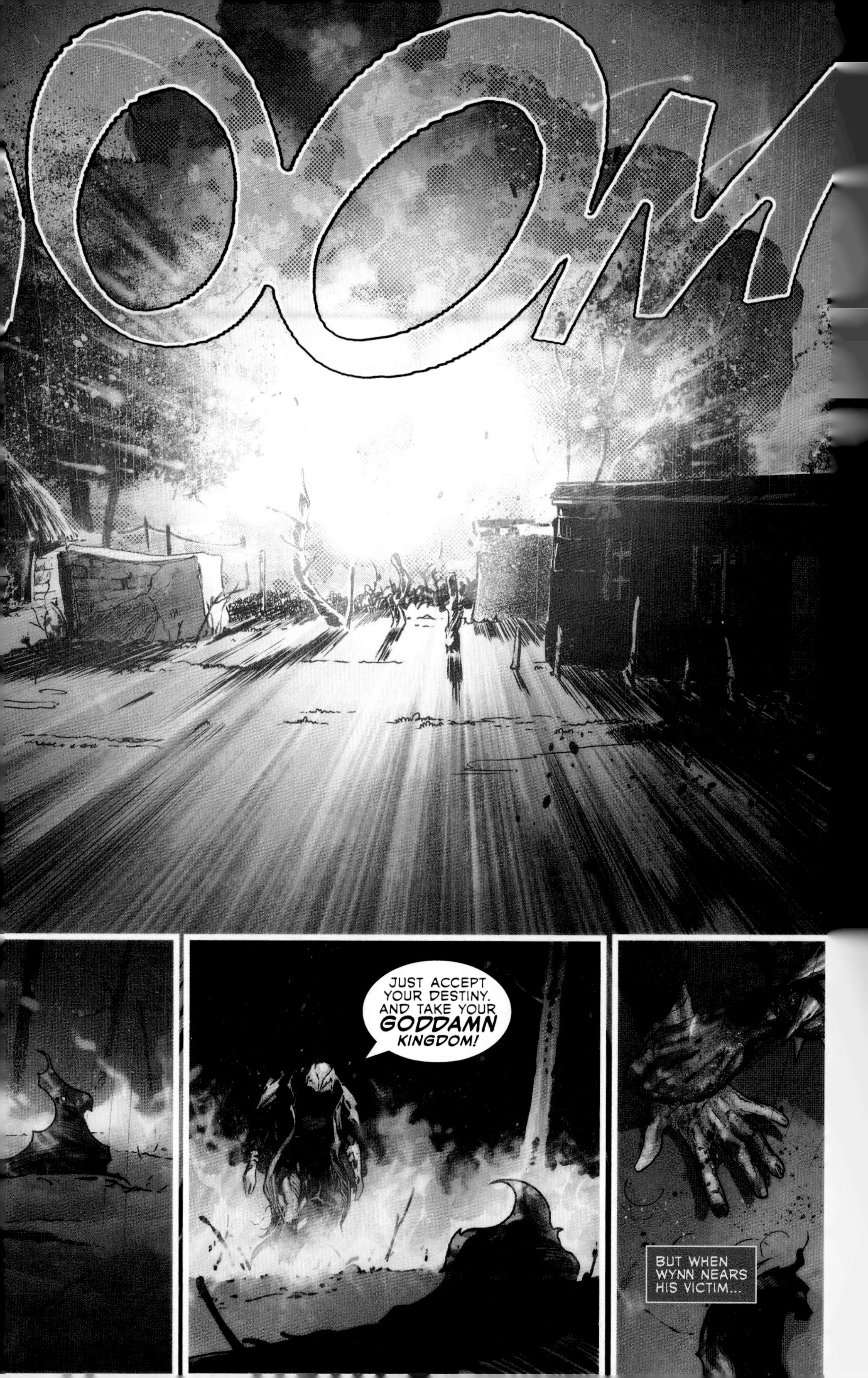

OOOM
JUST ACCEPT YOUR DESTINY. AND TAKE YOUR GODDAMN KINGDOM!
BUT WHEN WYNN NEARS HIS VICTIM...

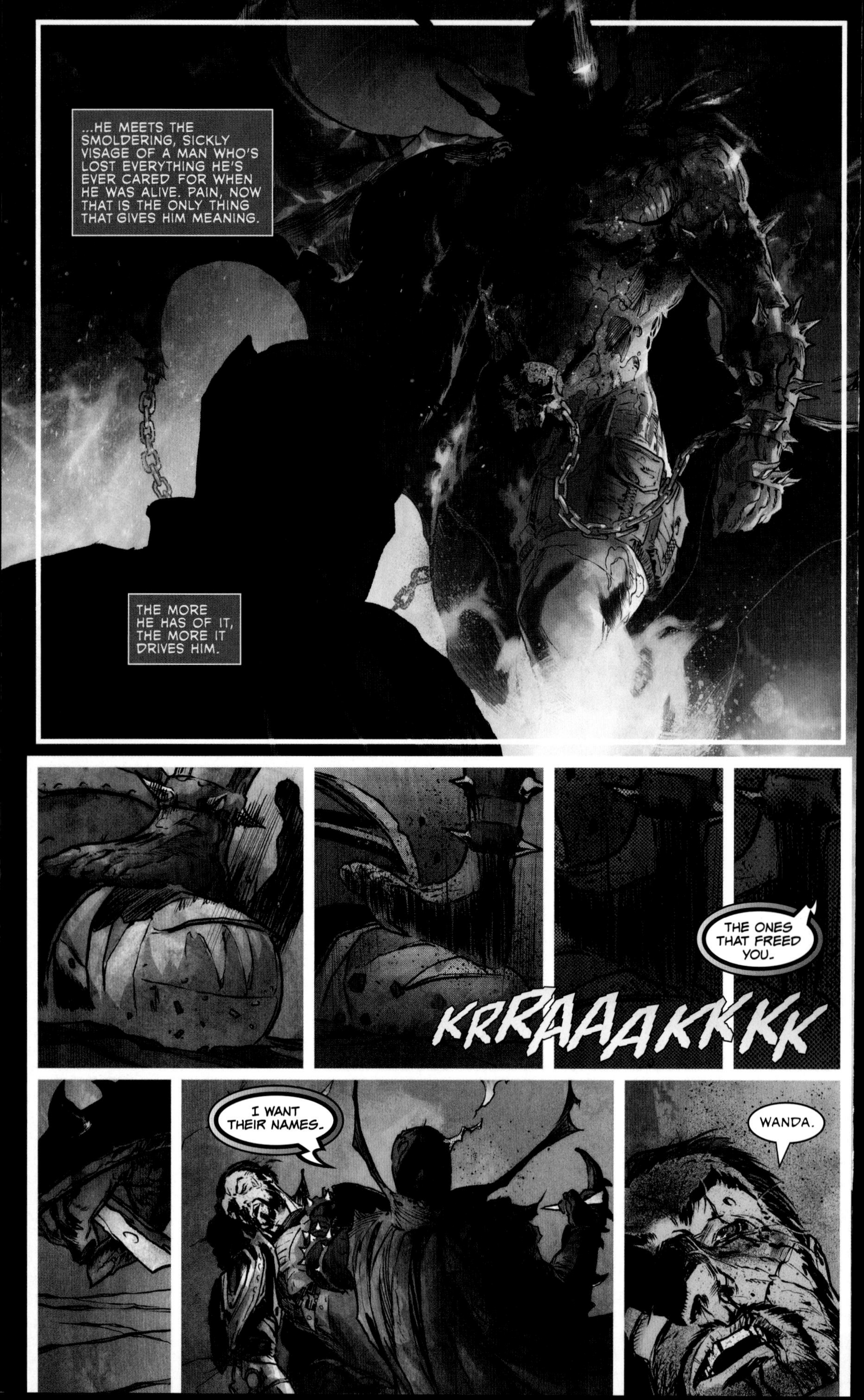
...HE MEETS THE SMOLDERING, SICKLY VISAGE OF A MAN WHO'S LOST EVERYTHING HE'S EVER CARED FOR WHEN HE WAS ALIVE. PAIN, NOW THAT IS THE ONLY THING THAT GIVES HIM MEANING.
THE MORE HE HAS OF IT, THE MORE IT DRIVES HIM.
THE ONES THAT FREED YOU.
KRKRAAAAKKKK
I WANT THEIR NAMES.
WANDA.

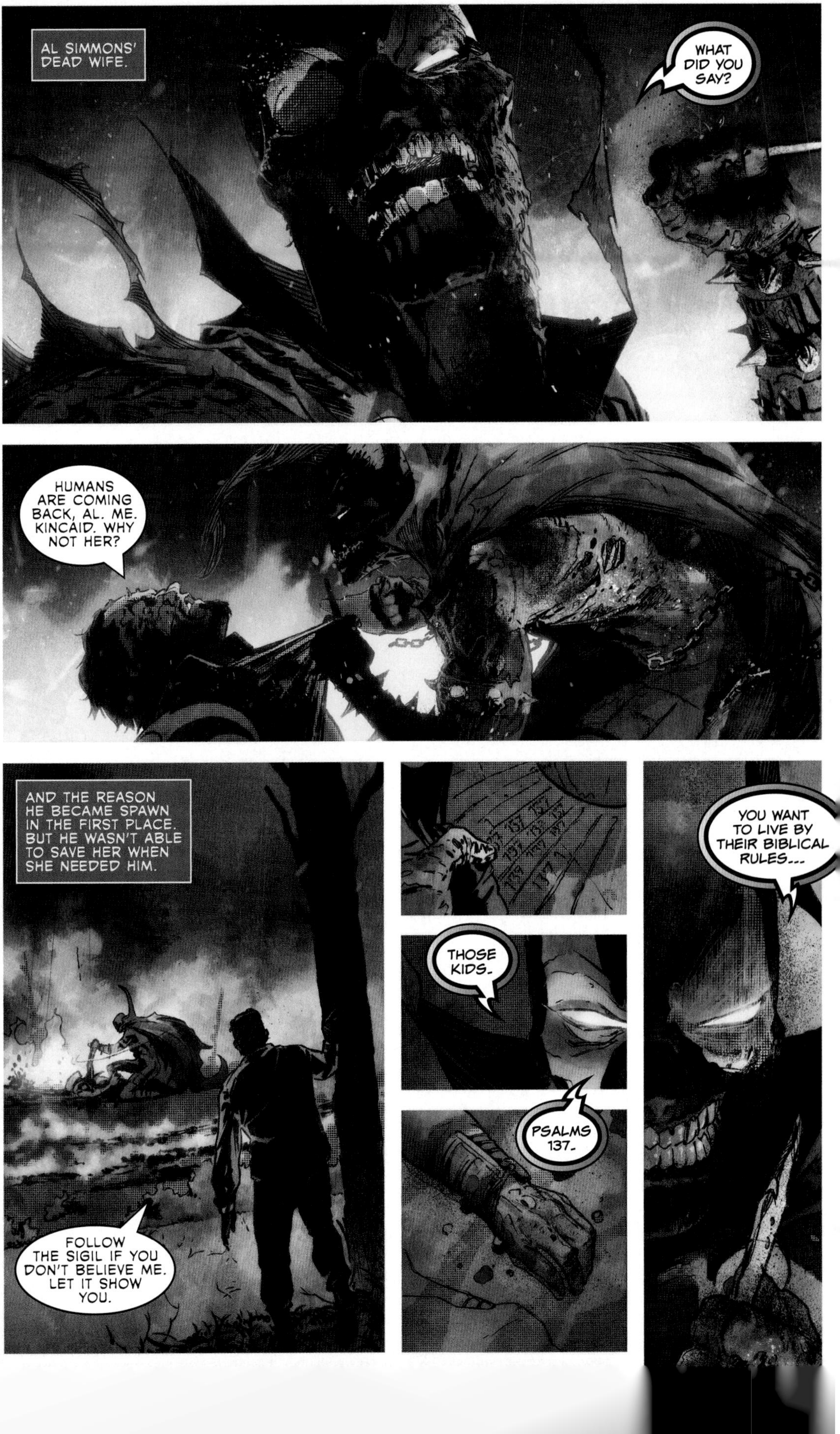
AL SIMMONS' DEAD WIFE.
WHAT DID YOU SAY?
HUMANS ARE COMING BACK, AL. ME. KINCAID. WHY NOT HER?
AND THE REASON HE BECAME SPAWN IN THE FIRST PLACE. BUT HE WASN'T ABLE TO SAVE HER WHEN SHE NEEDED HIM.
FOLLOW THE SIGIL IF YOU DON'T BELIEVE ME. LET IT SHOW YOU.
THOSE KIDS.
PSALMS 137.
YOU WANT TO LIVE BY THEIR BIBLICAL RULES...

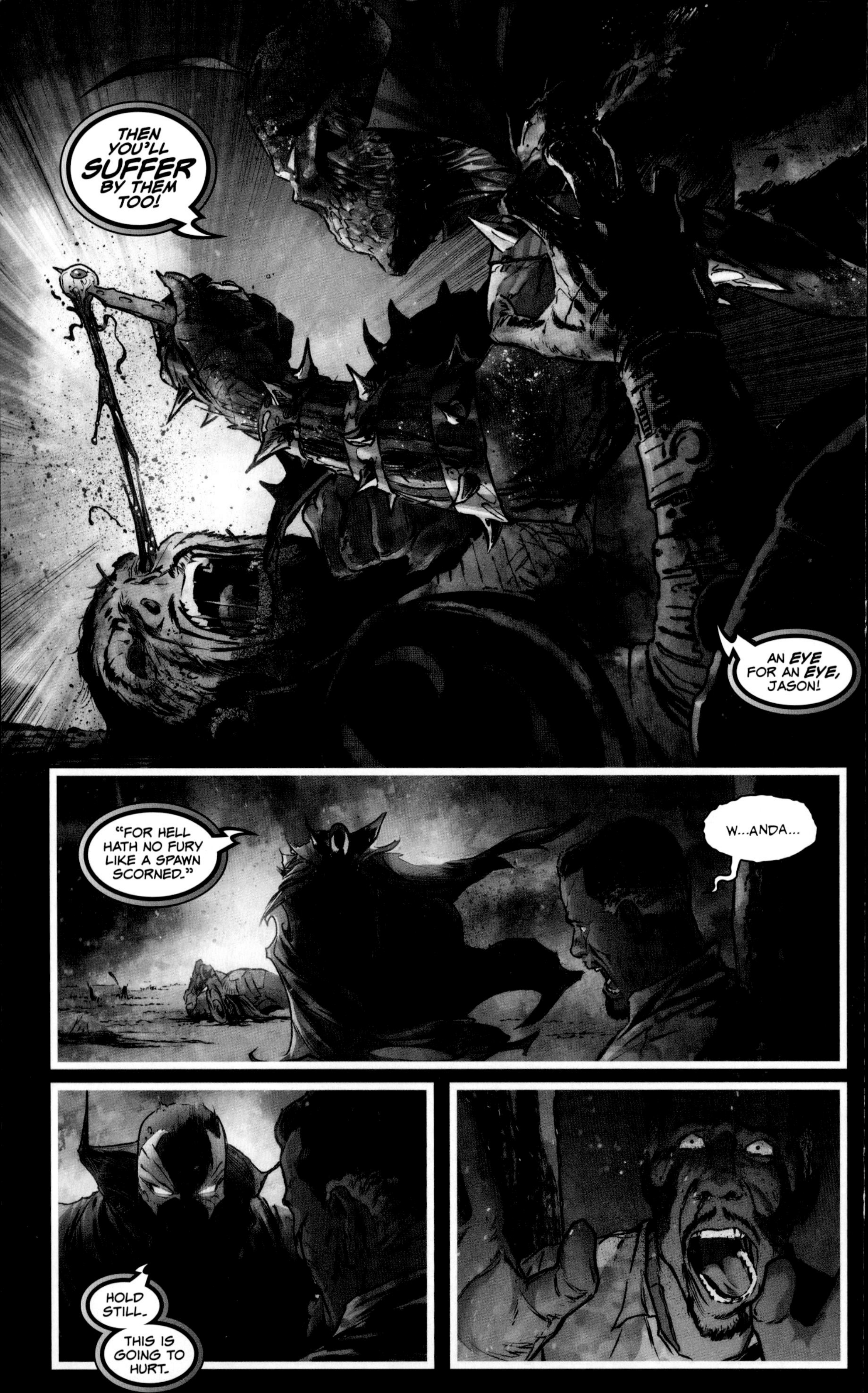
THEN YOU'LL SUFFER BY THEM TOO!
AN EYE FOR AN EYE, JASON!
"FOR HELL HATH NO FURY LIKE A SPAWN SCORNED."
W...ANDA...
HOLD STILL.
THIS IS GOING TO HURT.

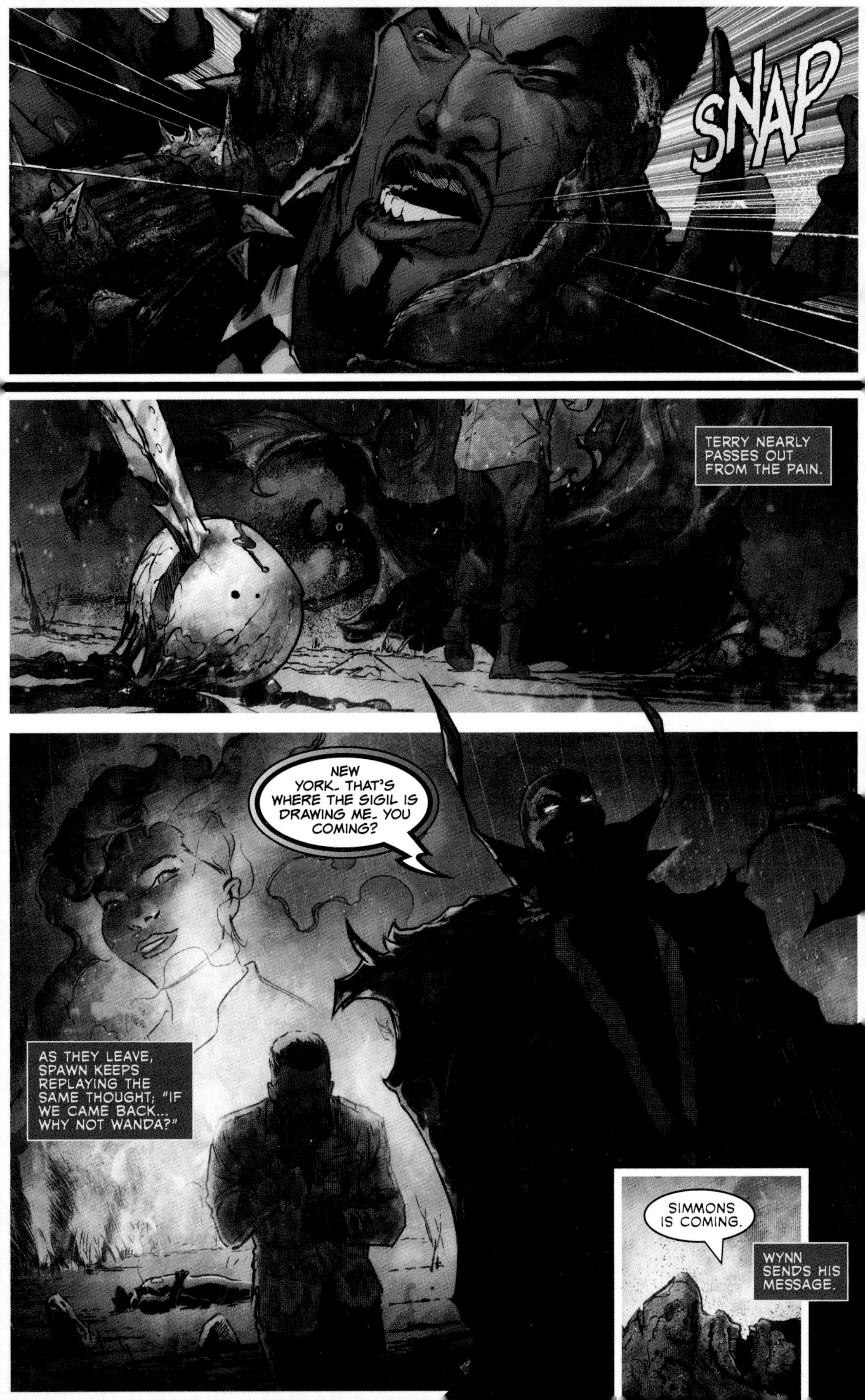
SNAP
TERRY NEARLY PASSES OUT FROM THE PAIN.
NEW YORK. THAT'S WHERE THE SIGIL IS DRAWING ME. YOU COMING?
AS THEY LEAVE, SPAWN KEEPS REPLAYING THE SAME THOUGHT; "IF WE CAME BACK... WHY NOT WANDA?"
SIMMONS IS COMING.
WYNN SENDS HIS MESSAGE.

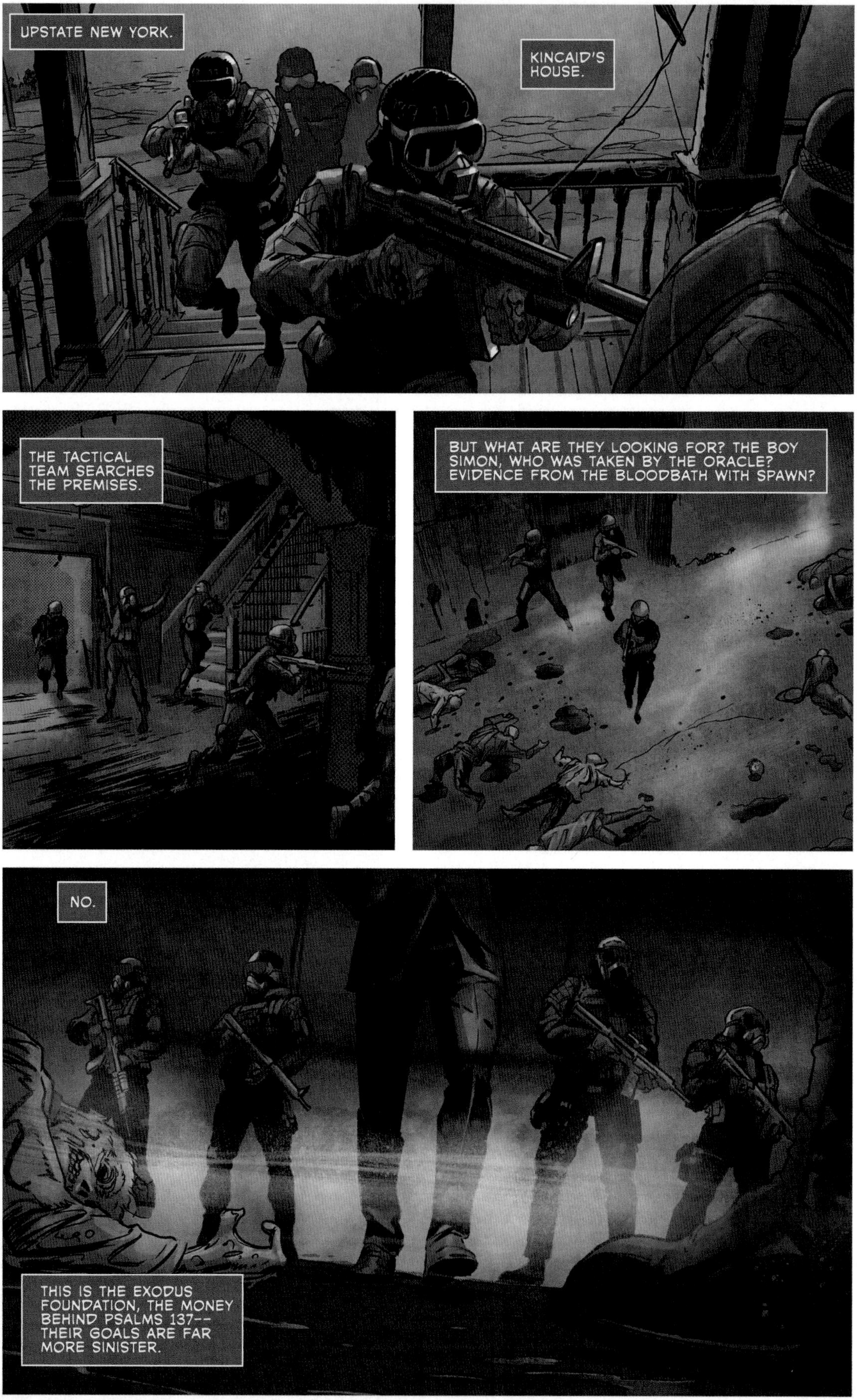
UPSTATE NEW YORK.
KINCAID'S HOUSE.
THE TACTICAL TEAM SEARCHES THE PREMISES.
BUT WHAT ARE THEY LOOKING FOR? THE BOY SIMON, WHO WAS TAKEN BY THE ORACLE? EVIDENCE FROM THE BLOODBATH WITH SPAWN?
NO.
THIS IS THE EXODUS FOUNDATION, THE MONEY BEHIND PSALMS 137-- THEIR GOALS ARE FAR MORE SINISTER.

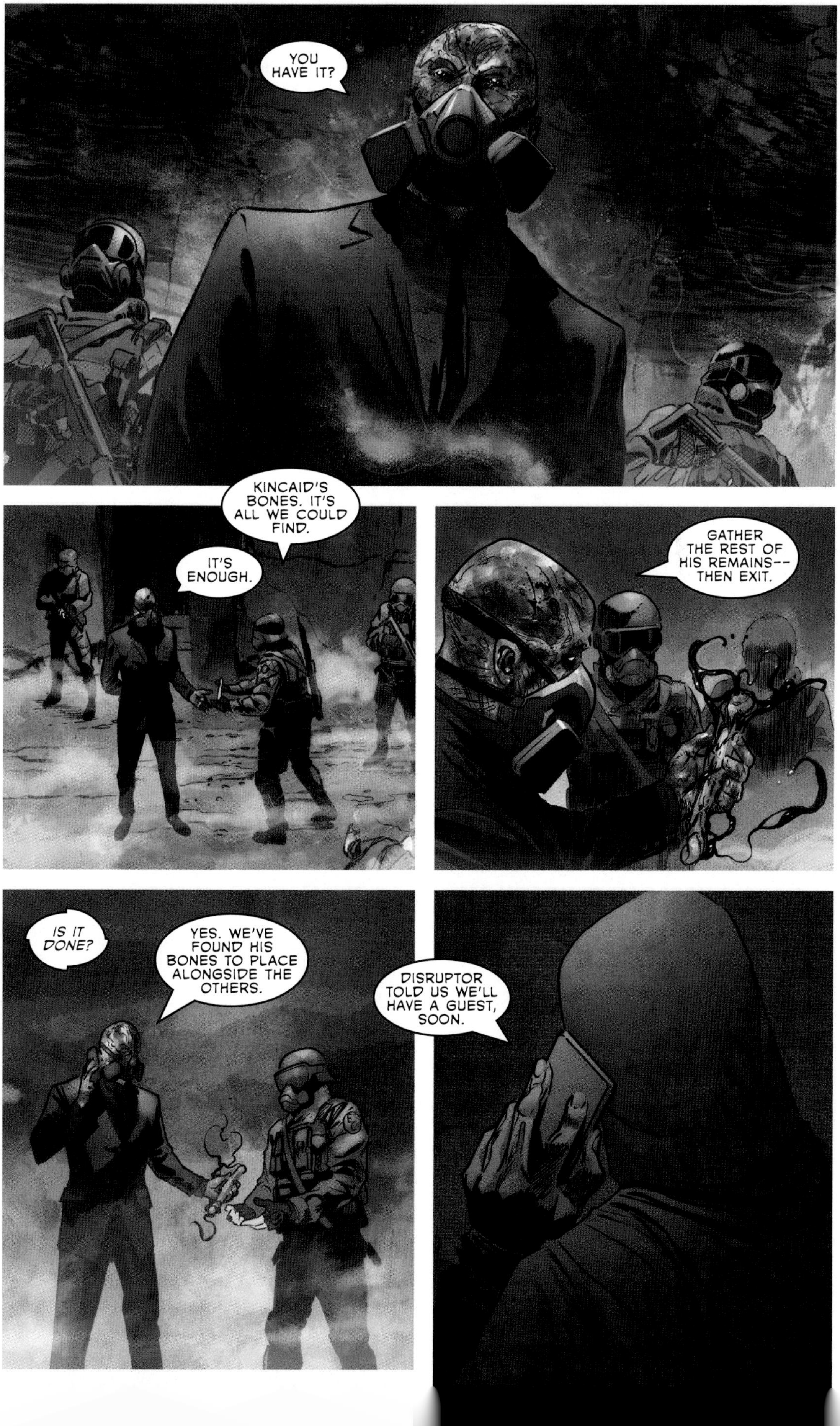
YOU HAVE IT?
KINCAID'S BONES. IT'S ALL WE COULD FIND.
IT'S ENOUGH.
GATHER THE REST OF HIS REMAINS-- THEN EXIT.
IS IT DONE?
YES. WE'VE FOUND HIS BONES TO PLACE ALONGSIDE THE OTHERS.
DISRUPTOR TOLD US WE'LL HAVE A GUEST, SOON.

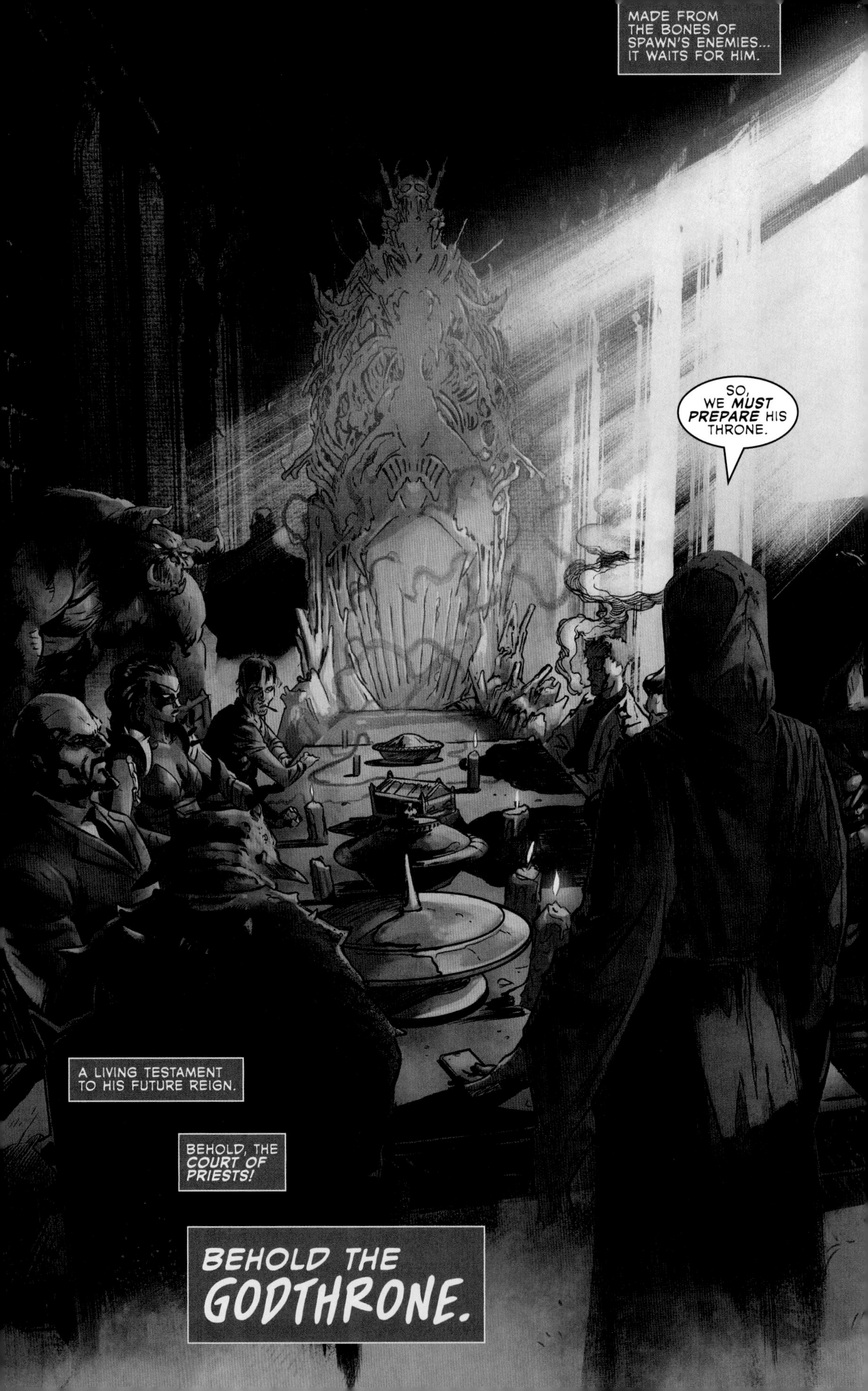
MADE FROM THE BONES OF SPAWN'S ENEMIES... IT WAITS FOR HIM.
SO, WE *MUST PREPARE* HIS THRONE.
A LIVING TESTAMENT TO HIS FUTURE REIGN.
BEHOLD, THE *COURT OF PRIESTS!*
BEHOLD THE GODTHRONE.

"Haunt"

* This story contined in the pages of **Spawn**

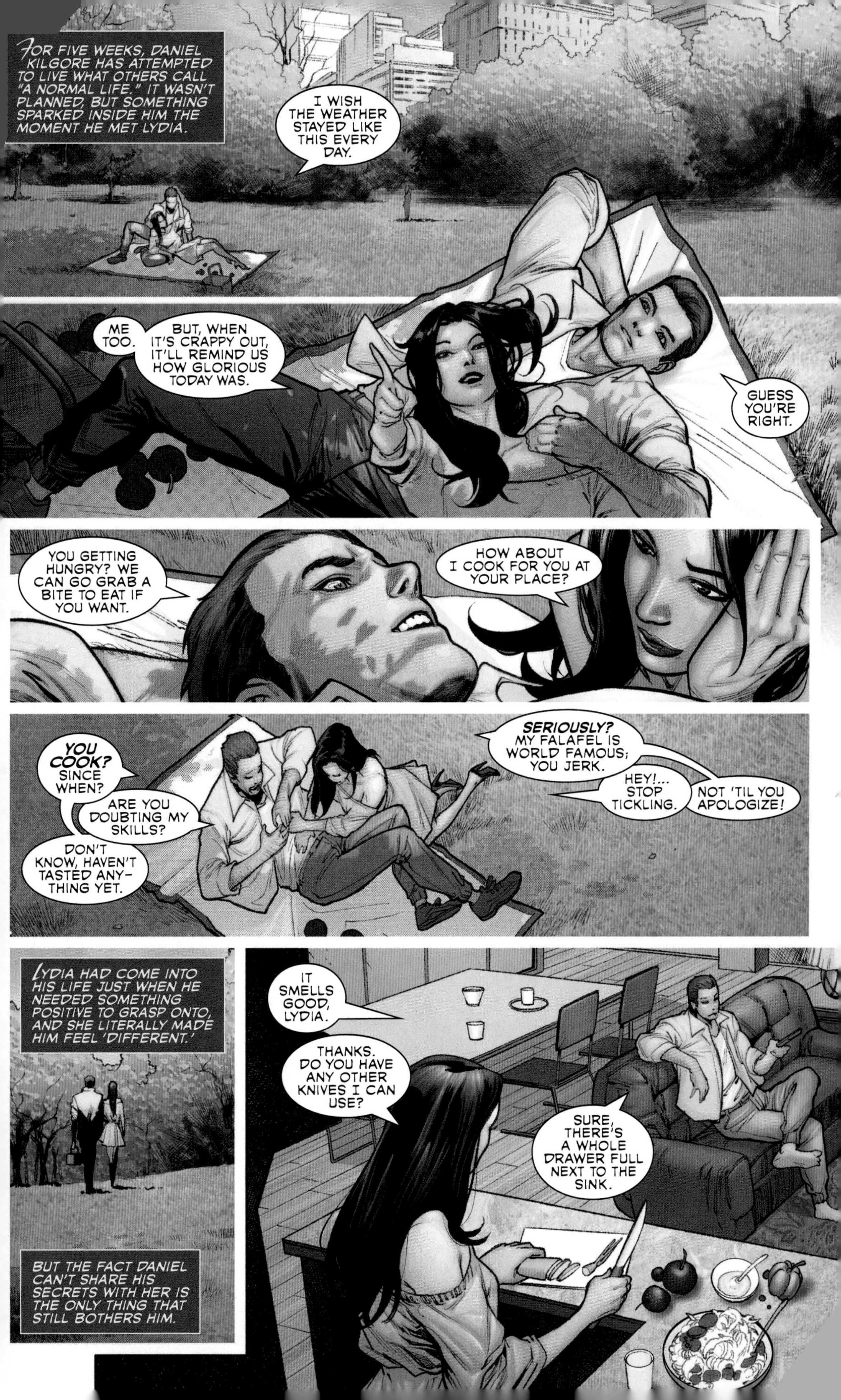

FOR FIVE WEEKS, DANIEL KILGORE HAS ATTEMPTED TO LIVE WHAT OTHERS CALL "A NORMAL LIFE." IT WASN'T PLANNED, BUT SOMETHING SPARKED INSIDE HIM THE MOMENT HE MET LYDIA.
I WISH THE WEATHER STAYED LIKE THIS EVERY DAY.
ME TOO.
BUT, WHEN IT'S CRAPPY OUT, IT'LL REMIND US HOW GLORIOUS TODAY WAS.
GUESS YOU'RE RIGHT.
YOU GETTING HUNGRY? WE CAN GO GRAB A BITE TO EAT IF YOU WANT.
HOW ABOUT I COOK FOR YOU AT YOUR PLACE?
YOU COOK? SINCE WHEN?
ARE YOU DOUBTING MY SKILLS?
DON'T KNOW, HAVEN'T TASTED ANY-THING YET.
SERIOUSLY? MY FALAFEL IS WORLD FAMOUS, YOU JERK.
HEY!... STOP TICKLING.
NOT 'TIL YOU APOLOGIZE!
LYDIA HAD COME INTO HIS LIFE JUST WHEN HE NEEDED SOMETHING POSITIVE TO GRASP ONTO, AND SHE LITERALLY MADE HIM FEEL 'DIFFERENT.'
BUT THE FACT DANIEL CAN'T SHARE HIS SECRETS WITH HER IS THE ONLY THING THAT STILL BOTHERS HIM.
IT SMELLS GOOD, LYDIA.
THANKS. DO YOU HAVE ANY OTHER KNIVES I CAN USE?
SURE, THERE'S A WHOLE DRAWER FULL NEXT TO THE SINK.

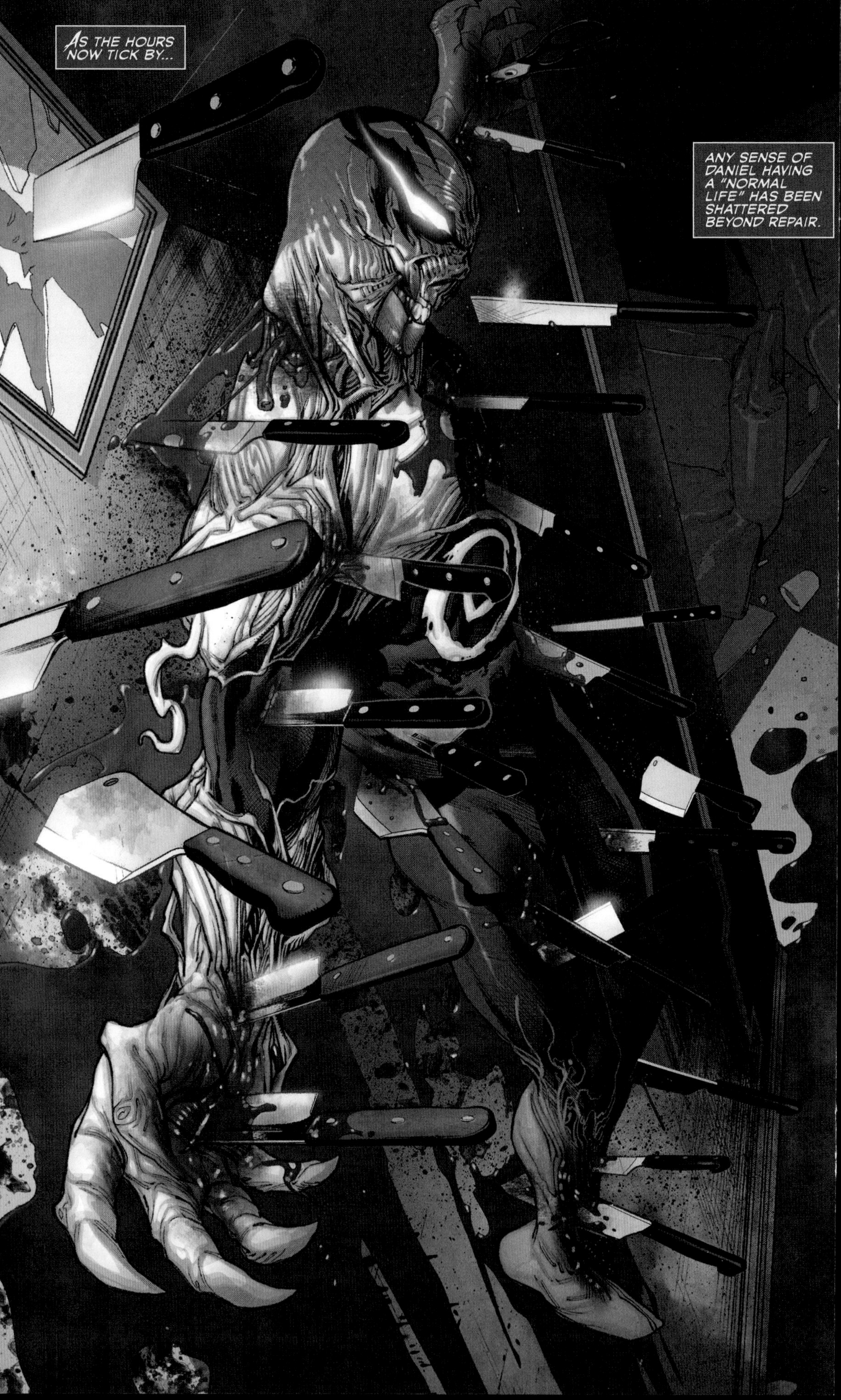
AS THE HOURS NOW TICK BY...
ANY SENSE OF DANIEL HAVING A "NORMAL LIFE" HAS BEEN SHATTERED BEYOND REPAIR.

IN THE BACK OF HIS MIND A VOICE WAS TELLING HIM, "THIS IS ALL TOO GOOD TO BE TRUE." BUT HE WAS SO DESPERATE TO CLING TO ANY NORMALCY, HE IGNORED THOSE INSTINCTS.

IDIOT.

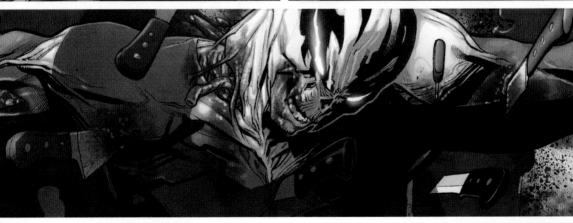

shup

THEY KNEW YOU'D FALL INTO THEIR TRAP.

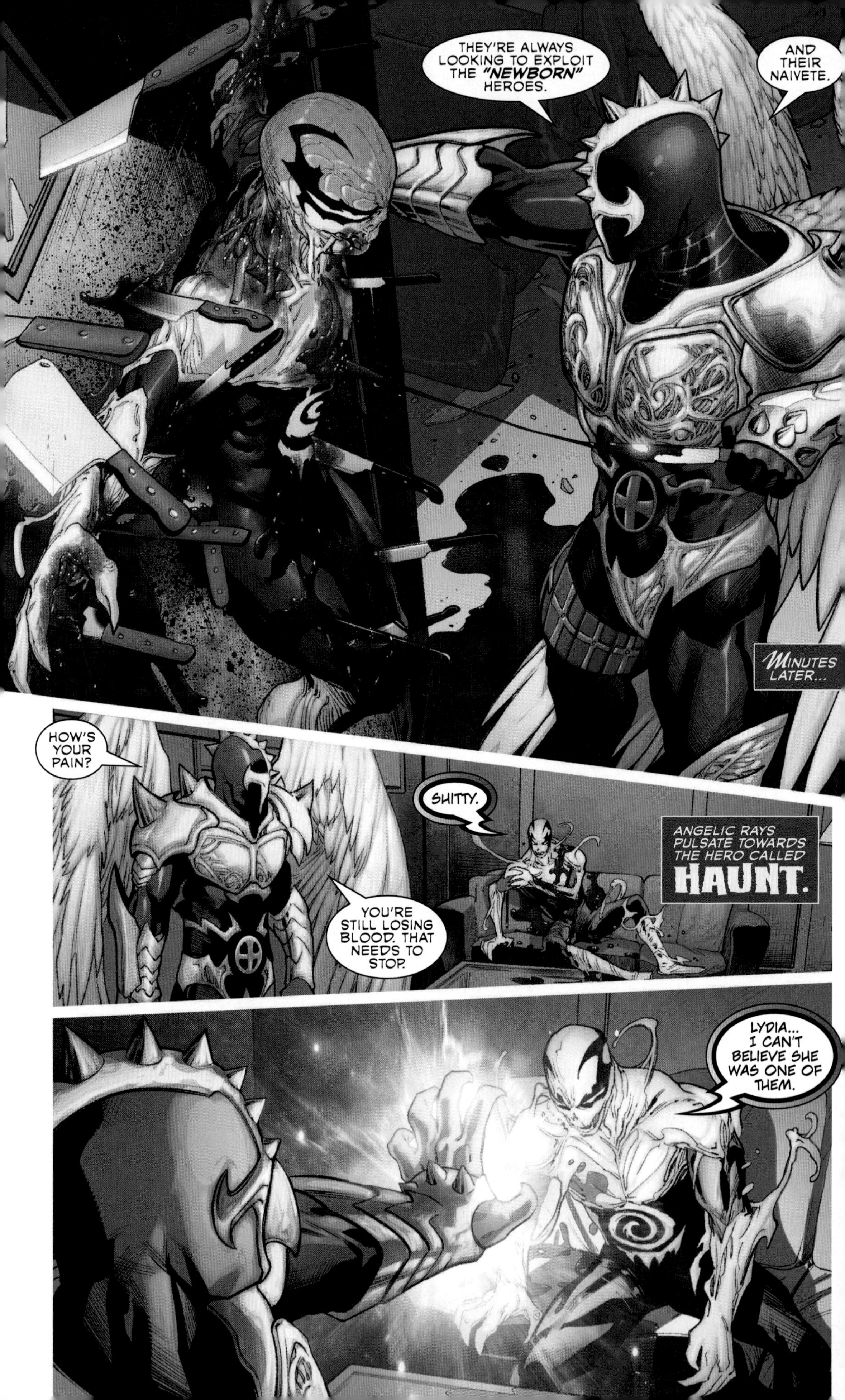
THEY'RE ALWAYS LOOKING TO EXPLOIT THE "NEWBORN" HEROES.
AND THEIR NAIVETE.
MINUTES LATER...
HOW'S YOUR PAIN?
SHITTY.
ANGELIC RAYS PULSATE TOWARDS THE HERO CALLED HAUNT.
YOU'RE STILL LOSING BLOOD. THAT NEEDS TO STOP.
LYDIA... I CAN'T BELIEVE SHE WAS ONE OF THEM.

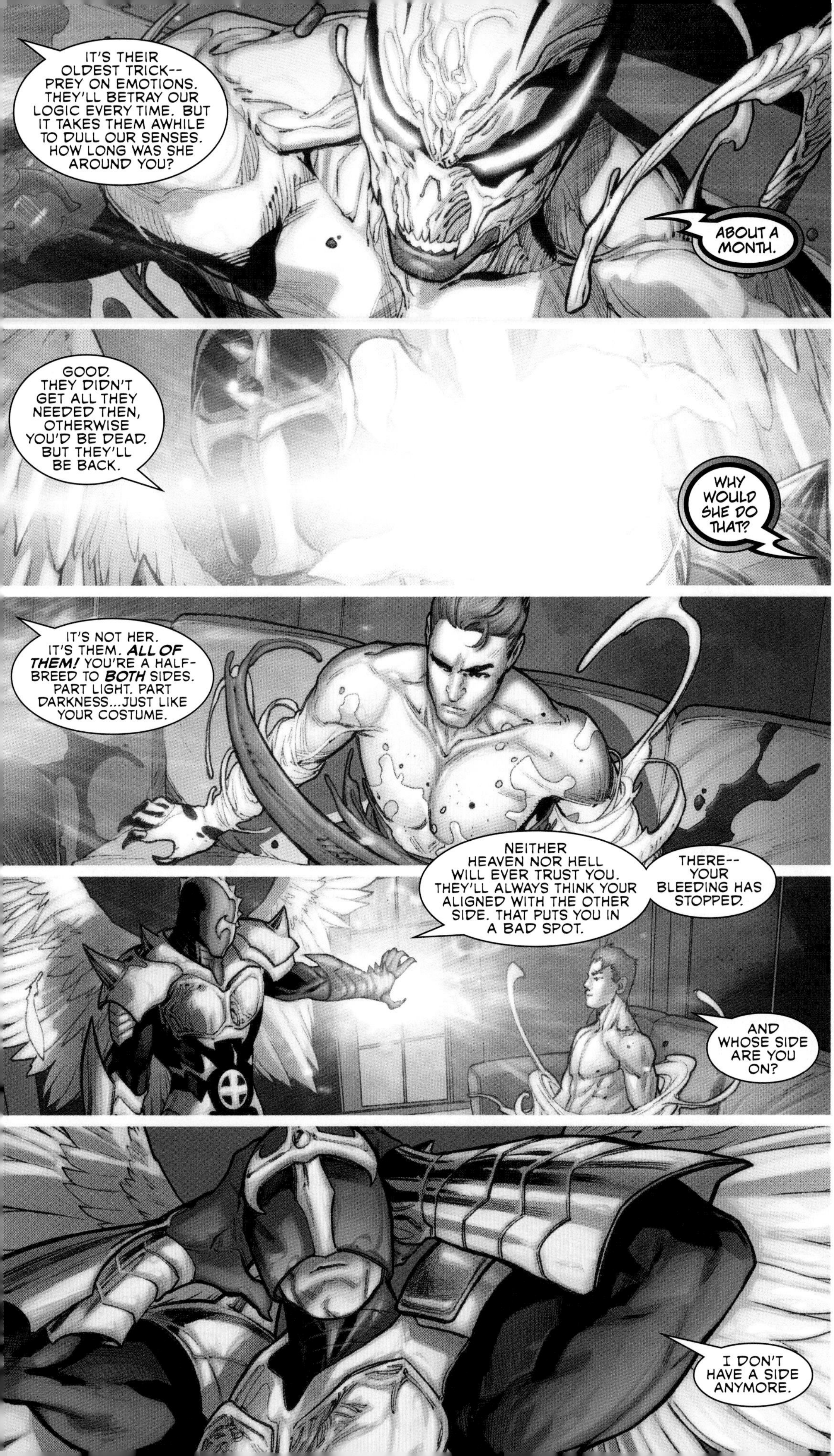
IT'S THEIR OLDEST TRICK-- PREY ON EMOTIONS. THEY'LL BETRAY OUR LOGIC EVERY TIME. BUT IT TAKES THEM AWHILE TO DULL OUR SENSES. HOW LONG WAS SHE AROUND YOU?
ABOUT A MONTH.
GOOD. THEY DIDN'T GET ALL THEY NEEDED THEN, OTHERWISE YOU'D BE DEAD. BUT THEY'LL BE BACK.
WHY WOULD SHE DO THAT?
IT'S NOT HER. IT'S THEM. ***ALL OF THEM!*** YOU'RE A HALF-BREED TO ***BOTH*** SIDES. PART LIGHT. PART DARKNESS...JUST LIKE YOUR COSTUME.
NEITHER HEAVEN NOR HELL WILL EVER TRUST YOU. THEY'LL ALWAYS THINK YOUR ALIGNED WITH THE OTHER SIDE. THAT PUTS YOU IN A BAD SPOT.
THERE-- YOUR BLEEDING HAS STOPPED.
AND WHOSE SIDE ARE YOU ON?
I DON'T HAVE A SIDE ANYMORE.

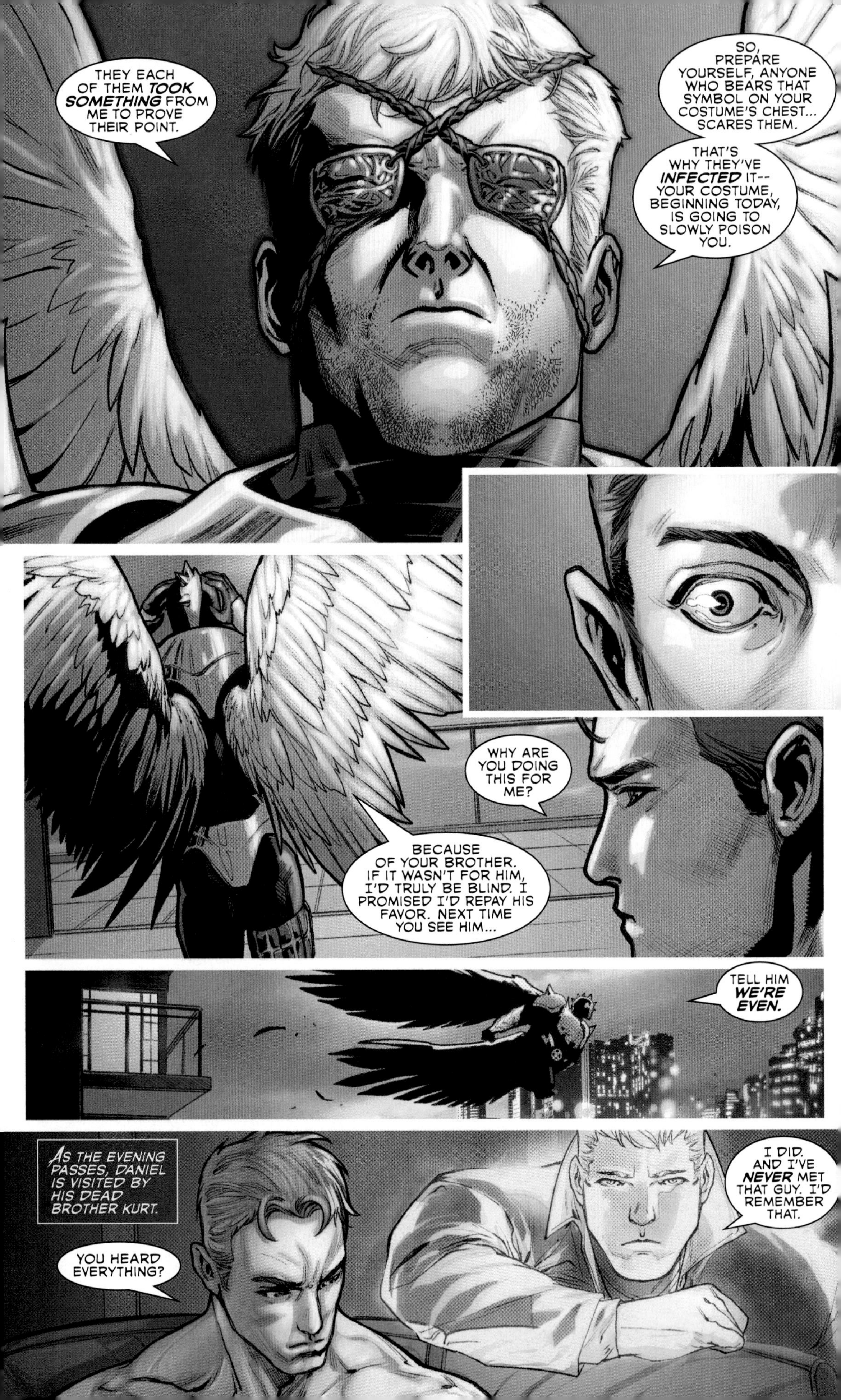

THEY EACH OF THEM TOOK SOMETHING FROM ME TO PROVE THEIR POINT.
SO, PREPARE YOURSELF, ANYONE WHO BEARS THAT SYMBOL ON YOUR COSTUME'S CHEST... SCARES THEM.
THAT'S WHY THEY'VE INFECTED IT-- YOUR COSTUME, BEGINNING TODAY, IS GOING TO SLOWLY POISON YOU.
WHY ARE YOU DOING THIS FOR ME?
BECAUSE OF YOUR BROTHER. IF IT WASN'T FOR HIM, I'D TRULY BE BLIND. I PROMISED I'D REPAY HIS FAVOR. NEXT TIME YOU SEE HIM...
TELL HIM WE'RE EVEN.
AS THE EVENING PASSES, DANIEL IS VISITED BY HIS DEAD BROTHER KURT.
YOU HEARD EVERYTHING?
I DID. AND I'VE NEVER MET THAT GUY. I'D REMEMBER THAT.

"Nightmare"

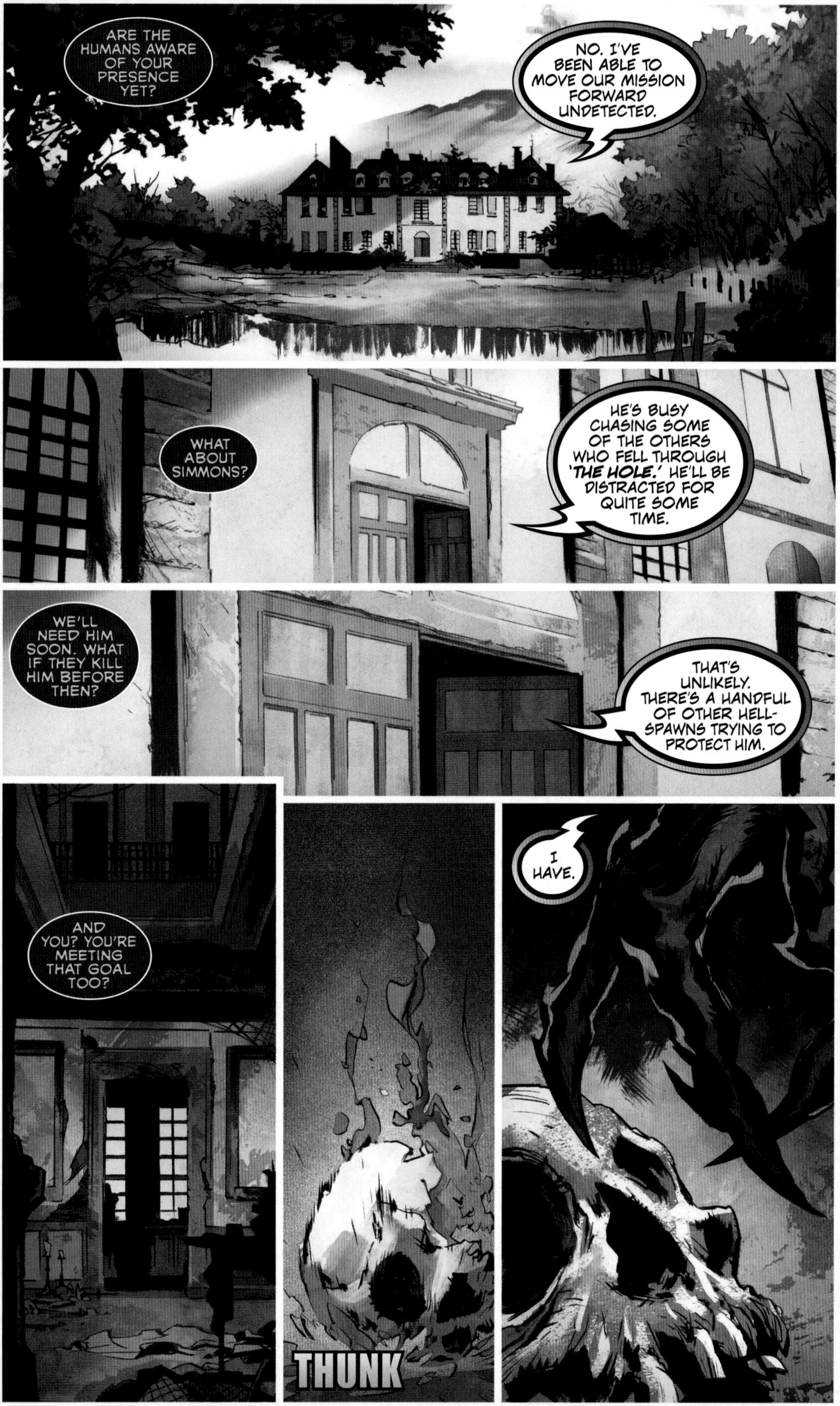
ARE THE HUMANS AWARE OF YOUR PRESENCE YET?
NO. I'VE BEEN ABLE TO MOVE OUR MISSION FORWARD UNDETECTED.
WHAT ABOUT SIMMONS?
HE'S BUSY CHASING SOME OF THE OTHERS WHO FELL THROUGH 'THE HOLE.' HE'LL BE DISTRACTED FOR QUITE SOME TIME.
WE'LL NEED HIM SOON. WHAT IF THEY KILL HIM BEFORE THEN?
THAT'S UNLIKELY. THERE'S A HANDFUL OF OTHER HELL-SPAWNS TRYING TO PROTECT HIM.
AND YOU? YOU'RE MEETING THAT GOAL TOO?
THUNK
I HAVE.

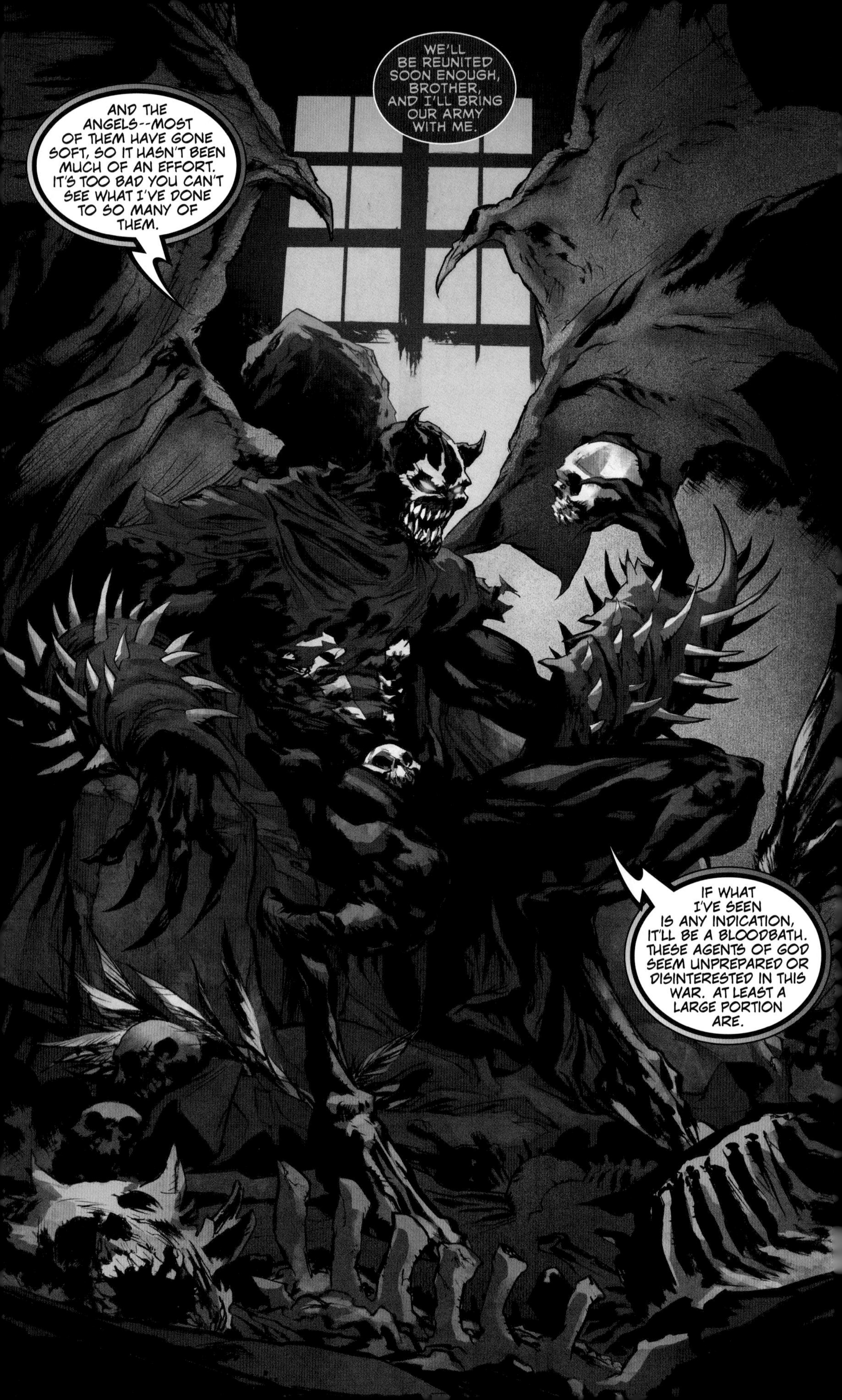
AND THE ANGELS--MOST OF THEM HAVE GONE SOFT, SO IT HASN'T BEEN MUCH OF AN EFFORT. IT'S TOO BAD YOU CAN'T SEE WHAT I'VE DONE TO SO MANY OF THEM.
WE'LL BE REUNITED SOON ENOUGH, BROTHER, AND I'LL BRING OUR ARMY WITH ME.
IF WHAT I'VE SEEN IS ANY INDICATION, IT'LL BE A BLOODBATH. THESE AGENTS OF GOD SEEM UNPREPARED OR DISINTERESTED IN THIS WAR. AT LEAST A LARGE PORTION ARE.

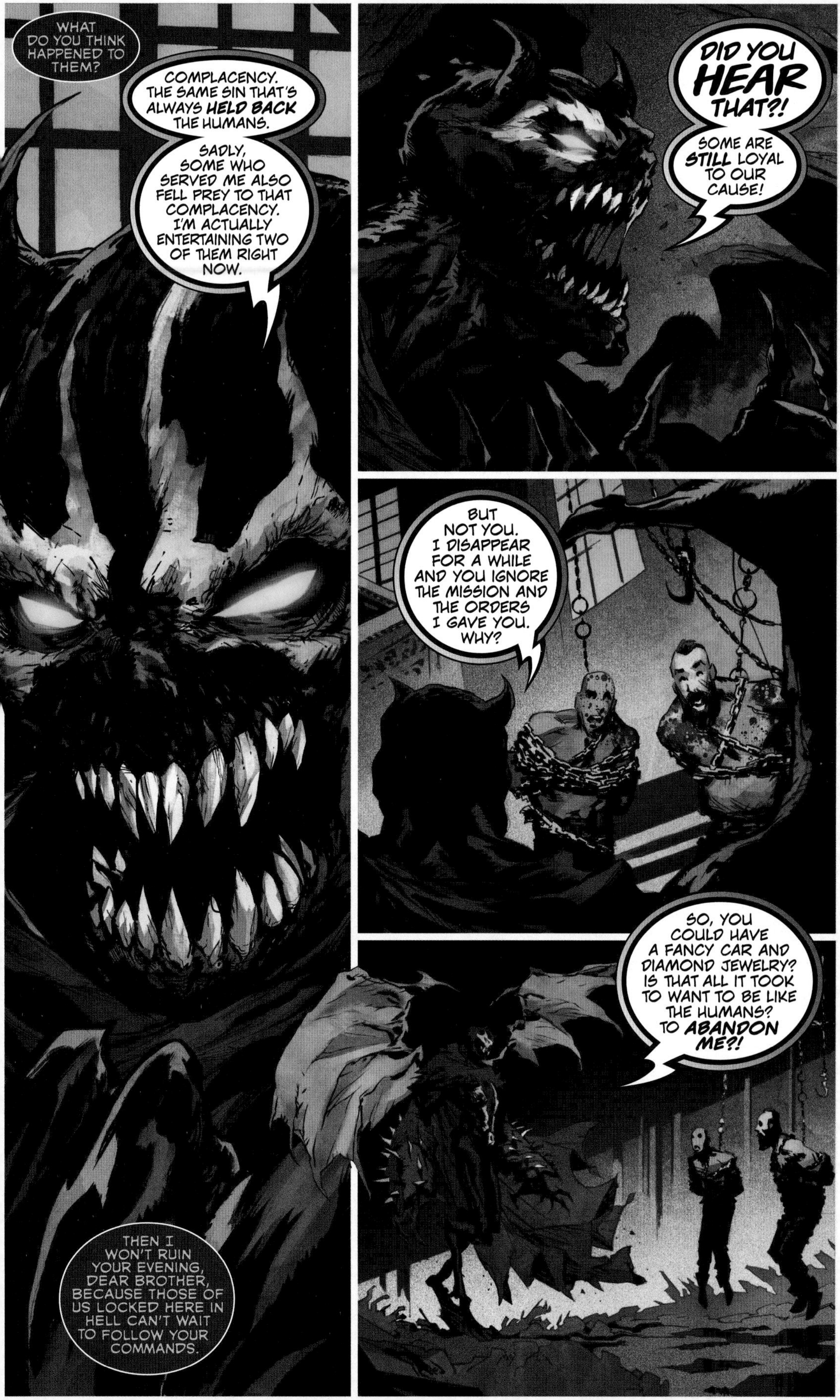
WHAT DO YOU THINK HAPPENED TO THEM?
COMPLACENCY. THE SAME SIN THAT'S ALWAYS HELD BACK THE HUMANS.
SADLY, SOME WHO SERVED ME ALSO FELL PREY TO THAT COMPLACENCY. I'M ACTUALLY ENTERTAINING TWO OF THEM RIGHT NOW.
THEN I WON'T RUIN YOUR EVENING, DEAR BROTHER, BECAUSE THOSE OF US LOCKED HERE IN HELL CAN'T WAIT TO FOLLOW YOUR COMMANDS.
DID YOU HEAR THAT?!
SOME ARE STILL LOYAL TO OUR CAUSE!
BUT NOT YOU. I DISAPPEAR FOR A WHILE AND YOU IGNORE THE MISSION AND THE ORDERS I GAVE YOU. WHY?
SO, YOU COULD HAVE A FANCY CAR AND DIAMOND JEWELRY? IS THAT ALL IT TOOK TO WANT TO BE LIKE THE HUMANS? TO ABANDON ME?!

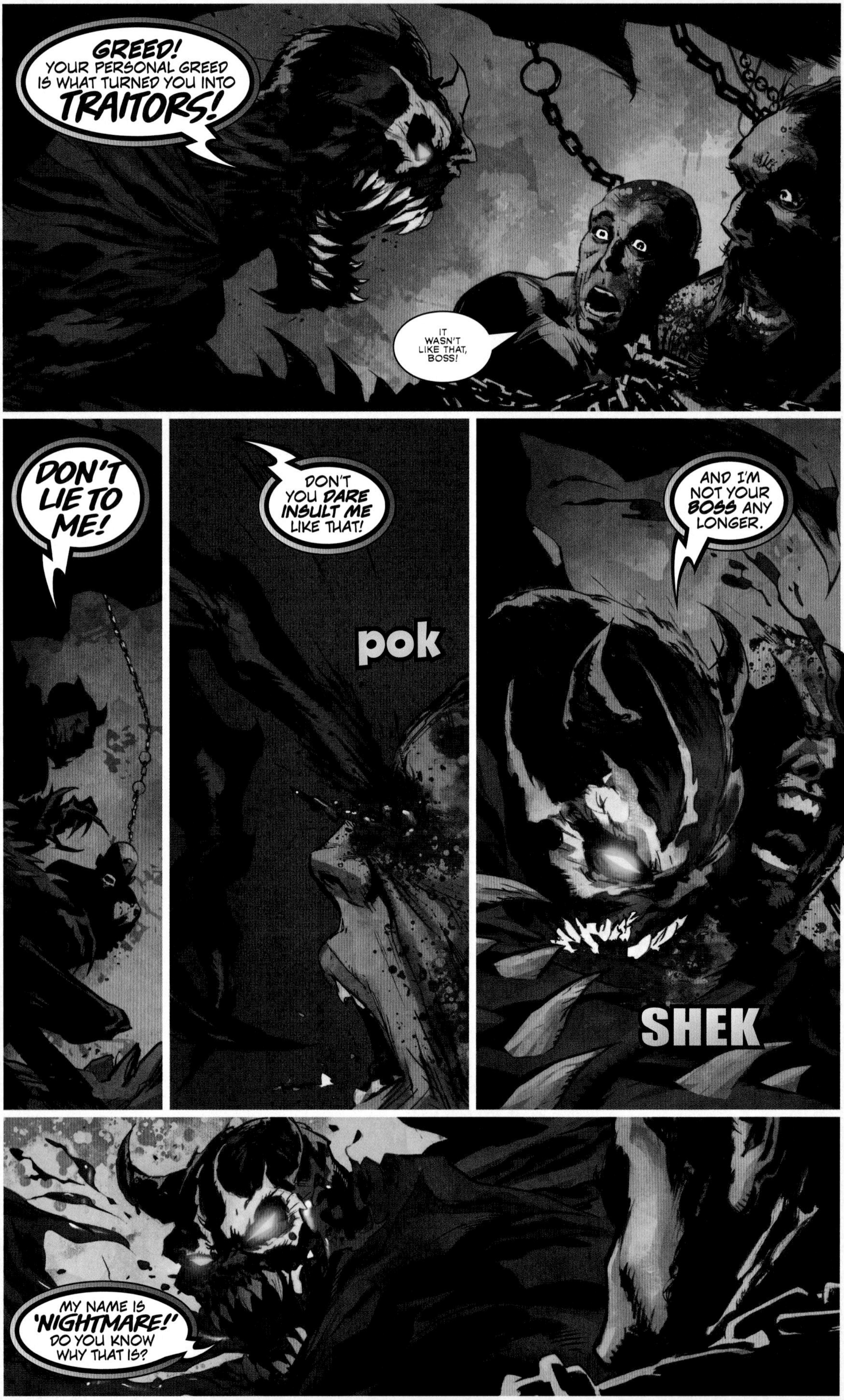
GREED! YOUR PERSONAL GREED IS WHAT TURNED YOU INTO TRAITORS!
IT WASN'T LIKE THAT, BOSS!
DON'T LIE TO ME!
DON'T YOU DARE INSULT ME LIKE THAT!
pok
AND I'M NOT YOUR BOSS ANY LONGER.
SHEK
MY NAME IS 'NIGHTMARE!' DO YOU KNOW WHY THAT IS?

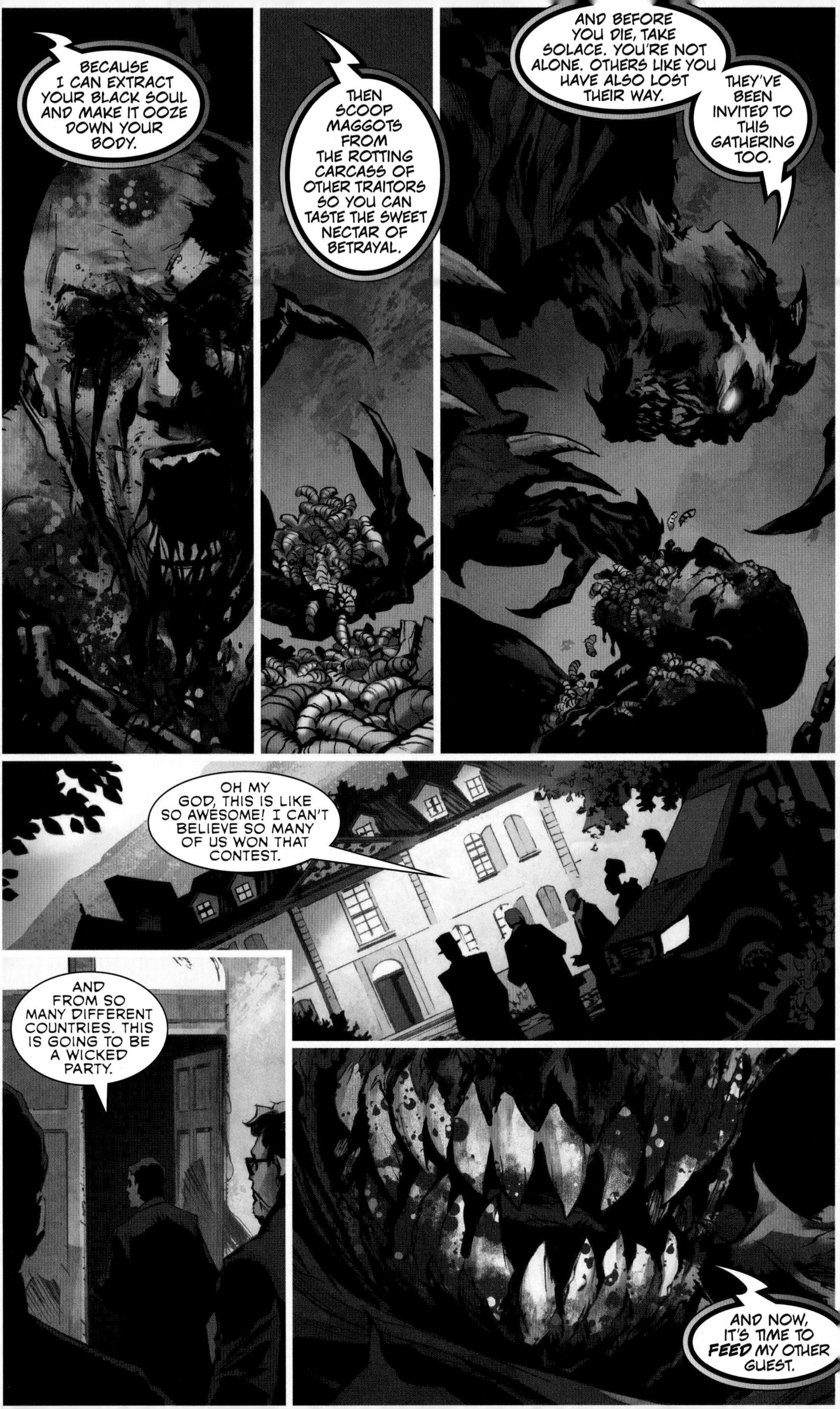

BECAUSE I CAN EXTRACT YOUR BLACK SOUL AND MAKE IT OOZE DOWN YOUR BODY.
THEN SCOOP MAGGOTS FROM THE ROTTING CARCASS OF OTHER TRAITORS SO YOU CAN TASTE THE SWEET NECTAR OF BETRAYAL.
AND BEFORE YOU DIE, TAKE SOLACE. YOU'RE NOT ALONE. OTHERS LIKE YOU HAVE ALSO LOST THEIR WAY.
THEY'VE BEEN INVITED TO THIS GATHERING TOO.
OH MY GOD, THIS IS LIKE SO AWESOME! I CAN'T BELIEVE SO MANY OF US WON THAT CONTEST.
AND FROM SO MANY DIFFERENT COUNTRIES. THIS IS GOING TO BE A WICKED PARTY.
AND NOW, IT'S TIME TO **FEED** MY OTHER GUEST.

"The Hero"

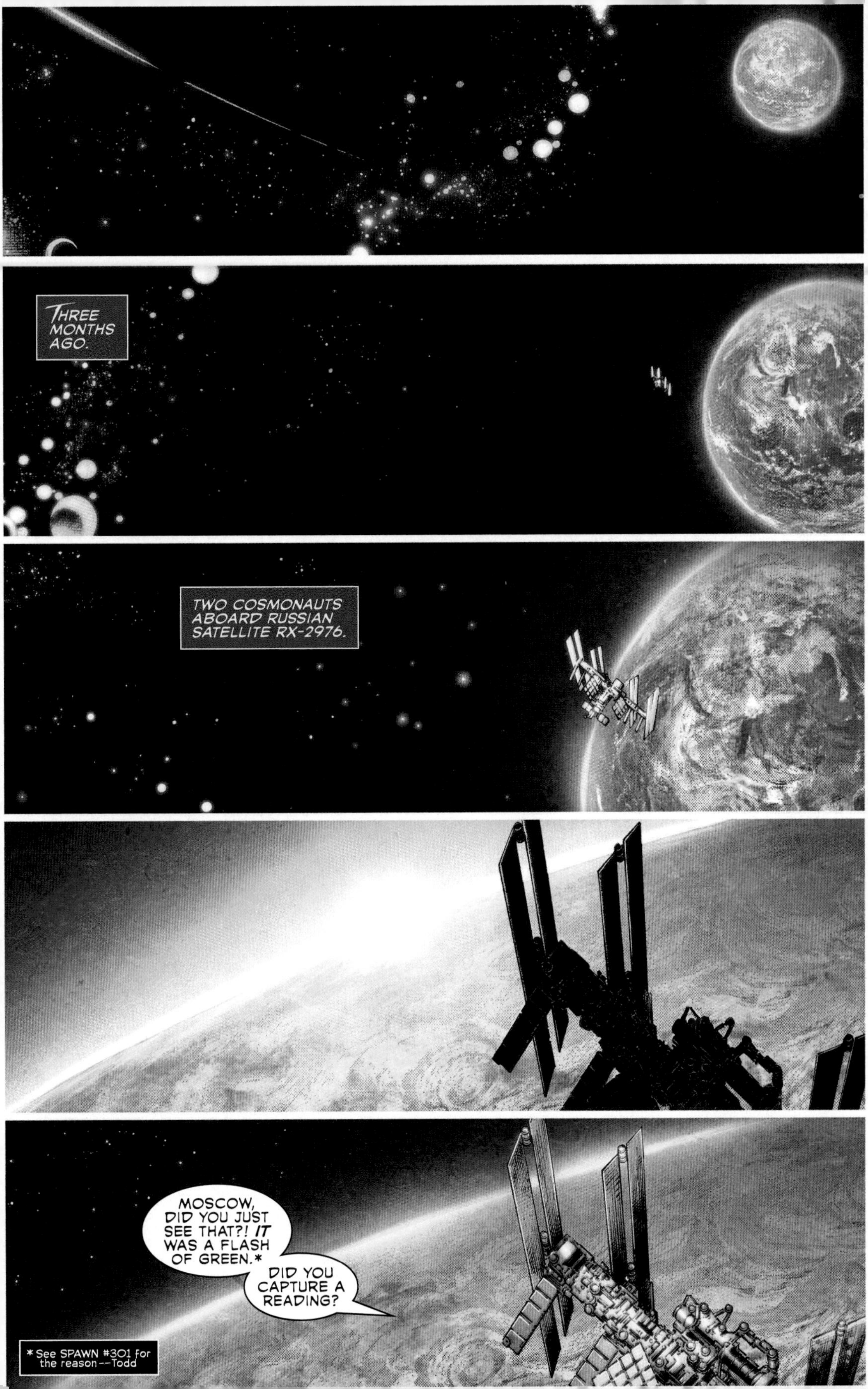
THREE MONTHS AGO.
TWO COSMONAUTS ABOARD RUSSIAN SATELLITE RX-2976.
MOSCOW, DID YOU JUST SEE THAT?! IT WAS A FLASH OF GREEN.*
DID YOU CAPTURE A READING?
* See SPAWN #301 for the reason--Todd

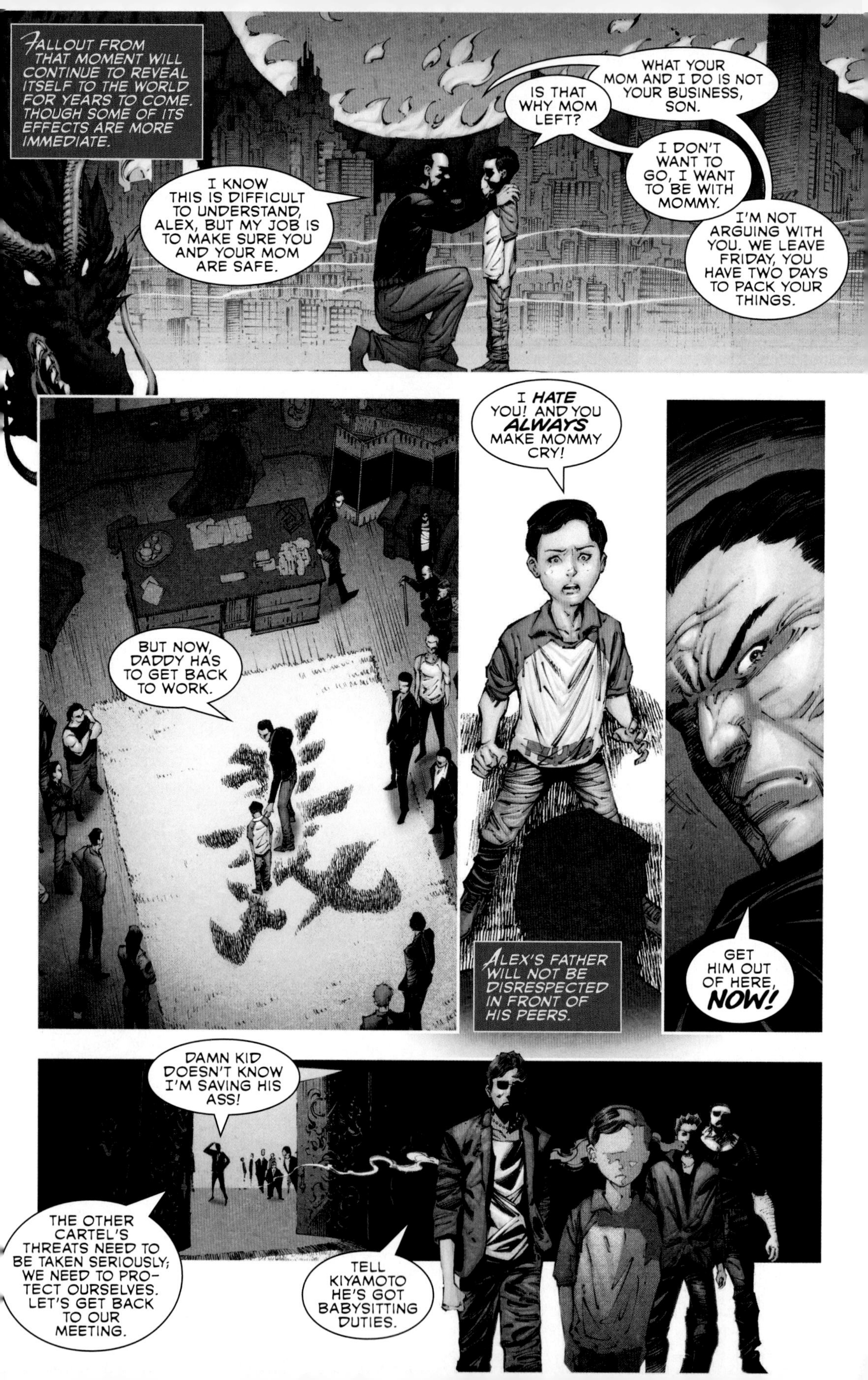
FALLOUT FROM THAT MOMENT WILL CONTINUE TO REVEAL ITSELF TO THE WORLD FOR YEARS TO COME. THOUGH SOME OF ITS EFFECTS ARE MORE IMMEDIATE.
I KNOW THIS IS DIFFICULT TO UNDERSTAND, ALEX, BUT MY JOB IS TO MAKE SURE YOU AND YOUR MOM ARE SAFE.
IS THAT WHY MOM LEFT?
WHAT YOUR MOM AND I DO IS NOT YOUR BUSINESS, SON.
I DON'T WANT TO GO, I WANT TO BE WITH MOMMY.
I'M NOT ARGUING WITH YOU. WE LEAVE FRIDAY, YOU HAVE TWO DAYS TO PACK YOUR THINGS.
BUT NOW, DADDY HAS TO GET BACK TO WORK.
I HATE YOU! AND YOU ALWAYS MAKE MOMMY CRY!
ALEX'S FATHER WILL NOT BE DISRESPECTED IN FRONT OF HIS PEERS.
GET HIM OUT OF HERE, NOW!
DAMN KID DOESN'T KNOW I'M SAVING HIS ASS!
THE OTHER CARTEL'S THREATS NEED TO BE TAKEN SERIOUSLY; WE NEED TO PROTECT OURSELVES. LET'S GET BACK TO OUR MEETING.
TELL KIYAMOTO HE'S GOT BABYSITTING DUTIES.

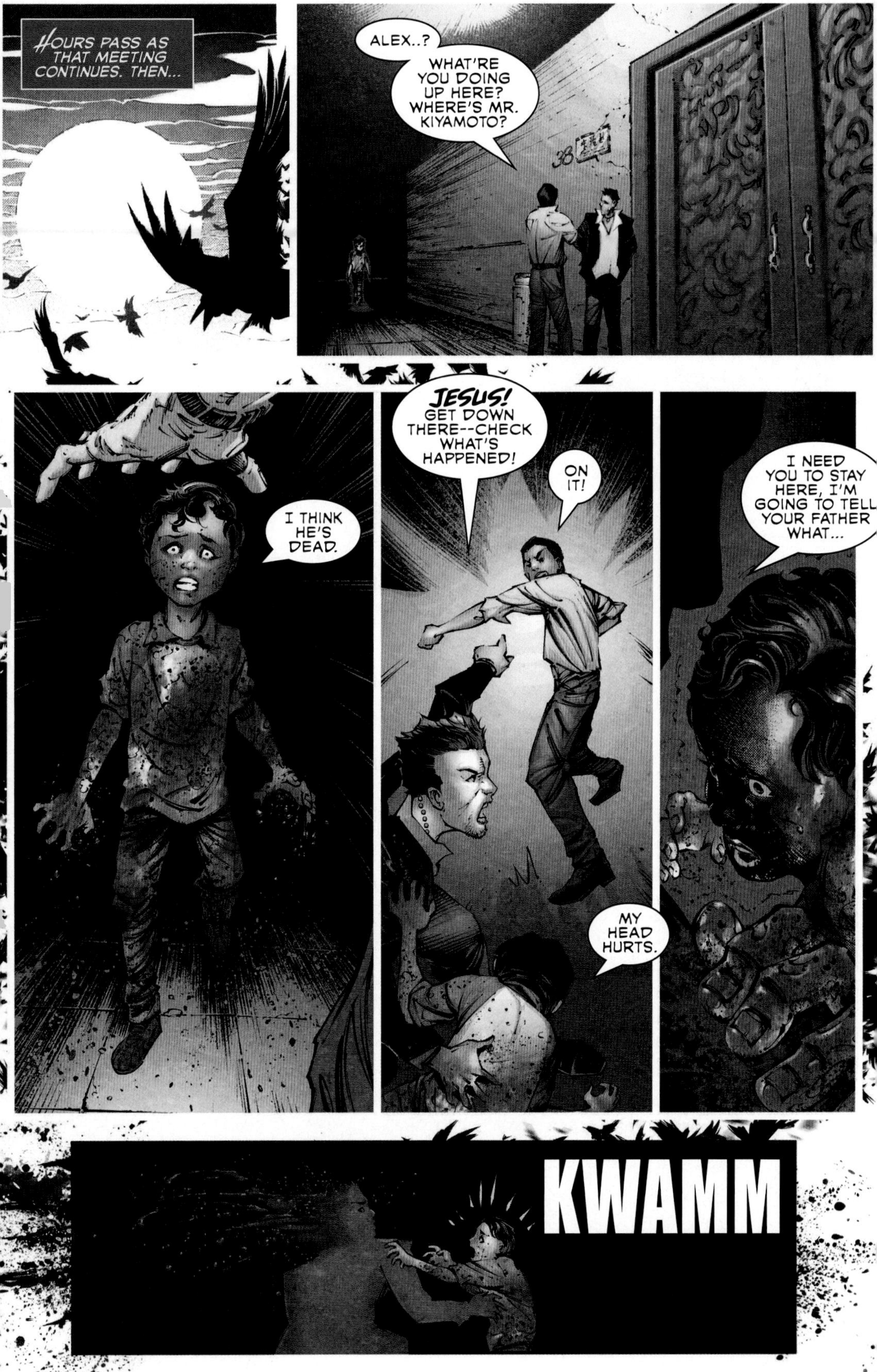
HOURS PASS AS THAT MEETING CONTINUES. THEN...
ALEX..?
WHAT'RE YOU DOING UP HERE? WHERE'S MR. KIYAMOTO?
I THINK HE'S DEAD.
JESUS! GET DOWN THERE--CHECK WHAT'S HAPPENED!
ON IT!
MY HEAD HURTS.
I NEED YOU TO STAY HERE, I'M GOING TO TELL YOUR FATHER WHAT...
KWAMM

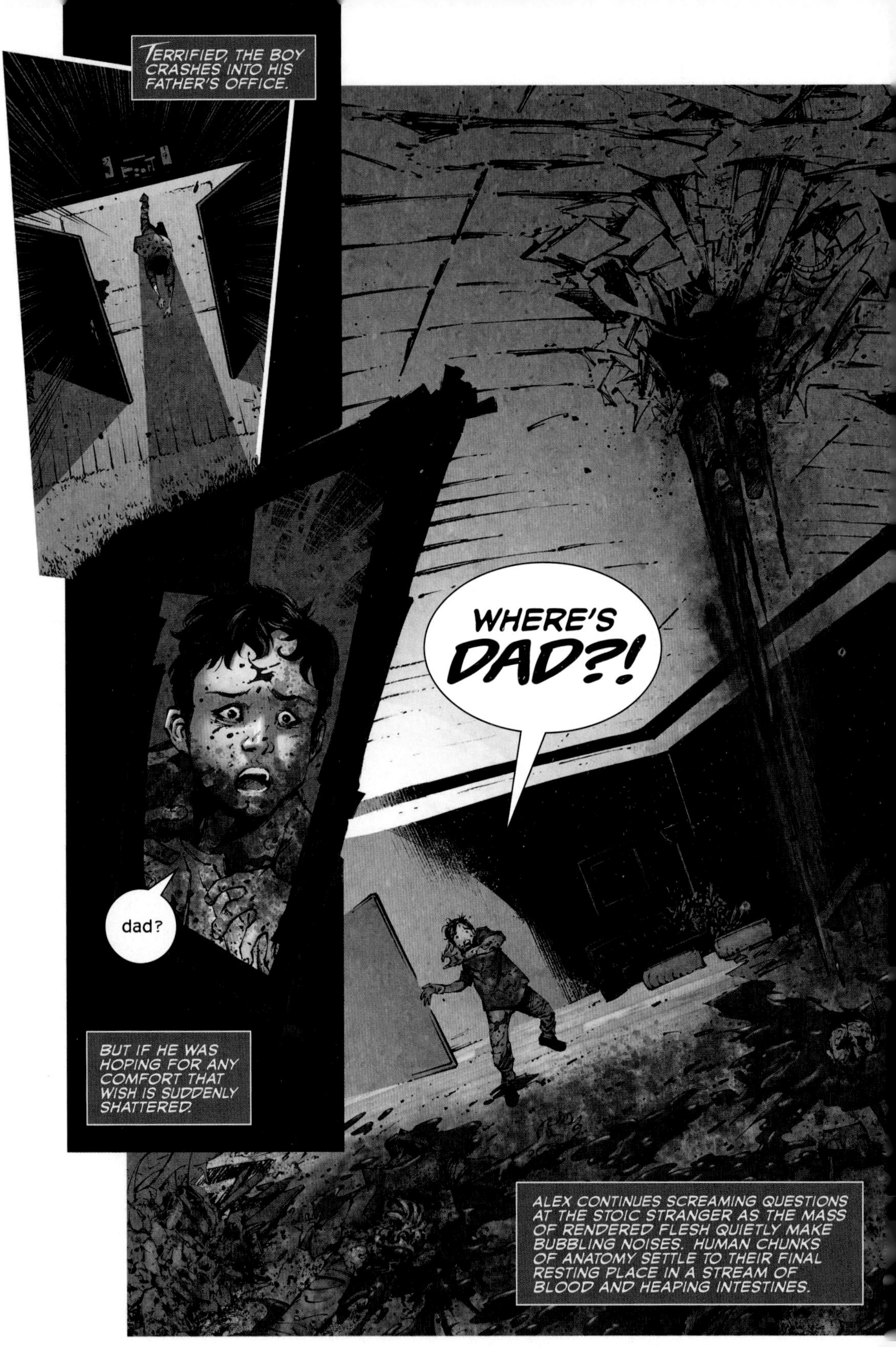
TERRIFIED, THE BOY CRASHES INTO HIS FATHER'S OFFICE.
dad?
BUT IF HE WAS HOPING FOR ANY COMFORT THAT WISH IS SUDDENLY SHATTERED.
WHERE'S DAD?!
ALEX CONTINUES SCREAMING QUESTIONS AT THE STOIC STRANGER AS THE MASS OF RENDERED FLESH QUIETLY MAKE BUBBLING NOISES. HUMAN CHUNKS OF ANATOMY SETTLE TO THEIR FINAL RESTING PLACE IN A STREAM OF BLOOD AND HEAPING INTESTINES.

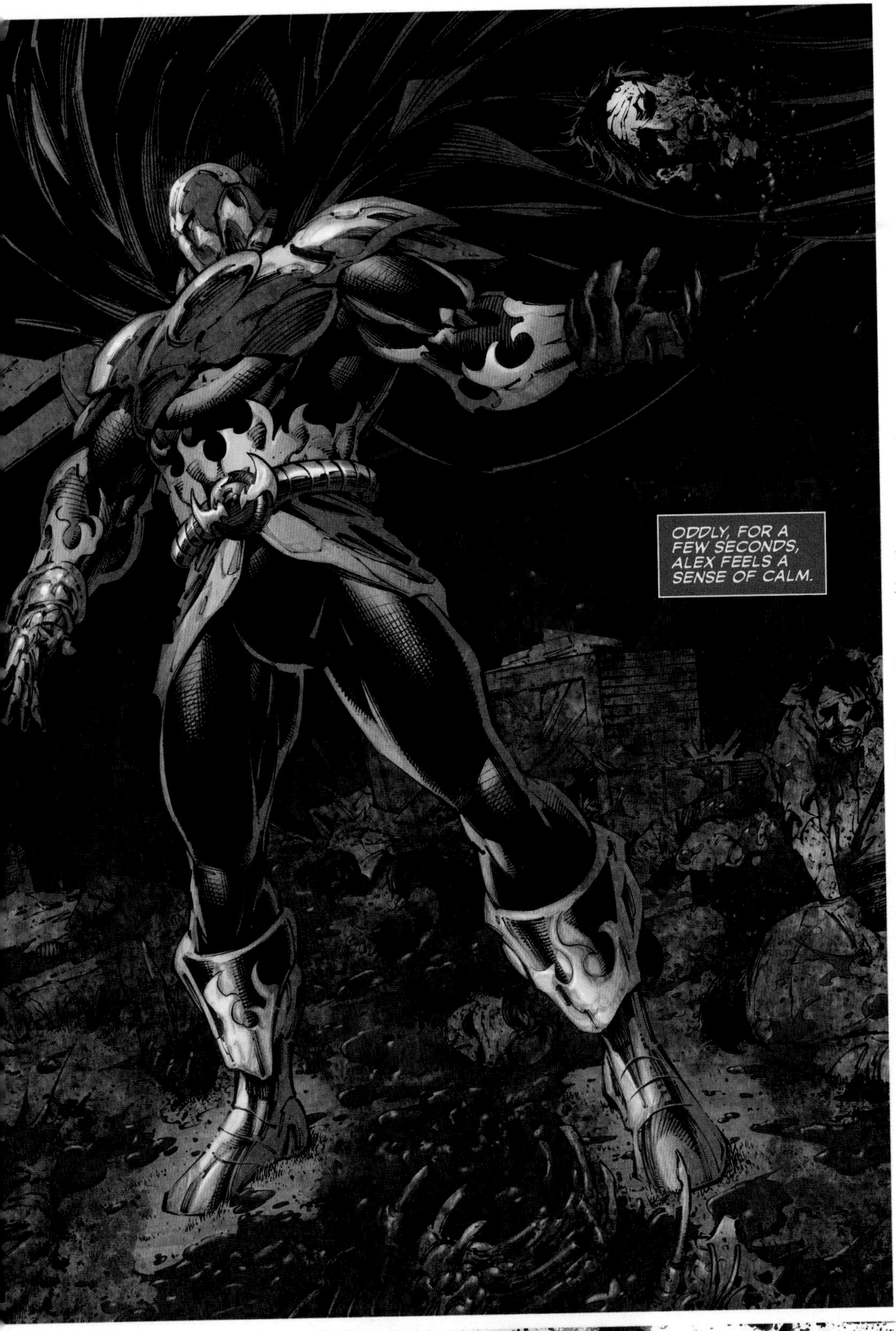
ODDLY, FOR A FEW SECONDS, ALEX FEELS A SENSE OF CALM.

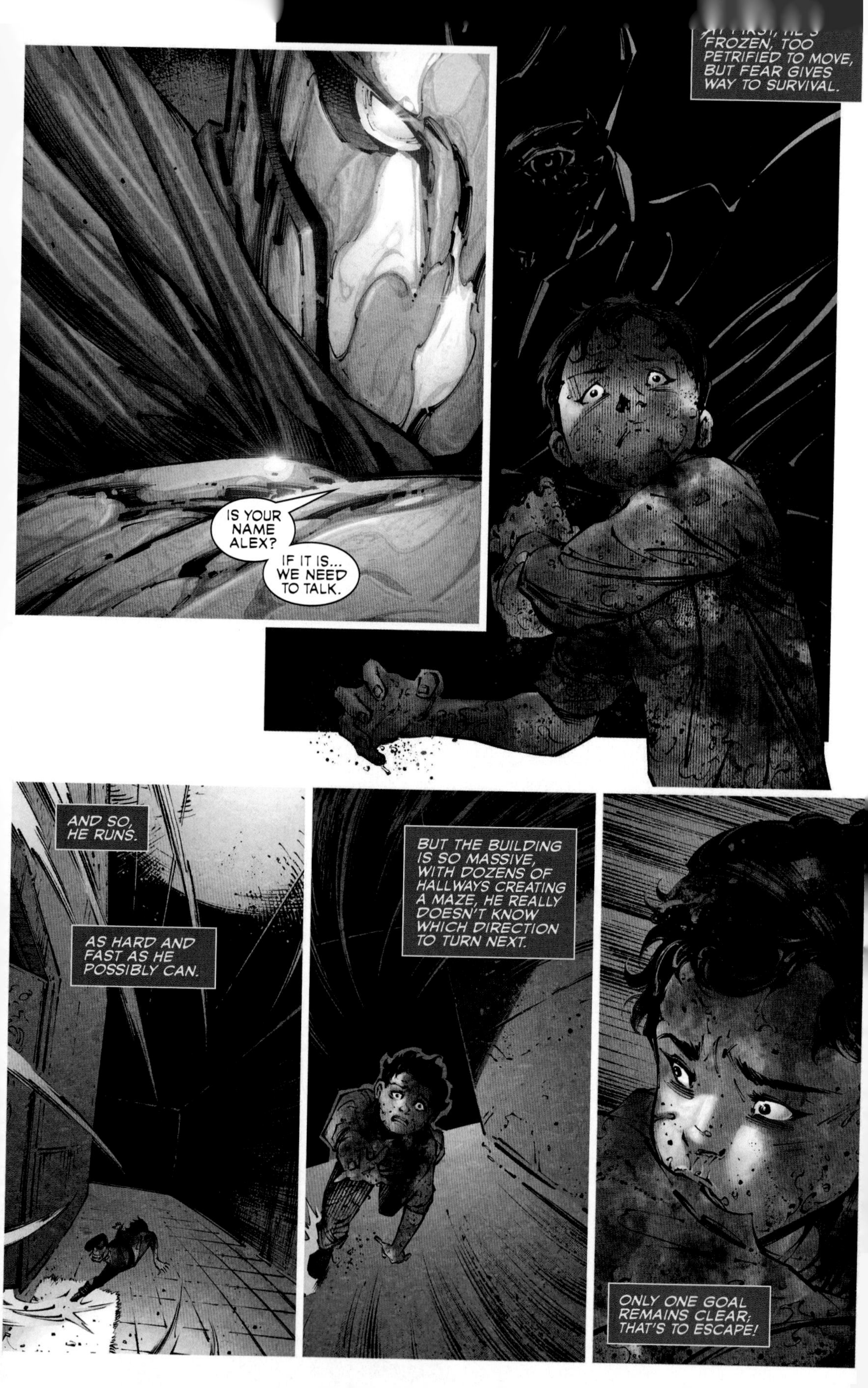
IS YOUR NAME ALEX?
IF IT IS... WE NEED TO TALK.
FROZEN, TOO PETRIFIED TO MOVE, BUT FEAR GIVES WAY TO SURVIVAL.
AND SO, HE RUNS.
AS HARD AND FAST AS HE POSSIBLY CAN.
BUT THE BUILDING IS SO MASSIVE, WITH DOZENS OF HALLWAYS CREATING A MAZE, HE REALLY DOESN'T KNOW WHICH DIRECTION TO TURN NEXT.
ONLY ONE GOAL REMAINS CLEAR; THAT'S TO ESCAPE!

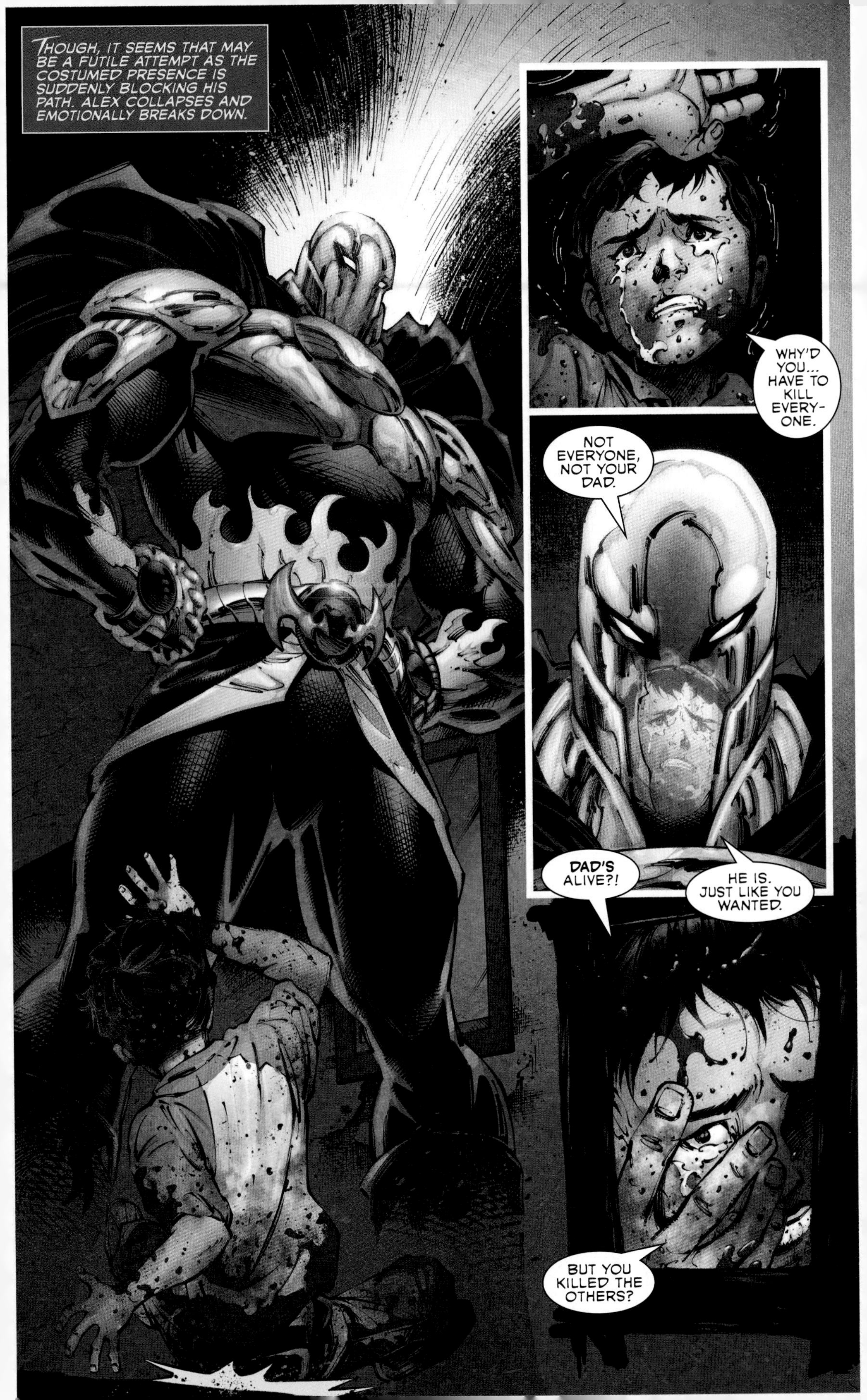
THOUGH, IT SEEMS THAT MAY BE A FUTILE ATTEMPT AS THE COSTUMED PRESENCE IS SUDDENLY BLOCKING HIS PATH. ALEX COLLAPSES AND EMOTIONALLY BREAKS DOWN.
WHY'D YOU... HAVE TO KILL EVERY-ONE.
NOT EVERYONE, NOT YOUR DAD.
DAD'S ALIVE?!
HE IS. JUST LIKE YOU WANTED.
BUT YOU KILLED THE OTHERS?

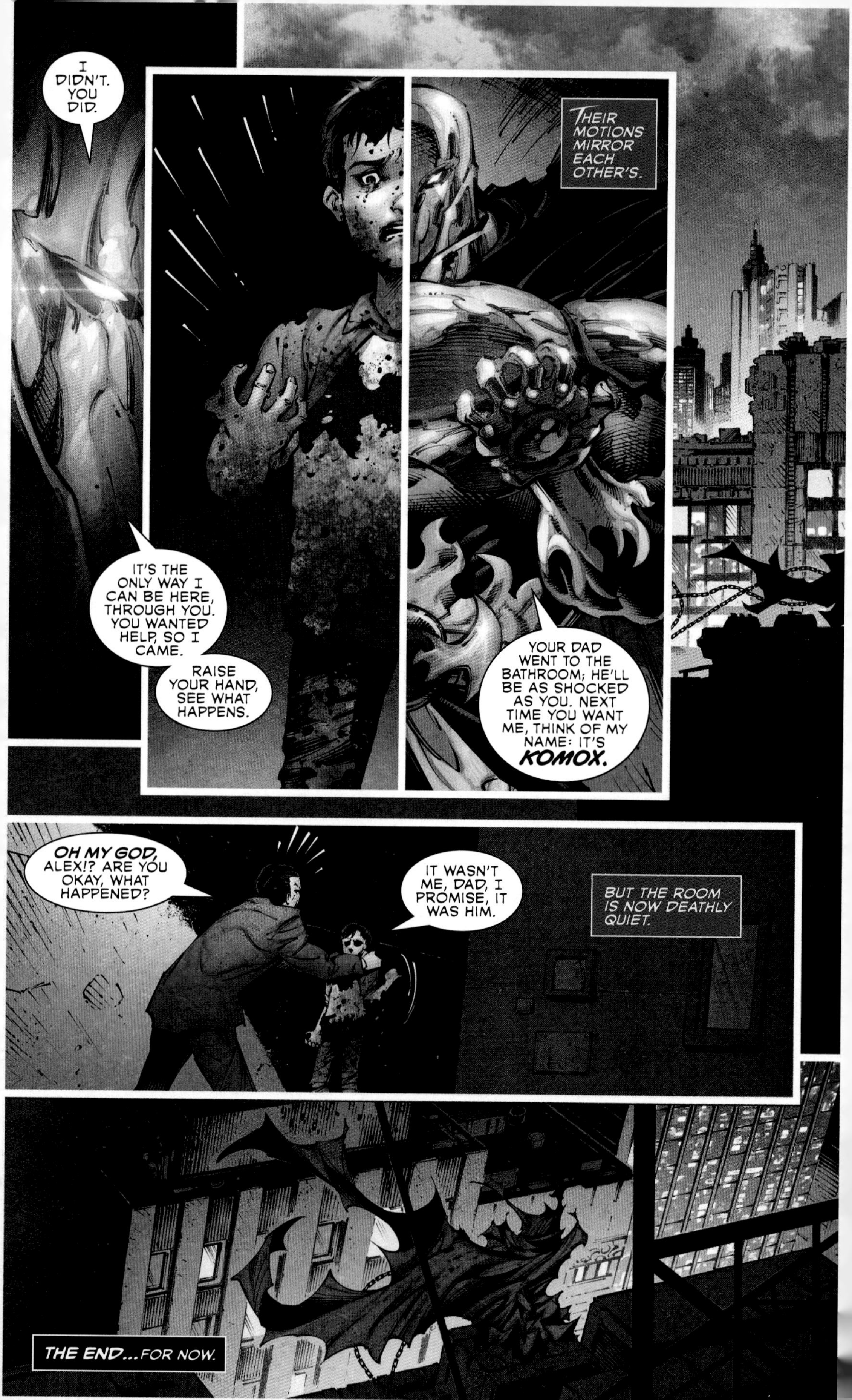
I DIDN'T. YOU DID.
THEIR MOTIONS MIRROR EACH OTHER'S.
IT'S THE ONLY WAY I CAN BE HERE, THROUGH YOU. YOU WANTED HELP, SO I CAME.
RAISE YOUR HAND, SEE WHAT HAPPENS.
YOUR DAD WENT TO THE BATHROOM; HE'LL BE AS SHOCKED AS YOU. NEXT TIME YOU WANT ME, THINK OF MY NAME: IT'S KOMOX.
OH MY GOD, ALEX!? ARE YOU OKAY, WHAT HAPPENED?
IT WASN'T ME, DAD, I PROMISE, IT WAS HIM.
BUT THE ROOM IS NOW DEATHLY QUIET.
THE END...FOR NOW.

"Gunslinger"

* This story contined in the pages of **Gunslinger Spawn**

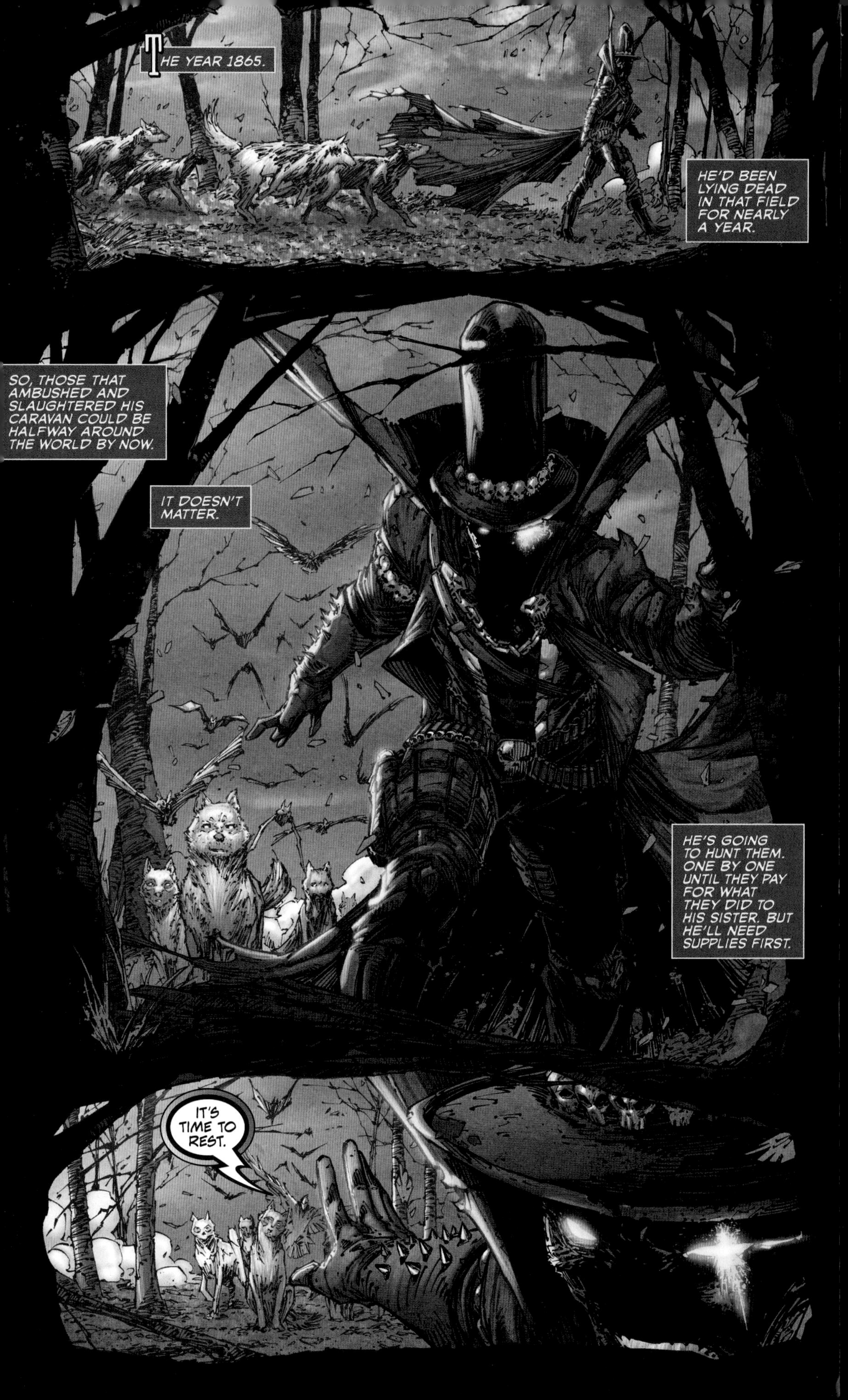
THE YEAR 1865.
HE'D BEEN LYING DEAD IN THAT FIELD FOR NEARLY A YEAR.
SO, THOSE THAT AMBUSHED AND SLAUGHTERED HIS CARAVAN COULD BE HALFWAY AROUND THE WORLD BY NOW.
IT DOESN'T MATTER.
HE'S GOING TO HUNT THEM. ONE BY ONE UNTIL THEY PAY FOR WHAT THEY DID TO HIS SISTER. BUT HE'LL NEED SUPPLIES FIRST.
IT'S TIME TO REST.

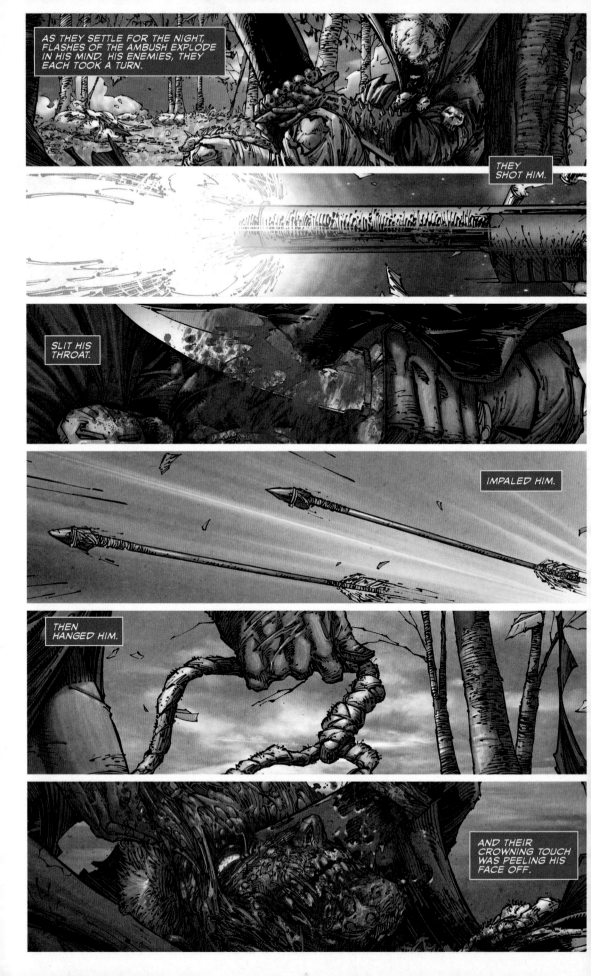

AS THEY SETTLE FOR THE NIGHT, FLASHES OF THE AMBUSH EXPLODE IN HIS MIND. HIS ENEMIES, THEY EACH TOOK A TURN.

THEY SHOT HIM.

SLIT HIS THROAT.

IMPALED HIM.

THEN HANGED HIM.

AND THEIR CROWNING TOUCH WAS PEELING HIS FACE OFF.

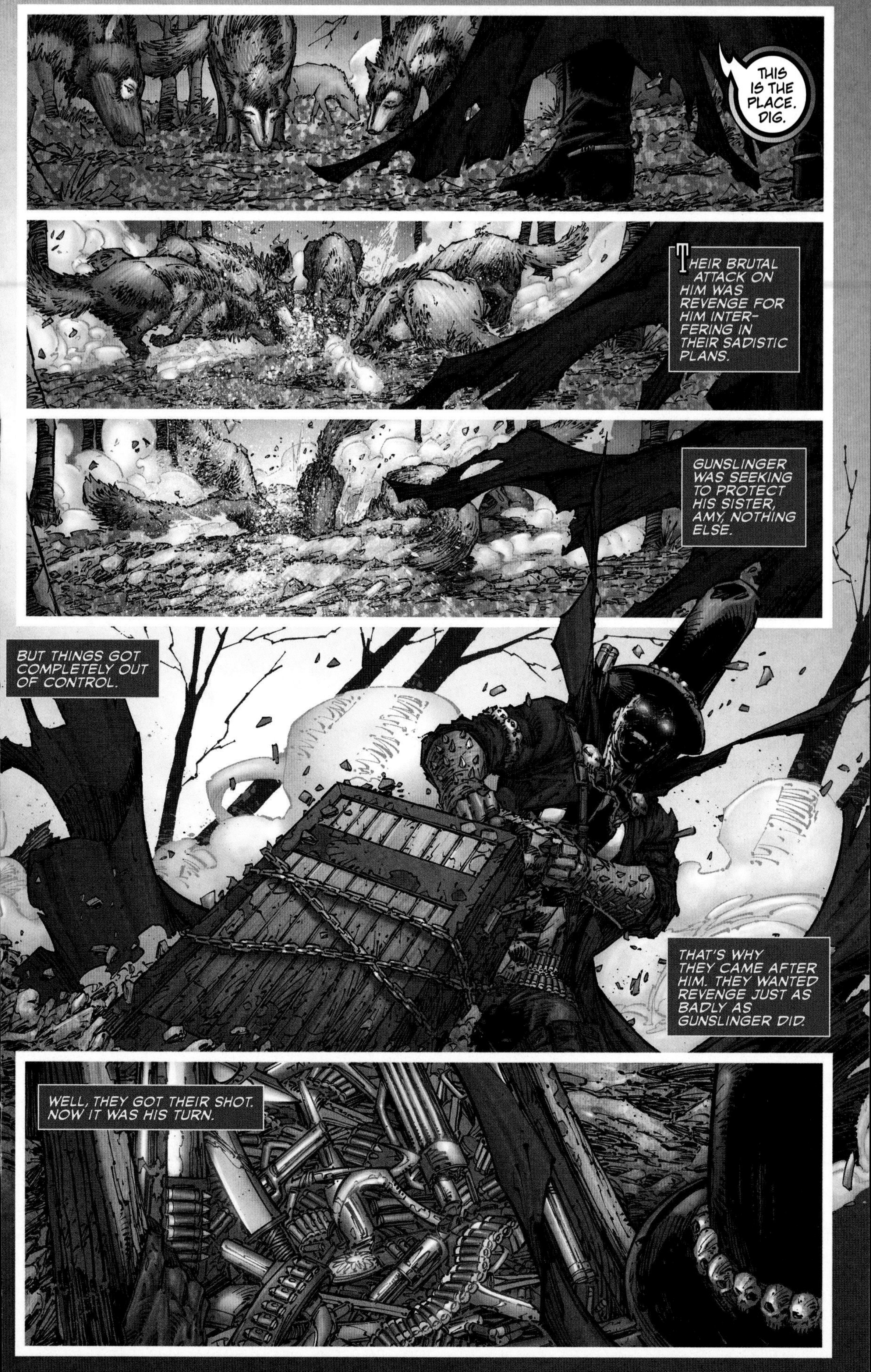

THIS IS THE PLACE. DIG.
THEIR BRUTAL ATTACK ON HIM WAS REVENGE FOR HIM INTER-FERING IN THEIR SADISTIC PLANS.
GUNSLINGER WAS SEEKING TO PROTECT HIS SISTER, AMY, NOTHING ELSE.
BUT THINGS GOT COMPLETELY OUT OF CONTROL.
THAT'S WHY THEY CAME AFTER HIM. THEY WANTED REVENGE JUST AS BADLY AS GUNSLINGER DID.
WELL, THEY GOT THEIR SHOT. NOW IT WAS HIS TURN.

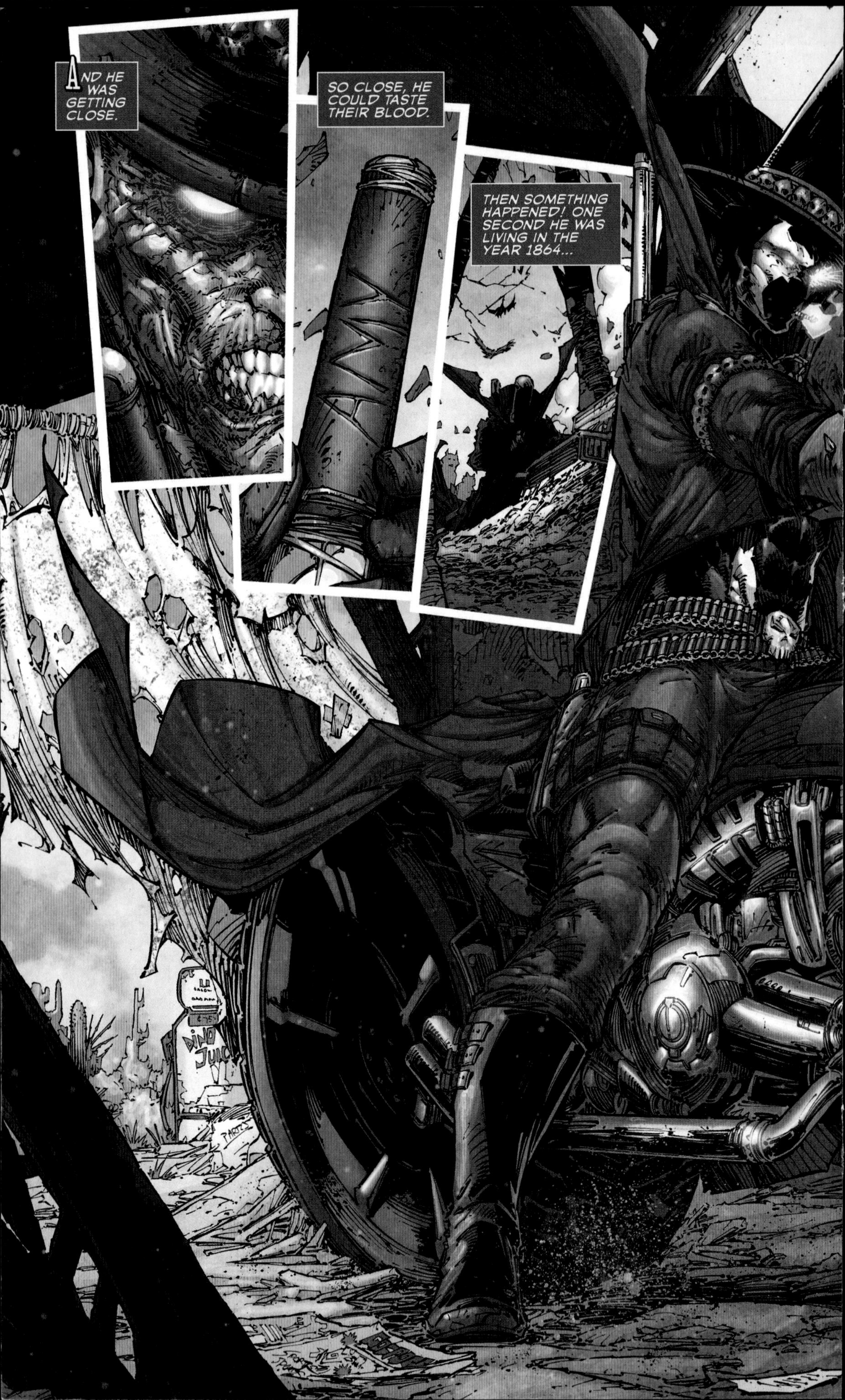
AND HE WAS GETTING CLOSE.
SO CLOSE, HE COULD TASTE THEIR BLOOD.
THEN SOMETHING HAPPENED! ONE SECOND HE WAS LIVING IN THE YEAR 1864...
DINO JUIC

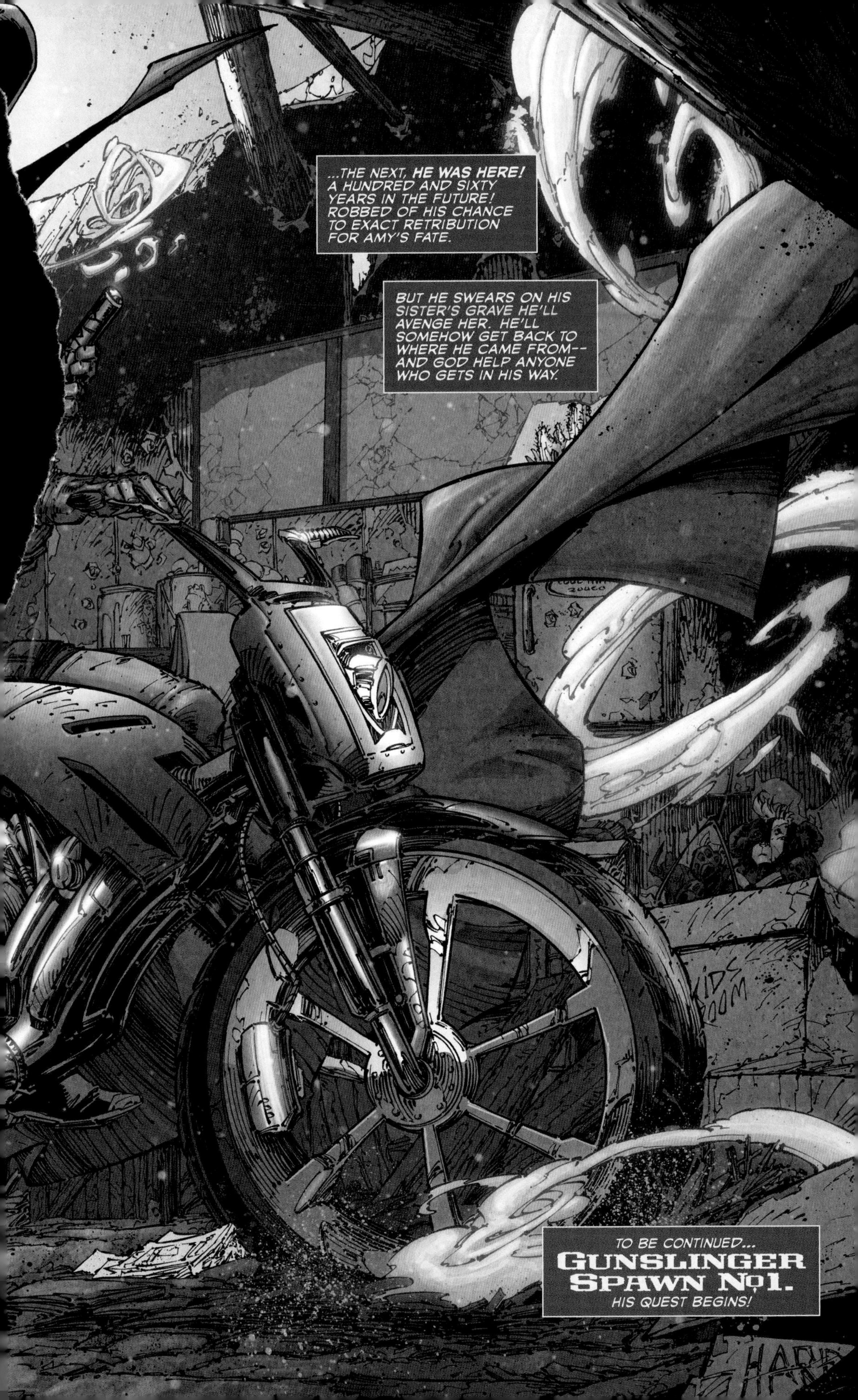
...THE NEXT, HE WAS HERE! A HUNDRED AND SIXTY YEARS IN THE FUTURE! ROBBED OF HIS CHANCE TO EXACT RETRIBUTION FOR AMY'S FATE.
BUT HE SWEARS ON HIS SISTER'S GRAVE HE'LL AVENGE HER. HE'LL SOMEHOW GET BACK TO WHERE HE CAME FROM-- AND GOD HELP ANYONE WHO GETS IN HIS WAY.
KIDS ROOM
TO BE CONTINUED...
GUNSLINGER SPAWN №1.
HIS QUEST BEGINS!

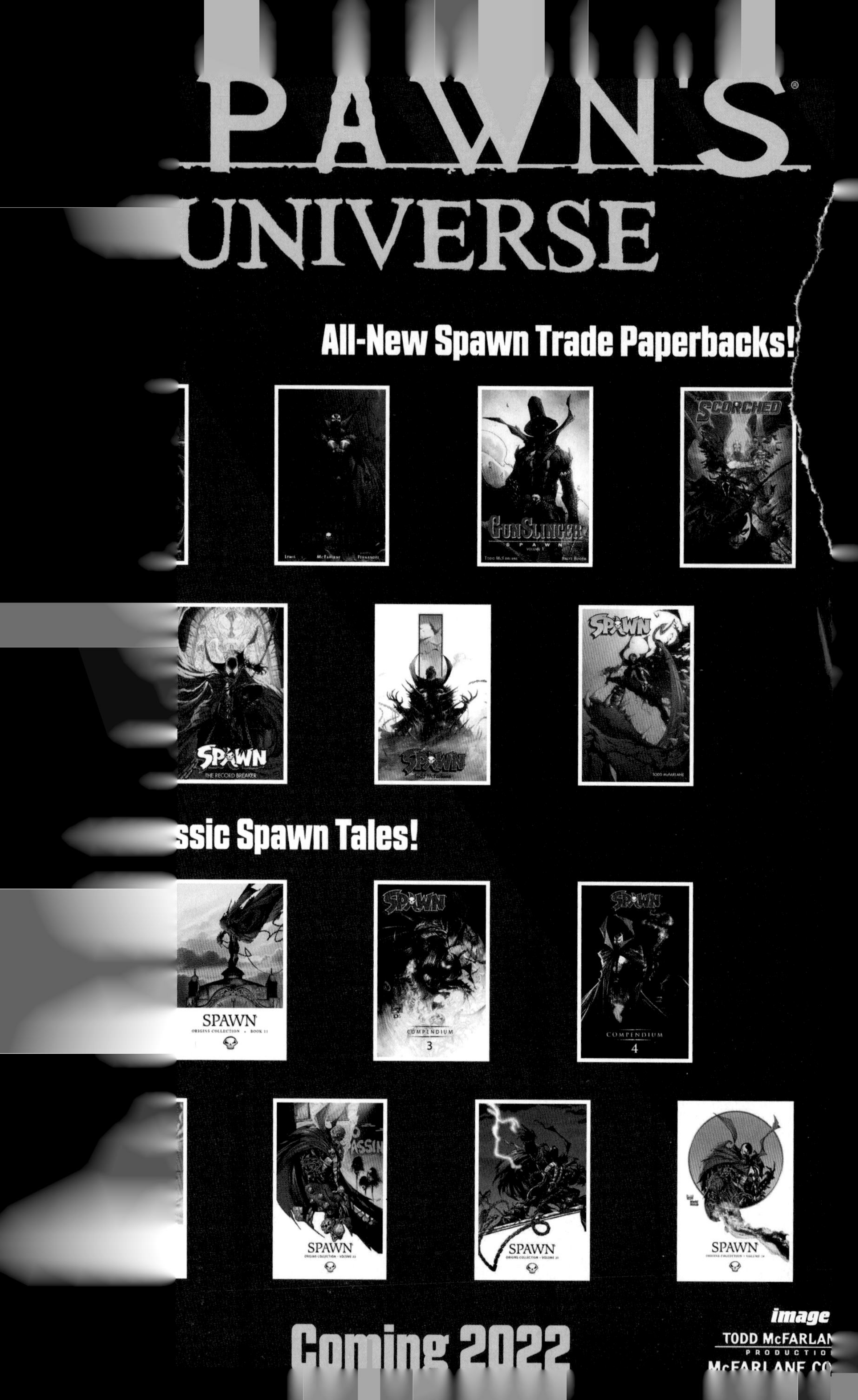

PAWN'S®
UNIVERSE
All-New Spawn Trade Paperbacks!
SCORCHED
GUNSLINGER
SPAWN
SPAWN
THE RECORD BREAKER
SPAWN
SPAWN
ssic Spawn Tales!
SPAWN
ORIGINS COLLECTION • BOOK 11
SPAWN
COMPENDIUM
3
SPAWN
COMPENDIUM
4
SPAWN
SPAWN
SPAWN
Coming 2022
image
TODD McFARLAN
PRODUCTIO